Oil, Power, and Principle

Contemporary Issues in the Middle East

Mostafa Elm

Oil, Power, and Principle

Iran's Oil Nationalization and Its Aftermath

Syracuse University Press

Copyright © 1992 by Syracuse University Press
Syracuse, New York 13244-5160

First Edition 1992
92 93 94 95 96 97 98 99   6 5 4 3 2 1

The paper used in this publication meets the minimum
requirements of American National Standard for Information
Sciences—Permanence of Paper for Printed Library Materials,
ANSI Z39.48-1984. ∞™

LIBRARY OF CONGRESS
CATALOGING-IN-PUBLICATION DATA

Elm, Mostafa.
   Oil, power, and principle : Iran's oil nationalization and its
aftermath / Mostafa Elm. — 1st ed.
      p.   cm. — (Contemporary issues in the Middle East)
   Includes bibliographical references (p.   ) and index.
   ISBN 0-8156-2551-0 (alk. paper)
      1. Petroleum industry and trade—Government ownership—
Iran.   2. Anglo-Iranian Oil Dispute, 1951–1954.
3. Mosaddeq, Mohammad, 1880–1967.   4. Iran—Politics and
government—1941–1979.   I. Title.   II. Series.
HD9576.I62E46   1992
338.2'7282'0955—dc20   91-12390

Manufactured in the United States of America

. . . could thou and I with Fate conspire
To grasp this sorry Scheme of Things entire,
Would not we shatter it to bits—and then
Re-mould it nearer to the Heart's Desire!

OMAR KHAYYAM

To the memory of Mossadeq
With the hope that Iran may yet weather the storms

O let me see our land retain her soul
Her pride, her freedom, and not freedom's shade

JOHN KEATS

Contents

Tables

Abbreviations

AGIP	Italian National Oil Company
AIOC	Anglo-Iranian Oil Company
APOC	Anglo-Persian Oil Company
ARAMCO	Arabian American Oil Company
BBC	British Broadcasting Corporation
BP	British Petroleum Company
CAB	Cabinet
CBS	Columbia Broadcasting System
CFP	Compagnie Française des Pétroles
CIA	Central Intelligence Agency
DEFE	Chief of Staffs Committee
DMPA	(U.S.) Defense Materials Production Department
FEC	First Exploitation Company
FO	Foreign Office
FR-US	Foreign Relations of the United States
GHQ	General Headquarters
HMG	His or Her Majesty's Government
IEA	International Energy Agency
IJC	International Court of Justice (World Court)
ILO	International Labor Organization
IPC	Iraq Petroleum Company
JCS	Joint Chiefs of Staff
MELF	Middle East Land Forces
MI6	British Foreign Intelligence
NATO	North Atlantic Treaty Organization
NIOC	National Iranian Oil Company
NSC	National Security Council

OPEC	Organization of Petroleum Exporting Countries
PAD	Petroleum Administration for Defense
PREM	Prime Minister's Office Records
RG	Record Group
Rls.	Rials

Preface

This book is an attempt to trace and analyze the remarkable events leading to the nationalization of British oil interests in Iran in 1951, the ensuing Anglo-American-sponsored coup that crushed the country's nationalist government in 1953 and ended in reinstating the Shah, and the formation of an American-dominated oil consortium in 1954. It then demonstrates that the United States' backing of an autocratic regime in Iran planted the seeds of the 1979 revolution in that country and contributed to further instability in the Persian Gulf leading to the Iraq-Iran war, the Iraqi occupation of Kuwait, and the Gulf war.

The 1951–54 episode contains all the elements of a powerful drama: kidnapping, political intrigues and assassinations, psychological warfare, riots by hired mobs, and covert operations by the Central Intelligence Agency and the British Foreign Intelligence. Dominating the whole scene is the extraordinary figure of the nationalist leader Mohammad Mossadeq.

The study is based on extensive study of documents recently declassified in Great Britain and the United States as well as Iranian private and public documents. Furthermore, it draws on interviews with Iranian, British, and American officials directly involved in the events of 1951–54.

The book could serve as an instructive case study of the rise of nationalism and the struggle for national independence and sovereignty over natural resources by third world countries during the twilight era of British imperial power. It shows how the Anglo-Persian Oil Company—a small British oil concern—grew into a giant international corporation by the name of British Petroleum mainly by reaping exorbitant profits from Iranian oil at the expense of the producer country. It demonstrates how this development brought about a conflict between Iranian nationalists led by Mossadeq and a British oil company that had become a pillar of Britain's economic and strategic power in the Middle East. It reveals how this dispute brought about a much wider conflict between the global interests of Britain, the United States, and international oil companies, a conflict aggravated further by fears that it might involve Britain and the United States in a catastrophic war with the Soviet Union.

In the midst of these conflicts, Britain succeeded in luring President Dwight D. Eisenhower to mount a CIA coup in Iran that crushed the national democratic government, reinstated the autocratic Shah, and brought Iran's oil resources under Anglo-American control. But these moves gave rise to a chain of disruptive events. The coup ultimately contributed to the 1979 revolt in Iran against the United States and the Shah. This in turn led to further instability in the Middle East. The study reveals how warped perceptions of national security and the pursuit of short-term gains gave rise to cataclysmic events that were detrimental to the West.

Few instances in recent history have so intensely involved such a host of leading world figures as Iran's nationalization of oil. Among the endless list of players in this drama, in which Mossadeq played the leading role, are Truman and Acheson, Attlee and Morrison, Eisenhower and Dulles, Churchill and Eden, while Stalin and Molotov are mysteriously standing in the wings. There are also the leading figures of many other countries, the heads of major international oil companies, and the chiefs of the intelligence services of the United States and Great Britain. And finally there is the active involvement of such major organizations as the United Nations, the International Court of Justice, and the World Bank.

The story of oil nationalization in Iran cannot be separated from Iran's fight for constitutional rule, aimed at curbing the power of autocratic kings who, among other arbitrary practices, granted concessions to foreigners for personal gain. To shed some light on the underlying causes of the Iranian dissatisfaction with local rulers and foreign concessions and to put the issues in proper perspective, the first three chapters deal with the internal and external forces at work in Iran in the perplexing period between 1870 and 1949 and the circumstances under which the Anglo-Iranian Oil Company operated in Iran. The remaining chapters deal with the events of 1950–54 and throw light on the repercussions of the Anglo-American-sponsored coup in Iran and the rest of the Middle East.

My work was greatly facilitated by the fact that I lived in Iran, witnessing for decades the rise of nationalism and later the traumatic events of the oil nationalization years, the angry demonstrations in Tehran and the riots in Abadan, the heated arguments in the Parliament and the press. However, a true picture of events could not have been drawn without access to documents concerning secret discussions in Tehran, London, Washington, and other world capitals and without knowing the views and recollections of those closely involved.

In the course of my research I have had helpful advice from the staffs of many libraries and archives in the United States and Great Britain. My special thanks are due to the staff of the British Public Record Office, the U.S. National Archives, the Library of the London School of Oriental Studies, and the Princeton University Library.

I also wish to express my thanks to those who generously gave of their time, in the course of long interviews, to throw additional light on the contents of documents recently declassified. In fact, many were themselves the authors of the documents. Among some seventy officials interviewed are former Iranian Cabinet ministers and members of Parliament, U.S. under secretaries of state, British and American ambassadors, and oil corporation presidents and consultants, as well as intelligence and army officers. The names of most appear in the relevant notes, though some preferred to remain anonymous.

My sincere thanks are also due to Albert Hourani, Emeritus Fellow, St. Antony's College, Oxford, who, throughout the writing of this book, provided me with valuable suggestions and comments. Since the subject of the book involves various international bodies, each chapter dealing with a specific organization was critically read by one or more persons familiar with that organization. My thanks are due to Cyrus Ghani, a legal expert, for his comments on chapters dealing with the International Court of Justice and the U.N. Security Council and for his assistance in identifying some of the obscure personalities involved in this drama. I am grateful also to

Khodadad Farmanfarmaian, a former governor of the Central Bank of Iran, and to Reza Moghadam, a former official of the International Monetary Fund, for their comments on chapters dealing with the World Bank and financial issues. However, I alone am responsible for the views expressed in this book.

I am also deeply grateful to my wife, Mahin, for her support, encouragement, and patience over the nine years that I was engaged in this work. Finally I would like to thank my son, Nader, who acted as my secretary and word-processing expert, organized a multitude of photocopies of documents, notes, and papers, and typed the manuscript of this book with great enthusiasm. The typing of the text, he says, gave him an opportunity to find out what happened to his country before his birth and why his homeland is in the state it is now.

Note on Transliteration

The system of transliteration adopted in this study is based on the way Persian or Arabic names are pronounced and not on the way such names appear in English-language writings on Iran, a point on which there is little uniformity. As an example, in British sources the name Mossadeq is generally rendered as Musaddiq but sometimes as Mossadak, Mossadiq, Mosadeq, or Mossaddegh. Except in quotations, I have used the form Mossadeq, which happens to be the way the name generally appears in American writings and documents.

In the rare case in which a form is uniformly used in English-language sources, such as Islam, I have used the accepted spelling even if it does not correspond to the Persian pronunciation. Readers will no doubt find certain inconsistencies, but such is the problem of transliterating names from one alphabet to another.

Oil, Power, and Principle

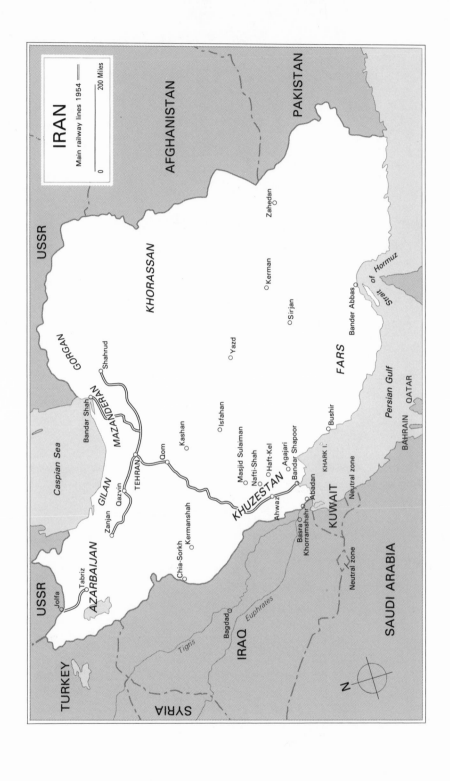

1

The Age of Autocracy and Concessions

"If His Majesty were to affix his glorious and august name to this Concession, he would, with one stroke of the pen, bestow upon this land and nation more glorious benefit and nobler existence than all the kings of Persia have done over the past thousands of years."

This is the final paragraph of a two-page report submitted in 1872 to Nasser ed-Din Shah, the autocratic ruler of Iran, by his sycophant ministers, giving their views on a concession demanded by Baron Julius de Reuter.[1] The concession concerned the exclusive right to the exploitation of practically every agricultural, industrial, and mineral resource in the country.

Reuter, a successful operator of a commercial news service in his home country, Germany, had moved his business to London, where he became a British subject in 1857 and later bought the title of Baron. The Iranian minister in London, Moin ol-Molk, attracted by the title and wealth of this new British citizen, interested him in making investments in Iran and told him of the great potential for quick gains if only he could come to terms with Iran's rulers.[2]

The days of great kings of Persia who ruled a vast empire had gone by. The country was ruled by ineffectual monarchs caught between the two great powers of the time, Britain and Russia. Britain, which had conquered next-door India, wanted Iran, the gateway to that colony, to be under her own sway. Russia had earlier taken the initiative by "steadily swallowing the Persian artichoke leaf by leaf," as Lord Curzon, the Viceroy of India, put it.[3] Britain had scarcely tried to halt Russian advances, but now felt the need to protect her vital interests. "Were it not for our possessing India," Lord Salisbury, the British Foreign Secretary, observed, "we should trouble ourselves but little about Persia."[4] Thus it was necessary for Britain to make sure that Russia did not swallow the remaining leaves of the Iranian artichoke, which separated Russia from India and the Persian Gulf.

The Shah was indifferent to the condition of his subjects, most of whom lived in poverty. His main concern was to look for funds to support his lavish life-style. "The extravagance of the Shah was only matched by his desperation for money."[5] Thus he did not need any encouragement to accept Reuter's proposal. He was badly in need of cash for a pleasure trip to Europe. Persian kings before him had never set foot outside the country except for foreign conquests. The last was Nader Shah, who invaded India in 1737, defeating a large Moghul army.

The concession signed by Nasser ed-Din Shah on July 25, 1872, gave Reuter the "exclusive and definitive right" for seventy years to construct railways and irrigation works in Iran as well as a monopoly on the exploitation of forests and uncultivated land throughout the country, the right to exploit most mineral resources (including oil), a first option on a national bank, and options on the construction of roads, public works, factories, etc. According to Reuter, what enabled him to obtain such an unprecedented concession was the payment of £180,000 to the Shah and his courtiers.[6]

The British Foreign Office considered the terms of the concession to be extravagant. Even a colonial figure like Curzon described its terms as "the most complete and extraordinary surrender of the entire industrial resources of a kingdom into foreign hands that has probably ever been dreamed of, much less accomplished in history."[7] But Nasser ed-Din Shah, the self-styled "King of Kings" and "Shadow of God," felt that he had struck a good bargain for personal gain.

Having found some cash, the Shah left for a five-month trip to Europe in May 1873. At the courts of Tsar Alexander II and Queen Victoria, the Shah found that his hosts were not at all pleased with Reuter's concession. The Russians suspected that the concession was a British plot to upset the balance of power between the two countries in Iran. The British, in their turn, were unhappy that Reuter had made an enormous deal with Iran without consulting them. Moreover, they had serious doubts about his loyalty to the British Empire and feared that he might renounce his acquired British nationality while auctioning off his concession to the Russians.[8]

On his return to Iran the Shah found that the nationalists and such disparate groups as the imperial harem, the princes, and the high mullahs all wanted the concession canceled. The monarch, being under great pressure, sent word to Reuter that since he had not taken any steps toward performing any part of his undertaking, the concession was considered null and void.[9]

Reuter realized that he had lost his concession because he had failed to obtain the support of the British government. With this lesson learned, he patiently won the confidence of Sir Henry Drummond Wolff, the British minister in Tehran, who revived two major portions of the lost concession. In January 1889 the Shah granted him a new concession for the formation of a state bank for a period of sixty years with the exclusive right of note issue in Iran while exempting him "from every kind of tax or duty." At the same time the bank was given the right to exploit all mineral resources throughout the country with the exception of gold, silver, and precious stones. Iran's share in mining was to be 16 percent of the net profits. The concession stipulated that if production did not start within ten years, his mining rights would be canceled.[10]

Baron de Reuter's son, George, who conducted the negotiations, presented a "gift" of £20,000 to the Shah for having signed the concession and gave other "gifts" to the prime minister and others.[11] Toward the end of 1889 the Imperial Bank of Persia was established under the Royal Charter.

Soon after signing the bank concession, Nasser ed-Din Shah departed for Europe while Iran was in turmoil. On his return to Iran, the Shah's thirst for cash and the British readiness to exploit his need prompted the beginning of a strong national movement against corrupt rulers who welcomed foreign exploitation for their own ends. In March 1890, a British entrepreneur by the name of G. F. Talbot, with the support of the British legation in Tehran, bought from the Shah a concession for the full control over the production, internal sale, and export of Iran's tobacco for a period of fifty years. In return he undertook to pay the Shah or his government a quarter of the annual net profits and an annual rent of £15,000.[12]

The Talbot concession, which threatened the interests of various groups dealing with tobacco, triggered an uprising throughout the country, fueled further by a nationalist figure living abroad named

Seyyed Jamal ed-Din Assad-Abadi, known as Afghani, who was a powerful Iranian reformist and pan-Islamist with a large following. Afghani, who had been exiled from Iran for opposing the Shah's autocratic rule, told Edward Browne, the well-known British orientalist, that "no reform was to be hoped for until six or seven heads were cut off," adding that the first two must be those of Nasser ed-Din Shah and his prime minister, both of whom in fact were assassinated later.[13]

Afghani, well aware of the great influence of Moslem religious leaders, wrote to Ayatollah Hassan Shirazi in Samarra to protest the Shah's concessions to the British and the Russians. His letter calls the Shah "corrupt" and condemns him for having chosen as his prime minister Amin ol-Sultan, of whom he says:

> He hath sold to the foes of our Faith the greater parts of the Persian lands and the profits accruing therefrom, to wit the mines. . . . Also the tobacco . . . with the chief centres of cultivation. . . . Lastly there is the Bank [concession granted to Reuter]: and what shall cause thee to understand what is the Bank? It means the complete handing over of the reins of the government to the enemy of Islam [and] the enslaving of the people to that enemy.

He finally warned the high ecclesiastic that if he did not rise to help his people, "the realms of Islam will soon be under the control of foreigners."[14]

The Ayatollah instantly issued a *fatwa* declaring the use of tobacco unlawful until the concession was canceled. The *fatwa* was fully obeyed in Iran, where there were violent uprisings against the Shah. The Shah yielded and canceled the concession, but was faced with a demand for compensation totaling £500,000. When the government could not come up with this amount, Britain's Foreign Office instructed the British Imperial Bank to supply it in the form of a loan to the Iranian government. The bank obliged by providing a loan at an interest of 6 percent repayable in forty annual installments while securing as collateral the customs receipts of Iran's Persian Gulf ports. These losses were imposed on the Iranian people, who were entirely ignored when the actual concession was granted. To quote Edward Browne: "And all this for the enrichment of a few greedy English speculators and a handful of traitorous Persian courtiers and ministers."[15] It is ironic that whereas the British Foreign Office talked from time to time of the need for reform in Iran, the British cultivated corruption by bribing the Shah and his courtiers to milk the country.

By arranging a loan that saddled Iran with forty years of repayment, the Foreign Office, as Geoffrey Jones put it, assisted the British Imperial Bank in establishing itself "as a permanent fixture in Persia" while using it "as a political instrument by the British government, a role which was to grow over the following three decades."[16] Thus Afghani, the Iranian nationalist figure, was not wrong in his forecast on what the British bank meant.

In the early 1890s opposition to Nasser ed-Din Shah's autocratic rule, spurred by nationalists, grew in momentum until he was shot dead on May 8, 1896, three days before the fiftieth anniversary of his reign. The assassin, a follower of Afghani, castigated the "corrupt" Shah and the "scoundrels" around him, who, he said, had trampled on the rights of the people and had given concessions to foreigners. But the assassin was wrong in thinking that killing the Shah would bring justice and reform. On June 8, 1896, the son of the deceased Shah, Mozaffar ed-Din Qajar, was crowned and continued to rule more or less in his father's fashion.[17]

These events did not shake the position of the Imperial Bank except for a short-lived drop in its shares. The bank sold its mining rights for £150,000 to a newly formed concern called the Persian Bank Mining Rights Corporation; George de Reuter was a member of the board. The corporation failed in its explorations for oil, and the concession, which called for profitable operation within ten years, came to an end in 1899.[18]

Meanwhile a French scientific team headed by Jaques de Morgan came to Iran, and the team's geologists were led by chance to oil seepages at Chia Sorkh in the northwest, close to the Turkish frontier. In 1892, after a detailed investigation of the area, they published a favorable report on its probable oil resources in the French mining publication *Annales des Mines*. This was followed in later years by further reports in which de Morgan's team maintained that geological formations confirmed the existence of oil. This led an Armenian named Antoine Ketabji Khan, the director of Iran's Cus-

toms Administration, to secure the monopoly of oil rights throughout the country. He then went to Paris where he contacted Sir Henry
Drummond Wolff, the former British minister in Tehran, and asked
for his assistance in finding British financiers who might be interested in venturing on Persian oil. Wolff later introduced him to a
William Knox D'Arcy, the son of an Irish solicitor who had gained
wealth in gold mining in Australia.[19]

Edward Cotte, formerly Reuter's agent, was sent as Ketabji's
representative to London, where he explained to D'Arcy's men the
findings of the French geologists. D'Arcy consulted Dr. Boverton
Redwood, a leading petroleum expert, who proposed sending a
well-known geologist named H. T. Burls to Iran for further surveys.
Burls went to Iran, and on his return presented a favorable report on
the possible existence of oil in Kermanshah and Khuzistan. His
report put the wheels in motion. In January 1901, after a dozen
meetings in Paris and London between D'Arcy, Ketabji Khan, Wolff,
and Cotte, the four agreed on the percentage share each would
obtain if, as a result of their efforts, an oil concession was secured.
No one foresaw the exceptional financial gains to be made from the
future concession, and those other than D'Arcy were later to regret
having agreed to small percentages.[20]

D'Arcy did not take any step until he was assured of his government's diplomatic support, after which he appointed Alfred Marriott, a cousin of his financial adviser, as his representative in Tehran. The Foreign Office obliged by providing him with a letter of
introduction to Sir Arthur Hardinge, the British minister in Tehran,
who had been instructed to extend his assistance. The real job of
paving the way in the Iranian capital, however, was undertaken by
Ketabji Khan, who "secured in a very thorough manner the support
of all the Shah's principal ministers and courtiers, not even forget-
ting the personal servant who brings His Majesty his pipe and
morning coffee."[21]

Ketabji Khan met in April 1901 with Ali Asghar Amin ol-Sultan,
the prime minister, "the Great Lord-Protector and Confidant of the
Sovereign," and discussed with him the draft agreement that had
been drawn up in London. Hardinge, too, paid a number of visits to
the prime minister urging him to support the draft agreement,
which called for the formation of a company with exclusive rights
for exploration and exploitation of oil throughout the country in

return for paying Iran 10 percent of annual net profits and 5 percent export taxes.

After significant bribes were promised and partly paid by Ketabji Khan to the prime minister and other Iranian officials, the draft was passed on to Mozaffar ed-Din Shah. But on May 20, 1901, the Shah exclaimed that he would not sign it unless there were a down payment of £40,000 and another £40,000 on the formation of the company. Moreover, he indicated that Iran's share of the net profits should be 16 percent rather than the 10 percent stated in the draft. Having delivered these views, he went off hunting.[22]

Meanwhile, the prime minister claimed to be concerned about possible Russian objections to such a concession. Ketabji Khan solved the problem by promising him a "gift" of another £5,000. This and other bribes were approved by D'Arcy, who told Marriott "Don't scruple if you can propose anything for facilitating affairs on my part."[23]

There was one more hurdle to overcome, and that was the Shah's demand for 16 percent of the net profits. But Marriott had no difficulty in juggling the figures in the draft concession; he simply accepted the Shah's demand and omitted the 5 percent export duty that was originally proposed to be paid to Iran.

On May 28, 1901, the Shah signed the concessionary agreement on behalf of his government and Marriott signed on behalf of D'Arcy. Under the agreement, D'Arcy was granted, for a period of sixty years, an exclusive right to explore, exploit, and refine oil throughout the whole country with the exception of five northern provinces close to the Russian border. The concessionaire was allowed to use free of charge all uncultivated land belonging to the state that might be necessary to his work. Imports of equipment and exports of oil and oil products were to be free of all taxes. The concessionaire was entitled to found one or several companies after giving prior notice to the Iranian government concerning their statutes and locations. The first company was to be established within two years if the concession were not to become null and void. Upon the founding of the first exploitation company, the Iranian government was to be paid £20,000 in cash and £20,000 in paid-up shares. The concessionaire also had to pay annually 16 percent of the net profits of any company or companies that might be formed.

The Iranian government was to appoint a commissioner, who

had to be consulted by the concessionaire and the directors of the companies to be founded. The commissioner was to undertake "such supervision as he may deem expedient to safeguard the interests" of the Iranian government. On the expiration of the concession in 1961, all physical assets were to become the property of the Iranian government free of charge. Disputes were to be submitted to a committee consisting of two arbitrators at Tehran, one appointed by each party, and an umpire appointed by the two.[24] Strangely enough, the Iranian government appointed as its commissioner Antoine Ketabji, the very same man who had actively worked for D'Arcy to obtain the concession and had been rewarded by him with a share in it.

Late in June 1901, when D'Arcy received the signed concession, he wrote to Lord Lansdowne, the Foreign Secretary, saying:

> I beg to offer your Lordship my sincere thanks for the great services you have rendered me. . . . I hope that this enterprise will prove advantageous to British commerce and to the influence of this country in Persia. I would therefore venture to ask for it the protection and countenance of His Majesty's Government in the hope that, if necessary, I may be allowed, as well as my Agents in Persia, to apply to the Foreign Office, and also to the Diplomatic and Consular Representatives of His Majesty in Persia to whose counsels I shall always endeavour to give effect.[25]

The Shah, too, pleased that the concession would bring him personal benefits, issued a royal decree announcing that he had granted D'Arcy and "all his heirs and assigns and friends, full powers and unlimited liberty for a period of sixty years to probe, pierce, and drill at their will the depths of Persian Soil" for oil, and that "all officials of this blessed kingdom" should do their best to assist him since he enjoys "the favour of our splendid court."[26]

Iran at the time had no parliament, and negotiations on an agreement that was to influence the fate of the nation for decades to come had been kept secret from the people. Other governments, too, were kept in the dark. The Russians, however, found out about the concession and put intensive pressure on Iran to nullify or at least modify it, but to no avail.

With the concession in his pocket, D'Arcy looked for a man who could conduct drilling operations in Iran and found George Bernard Reynolds, a tough Royal Engineer who had previously drilled for oil in the Dutch East Indies. Reynolds left for Iran, where he employed a team of Polish drillers who had worked in the Russian oil fields of Baku. The equipment, provisions, and supplies took months to arrive in carts and wagons from England, and drilling finally started at Chia Sorkh in the autumn of 1902.[27] In December of the same year Antoine Ketabji died and his son Vincent took over as Iran's commissioner.

Under the terms of the concession D'Arcy had to form the first company by the end of May 1903. But no oil was struck by then. However, a week before the deadline, D'Arcy formed the First Exploitation Company (FEC), with an issued capital of £600,000 in £1 shares. As required by the concession, he gave the Iranian government, or rather the Shah, £20,000 in shares and £20,000 in cash. In addition, he had other "debts of honour" to those "leading personalities" in Iran who had secured the concession, to whom he paid a total of £49,000, of which £19,000 was in cash and £30,000 in shares. Of these shares £20,000 worth went to the prime minister, the minister of mines, and the foreign minister, all of whom had received some cash before the signing of the concession.[28]

D'Arcy soon realized that his assets and those of the FEC might not meet the heavy cost of drilling in a far-off land. When he approached the British investors, they showed hardly any interest, but the French Baron Alfonse de Rothschild expressed willingness to consider the venture. When D'Arcy left for Cannes with the intention of selling the concession to Rothschild, the British government woke up to the idea that the concession was on the point of slipping out of British hands. Ernest Pretyman, the Admiralty secretary, accordingly wrote to D'Arcy urging him not to sell the concession.[29]

Sir John Fisher, who in 1904 became First Lord of the Admiralty, was eager to convert the Royal Navy's fuel from coal to oil, and a committee headed by Pretyman was formed to look into the prospects of bringing new oil resources under British control. In his capacity as oil consultant, Boverton Redwood told the committee of the Persian oil possibilities. But the government was reluctant to enter into substantial private ventures. Under these circumstances

Pretyman looked for a respected figure in financial circles who could attract rich investors. He found his man in the person of Lord Strathcona, the founder and director of Canadian Pacific Railway and the Bank of Montreal, who in 1896 had taken the mantle of Canadian High Commissioner in London. The Admiralty along with Lord Strathcona encouraged Burma Oil Company to assist D'Arcy in his venture. Early in 1905 a concessions syndicate was formed with a share capital of £100,000, of which Burma took £95,000 and Lord Strathcona £5,000. The Admiralty thus succeeded in keeping the D'Arcy concession in British hands.[30]

Back in Iran a new problem cropped up in the south. When Reynolds and his men brought their drilling equipment to Masjid Sulaiman, the Temple of Solomon, they found themselves faced with local Bakhtiari tribesmen who would not honor the concession granted by the central government. They made it clear to the drilling team that they would not allow them to operate there unless their masters undertook to pay them 10 percent of the profits of any oil extracted in what they called their own territory. Instead of referring the matter to the Iranian government, the Foreign Office "loaned" John Richard Preece, the British consul general in Isfahan, to the D'Arcy group to help them resolve the dispute. Preece persuaded the Bakhtiari Khans to decrease their demands. On November 15, 1905, the Khans agreed to accept 3 out of every 100 ordinary shares of any company or companies formed that would deal with oil operations in the Bakhtiari area. They were also to be paid sums for providing guards for drilling and pipe-laying operations. The agreement with the Bakhtiari Khans led to the formation of the Bakhtiari Oil Company as a producing concern.[31]

In 1906 the syndicate was faced with a new critical element. The nationalist sentiments that had lain dormant since the cancellation of the tobacco concession reemerged on the Iranian scene, taking the form of increased opposition to the autocratic regime of Mozaffar ed-Din Shah and strong demands for a constitution that would guarantee parliamentary rule. Under great nationalist pressure, the Shah agreed to the drafting of such a constitution. By the time it was drafted, he was on his deathbed. The clergy begged him to "remember that he was about to meet his God, and should strive to take with him . . . some deed of great merit which might counterbalance his sins." This appeal moved him to sign the constitution on January 1, 1907, which brought great rejoicing by huge crowds in the capital.[32]

A week later Mozaffar ed-Din Shah died and was succeeded by his son, Mohammad Ali Mirza, who proved to be much less sympathetic to the constitution than his father and was determined to exercise the same autocratic powers that his predecessors had enjoyed. Meanwhile Russia and Britain, concerned with the impact on their interests of the constitutional struggles in Iran, set aside their rivalries and signed a treaty on August 31, 1907, in St. Petersburg dividing Iran into two zones of influence. By this treaty Britain undertook not to interfere with the interests of Russia in the northern half of the country, and the Russians agreed not to interfere in the south and the Persian Gulf area, which were vital to British domination in the Near East and India. This agreement provided the nationalists with a powerful weapon with which to fight against the domination of its signatories.[33]

On the day this treaty was concluded in St. Petersburg, Amin ol-Sultan, the all-powerful Iranian prime minister, was assassinated in Tehran. The assassin shot himself and died instantly. When the details of the Anglo-Russian agreement became known later in Iran, the assassin was venerated as a patriot. Those involved in the constitutional struggle did not challenge the D'Arcy concession. The nationalists were too busy with their endeavors in establishing the constitution to allow themselves to quarrel with the British.

D'Arcy's men went on drilling in the Masjid Sulaiman area. For their protection, the British government sent a detachment of twenty Indian troops under the command of a young lieutenant, Arnold Wilson, later to become Sir Arnold. Meanwhile, financing the operation became a critical problem. Early in 1908, in an effort to decide whether it was worth continuing the operation, Burma Oil sent an investigator to Iran who on his return reported that any further exploration would be unproductive. A cable was sent from London to Reynolds instructing him to stop work, dismantle the equipment worth the cost of transporting, and return home.

Reynolds was greatly upset. So was Lieutenant Wilson, who noted with bitterness in his diary: "I am tired of working here for these stay-at-home businessmen . . . masquerading in top hats as pioneers of Empire." Reynolds, however, decided to keep drilling until the receipt of written confirmation of the cable telling him to stop. And he was well rewarded. At 4 A.M. on the morning of May 26, 1908, oil was struck at a depth of 1,180 feet and a gusher of some fifty feet shot into the sky. At the end of May D'Arcy received a telegram about this long-awaited oil strike. He was so delighted that he promised his wife, Nina, a £1,500 Rolls Royce automobile, one of the first few hundred models to be manufactured.[34]

British enterprise, along with a total capital expenditure of £400,000 over eight years, had led to the discovery of oil in Iran. When it became certain that commercial quantities of oil were available, concern over financial problems evaporated. The task was to design a proper company with adequate financing to run all aspects of the operation. After months of discussions and negotiations between Lord Strathcona, D'Arcy, Burma Oil, bankers, technicians, and solicitors, the framework for the Anglo-Persian Oil Company (APOC) was drawn up. However, before the formation of such a company, D'Arcy, who was the owner of the concession and had spent much of his personal funds on its operations, had to be compensated.

Late in March 1909 an agreement was reached between him and the Burma Group under which he agreed to sell his concession, along with his rights and shares in various related agreements, for £203,067 19s 6d in cash and 170,000 fully paid ordinary shares of Burma Oil. Thus D'Arcy not only recouped his outlay but made a "profit" of £895,000, this being the value of his Burma Oil shares. The transfer of the concession from D'Arcy to another party could not take place without the approval of the Iranian government; but luckily for D'Arcy, Vincent Ketabji was both the Iranian commissioner and his partner. To obtain Ketabji's consent, D'Arcy gave him 11,900 of the Burma Oil shares allotted to himself.[35]

The way was now clear for the formation of the Anglo-Persian Oil Company, which on April 14, 1909, was incorporated with an authorized capital of £2 million, half in ordinary shares of £1 each and half in 6 percent preferred stock. The ordinary shares (common stock), allotted as fully paid, were transferred to Burma Oil (570,000), the concessions syndicate (400,000), and Lord Strathcona, who received 30,000 shares and was named chairman of the company. The preferred stock was offered to the public in April and snapped up within half an hour.[36]

The company's seven-member board, headed by Lord Strath-cona, included D'Arcy and Sir John Cargill, who was also a member of the Burma Oil board and had been active in negotiations with the Admiralty concerning the formation of APOC. The company's prospectus noted that "substantial contracts for fuel oil may be confidently looked for from the Admiralty," while pointing out that the outlet of the APOC's pipelines "will be at the head of the Persian Gulf, and so under British control." Lord Strathcona for his part acknowledged at the company's opening meeting "the valuable assistance received from the Foreign Office and the British Consul in Persia." "So began," remarks Elwell-Sutton, "the industry that was to see the Royal Navy through two world wars, and to cause Persia more trouble than all the political manoeuvrings of the great powers put together."[37]

During the years 1908 and 1909, when oil was discovered and APOC incorporated, Iran was in the throes of a constitutional struggle. Although Mozaffar ed-Din Shah had signed the constitution, which enabled Iran to send elected representatives to the National Assembly (Majlis), his son and successor, Mohammad Ali Shah, hated any institution that challenged his absolute power. His opposition to constitutional rule led to a revolt against him by constitutional forces, which mainly consisted of two classes. One was the traditional middle class, whose interests were threatened by monarchs who left the country at the mercy of foreign exploitation. The other was a new professional middle class with Western ideas. This class "espoused not the divine right of kings but the inalienable rights of man. . . . They venerated not the Shadows of God on Earth [kings] but the triumvirate of Equality, Liberty and Fraternity." The driving force behind both groups was a number of reformists, writers, and journalists who considered constitutionalism and nationalism vital for the establishment of a strong modern Iran.[38]

There were no political parties at the time. But those supporting constitutional rule had formed some one hundred political societies whose members met to exchange views and consolidate forces. These meetings resulted in the establishment of an intersociety "War Committee" to devise plans to fight against autocratic rule. A young man in his mid-twenties by the name of Mohammad Mossadeq, at that time vice-chairman of Majma'e Ensaniat (Society of Human-ity), became a member of this committee. Thus began the political life of the man who was to nationalize Iran's oil industry some forty years later.[39]

Mohammad Ali Shah, determined to do away with the Majlis, instructed Colonel Vladimir Liakhoff, a Russian officer who com-manded the Persian Cossack brigade, to wipe out the constitutional-ists. Liakhoff and his men dutifully did so by shelling the Majlis and the adjoining square, killing several hundred constitutionalists. This prompted an uprising against the Shah throughout the country and rallied new adherents to the nationalist cause. In July 1909 na-tionalist forces defeated the royalists and the Cossacks and oc-cupied the capital.

The Shah, finding himself in danger, took refuge in the Russian legation along with his family. After such a degrading flight he could not return to his throne. His twenty-year-old son, Prince Ahmad, left the sanctuary of the Russian legation on July 10, 1909, and took his oath as a constitutional monarch. The dethroned Shah, accom-panied by his wife, four children, ten women of the harem, and a number of other companions, departed for Odessa.[40]

The confusion in the capital hardly affected the southern areas of the country where oil was being produced. APOC confidently went on to plan for the construction of a pipeline to Abadan, at the northern tip of the Persian Gulf, and for building a port and refinery there. The Abadan area was inhabited mostly by ethnic Arabs and governed by Khaz'al, known as the Sheikh of Mohammerah, who, although nominally under the Iranian government, exercised auton-omy with British support. But the possible emergence of a constitu-tional government in Tehran endangered the Sheikh's autonomous rule. To remove his worries, Major Percy Cox, the British political resident in the Persian Gulf, in May 1909 offered the Sheikh "a guarantee that Britain would not allow the Persian Government to disturb the *status quo* of himself or of his heirs and successors." The Sheikh had no reason to doubt his assurances, since the political resident was "the uncrowned King of the Gulf."[41]

Major Cox's next step was to obtain from the Sheikh, at an annual rent of £650, a square mile of land in Abadan that APOC needed for the construction of a port and a refinery. This earned Cox the warm compliments of Sir Edward Grey, the Foreign Secretary, and the APOC directors for his faithful defense of the company's interests.

With the arrangements made with the Sheikh and earlier with Bakhtiari Khans, the British government strengthened autonomy in APOC's areas of operation against the authority of the central government. In fact Lord Strathcona, APOC's chairman, said as much at the general annual meeting in 1911: "As our part of Persia is within the Territories under the influence of the Sheikh of Mohammerah and the Bakhtiyari chiefs . . . we are fortunately able to view the present political situation in Persia with perfect equanimity. (Cheers.)" The Iranian government repeatedly objected to APOC about its business arrangements with the Sheikh and the Bakhtiaris, but to no avail.

With Abadan leased at less than £13 a week, engineers, refinery artisans, and workers from many nations—Persians, Arabs, Chinese, Burmese—poured in and built a refinery. The year 1912 was a banner year in the history of APOC as the pipeline between Masjid Sulaiman oil fields and the Abadan port and refinery was completed. The pipeline had an annual capacity of 400,000 tons, and 43,000 tons of crude oil were exported for the first time. By 1914, when World War I broke out, the export figure reached 274,000 tons. In that year the production of two wells alone, out of thirty drilled, was more than the pipeline could take. When the storage tanks were full, APOC set on fire the rest of the oil extracted and called a temporary halt to further drilling. One well, known as F.7, spouted 6.5 million tons of oil in its twelve-year life.[42]

As the Iranian oil fields developed, the British government became aware of the tremendous resources at APOC's disposal. In 1911, when Winston Churchill became the First Lord of the Admiralty, he revived the idea of converting the Royal Navy's fuel from coal to oil. To verify whether or not APOC was in a position to furnish adequate supplies to the Admiralty, a mission headed by Admiral Sir Edmond Slade, a former director of the Admiralty's Intelligence Division, was sent to Iran. A member of this mission was John Cadman, petroleum adviser to the Colonial Office and professor of mining at Birmingham University (who later became

APOC's chairman). The supply of oil in Iran was found to be abundant, and the mission recommended in 1914 that the Admiralty secure control of APOC.

As a result of this recommendation, Churchill urged that £2 million be spent to acquire 51 percent interest in APOC for the Admiralty. Some members of Parliament were concerned that the acquisition by the British government of a controlling interest in the company might provoke the Russians to occupy Iran's northern provinces, but the measure was approved in spite of these objections. As it happened, approval came forty-eight days before the start of World War I, in the course of which the Allied armies, as Curzon put it, floated to victory on a wave of oil.[43]

APOC increased its ordinary shares by the £2 million the British government had injected, and began expanding production facilities to meet the increasing fuel oil needs of the Admiralty. Meanwhile the British government appointed two members to the APOC board.

To quote Dr. Ferrier, the British Petroleum historian: "It is undeniable that the government shareholding in the Company changed the spirit of the D'Arcy Concession and had a profound impact on its standing within the context of international relations. The Company, however much it proclaimed its independence, was considered to be no longer just a private organisation, but a national enterprise for a national purpose." Thus many governments, including Iran's, believed that "the hidden hand of the British Government was to be detected behind most, if not all, of the activities of the Company."[44]

In May 1914 the Admiralty concluded a contract with APOC for the purchase of some 500,000 tons of fuel oil per year for a period of twenty years. The price was agreed to be 30s per ton f.o.b. Abadan, subject to rebates when the company's profits were higher than 10 percent on ordinary shares. The minimum price, however, was to be no less than £1 per ton. It was also agreed that in times of war the Admiralty would have the first option to obtain all the oil it required, no matter how much that might be, on the same favorable terms.[45]

When World War I broke out, the Admiralty's fuel oil requirements rose sharply. Thus the Abadan refinery increased its throughput while gearing up to produce the highest possible percentage of fuel oil, a figure that was to reach 65 percent. It was cheap Persian oil that fueled the British war machine during the war.

Churchill estimated that the Admiralty contract produced within eight years a saving of about £7.5 million "on the purchase price of oil as compared with current prices." To this figure he added three other major returns: £16 million for the appreciation in value of the government's shares over its original investment; £6.5 million in government receipts of dividends, interest, taxes, etc.; and £10 million from other factors, including the reduced price of oil supplied by other companies to Britain by reason of having to compete with APOC. In short, he concluded that the British government had gained, within a short period, a total of £40 million out of Iran's oil. Churchill went on to point out that the realized and potential profits of the British government's investment in APOC were such that "we may not unreasonably expect . . . to claim that the mighty fleets laid down in 1912, 1913, and 1914, the greatest ever built by any Power in an equal period, were added to the British Navy without costing a single penny to the taxpayer." Thus it is not surprising to find Churchill jubilantly saying: "Fortune brought us a prize from fairyland far beyond our brightest hopes."[46]

What was Iran's share out of her own fairyland? The total royalties paid to Iran from 1912, when oil exports began, up to 1924 were £3.7 million (see Table 1). The amount is so small because APOC did its utmost to reduce payments to Iran so as to maximize profits and expand its operations worldwide.

A major step by APOC to expand its overseas operations was the acquisition of the British Petroleum Company Ltd. (BP), a subsidiary of the European Petroleum Union of Bremen, which distributed Shell products in Britain. On the outbreak of World War I, BP and its associated firms were classed by the British government as enemy concerns because of their German connections. This helped APOC to purchase BP at a cost of £2 million, paid mainly in annual installments. The purchase included seven tankers, fifteen ocean installations, and hundreds of inland depots and railway tank wagons. This acquisition, together with the formation of the British Tanker Company, with a capital of £3 million, enabled APOC to possess its own shipping fleet and to evolve its own marketing strategy.[47] Thus APOC joined the big league of oil companies, along

TABLE 1

Iran's Oil Production, APOC Profits, and Royalty Payments to Iran,
1912–31

Year[a]	Oil production, 000 long tons (1)	AIOC profits,[b] £000 (2)	Royalty to Iran, £000 (3)
1912–13	80		
1913–14	274	27	10
1914–15	376	62	
1915–16	459	55	
1916–17	644	458	
1917–18	897	2,113	
1918–19	1,106	2,652	325[c]
1919–20	1,385	1,849	469
1920–21	1,743	3,264	585[d]
1921–22	2,327	3,779	593
1922–23	2,959	3,431	533
1923–24	3,714	3,517	411
1924–25	4,334	4,067	831
1925–26	4,556	4,397	1,054
1926–27	4,832	4,800	1,400
1927–28	5,358	4,106	502
Apr. 1 to Dec. 31, 1928	4,290	3,689	529
1929	5,461	4,274	1,437
1930	5,939	3,786	1,288
1931	5,750	2,413	307[e]

Sources: Col. (1), Fateh, *Panjah Sal,* p. 274. Cols (2) and (3), APOC Annual Reports and Mikdashi, *Middle East Oil Concessions,* pp. 45–46.

[a]From 1912 to 1928 the financial year ended on March 31. In 1928 the financial year changed to end on December 31.

[b]Profits after deduction of expenses, debenture and preferred stock interest, and royalty payments to Iran.

[c]The figure is the sum total of royalties paid to Iran during the six-year period 1913–14 to 1918–19.

[d]The amount does not include payment of £1 million in partial settlement of past claims.

[e]Under the 1933 Agreement this amount was adjusted to £1,339,132.

with Shell and Standard Oil of New Jersey. Its distributing organization soon spread to Europe, India, Australia, and South and West Africa, and later covered the whole world.

The company's expansion overseas was not confined to marketing and transport facilities alone. In 1921 it formed National Oil Refineries Ltd., building refineries at Llandarcy in Wales and Grangemouth in Scotland. This was followed by the acquisition of refineries in France, Belgium, Italy, and Australia. Until 1914

APOC's fixed assets were all in Iran, but the situation changed rapidly when internally generated funds were used to build a tanker fleet and refineries abroad.[48]

What made this great expansion possible was that Iran's oil wells proved to be tremendously productive. In the APOC report for the year 1917, the chairman proudly revealed that the annual production of 4 million tons of oil from fifteen wells of Masjid Sulaiman was made possible by an investment of £4 million only, whereas before the war some 2,000 wells in the Rumanian and Galician oilfields had produced less oil at an investment of £40 million.

Nevertheless, APOC used every possible device to reduce Iran's royalty payments. In February 1915, during World War I, Bakhtiari tribesmen (instigated by German agents) blew up the pipeline joining the oilfields to the Abadan refinery. APOC declared that it considered the Iranian government responsible for the incident and lodged a claim for £614,489 3s 1d, of which £402,887 was claimed for the cost of repairs and the balance for the loss of production. Furthermore APOC announced that it would withhold royalty payments until the matter was settled. By giving so precise a figure, the company apparently wanted to impress the Iranians with its scrupulousness in calculation. Yet, as shown later, both the amount and the nature of the claim were baseless.[49]

Under the terms of the D'Arcy concession of 1901 the Iranian government demanded that the matter be submitted to arbitration. The British minister in Tehran announced that APOC would not allow anyone to question either its right to damages or its right to withhold royalties. Meanwhile, APOC withheld the payment of royalties for 1916 and 1917, which totaled £44,347. Considering the large sum claimed for repairs and loss of production, it looked as if APOC, backed by the British government, intended not to pay any royalties to Iran for a decade or more; and the Iranian government accordingly decided after the war to challenge the company's claims. Late in 1919 Iran asked Sydney Armitage-Smith, her British financial adviser, to look into the matter. Armitage-Smith, a former assistant secretary to the British Treasury who had come to Iran under an agreement reached in August 1919 (see Chapter 2), employed William McLintock, a leading chartered accountant, to look into the company's accounts.

McLintock completed his report in February 1920. He found that the damage to the pipeline, which the company had assessed at £402,887, amounted to no more than £20,000. Moreover, he contended that the damage was not the responsibility of Iran, which had declared neutrality in the war only to be invaded by the British, but was the work of Britain's enemies, who knew the importance of the pipeline to the Royal Navy. McLintock also discovered that APOC, while claiming damages from Iran, had at the same time charged £10,000 a year for these damages as operating expenses, thus lowering its nominal profits and also lowering the royalties payable to Iran.[50]

McLintock's job was also to find out whether the company in fact paid Iran 16 percent of the net profits as specified by the terms of the 1901 D'Arcy concession. He found numerous irregularities in APOC's bookkeeping methods. The company had deducted each year a sum from its net profits, on which Iran's royalties were based, for a sinking fund to which Iran was not obligated to contribute. It had also deducted yearly interest on debentures issued by its subsidiaries while at the same time claiming that the Iranian government had no right to share in the profits of such subsidiaries; this claim was in violation of Article 10 of the 1901 concession, which said that Iran had to be paid annually "a sum equal to 16 percent of the annual net profits of any company or companies that may be formed."

Another bookkeeping gimmick concerned First Exploitation Company (FEC), in which Iran was a shareholder. APOC reduced the profits of FEC by charging against it all the construction costs of the APOC organization as a whole. It also made FEC, as primary producer, sell oil below cost price to Bakhtiari Oil Company, which in turn sold it to APOC at normal prices. Also improperly deducted from royalties payable to Iran were the amounts APOC paid to Bakhtiari chiefs for protecting the pipelines, plus 3 percent of the profits of operations in their area. Yet another way that APOC reduced the sums due to Iran was by selling fuel oil at cut prices to the Admiralty.[51]

McLintock's report upset APOC by revealing its "artificial" transactions and bookkeeping methods. It not only rejected APOC claims but, in the words of Armitage-Smith, "disclosed certain undoubted errors and irregularities of accounting, which had resulted in under-payment of royalty" to the Iranian government. An important point raised by McLintock was that Iran was "entitled to claim 16 percent on the profits of all the subsidiary companies of the Anglo-Persian Oil Company carrying on business outside Persia." APOC chairman Charles Greenway, finding his company caught red-handed, did not reply to specific points raised in McLintock's report. Instead, he wrote to Iran's foreign minister, Nostrat od-Dowleh, dropping APOC's claim for damages and offering to settle Iran's claims up to March 1919 by making a lump-sum payment of £500,000. This amount was later raised to £1 million. He also resumed paying royalties to Iran. Although APOC, by offering a settlement, admit-ted to its wrongdoing, it did not address the subject of Iran's share in its subsidiaries.[52]

When Iran's pressure on this point grew, APOC argued that the terms of the concession drawn up twenty years earlier had become irrelevant to changing circumstances. It threatened that if Iran claimed a share of profits in subsidiary companies, APOC would detach them from the parent body, thus nullifying Iran's claims. Although this threat was farfetched, it helped pave the way for a compromise. In December 1920 Armitage-Smith and APOC con-cluded a draft agreement that constituted a major revision of the D'Arcy concession.

Under this agreement, the Iranian government was entitled to 16 percent of the profits from all operations carried out by APOC in Iran; but with regard to subsidiaries outside Iran its royalties were to be based only on that portion of profits "defined and calculated" by APOC as being associated with Iranian oil. Not only did this arrangement leave a lot to APOC's discretion, but also it ignored the important fact that the subsidiaries had been formed with the profits from Iranian oil. Furthermore, large deductions granted to the company in calculating Iran's share of the profits in the subsid-iaries induced APOC to establish refineries outside Iran so as to reduce Iran's share of the profits.[53]

Armitage-Smith, considering himself to be the full representative of the Iranian government, signed the agreement with APOC on December 20, 1920. When the agreement was passed on to a firm of London solicitors to check its contents, they reported to Iran that

Armitage-Smith had exceeded his instructions by offering deductions to APOC in violation of the terms of the concession that called for a full 16 percent of the profits of APOC and all subsidiary companies "formed for the purpose of working the Concession or any part thereof."[54]

Representing as it did a substantial modification of the 1901 concession, the new agreement required ratification by the Majlis. This did not occur. Yet APOC, paying no heed to Iran's objections, considered the agreement valid and adjusted its royalty payments according to its terms. Iran had little choice. After all, the company was much stronger than the Iranian government.

2

Reza Shah and the 1933 Concession

The Russian Revolution of 1917 and the collapse of the Tsarist regime created an opportunity for Britain to look for absolute political and economic supremacy in Iran. Lord Curzon, who succeeded Arthur Balfour as Foreign Secretary in 1919, argued that

> we possess in the south-western corner of Persia great assets in the shape of oil fields, which are worked for the British Navy and which give us a commanding interest in that part of the world. . . . [Persia's] geographical position, the magnitude of our interests in the country, and the future safety of our Eastern Empire render it impossible for us now . . . to disinterest ourselves from what happens in Persia.

Curzon's scheme was to put Iran's civil and military administration under British direction. In 1919 he instructed Sir Percy Cox, then promoted to the rank of British minister in Tehran, to arrange the conclusion of an agreement that would bring Iran under full British control.[1]

Under the draft agreement prepared in London, Britain was to furnish Iran with military and administrative advisers "endowed with adequate powers" to equip and train the Iranian Army, to direct the country's finances and customs, and to construct roads and railroads—all at Iran's expense. Britain, however was to lend Iran £2 million secured by customs revenue and "other sources of income at the disposal of the Persian Government," which meant oil. In brief, the suggested agreement put Iran under British tutelage—a tutelage that was to be financed by Iran.[2]

For a number of reasons Britain was certain the Iranian government would approve this agreement. British forces were still in Iran after the European war. They had arrested Iranians unfriendly to the British, and Ahmad Shah had been forced to appoint anglophile ministers. The British government paid the Shah a monthly subsidy of £5,000 to keep the ardent anglophile, Vosuq od-Dowleh, as prime minister, and it was with Vosuq and two other anglophile ministers that Cox would be negotiating.[3] As a final precaution these three ministers were bribed £131,000 to arrange the conclusion of the agreement, a sum quietly charged against the first installment of the £2 million loan. The three ministers, who knew that the agreement would be unpopular and might cause them trouble, took the precaution of obtaining written guarantees from Percy Cox that they would be afforded "asylum in the British empire should necessity arise."[4]

The agreement was eventually approved by the Iranian Cabinet on August 9, 1919. Britain, taking Majlis approval for granted, lost no time in sending military and financial advisers, among them Armitage-Smith, to implement the agreement. But British optimism proved to be premature. Iranian nationalists, supported by the general public, began a concerted attack on the government for having signed such an agreement. Severe criticism also came from other countries, including not only Russia but also the United States and France. The agreement was not ratified by the Majlis in spite of British pressure.

Curzon could not have chosen a worse time for his scheme. It was precisely when Russia was trying to weaken European powers in Asia by supporting nationalist movements there. On January 14, 1918, Leon Trotsky had annulled the 1907 Anglo-Russian treaty that divided Iran into two zones of influence, "in view of its inconsistency with the freedom and independence of the Persian nation." Furthermore, a Russian note to Iran on June 26, 1919, in which Tsarist Russia and Britain were accused of "devastation" and "oppression" in Iran, expressed readiness to compensate Iran "for losses incurred by Russia" while hoping that Iran would claim damages from "the English Imperialist Government."[5] Russia's show of sympathy with Iran led to negotiations that ended in the conclusion of a treaty of friendship between the two.

Britain, however, decided to strengthen her position in Iran while the British forces, under the command of Major General Edmond Ironside, were still in that country. In January 1920, Ironside obtained the Iranian government's agreement to refit the Persian Cossacks, a force of 3,000 Iranians under Russian officers stationed near Qazvin. Ironside dismissed the Russian officers and put Reza Khan, an Iranian officer, in command, under the watchful eye of Colonel Henry Smyth, a British officer placed in charge of the Cossacks' administration and finance. Ironside wanted to use the force to oppose any attempt by the Russian Bolsheviks to attack the British forces in the course of their withdrawal or possibly to occupy Tehran and take over the government.

On his choice of Reza Khan, Ironside noted in his diary: "He seemed to me a strong and fearless man who had his country's good at heart." Although he told Reza Khan "not to take or allow to be taken any violent measures to depose the Shah," he despised Ahmad Shah as "a wretched specimen of a man in so great a position." Iran, he wrote in his diary, "needs a strong man to bring her through." In another entry he added: "In fact a military dictatorship would solve our troubles and let us get out of the country without any trouble at all."[6] As we shall see, the appointment of Reza Khan had a major impact not only on the history of Iran but on the future course of APOC.

Having completed his mission in Iran, Ironside left for Bagdad. Meanwhile in Tehran an anglophile journalist, Seyyed Zia ed-Din Tabatabai, in cooperation with three members of the British legation, plotted a coup against the government to be carried out with the help of the Cossack Brigade. When Reza Khan and Colonel Smyth proved agreeable, Zia, backed by his friends at the British legation, obtained funds from the British Imperial Bank to pay off Reza Khan and the Cossacks.[7]

On February 20, 1921, Zia, along with Reza Khan and his Cossack forces, marched on Tehran, meeting hardly any resistance. Five days later Zia became prime minister and Reza Khan commander of Iran's armed forces. In Bagdad, Ironside noted in his diary: "I fancy that all the people think I engineered the coup d'etat. I suppose I did strictly speaking."[8] Colonel Smyth credited himself for the operation, saying that "he had organised the Cossack coup in Tehran . . . with the knowledge of British legation."[9] However, Herman Norman denied that he, as the British minister in Tehran, had been involved in any way.[10]

To make himself popular, Zia denounced the 1919 Anglo-Persian agreement and on February 26, 1921, concluded the Russian-Persian Friendship Treaty agreement which strengthened the hand of nationalists against British domination in Iran. In it the Soviet Republic declared null and void all previous treaties with Britain and other European powers that affected Iran and made her "a prey to the cupidity and tyranny of European robbers." It also nullified all previous treaties and conventions between Tsarist Russia and Iran and renounced Russia's rights to the repayment of loans granted to Iran.[11]

It was, however, Article 6 of this treaty that protected Iran from British territorial domination and at the same time exposed her to Russia. The article says that if a third party attacks Persia or seeks "to use Persian territory as a base for operations against Russia . . . and if the Persian Government should not be able to put a stop to such menace . . . Russia will have the right to advance her troops into the Persian interior for the purpose of carrying out military operations necessary for its defence." As we shall see, it was this article that prompted the United States to prevent Britain from occupying Abadan in 1951, after the nationalization of the oil industry in Iran.

Having denounced the Anglo-Persian agreement and signed the Russian-Persian Treaty, Zia lost the support of the British and his government soon fell. The Cabinet that replaced Zia's in June included three prominent figures who over the next twenty years were to play a crucial role in changing Iran's relations with APOC. The new prime minister was Ahmad Qavam, an aristocrat. The other two, both chosen by Qavam, were Mohammad Mossadeq as finance minister and Reza Khan as minister of war.

As minister of war, Reza Khan, with great skill and stamina, soon succeeded in restoring order and security throughout the country. His determination to strengthen the central government, however, clashed with Britain's desire to support the autonomous Bakhtiari Khans and Sheikh Khaz'al, with whom APOC dealt directly (see Chapter 1). To calm British concerns, Reza Khan told Sir Percy Loraine, who had replaced Norman as British minister in Tehran, that it would be in the British government's interest to support internal security in Iran. Loraine, who had great admiration for Reza Khan's "personal vigour and his singleness of purpose and his patriotism," believed that he could be trusted to protect British interests.[12] He had developed friendly relations with Reza Khan; the two had frequent poker games at the legation, which Reza Khan engaged in to show his friendship with the British.[13]

As Reza Khan's power increased, he tamed the Bakhtiari Khans and brought them under the control of his war ministry. Loraine, who knew that soon Sheikh Khas'al would also be brought under submission, advised the Foreign Office "to encourage internal security and to entrust the protection of British interests to the Imperial [Iranian] authorities." But some in London felt otherwise. The India Office suggested dispatching a gunboat to Mohammerah to support the Sheikh. Others doubted the wisdom of taking such action.[14]

Meanwhile Reza Khan, backed by the army, took advantage of Ahmad Shah's weakness and made himself prime minister on October 29, 1923. The Shah left for Europe never to return. Britain, divided between giving protection to Sheikh Khaz'al and maintaining good relations with Reza Khan, took no specific measures. Consequently in April 1925 Reza Khan's forces captured Sheikh Khaz'al and took him to Tehran, thus ending the autonomous rule of a man to whom the British had given assurances of full protection and who had been invested for his services as a Knight Commander of the Most Eminent Order of the Indian Empire (KCIE). He died in Tehran as a virtual prisoner in 1936.[15]

Reza Khan's ambitions did not end with the premiership. He aimed at becoming head of state as president. When the clergy advised him against changing the institution of monarchy, he decided to terminate the Qajar dynasty and crown himself king. To gain British support, he discussed his scheme with Loraine, who, after consulting the Foreign Office, told him that the British government was determined "to leave Persia absolutely free to settle internal affairs," adding that, "in return we did expect our questions to be taken in hand and settled as soon as possible." Reza Khan gave his assurances.[16] Meanwhile, by a mixture of solicitation and intimidation, he won over a majority of the deputies in the Majlis, whose approval was required for his takeover of the throne. In October 1925 the Majlis was presented with a bill terminating the Qajar dynasty and establishing the Pahlavi dynasty beginning with

Reza Khan. During the debate, Mossadeq, then a Majlis deputy, strongly opposed the bill. He considered such a move to be unconstitutional, leading to dictatorship.[17]

In spite of his objections and those of three others, the bill was ratified by the Majlis, and less than six months later, on April 25, 1926, Reza Khan crowned himself as the first king of the Pahlavi dynasty. Lady Loraine assisted the new Shah in his coronation, and the British government was the first to recognize his regime. In Iran itself the change was welcomed by the majority of the people as promising an end to insecurity and disorder.

The new Shah started a program for modernization of the country and its armed forces. To have a free hand in the affairs of state, he began a campaign to eliminate local and foreign privileges. He subdued the power of politicians, landlords, mullahs, and the tribes and then, to Britain's surprise, concentrated on limiting the influence of the British and their institutions in Iran. Although he had come to power with Britain's blessing, as king he considered it essential to liberate his country from Britain's grip. In 1928 he founded Bank Melli Iran, the country's national bank, and two years later he transferred to it the Imperial Bank's right to issue notes. But APOC proved problematic.

In Iranian eyes APOC represented "the epitome of foreign intervention" as it controlled and exploited Iran's greatest natural asset while giving her "a miserable pittance in return for the millions it took away."[18] This was unacceptable to Reza Shah. Furthermore he was unhappy that the British government had a majority share in the company while Iran had none. He was convinced that APOC's worldwide position had its origins in Iranian oil and thus felt that Iran was justified in demanding her proper share in the entire operations of the company.

In July 1928 Reza Shah sent Abdol-Hossein Teymurtash, his influential court minister, to London for discussions with Sir John Cadman, who was then chairman of both APOC and the newly established Turkish Petroleum Company, later to be called the Iraq Petroleum Company (IPC). In a series of meetings Teymurtash tried to convince Cadman of the need for a new relationship between APOC and Iran. He told him that if the Iranians were given a fair share of the business, they would extend every assistance in furthering the company's development and progress. Teymurtash's main proposal was for the Iranian government to receive 25 percent of APOC's common stock free of charge and a royalty of 2s per ton on the quantity of oil produced. His aim was for Iran to earn an annual sum of £1 million.[19]

Cadman, unlike his predecessors, was sympathetic to the Iranian cause. He knew that many vocal critics in Iran resented that it was Britain that benefited most from Iranian oil. He also understood Iranian resentment of the fact that the British government was a majority shareholder in APOC while Iran—which owned the oil resources—was conspicuously absent as a shareholder. He believed that making Iran a partner in the industry's fortunes would preserve the future of the concession.[20]

Meanwhile, Reza Shah sent a message to Cadman through Mostafa Fateh, APOC's highest-ranking Iranian official, saying that "Iran can no longer tolerate watching huge oil revenues go into the pockets of foreigners while she is being deprived of them."[21] The Iranian press followed this up with a campaign against the company. One wrote that the 1901 D'Arcy concession was granted by a corrupt ignorant government bribed by unscrupulous financiers to swindle Iran.[22]

Cadman, after protracted discussions with his board, succeeded in obtaining approval of Iran's participation in APOC as a shareholder, provided that her shares be inalienable and nonvoting. With Cadman's persuasion, Winston Churchill, then Chancellor of the Exchequer, consented to the scheme. Cadman went to Tehran in February 1929 with a team of legal and financial advisers and presented the draft of a new agreement, which called for APOC to provide Iran with 20 percent of its common stock free of charge, to pay Iran 2s per ton on the quantity of oil produced, to reduce its area of the concession to 100,000 square miles, and in return to obtain a thirty-year extension of the concession.

Although earlier negotiations with Cadman were conducted solely by Teymurtash, the Shah now instructed A. A. Davar, minister of justice, and N. D. Firuz, minister of finance, to join him. As a result, Teymurtash, in an effort to gain the Shah's esteem, saw fit to take a very hard line with the British. He proposed that the Iranians receive 25 percent of the common stock, a guaranteed minimum annual revenue, and all relevant taxes and duties, and that they retain their share and interest after the expiration of the concession. In return Iran would grant APOC a twenty-year extension.[23]

Cadman considered the Iranian demands exorbitant and returned to London to discuss the matter with his board. Sir William Fraser and other board members who, out of respect for Cadman, had reluctantly agreed to giving Iran 20 percent of the stock, rejected the new proposals. Meanwhile the New York Stock Exchange collapsed and the price of oil fell sharply. Because of the resulting uncertainty, APOC was no longer interested in pursuing negotiations for Iranian participation. On August 7, 1931, Cadman wrote to Teymurtash saying that no settlement could at present be worked out owing to "an excessive difference between the views of the Persian Government and the Company as to what is possible and equitable." He added that "the whole question . . . can only be effectively discussed when . . . the present chaotic condition of the oil industry has disappeared."[24]

There was a fleeting moment when all the elements needed for a fair settlement of the oil dispute were in place. Reza Shah, in full control of Iran, wanted an honorable settlement, and Lord Cadman was all for Iran's partnership in APOC. The conclusion of an agreement that made Iran a participant in the company's interests would have dissipated, or at least delayed, the traumatic disputes that led to oil nationalization in 1951. But that fateful moment passed thanks to Teymurtash's mistaken belief that Iran had time to bargain for more. He had gambled for high stakes and Iran had lost.

The Shah's inconsiderate haste in military buildup and public works had put severe strains on the government's finances. APOC was fully aware of Iran's financial difficulties and knew that the Shah had no alternative but to come to a settlement.

In September 1931 Teymurtash went to Switzerland to place Crown Prince Mohammad Reza in a school there. He met Cadman in Lausanne for further negotiations, which later continued in Paris and London. This time their discussions did not deal with Iranian participation in APOC, which the company was no longer ready to contemplate, but with providing a new basis for the payment of royalties and taxes. The negotiations led to the drafting of an agreement that raised APOC's royalty payments from 16 percent to

20 percent of the net profits on all operations connected with Iranian oil conducted by APOC and its subsidiaries. The additional 4 percent was in lieu of Iranian taxes. After numerous amendments, a draft agreement was initialed on May 22, 1932, by Cadman and Isa Khan, Iran's commissioner in London.[25]

Just as the scene was set for approval of this agreement in Tehran, Teymurtash learned that royalty payments for 1931 would be only £306,870, less than a quarter of the royalties of the year before and the lowest figure since 1917. Iran's oil production, which in 1930 was 5.9 million tons and earned £1.3 million in royalties, had dropped by only 3.2 percent to 5.75 million tons in 1931; but the corresponding royalties had dropped by 76.2 percent (see Table 1, p. 18). The reason for such a disproportionate fall was that APOC had sharply reduced its royalty per ton in 1931. True, the depression had reduced the company's profits by 37 percent but not by 76 percent. The Iranian press began a concerted attack against the company, alleging that it falsified accounts to defraud the Iranian Treasury. The government demanded that its representatives be allowed to examine the accounts and that APOC's representatives come to Tehran for discussions over the draft agreement. The company's response to both demands was negative. It used delaying tactics for months.

Reza Shah, whose country was in the middle of a financial crisis, was furious. At a Cabinet meeting on November 26, 1932, he told Teymurtash to bring in APOC's file. When the file was given to him, "he threw it in the fireplace and told us not to leave until we have cancelled the Concession."[26] On the following day, H. Taqizadeh, who had replaced Firuz as finance minister, sent a note to T. L. Jacks, APOC's resident director in Tehran, declaring the D'Arcy concession of 1901 null and void because it did not secure Iran's interests. The note added, however, that if the company was prepared to change its attitude by keeping Iran's interests in mind, the government would not refrain from granting it a new concession. Three days later, to the joy of the public, the Majlis unanimously approved the cancellation of the concession.[27]

The British Cabinet and the APOC board were thrown into a state of frenzy. After consultations between the two, Sir Reginald Hoare, the British minister in Tehran, sent a strong note of protest to the Iranian government. What followed bore a remarkable similarity to what would occur later during the nationalization of the oil industry in 1951. The British government took up APOC's cause and declared that the cancellation of the concession was an inadmissible breach of its terms. It demanded "the immediate withdrawal of the notification" of cancellation.[28]

Meanwhile Hoare suggested that the Foreign Office stem the crisis instantly by sending units of the East Indies Squadron to the Persian Gulf, putting Indian troops in the area on alert, and giving both these moves wide publicity. His proposals were presented to the Cabinet. The military option was referred to the Chiefs of Staff, who noted that the fleet could move quickly to the area if needed.[29]

When the Iranian government refused to withdraw its notification, Hoare wrote back on December 8, 1932, saying that the cancellation was a breach of international law and that his government would refer the matter to the Permanent Court of International Justice at The Hague. The note added that in case of any damage to APOC's interests, "His Majesty's Government will regard themselves as entitled to take all such measures as the situation may demand for that Company's protection." The Foreign Office knew that the Permanent Court dealt with treaties and conventions between governments and not with concessions granted to a private company; its purpose was simply to frighten Iran with a clear hint of military action. In a note of December 12, Iran's foreign minister, M. A. Foruqi, deplored the British government's "threats and intimidation." Pointing out that the Permanent Court was not competent to deal with the matter, he added that the Iranian government would consider it "within their rights in bringing to the notice of the Council of the League of Nations the threats and pressure which have been directed against them."[30]

The British Cabinet decided on December 14 to refer the matter to the League of Nations before Iran could do so. The feeling was that there were certain advantages in being the plaintiff rather than the defendant. Sir John Simon, the Secretary of State for Foreign Affairs, who happened to be in Geneva, "hurried in person to the Secretary-General—Geneva gossip had it that he actually ran in order to be sure of getting there first—with a formal demand that the question should be placed on the agenda of the Council."[31]

The proceedings before the Council started in January 1933. The Iranian delegation, headed by Minister of Justice A. A. Davar, told the Council that the 1901 D'Arcy concession had been obtained by devious means from an autocratic Iranian government that had no constitutional base. It contended that APOC had evaded proper payment of royalties and refused payment of Iranian taxes while using its "illegal" gains for enormous investments in other parts of the world. Furthermore, APOC had not permitted the Iranian government to inspect its accounts, had failed to employ Iranians except as laborers and petty staff, and had refrained from training local staff, sending only two Iranians as students to Britain over the years. Davar stressed that the Armitage-Smith agreement was not valid, having never been ratified by the Majlis—yet APOC had based Iran's payments on it. And finally, the Iranians pointed out that even if APOC was allowed oil free of charge and had to pay only the applicable local taxes and customs duties, the amount would have been £19 million instead of the £11 million so far received in royalties. The Iranian delegation concluded that since APOC had in every possible way failed to act according to the terms of the 1901 concession, the government's only course was to cancel it.[32]

The British delegation, headed by Sir John Simon, denied all these points, calling them pure allegations. The cancellation of the concession, Sir John said, was contrary to international law. If the Iranian government did not consider the Armitage-Smith agreement valid, he asked, why did it accept a settlement of £1 million based on that agreement? He considered the royalty payments fair and contended, incorrectly, that the Iranian government had regularly examined APOC's books.[33]

Britain was concerned that the matter might be referred to arbitration, which would oblige the company to open its books for inspection. The Iranians, unaware of this worry, did not ask for arbitration, feeling that if they did so Britain would overwhelm them through her power and influence.[34] The Council, after hearing both sides, instructed Dr. Eduard Beneš of Czechoslovakia, who was appointed as rapporteur, to see if he could reconcile the two parties. Beneš persuaded both parties to open direct negotiations for the purpose of drafting a "new concession."

Early in April 1933, negotiations began in Tehran. APOC's leading negotiators were Sir John Cadman, his deputy Sir William Fraser, and Dr. M. Y. Young, the company's physician in Iran, now a deputy director. The Iranian team was composed of M. A. Foruqi, foreign minister; A. A. Davar, minister of justice; H. Taqizadeh, finance minister; and Hossein Ala, president of Bank Melli. Teymurtash, who had conducted the previous negotiations, was conspicuously absent. The Shah had become suspicious of him and had put him under arrest.

Before leaving London, Cadman received a letter from Lord Greenway, his predecessor, in which he said, "With the [British] Government behind you, you will be in a strong position . . . and I have no doubt that you will be able to pull off a new agreement that will be in every way satisfactory to APOC."[35] Both the APOC board and the British government told Cadman to shake off his sympathies for Iran and to press hard for maximum gains. To make sure that the board's wishes were kept in mind, it sent William Fraser, a tough Scotsman, along with Cadman. In fact, Cadman, saying that he did not feel well, generally left it to Fraser to conduct the negotiations.

By canceling the D'Arcy concession of 1901, the Shah stated, he wanted to "wipe out the slate clean and enable a new concession to be worked out" that would set a fair basis for Iran's relations with APOC. The company, for its part, wanted to take advantage of the occasion to eliminate certain troublesome parts of the concession and replace them with new ones that would be more favorable to itself. Now that its operations were not confined to Iran but extended to the rest of the world, APOC's intention was to avoid giving Iran a share in the profits of its subsidiaries, as the concession called for; rather, it proposed to base royalty payments only on the quantity of oil produced in Iran. Iran, however, wanted a mixed balance between the two and insisted on limiting the area of the concession and the cancellation of APOC's exclusive right on laying pipelines to the Persian Gulf. With such contradictory demands, the two parties found that they were far apart.[36]

Cadman met the Shah and reminded him that in 1929, when Iran had rejected APOC's offer of 20 percent shareholding, it had been agreed to reopen negotiations after the depression passed. Unfortunately for the Shah, he could not wait that long; needing substantial funds right away, he insisted on negotiations at a time when the company was in no mood to improve its terms. While expressing his unhappiness with the British government's intervention in the matter, he asked Cadman "to assist him in opening a new page in Persian history and to start with a clean slate." The Shah's plea, however, did not move Fraser, who had taken charge of APOC's negotiations and "was not prepared to meet any sort of compromise." The problem was aggravated by the fact that the Iranians, fearful of the Shah, did not dare to express their opinions. Cadman reported to the Foreign Office: "The atmosphere here is dreadful, the Persian ministers seem afraid for their necks and are almost terrified to speak to or be seen with me or any of my party."[37]

When negotiations came to a stalemate, Cadman made a shrewd move. As he put it, he "had come to the conclusion that the only way to break the deadlock was to present the Shah with a shock decision." He sent word that he intended to leave. The Shah, disturbed, invited him to his palace and asked him to stay on. Cadman, who knew that in the Shah's presence his ministers would lose every initiative, suggested that "the Shah should take the chair which could be the final attempt to resolve the deadlock."[38] The Shah agreed, and a meeting took place at the palace with him at the head of the table.

Cadman's astute strategy, the Shah's authoritarian attitude, and the timidity of the Iranian team at the meeting were central to the atmosphere in which decisions on the 1933 agreement were reached. The Shah, opening the meeting, suggested that the differences between his ministers and APOC should be fully set out. Cadman, in his own words, "side-stepped this desire and suggested that the Company's new terms should be considered first." The Shah agreed. The ministers were "taken by surprise" but did not dare to contradict their sovereign and "sat in subdued silence."

Addressing his ministers, the Shah said "they were down on the ground and could not see very far beyond their own noses whereas he was placed on a pinnacle and could see the great world around him." With these words from their absolute monarch, they knew that if they wanted to keep their heads they had to keep silent and let him make the decisions. The Shah listened only to APOC's men and did not trouble to ask his ministers for their views.[39]

On April 25, when the two sides met again, there was only one text on the table to discuss: the draft agreement prepared by APOC. Cadman, who had found his first shock treatment of the Shah effective, now tried a second. He suggested that the period of the new concession should be "at least seventy-five years to assure continuity."[40] The D'Arcy concession of 1901 was to terminate in 1961, but Cadman wanted a new one to run until the year 2008. The Shah, upset by such an unexpected demand, responded: "This is impossible. For thirty years we have cursed our predecessors for granting this [D'Arcy concession]. Do you want us to be cursed . . . by future generations?"[41] However, faced with the persistence of the company team and his fear of British military intervention, the Shah finally agreed to give APOC a new concession for a period of sixty years, while the company agreed to reduce the concession area to 100,000 square miles.

The Shah, almost the only one on the Iranian side to talk, raised only a few comparatively trivial points, one being that the people in the northern provinces "had no oil for their lamps . . . and they often had to burn tallow at night"; he wanted APOC to supply them with kerosene. Ignorant as he was of the complicated issues in a sixty-year oil agreement, he did not raise any essential questions, while his ministers, fearful of giving him advice, kept silent. APOC's draft was finalized in no time with some modifications, among them the change of name from Anglo-Persian to Anglo-Iranian Oil Company (AIOC). The Shah did not like Iran to be called Persia. On April 29, 1933, the new concession was signed by both parties.[42]

On Cadman's arrival in London, letters of congratulation poured in. The British were jubilant that he and Fraser had pulled off a new agreement that would secure the company's operations in Iran for the next sixty years with much higher benefits. But, as things turned out, their deal was too shrewd to last. True, Iran gained a reduction of the company's area of operation from 500,000 square miles to 100,000 and the elimination of the company's exclusive right to construct pipelines to Iran's Persian Gulf coast. As to the financial gains, they were inconclusive. Whereas Iran's royalties under the D'Arcy concession were 16 percent of the net profits of any company formed, the new concession based payments on a combination of tonnage royalty and profit-sharing. AIOC was to pay Iran royalties of 4s per ton based on the price of gold to cover against possible sterling devaluation. The tonnage payment was on oil sold for consumption in Iran or exported. This meant that AIOC could use, free of charge, vast quantities of oil required in its Iranian operations and by its ocean tankers. As an example, in 1947 consumption for these purposes amounted to 1.5 million tons, which could have brought Iran a tonnage royalty of £300,000.

Iran was also to have a share in AIOC's overall profits around the world equivalent to 20 percent of dividends distributed among holders of common stock in excess of £671,250. But Iran had no means of ensuring whether AIOC, in calculating Iran's share, had included all its subsidiaries. In fact the company's statement of December 31, 1950, noted: "The accounts of fifty-nine subsidiary companies . . . have not been included in the Consolidated Accounts since your Directors are of the opinion that such consolidation would be misleading."[43]

At the expiration of the concession the company also had to pay Iran 20 percent of the amount by which its general reserves exceeded the 1932 level. Iran, however, had no control over the allocation of net profits between dividends and reserves. In fact the British government set limits on the distribution of dividends during and after World War II. Most important of all, Iran was left at the mercy of the British government, which by increasing AIOC's taxes decreased the company's net profits and thus Iran's 20 percent share in dividends and general reserves.

In lieu of taxation, AIOC had to pay Iran annually $9d$ per ton for the first 6 million tons and $6d$ on every additional ton for the first fifteen years. These amounts were to be increased respectively to $15d$ and $9d$ during the following fifteen years. Thus Iran's taxes on AIOC were fixed and frozen for the next thirty years while the British government could and did greatly increase its taxes. As an example, in 1947 AIOC paid Iran £308,000 in lieu of taxation, whereas it paid £14.8 million in taxes to the British government. This was more than double the sum of £7.1 million, the total receipts of Iran from AIOC in that year (see Table 2).

Without doubt, Iran's most significant blunder was extending the company's concession by thirty-two years over the previous one. Iran would have done better to press the company to abide by the terms of the D'Arcy concession. Then on the expiration of the

TABLE 2
TABLE 2

Iran's Oil Production, AIOC Net Profits, British Taxes, and Payments to Iran,
1932–50

Year	Oil production, 000 long tons	AIOC net profits, £000[a]	British taxes, £000	Payments to Iran, £000
1932	6,446	2,380	195	1,525
1933	7,087	2,654	305	1,812
1934	7,537	3,183	512	2,190
1935	7,488	3,519	409	2,221
1936	8,198	6,123	911	2,580
1937	10,168	7,455	1,652	3,525
1938	10,195	6,109	1,157	3,307
1939	9,583	2,986	1,956	4,271
1940	8,627	2,842	2,975	4,000
1941	6,605	3,222	2,921	4,000
1942	9,339	7,790	4,918	4,000
1943	9,706	5,639	7,663	4,000
1944	13,274	5,677	10,636	4,464
1945	16,839	5,792	10,381	5,624
1946	19,190	9,625	10,279	7,132
1947	20,195	18,565	14,800	7,104
1948	24,871	24,065	28,310	9,172
1949	26,807	18,390	22,480	13,489
1950	31,750	33,103	50,707	16,032

Sources: AIOC Annual Reports; Fateh, *Panjah Sal,* pp. 281, 307, 319–20; Mikdashi, *Middle East Oil Concessions,* pp. 109–10.

[a]After deduction of taxes and royalties.

concession in 1961, the company's physical assets would have been reverted to Iran and the Iranians would have had the freedom to operate the industry themselves or to contract it out on better terms. Instead under the new agreement Iran had committed herself until 1993 to the very same company with which she had been so unhappy for decades.

What brought about this unfortunate outcome was the Shah's desperate need for money and great concern about the presence of British warships in the Persian Gulf. Moreover, as Cadman notes, the Shah was "intensely suspicious of the Company's activities in Southern Persia . . . and in Persian Kurdistan."[44] Reza Shah's fears of British-instigated revolts by ethnic Arabs in oil-producing areas and possible British military intervention compelled him to accept British negotiators' terms.

Taqizadeh, who had been present at the 1933 negotiations, admitted fifteen years later that it was a grave mistake to cancel the D'Arcy concession. Under pressure from the Majlis to explain why such onerous terms had been accepted, he said that when the company team threatened to break off negotiations, "the Shah became apparently fearful of the consequences" and tried to mediate himself. "No one in the country had any authority and no resistance against the will of the absolute power of the time was either possible or could bear fruit." Trying to acquit himself of any wrongdoing, Taqizadeh said: "If there has been any failure or mistake, the fault should be laid at the feet not of the agents, but rather of the principal [the Shah]."[45] Hossein Ala, another participant in the 1933 negotiations, expressed similar views.

Others who had a hand in the oil negotiations did not survive. Firuz and Teymurtash were assassinated in jail by the Shah's men. Davar, of whom the Shah was suspicious, made his job easier by committing suicide.

The fifteen-year period of Reza Shah's reign, which ended in 1941, was characterized by both dictatorship and development. During this period, oil revenues, which totaled £41 million, played no significant part in the country's economic development, being mostly spent on arms and ammunition. The new railways, roads, and industrial plants were financed mainly by taxes on consumption. As an example: the trans-Iranian railway, which took ten years to build and joined Bandar Shapoor on the Persian Gulf to Bandar Shah on the Caspian Sea, was financed mainly with the proceeds of taxes on sugar and tea. This line was useful to AIOC transporting oil throughout the country.[46]

To Reza Shah modernization was "the condition and the proof of progress." He tried to remold the country into European shape, and in his boundless haste to do so he created an authoritarian state. But World War II upset his grand design as well as his rule, which had no constitutional base.[47] The war also upset, though provisionally, AIOC's vast empire. With the outbreak of war, the company lost some of its markets and oil production fell temporarily, resulting in a fall of Iran's oil revenues. The Shah asked for compensatory payments and AIOC agreed to make a flat annual payment of £4 million, which it did for the four years 1940–43. This was no particular sacrifice for AIOC. Although Iran's oil production fell from 9.6 million tons in 1939 to 6.6 million tons in 1941, it soon rose again, reaching 9.7 million tons in 1943 and 16.8 million tons in 1945. Nevertheless, the fact that Reza Shah had pressed for such payments aroused the British government's enmity toward him.[48]

Britain, however, had greater worries at the time. The German invasion of Russia in June 1941 created serious concern in Britain over a possible German pincer movement toward the Middle East, threatening the Iranian oil fields and the Persian Gulf. If Stalingrad fell, the British felt, there was hardly any obstacle to a German advance into Iran from the north. If Russia was to avoid defeat, she had to be supported with ample war supplies, and the best supply route was through Iran. But this was problematic because Iran had declared her neutrality in the war. Another problem was that the Shah had shown an inclination toward Hitler's Germany. To quote his daughter, Princess Ashraf, "he did derive some satisfaction from seeing the German challenge to Britain and Russia, Iran's long-standing enemies."[49] Moreover, in his wishful thinking, Reza Shah felt that if Germany won the war in Russia, she would return to Iran those parts of the Caucasus and Turkmenistan that Russia had taken by force from Iran long before.[50]

There were German technicians in Iran providing assistance to new industries, and no doubt among them were some spies. The British worried that they might sabotage the oil installations. A Royal Air Force intelligence officer in Habbania asserted that there were about 4,000 Germans in Tehran alone ready to be called into action at a moment's notice. It was proved later that there were no more than 650 Germans throughout the country as a whole.[51]

On August 25, 1941, Britain and Russia used the presence of Germans in Iran as a pretext to make a coordinated attack on the country. Their real purpose, however, was to provide a supply route to Russia and to occupy the oil fields. When news of the invasion reached the Shah, he beseeched British and Soviet representatives in Tehran to recall the invading forces, saying that if the purpose of the attack was to get rid of Germans in Iran, he would expel them himself within one week. He received no reply.[52] British forces consisting of two divisions of the Indian Army occupied Abadan, where they opened fire on any Europeans they saw, presuming them to be German saboteurs. Thus a number of AIOC's British employees were killed.[53]

With the simultaneous attack from the north and the south, the Shah's military machine, built with oil money over fifteen years, collapsed within a few days. Britain decided to force him to abdicate, and the Foreign Office began to consider who would best serve Britain's interests as his replacement. It turned out that there was "no outstanding General or politician to supplant" Reza Shah,[54] since as a precautionary measure he had eliminated all such persons. What Britain did about a replacement greatly influenced the course of events during the oil nationalization years in 1951–54.

As L. S. Amery, then secretary of state for India in Churchill's Cabinet, notes in his diaries, the matter was discussed at a Defence Committee meeting on September 8, 1941. Anthony Eden, the foreign secretary, "was quite disposed to give serious consideration" to the Qajar pretender, Prince Mohammad Hassan, the brother of the late Ahmad Shah, who had been dethroned by Reza Khan. In order to assess this possibility, Eden and Amery lunched with Prince Hassan and his son, Hamid, who had joined the British Royal Mail shipping company as a cadet under the name of David Drummond. Later it was arranged that two men with experience in Iran, Sir Horace Seymour, the under secretary in charge of the Middle East at the Foreign Office, and Harold Nicolson, director of British Broadcasting Corporation (BBC) and a member of Parliament, meet the princes and judge whether they were "worth restoring to the throne." They found both men charming but discovered that Prince Hamid, whom Eden preferred, did not know a word of Persian. They felt this would make it difficult for him to occupy the throne of a Persian-speaking country.[55]

Meanwhile Sir Reader Bullard, the British minister in Tehran, after consulting M. A. Foruqi, Iran's prime minister, advised against installing the Qajars. "In consequence the British decided to give the young Crown Prince, Mohammad Reza Pahlavi, a chance to prove himself—he could always be got rid of if he did not come up to expectation." This decision was made in consultation with Moscow.[56]

Born on October 26, 1919, Mohammad Reza attended primary school in Tehran. In September 1931 his father, Reza Shah, sent him along with Hossein Fardust, a schoolmate, to Le Rosey school near

Lausanne in Switzerland. According to Fardust, the crown prince was a poor student in all subjects except athletics; Fardust had to do all his homework. In 1936 Mohammad Reza completed his secondary school studies in Switzerland and returned to Tehran, where he had two years of training at the Military College.[57] Soon afterward, in 1938, he married Fawzia, a sister of King Farouk of Egypt. (This marriage was dissolved in 1948. In January 1951 Mohammad Reza married Soraya Esfandiari, the daughter of a Bakhtiari tribesman and his German wife.)

Unlike his twin sister, Ashraf, Mohammad Reza was weak in character. This was well known to Reza Shah, who told his confidants that he wished Ashraf was male and eligible to become crown prince.[58] (Under the 1907 constitution only a male descendant of the monarch could be appointed crown prince.) As we shall see, this weakness of character, coupled with the knowledge that without Britain's approval he could not have occupied the throne, made Mohammad Reza unwilling to cross the British.

On September 15, 1941, twenty days after the Allied invasion, Reza Shah, who had wielded absolute power for fifteen years, abdicated. His possessions, which he had amassed by extortion, were left to his successor to be returned to their rightful owners or to the public at large. Reza Shah was exiled by the British to Mauritius and later transferred to Johannesburg, where he died in July 1944.

During the war the country was divided between the two occupying forces, the Soviets in the north and the British in the south, which included the oil fields and the refinery. The two forces, joined later by American troops, took over Iran's railway and port facilities for the transport of arms and ammunition from the Persian Gulf to the Soviet Union. Meanwhile Iran was faced with famine. The acute shortage of food was blamed on the British, who were said to have bought up local supplies for their own troops. The U.S. State Department cautioned the British: "One could not possibly win the love of the Iranians by starving them." To forestall possible rebellions, the British arrested some 200 Iranian nationalists, politicians, and persons with German leanings. Among them was General Fazlollah Zahedi, commander of the Isfahan garrison—the same man who twelve years later would take over Iran's premiership from Mossadeq with British support. Suspecting Zahedi of planning an army uprising against the Allied occupation in cooperation with the Germans, British military intelligence abducted him and flew him to Palestine, where he was held until the end of the war.[59]

The Iranian leaders, who distrusted British and Russian ambitions in Iran, asked U.S. assistance to ensure that their country would be evacuated after the war. Britain and Russia were not willing to make such a pledge. But in December 1943 when Roosevelt, Churchill, and Stalin met in Tehran to decide on their future war plans, Roosevelt, who believed that the purpose of the U.S. entry into the war was to ensure the freedom of nations from slavery and domination, pressed the other two to join him in such a commitment. The result was a joint declaration by the Big Three in which they expressed their intention to maintain the independence, sovereignty, and territorial integrity of Iran. In addition, the British and the Russians agreed to evacuate their forces not later than six months after the end of the war. Soon after the Tehran conference, the three participants raised the status of their legations to embassies.

During the war, Iran's oil helped fuel the Allied war machine. Another valued prize for the Allies was the trans-Iranian railway, over which they transported four million tons of military and other supplies to Russia, while another one million tons were shipped by road. With such lines of communication for the Allied war efforts, Iran became known as the "Bridge of Victory." Iran's share, by contrast, was nothing but famine and the miseries of occupation in spite of her neutrality. The Iranians felt that they had been victims of Britain and Russia in both peace and war. The accumulation of resentment against both countries was to manifest itself in due course.

3

Iran Defies Russia and Britain

The fall of Reza Shah's dictatorial regime and the occupation of Iran gave rise to two major forces in the internal politics of the country in the 1940s. The first liberated the democratic forces who fought for constitutional rule. The second widened the influence of Britain and Russia in the internal affairs of Iran during the occupation while fueling nationalistic sentiments. In 1944, these forces left their mark in the elections of the Fourteenth Session of the Majlis, in which oil became a major issue.

Soon after the fall of Reza Shah, the ban on forming political parties was lifted and 1,300 political dissidents were released from prison. Numerous new parties were formed, and some succeeded in sending deputies to the Majlis. These deputies consisted mostly of a number of lawyers, former civil servants, tribal chieftains, and landed aristocrats (among them Mohammad Mossadeq), who had been treated harshly for expressing their dislike of Reza Shah's dictatorial rule. However, some deputies were royalists and others, supported in their election by the occupying powers, were pro-Soviet and pro-British. In all, the Majlis had seven factions, ranging in ideology from capitalist conservatism to Marxist communism.[1] But of the 126 deputies, the majority were nationalists who had two common goals: to fight for constitutional rule and to eradicate foreign domination. Mossadeq became the informal leader of a loose coalition of sixteen "independents" dedicated to these two goals. It was against this background that the oil issue came to the Majlis, but the story began with something that had very little to do with British oil interests in the country.

During the occupation, Iran became a hunting ground for oil concessions. In 1943 Royal Dutch Shell sent its representatives to Tehran to negotiate an oil concession outside AIOC's area of opera-

44

tion. At Shah Mohammad Reza's encouragement, some American oil companies came in, too, to seek concessions, and the Russians lost no time in joining the race. In September 1944, Sergei Kavtaradze, Assistant People's Commissar for Foreign Affairs, came to Tehran asking for an oil concession covering the five northern provinces of Iran neighboring the Soviet Union. The Iranian government, however, ruled that no concessions would be granted until the end of war; otherwise it would be interpreted that Iran was put under duress. But the Tudeh (communist) party deputies in the Majlis argued that Iran should strive for a political balance between Russia and the West. Since the British were given an oil concession in the south, they said, there was no reason to deny the Russians one in the north.

Mossadeq rejected this argument. He said that Iran should follow a policy of "negative balance" by not granting any privilege to one foreign power that called for giving one to another. Elaborating on this theme, he told the Majlis late in October 1944: "If we follow a positive balance we should grant [the Soviet Union] a 92-year oil concession in the north. However, if Iran does so, her action would resemble that of a person with one hand amputated who, in pursuance of balance, would consent to his other hand being amputated." Mossadeq stressed that no oil concessions should be given to foreigners either during or after the war. Iranian oil resources, he said, should be developed by Iranians themselves. He then submitted a bill to the Majlis that banned all government officials from discussing oil concessions with foreigners; violators would be sentenced to solitary confinement for three to eight years. In spite of opposition by the Tudeh deputies, the bill was approved by a large majority.[2]

Kavtaradze left Tehran in anger, though with a Russian force of 30,000 still in Iran, he felt that the Soviet Union was still in a good position to obtain an oil concession. In February 1945, when the Allied foreign ministers met at Yalta, V. M. Molotov, the Soviet foreign minister, believing that the British were opposing Soviet efforts to obtain an oil concession in Iran, raised the matter with Eden. Not at all, said Eden. "It was no part of the British policy . . . to prevent the Soviet Union from obtaining oil in northern Iran"; indeed, the Soviet Union is "a natural consumer for Iranian oil." He pointed out, however, that the matter should be dealt with after the withdrawal of Allied troops from Iran.[3]

Some in the British Foreign Office believed that it would harm good relations with the Soviets to oppose Russian oil demands, especially since "we have the oil-fields in South Persia."[4] With this line of argument, some in the British government advocated a rapprochement with the Soviets on this issue.

Meanwhile the Russians showed no signs of withdrawing their troops from Iran in March 1946 as earlier agreed. Moreover, they had established autonomous rule, through pro-Soviet Iranian elements, in two northern provinces of Iran across the Soviet border. The U.S. government became concerned, and in December James Byrnes, the U.S. Secretary of State, raised the matter personally with Stalin, reminding him of the Allies' 1943 pledge regarding the sovereignty and territorial integrity of Iran. Stalin, who thought little of the pledge, said: "The Baku oil fields in the South of Russia lay close to the border [of Iran] and this created a special problem. These fields had to be safeguarded against any possible hostile action by Iran against the Soviet Union, and no confidence would be placed in the Iranian Government. Saboteurs might be sent to the Baku oil fields and set them on fire."

Byrnes found that Stalin had offered a "poor excuse for maintaining a large army inside the borders of Iran."[5] The American troops left Iran by the end of 1945, and the British announced that they would withdraw in March 1946, but the Soviets refused to pledge withdrawal. It looked for a time as if Iran might fall behind the Iron Curtain. Faced with this dire prospect, the Iranian government, with American support, submitted the matter in January 1946 to the United Nations. This was the first issue to come up before the newly formed world body and the first confrontation between the United States and the Soviet Union after the war. It marked the dawn of the "Cold War."

With hints from the Soviets that they would be willing to discuss the matter with Iran if Ahmad Qavam were prime minister, the Majlis obliged by voting him this office, although no one seemed to know what line this enigmatic politician would take. In February 1946 Qavam went to Moscow and convinced Stalin that if Russia evacuated Iran's northern provinces he would support a Soviet oil concession in that area. On his return to Tehran, Qavam signed an agreement with Ivan Sadchikov, the Soviet ambassador, under which the Russians agreed to evacuate their troops and Qavam agreed to present the Majlis a draft agreement on a joint Irano-Soviet oil company. This measure, along with a stiff message from Truman to Stalin to honor his pledge, resulted in the evacuation of Soviet troops from Iran in May 1946.[6]

Qavam, however, brought three communist members into his cabinet and continued to accept the Soviet puppet regimes in the north, claiming that these moves were aimed at calming the Russians. But Robert Howe, an undersecretary at the Foreign Office, expressed his concern that the Russians, if not opposed, might eventually expand their control over the whole of Iran, saying that this would have "far-reaching effects generally in Persia and in the Middle East and particularly as regards the Anglo-Iranian Oil Company." He suggested that Britain "adopt Russian tactics and encourage an autonomy movement in South-West Persia" pointing out that "Persian independence is already a thing of the past."[7]

Soon Britain was making contingency plans for the occupation of the oil-producing province of Khuzistan. In July 1946, British troops in the Iraqi city of Basra were reinforced and two warships were sent to Abadan to support pro-British elements in the south.[8] In October, with the encouragement of the British, the Qashqai tribes, joined by some other tribal forces, occupied government garrisons in Bushir and Kazerun. Qavam's reaction was to arrest pro-British elements as well as Bakhtiari tribal chiefs who cooperated with the Qashqais.[9]

While the country disintegrated under Soviet and British pressures, no one could be sure where Qavam stood. The Shah did not know; neither did the Americans. To the Americans he looked like a quisling playing a double game.[10]

The Americans, however, suspected that the British, in order to save their interests in Iran and to avoid open conflict with the Russians, were preparing "a tacit deal" to divide Iran between Britain and Russia. The U.S. government, which was categorically opposed to such arrangements, informed Qavam that the United States would assist him in getting rid of foreign influences. Heartened by this assurance, Qavam removed Tudeh ministers from his

Cabinet and made an alliance with the Qashqai and other tribal chiefs, who gave up their rebellion. Finally, in December 1946, he sent troops to overthrow the two pro-Soviet autonomous regimes in the north. The Russians did not interfere because they felt that the promised oil concession in the north would give them whatever influence they needed in the area. By the end of December the country was free from pro-Russian and pro-British forces.

Qavam's next move was to stage-manage the elections of the Fifteenth Session of the Majlis, which was to decide on the Soviet oil concession. With the powerful party machine he had built, his party won the majority of seats while the pro-Russian Tudeh found it futile to participate in the elections. Qavam also successfully blocked the election of those whom he disliked, among them Mossadeq. Nevertheless, Mossadeq remained the unofficial leader of a number of deputies who won seats in the Majlis as "independents."

Meanwhile the Americans campaigned against possible ratification of the Soviet oil concession. The Russians had been promised that a draft of the Irano-Soviet oil agreement would be submitted to the Majlis. Instead, in October 1947 a number of Majlis deputies submitted a bill rejecting Qavam's discussions on oil with the Soviets and calling his action contrary to the October 1944 act initiated by Mossadeq, which prohibited such discussions. Interestingly enough, the 1947 bill was prepared secretly in close cooperation with Qavam himself.[11] In this he was prompted not only by American pressure but also by pressure from the "independent" deputies, guided by Mossadeq, and others who feared that a concession to the Russians would be followed by Russian penetration in the north resembling the British penetration in the south.

The bill, ratified on October 22, 1947, had important implications for the future of AIOC. It not only forbade granting oil concessions to foreigners or participation with foreigners in such concessions, but also instructed the government to take all necessary measures to secure Iran's rights to her national resources where such rights had been violated, "with special reference to the Southern oil."[12]

In response, the Soviet ambassador sent a note to Qavam stating that in view of the British oil concession the rejection of the Russian oil agreement was a blatant instance of prejudice against the Soviet

Union. The Russians realized that Iran meant business, and that Qavam had skillfully misled them with the promise of oil so that they would move their forces out of Iran. The British, by contrast, did not take the act seriously. They assumed the legislators had made a passing reference to their concession merely to maintain a balance but with no intentions of changing the status quo. They were wrong.[13]

Many in the Majlis supported the rising tide of nationalism, and all were fully aware of the rampant dissatisfaction with AIOC. The general feeling was that the time was ripe for Iran to reassert her dignity. The government would no longer be a bystander while the country's national wealth was taken away to enrich a distant land. The war had weakened Britain and compelled her to give up a good part of her empire. The United States, which had emerged as a world power, opposed imperialism and represented herself as the custodian of freedom and democracy.

The situation in the oil fields was unstable. AIOC's Iranian labor force of over 60,000 was no longer prepared to tolerate low wages, inadequate housing, and the refusal to train them for more highly skilled jobs, which were invariably held by the British. While British employees enjoyed luxurious facilities, the local labor force was kept segregated, living mostly in slums. English women who married Iranians were considered odd and were shunned by their country-men. All in all, Iranians were considered an inferior race. The British employees' method of handling even their Iranian social equals was "to browbeat them, to cow them into submission."[14] Such behavior understandably fueled the Iranians' sense of nationalism.

Labor unions banned during Reza Shah's reign came back to life after his fall. Furthermore, during the Russian occupation, the Tudeh party became active throughout the country. In the oil-producing province of Khuzistan, the party instigated workers to press their demands for higher wages and improved living condi-tions.

Soon after the evacuation of British forces in March 1946, the oil workers launched a series of demonstrations and strikes. Early in July 1946, thousands of oil workers went on strike demanding proper housing, health, and transport facilities and full observance by AIOC of Iran's labor law, with its provisions for minimum wages

and decent working conditions. The company responded by encouraging Arab ethnic groups to form a union whose goal was autonomous rule in Khuzistan. This infuriated the Iranian labor force,
which clashed in mid-July with the Arab union, killing two of its
members. Rioting ensued throughout Abadan, forcing a confrontation with Iranian troops, who opened fire on rioters. In the fight, 47
people on both sides were killed and 170 were injured; but the
government finally compelled AIOC to abide by Iran's labor law.
Meanwhile British warships anchored in Iraqi waters off Abadan.
The British government announced that Indian troops had been
sent to Basra so as to be close to Abadan for the protection of
"British, Indian and Arab lives." [15]

AIOC, complacent for four decades, was shocked to find native
workers challenging its might with nationalistic fervor. At the Foreign Office, however, some had foreseen the rise of nationalism. As
early as 1943 R. M. A. Hankey of the Middle East Department had
declared that Britain "must cooperate with the Nationalists," and
that AIOC must act to raise Iran's standard of living to avoid an
explosion. Ernest Bevin, the Foreign Secretary, observed: "Although
we have a Socialist Government in this country there is no reflection
of that fact in the social conditions in connection with this great oil
production in Persia." He told Sir William Fraser, AIOC's chairman,
that his company's pay policy was not progressive. "A British company," he said, "should go out of their way to improve [pay condi-
tions] . . . and establish every possible relationship with the people
in order to develop confidence between them and the company." [16]
Bevin, however, could not compel AIOC to change its ways. Although the government was a majority shareholder, it had a binding
arrangement that gave the company full freedom of action.

Fraser paid little attention to Bevin's advice. As to establishing a
"relationship with the people," he decided that what AIOC needed
was a public relations office in Iran; and in 1947 such an office was
established. The only substantial step the company took to improve
conditions for its Iranian workers was to appoint Mostafa Fateh, a
graduate of Columbia University and its highest-ranking Iranian
official, as assistant general manager in Abadan to deal with the
workers' welfare. Fateh succeeded to some extent in improving
working conditions but had no success in getting the company to

train more Iranians or to put royalty payments on a fair basis. AIOC officers felt that as long as they could influence the Shah, who owed his throne to British blessings, and pro-British officials who occupied positions of power, there was no need to change.[17] Future events proved their shortsightedness.

Late in 1947, the Shah became increasingly annoyed at Qavam, who had frustrated his desire to have a voice in the affairs of state. Thanks to the efforts of his twin sister, Princess Ashraf, a majority of Majlis deputies voted to remove Qavam from premiership. She believed that "a strong and ambitious prime minister, like Ahmad Qavam, could pose a serious threat to the monarchy," since he "could, if he chose, overthrow the Shah."[18]

During the next two years the Shah chose weak prime ministers who were amenable to his personal rule. This made him a target of attack for having no regard for the constitution. One event, however, provided him with an occasion to silence his critics: early in February 1949, he was shot and wounded by a news photographer. The would-be assassin was killed on the spot by the Shah's security men, and thus his motives remained a mystery. However, there were allegations that he was a member of a procommunist union. The Shah used the occasion to proclaim martial law, outlaw the Tudeh party, and arrest Tudeh leaders. In addition he deported Ayatollah Abol-Qassem Kashani, an influential religious leader, and put Mossadeq under house arrest.

The Shah favored an autocratic regime like his father's. He told British ambassador John Le Rougetel and American ambassador George Allen that democracy would hamper Iran's progress, that what was needed was an autocracy that would gradually introduce democracy as the country progressed. The British, who preferred to deal with one man rather than with a host of ministers and legislators, had no objection to his scheme. The Americans, partial though they were to democracy, had to agree in 1949 that the stability of a country bordering the Soviet Union would better be assured by an authoritarian regime.[19] This was a mistake for which the United States would pay a heavy cost decades later.

In April 1949 the Shah arranged to have the constitution amended to give him power over the legislature, including the power to dissolve the Majlis whenever he wished. This put the fate of the

Majlis and consequently the Cabinet at the mercy of the Shah and put him at the center of every major decision in the country, including decisions concerning oil.

The combination of an autocratic Shah and weak prime ministers, both responsive to British desires, suited Britain very well, but it was something that Iran's nationalists and educated class could not tolerate. What incensed them further was a host of economic problems that they considered to be the by-products of government corruption and foreign exploitation.

To remedy the country's economic ills during World War II, Iran hired Dr. Arthur Millspaugh, a former economic adviser to the U.S. State Department. Millspaugh arrived in Tehran in January 1943 and was joined later by a team of seventy advisers. Though given extraordinary powers to administer Iran's finances, Millspaugh achieved very little because he could not bring about institutional reforms. He was forced to resign in February 1945.

As economic problems persisted, the Iranian government in 1946 devised a comprehensive Seven-Year Development Plan with the assistance of U.S. consulting firms. The plan had a total projected cost of $656 million with a foreign exchange component of $210 million, which was expected to be financed with oil revenues.[20] But the royalties AIOC paid did not even meet the routine foreign exchange needs of the country. As awareness about AIOC's exorbitant profits grew, the Majlis increased its criticism of the company and the disproportionately small amounts it paid to Iran.

In June 1948, when Abdol-Hossein Hajir took over as prime minister, he was urged by some Majlis deputies to secure Iran's rights in the southern oil as called for under the 1947 act. When negotiations with AIOC proved futile, Abbas Eskandari, a pro-Soviet deputy, demanded that the company be nationalized. Most deputies, however, preferred that the government continue its discussions with the company. To find out the areas in which the company had evaded its obligations under the concession, the government employed Gilbert Gidel, professor of international law at the University of Paris and president of the Academy of International Law at The Hague. Gidel and his colleague Jean Rousseau, along with Iranian experts, drew up a fifty-page memorandum under twenty-five headings specifying the points to be discussed

with AIOC.[21] Thus began the chain of events that led to the nationalization of Iran's oil industry.

The memorandum made a number of major points. One was that
AIOC had not abided by the gold guarantee clause in the 1933
concession. In 1933 the royalty figure of 4s per ton represented one-
eighth of the price of Iran's crude oil, whereas in 1947, considering
the gold guarantee, it represented less than one-sixteenth; thus
Iran's royalties in relation to the price of oil exported dropped from
33 percent in 1933 to 9 percent in 1947.[22] Another point was that in
fairness Iran should be granted the same terms as Venezuela, which
under its concession agreement with Creole Oil, a subsidiary of
Standard Oil of New Jersey, received 50 percent of that company's
profits. Iran received £7 million in royalties in 1947, but by the
Venezuela basis Iran would have received royalties of about £1 per
ton, or £22 million. Further, the experts contended that Iran should
have been exempted from British taxation on its share in AIOC's
annual profits, which in 1947 alone amounted to £2.5 million; and
Iran should not have been subjected to the limitations set by the
British government on the distribution of dividends, which resulted
in a major portion of Iran's share being held in the company's
general reserves.

That was not all. AIOC, in disregard of its commitments to Iran's
interests, had concluded agreements with the British Admiralty and
American oil companies, selling them oil products at high discounts
and refining a major portion of Iranian oil abroad while depriving
Iran from the profits of its operations overseas. AIOC had not paid
any royalties to Iran in connection with oil products consumed in
the process of its operations. The company had consistently resisted
Iran's demands to inspect its books in order to ascertain whether the
Iranian government received its proper royalties. AIOC had let gas
go to waste in its operations and had paid no attention to Iran's
repeated demands either to retain the gas in wells or to construct gas
pipelines to cities. Finally, the company had repeatedly ignored
demands by the Iranian government that it improve the working
conditions of the Iranian work force and train Iranian staff to
replace foreign employees in skilled jobs.

When AIOC again showed utter indifference to the points raised
by Iran, the Majlis lost patience. Ten deputies submitted a bill on

January 20, 1949, calling for the cancellation of AIOC's concession. This led to new negotiations in February between a delegation headed by Neville Gass, one of the company's directors, and an Iranian team headed by Finance Minister Abbas-Qoli Golsha'ian. The Iranians emphasized the need for royalties to match those of the Venezuelan concession. Furthermore, they stressed that a concession running for another forty-five years should be subjected to periodic reviews: "we cannot, with tied hands, capitulate Iran's interests to the Company for half a century."[23]

When discussions with Gass proved fruitless, the government invited AIOC chairman Sir William Fraser to come to Tehran. He agreed to do so provided that he would negotiate with Prime Minister Mohammad Sa'ed himself. At their meeting on May 5, 1949, Fraser handed Sa'ed the draft of a so-called supplemental oil agreement, which was couched as a supplement to the 1933 concession. In brief, under the draft AIOC offered Iran a mix of payments that in an ordinary year would amount to 12/6 per ton. This included royalties, taxes, and Iran's 20 percent share in dividends and reserves. The Iranian government, which had originally asked for £1 per ton, considered the company's offer to be unacceptably low.[24]

Golsha'ian reported to Sa'ed that both his team and their foreign advisers felt that the matter should be referred to arbitration; otherwise there was little chance that AIOC would improve its offer. The Shah then instructed the Cabinet not to seek arbitration, leaving Golsha'ian no choice but to ask AIOC to improve its offer of 12/6 per ton to 16/4. Fraser replied that the company would not add a penny to what it had already proposed. Then, using the walkout tactics of his predecessor, Sir John Cadman, he stated that he had to return to London with his special plane.[25]

Meanwhile Mostafa Fateh, AIOC's Iranian assistant general manager in Abadan, wrote a private letter to Majlis deputy Taqizadeh (a participant in the 1933 oil negotiations), urging him not to let the government accept AIOC's terms. Fateh, though regarded by the general public as the company's front man and pro-British, proved in his letter to be otherwise. He wrote that "we were hoodwinked" by APOC in the negotiations leading to Iran's 1933 concession, and that "the Company's present proposals resemble that of a covetous lender who exploits the dire needs of his neighbour by taking his property as collateral for giving him a loaf of bread." He added that if those in power did not care about the millions of naked and hungry compatriots, at least Taqizadeh should "make your voice heard to stop the Government from this tyranny." If nothing could be achieved now, he concluded, it would be preferable to break off negotiations and wait for the international political climate to become more favorable to Iran.[26]

Taqizadeh was too conservative to take a firm stand, but Golsha'ian made it clear to his government that AIOC's proposals did not meet Iran's rights. Nevertheless, the Shah instructed the Cabinet to accept AIOC's offer of 12/6 per ton with no rights to revise the concession, and on July 17, 1949, Gass and Golsha'ian signed the Supplemental Agreement.[27] Fraser thought that his tough stand had worked and that the Iranians would remain silent for decades to come.

Finance Minister Golsha'ian privately complained that "were it not for the intervention of the Prime Minister [Sa'ed] and His Majesty," whose cautiousness out of "political considerations" robbed them of their freedom in negotiations, better terms could have been obtained. He lamented that "the British want the whole world for the furtherance of their own policy." Indeed, both Sa'ed and the Shah had been under constant pressure from the British ambassador to accept AIOC's terms.[28]

The new agreement awarded Iran between 32 percent and 37.5 percent of total net profits, depending on calculations relating to foreign exchange differential and other costs. But AIOC began a publicity campaign congratulating itself on its generosity and claiming that the agreement provided Iran with higher gains than the Venezuela concession, which was based on equal division of profits. This was not true. In 1951 Gass admitted to Victor Butler of the ministry of fuel that Iran's "net benefits" for 1950 would have been £40 million under a 50-50 arrangement instead of the £30 million, or 37.5 percent of total net, awarded under the Supplemental Agreement.[29]

AIOC ignored most of the twenty-five points that Iran had raised in her memorandum. If the Iranians thought that the company had at least given them better financial terms, they were wrong. Anticipating the sterling devaluation later that year, AIOC had been eager to clinch a deal so that Iran would not be in a position later to make any demands. As Gass told the Foreign Office, the Supplemental Agreement was "a voluntary revision by the Company primarily to take account of devaluation."[30] What Gass and Fraser had not anticipated was that the agreement would not be enacted by the Majlis before the sterling devaluation.

The agreement reached the floor of the Majlis in the form of a bill on July 23, four days before the end of its two-year term. AIOC expected that with the assistance of pro-British and royalist deputies in the Majlis and with the blessing of the Shah, the agreement would be ratified in no time. But the company was mistaken. The small opposition in the Majlis knew that if the bill came to a vote it would be passed by the majority, many of whom feared if they voted against the bill the Shah and the British would see to it that they were not reelected. To forestall a vote, the opposition, headed by Hossein Makki, conducted a filibuster. For four days Makki talked about the country's tortuous experience with AIOC and the shortcomings of the bill, while asking Finance Minister Golsha'ian to explain various points. Golsha'ian, who at heart was not happy with the agreement, did not try to defend it. Four days later, when the term ended, the debate had reached no conclusion. The fate of the bill remained to be decided by the next Majlis.[31]

On September 18, 1949, the British pound was devalued sharply by the Bank of England, falling against the dollar by 30.5 percent. Prime Minister Sa'ed met Bevin and Fraser in London in October. He told them that the increase in payments projected under the Supplemental Agreement had been wiped out by the devaluation and that a revision was accordingly required to make the agreement acceptable to the Majlis. Bevin, reflecting Fraser's assertion that AIOC had made a sufficient sacrifice, told Sa'ed that the agreement was "eminently reasonable to both parties."[32]

With the oil bill at stake, the British were moved to do their utmost to influence Iran's general elections. The Shah, too, had a stake in the elections; he wanted to strengthen his power base by putting his own men in the Majlis. To ensure that he would not be scuttled by the British, he avoided raising objections to the Supplemental Agreement. Thus the mutuality of interest between the British and the Shah was confirmed. Court Minister Abdol-Hossein Hajir, appointed by the Shah to supervise the elections, expected the

Majlis candidates to have two objects: to support the Shah and to endorse the oil agreement.[33] With this aim in mind he placed electoral supervision in the hands of royalists. To secure his position further, the Shah decided to convene the Senate, or the upper house, as stipulated in the 1907 constitution.

From 1907 until 1949, Iran's Parliament consisted solely of the National Assembly (the Majlis), whose members were elected by the people. For the Senate, however, the constitution required that half of its members should be elected and the other half appointed by the monarch. (This was a concession to Mozaffar ed-Din Shah to induce him to sign the constitution in 1907.) In 1949 Mohammad Reza Shah felt that convening the Senate would work in his favor because all acts of the lower house would then need the endorsement of the upper. Thanks to the Shah's methodic manipulation, the first Iranian Senate, convened in 1949, was packed with veteran royalists, though some were of an independent mind.

Mossadeq, however, considered the Senate "an aristocratic club" with no significance in Iranian politics. It was the Majlis, he said, that determined the destiny of the nation. In a move to stop irregularities in the Majlis elections, Mossadeq issued a statement calling on those who supported the constitution to meet in front of his home on October 14 and march to the Shah's palace. Thousands of people, including university professors and students, lawyers, civil servants, bazaar merchants, and shopkeepers, joined the march. They chose a delegation of twenty, headed by Mossadeq, to present their grievances on electoral malpractices to Court Minister Hajir. The twenty men entered the palace and refused to leave until they received a positive response. Three days later, on October 17, Hajir finally promised to eliminate electoral irregularities: the Shah, who was leaving in November for Washington for a state visit, wanted to portray himself as a democratic leader.

The delegation then made a momentous decision right there in the palace: they would cooperate fully in future challenges to the constitution. Their decision would change the political character of Iran for the next three years. One delegate, Hossein Makki, suggested that because the twenty men were members of various groups and parties, they should form a broad coalition and call it the National Front. Mossadeq welcomed the idea, saying that he would prefer to address the whole nation rather than a specific party. The group elected Mossadeq as its chairman and appointed a committee to draw up the National Front's program and charter. The program, once published, said nothing about oil; its concerns were more general, the pursuit of constitutional rule and social justice. The group, under its charter, set up a central council and invited political parties and professional organizations to join.[34] (For the composition of the National Front and the political parties it represented, see Chapter 6.)

The choice of Mossadeq as the leader of the National Front was welcomed by the public at large. His political integrity and his singleness of purpose in trying to save the country from local autocracy and foreign intervention were well-known. Born in 1882, Mossadeq was the son of a landed aristocrat.[35] Though related to the Qajars, he hated their autocracy and corruption. In 1906 he joined the constitutionalists who fought for parliamentary rule. When they succeeded temporarily, he was rewarded by being elected to the first session of the newly formed Majlis; but being younger than thirty, the minimum age required for Majlis membership, he could not take the position. He went to Neuchâtel University in Switzerland, where he received a doctorate in law in 1914.

On his return, he taught at the School of Political Sciences in Tehran and wrote several books on law, including one, *Capitulations and Iran*,[36] that had significant political impact. In this book he attacked Iran's agreements with some foreign governments under which their nationals were immune from prosecution by Iran's courts. The publication of this book did not please the British and the Russians, who enjoyed such privileges. Mossadeq's clash with the British intensified with the conclusion of the abortive Anglo-Persian agreement of 1919, which aimed at bringing Iran under British tutelage. Thanks to his persistent campaign against that agreement, along with other nationalists, it was not ratified by the Majlis.

Between 1917 and 1924 he held various government posts. As finance minister in 1921 he launched an anticorruption campaign that antagonized the influential but won him the admiration of the general public. Later, as governor of the province of Azarbaijan, he refused to give capitulatory privileges to Soviet nationals. As foreign minister, he fought against giving such privileges to the British and against foreign subjugation generally. Between 1924 and 1928, when he was a Majlis deputy, he fought against autocratic rule. When Reza Shah came to power, Mossadeq attacked his dictatorial regime and what he called the Shah's superficial drive for Westernization. In response Reza Shah put him under house arrest on his farm outside Tehran. Later, in 1940, the Shah sent Mossadeq to jail, where he had to share a cell with criminals and was physically maltreated. After his release from jail, he was extremely weak and unable to walk. He suffered occasional fits of fainting, which afflicted him for the rest of his life. He was put under house arrest again until 1941, when the Allies forced Reza Shah to abdicate. His years of suffering ended, but the hardships he had undergone crystallized his convictions.

During his formative years, Mossadeq had seen how Iran was a helpless prey of the British and the Russians and at the same time the victim of the Qajar kings, who were autocratic toward their people, yet meek toward foreign powers. Later, under Reza Shah, he had seen Iran subjected to a dictatorial regime in which the concept of government responsibility to the people was ignored and the operation of government agencies was aimed at strengthening the ruler rather than serving the people. He concluded that Iran could progress only when the twin evils of local autocracy and foreign interference were uprooted.

In 1944, when Mossadeq was elected to the Majlis, he had two aims: to end Iran's subjection to foreign powers and to establish parliamentary rule so that representatives of the people—and not a single sovereign ruler—would control the affairs of state. His persistent struggle to achieve these aims made him the symbol of Iranian aspirations for freedom and independence.

The first priority of the National Front leaders in 1949 was to get elected to the Majlis as a means of achieving their goals. As the general elections began, it became clear that the royal court was bent on producing its own men out of the ballot boxes; and that Court Minister Hajir's promises of fair elections had not been genuine. On November 4 Hajir was assassinated by an Islamic extremist. In response, Prime Minister Sa'ed stopped the elections and ordered the renewal of voting in Tehran. Meanwhile Iran was left without a legislature.

On November 16, 1949, in the midst of these electoral struggles, the Shah went to Washington. In his meetings with President Truman, Secretary of State Dean Acheson, and George McGhee, Assistant Secretary of State for Near Eastern, South Asian, and African Affairs, the Shah talked of Iran's need for U.S. military assistance to resist Soviet domination. Acheson disagreed, saying that the Iranian Army could not withstand Russian aggression. The Shah, he said, would do better to make economic and social reforms to avoid communist penetration. The Shah, pointing out that oil royalties were inadequate for these purposes, asked for U.S. economic aid. Acheson, however, felt that Iran's financial problems could be solved if she could obtain a fair deal with AIOC.[37]

The Shah left Washington empty-handed and embarrassed that his countrymen might interpret his failure to receive aid as indicating that he lacked American support. Following his departure, Hossein Ala, Iran's ambassador to Washington, repeatedly pressed the State Department to extend U.S. military aid to Iran. McGhee told him that "Iranian requests for assistance outnumbered those of all the rest of the [eighteen] countries in the Near East area put together," adding that it was not U.S. policy "to assist foreign countries to increase the size of their armed forces."[38]

The United States, however, was not indifferent to the fate of Iran. Two weeks after the Shah's departure, McGhee went to Tehran on a fact-finding mission. Iran was seen as a target of Soviet subversion, and the United States was determined to frustrate Soviet moves. Since the war the United States had expanded its relations with Iran and had sent a military advisory mission there.[39] McGhee knew, however, that it was still the British who wielded the real power in Iran, and that indeed their embassy and AIOC "largely controlled the press and the Majlis." Moreover, General Ali Razmara, the armed forces chief of staff, was at the time lobbying for the premiership with strong British backing.

McGhee reached several conclusions after meeting the Shah and other leading figures in Tehran, along with Ambassador John Wiley. One was that the Shah had "an insatiable appetite for military equipment," partly because he saw it as "a source of prestige to strengthen his regime." Another was that to counter Soviet subversion Iran was in need of social and economic reforms, not arms. Finally, Iran's most important asset was oil, which had produced little benefit for the country. "The annual income to Iran from the Company was currently only some $30 million a year," which according to the Iranians "was less than their expenses in providing security for AIOC installations."[40]

Shortly after his return to Washington, McGhee arranged a meeting at the State Department on January 24, 1950, with AIOC officials, including Richard Seddon, the company's newly appointed representative in Tehran. When McGhee asked them to improve the terms of AIOC's oil agreement with Iran, he was told that the company had already made "liberal concessions" and that any more would leave "nothing in the till." McGhee, who had his own oil firm and was well aware of AIOC's enormous financial gains, told them, "as one oil man to another, profits were still far from disappearing." He said that Iran was "perfectly aware of the more favorable concession terms not only in the western hemisphere but even in the Persian Gulf," adding that AIOC should "deal with the situation realistically by recognizing the legitimate demands of oil producing states."[41] AIOC officials not only failed to appreciate McGhee's remarks but, as we shall see, tried, in cooperation with the Foreign Office, to remove him from the State Department.

Meanwhile, in Iran the general elections were completed early in 1950. The National Front headed by Mossadeq won eight seats. Ayatollah Kashani, exiled by the Shah, was also elected and returned to Tehran to receive a tumultuous welcome. The Majlis also contained 40 "independent" deputies. Of the 131 elected, however, the majority were royalist and pro-British. Thus the Shah had no difficulty in choosing Ali Mansur, a close ally of the court, as prime minister.

The British were now anxious to obtain approval of their oil agreement. The Shah, having filled all the Cabinet posts with his men, was bent on gaining full control of the government and the Majlis and ruling without opposition or obstruction. But Mossadeq could not accept such a violation of the constitution. In his first major address to the new Majlis, he stated that when he was released from Reza Shah's political detention in August 1941, he had advised the young Mohammad Reza Shah to follow the example of the British monarchy: to stand above politics and not interfere in the appointment of ministers and the election of Majlis deputies. It is these high qualities in the British political system, he said, that cultivate capable statesmen and patriotic citizens, without whom the country would lack everything. He added that Iran did not belong to one man or a small minority but to all the people.[42]

As to the oil bill, presented by Prime Minister Mansur to the Majlis in April 1950, Mossadeq and his National Front colleagues considered it a humiliating document; to approve it was to accept Iran's subjugation to foreign interests. The Majlis referred the matter for further study to a parliamentary committee of eighteen, five of whom, including Mossadeq, were members of the National Front. The British were unhappy with Mansur's handling of the oil bill because he did not defend it in the Majlis.

The Americans, too, did not like Mansur, though for other reasons. John Wiley, the American ambassador, was of the opinion that he had "notoriously sticky fingers" and was not the type of man who would push for reforms. Mansur's position became even shakier when General Razmara promised the U.S. embassy that if he headed the government, he would pursue an "anti-corruption campaign to eliminate . . . members of the old guard." This pleased the Americans, who favored political and economic reforms as a way of countering communist threats in Iran. Wiley reported to Acheson that Razmara was "very clean" and as chief of staff "holds the Iranian Army in the palm of his hand." As to Razmara's ambitions, Wiley felt that "he would not want to become Shah. He would probably want to play the role of Richelieu. He is ambitious, utterly cold-blooded, ruthless and cinquecento."[43]

Britain, too, felt that a strong man was needed at the helm. Sir Michael Wright, assistant under secretary of state in charge of Middle Eastern affairs, did not consider the Shah a strong man. To be sure, the Shah was "well disposed towards the West" and "anxious to press ahead with reforms," but "the danger is that he will act clumsily or overeagerly, and by imposing . . . a military dictatorship, precipitate a crisis in which he will fail to carry the country with him."

Wright felt that Britain should assist the Shah in choosing a strong man as prime minister, one who would not ignore British interests. Following this line, Ambassador Le Rougetel tried to impress upon the Shah "the importance of having a real Government led by a man of strong personality," but the Shah was "averse to this."[44]

Sir Francis Shepherd, who replaced Le Rougetel in April 1950 as British ambassador to Tehran, followed up the matter. Shepherd, who had held consular posts between 1920 and 1949, mostly in countries with dictatorial or colonial regimes such as Peru, Haiti, El Salvador, the Belgian Congo, and the Netherlands East Indies, believed that Iran, too, needed an authoritarian regime. Like Wright and Le Rougetel, he stressed the need for a strong prime minister.[45] Thus Razmara emerged as a candidate for the premiership who had both American and British support.

The Shah and his court distrusted Razmara, considering him a threat to the throne and "a snake in the grass." But the Shah later concluded that the only way to face opponents like Mossadeq and other nationalists (whom he considered more dangerous to his throne) was to appoint a powerful military man. He thus agreed to meet British and American demands for Razmara's appointment, particularly when Mansur proved a disappointment to him.

Shepherd reported to Foreign Secretary Bevin that Mansur's "instructions from the Shah included an order to secure as soon as possible the passage of Supplemental Oil Agreement," adding that since Mansur had "no intention of carrying out his master's orders" he faced dismissal.[46]

Hearing speculation about his removal, Mansur tried to secure his position with the help of AIOC, which he considered the real power in Iran's politics. He sent word to E. G. D. Northcroft, the company's representative in Iran, saying that he would henceforth be more active in steering the oil bill through the Majlis and "would give it the fullest support." He added that he was unhappy to find the American embassy actively engaged in replacing him with Razmara. "But he was both surprised and grieved to hear . . . that the British Embassy was apparently pursuing a similar line of policy. He considered this . . . as unfair to him and dangerous to the future of the Supplemental Agreement." Northcroft sent word to Mansur assuring him that "the Company fully supported the present Government."[47] But his assurances were not genuine. A week later on June 26, 1950, the Shah dismissed Mansur and, as promised, appointed General Razmara prime minister.

The British now expected Razmara to pay them back, and they were confident that the general would have enough coercive power to force the ratification of the oil bill through the Majlis. But they had underestimated the growing strength of nationalism among the masses and the buildup of public resentment against them during the first half of the twentieth century. Thus they could not foresee the crisis ahead.

4

The General's Mission

The choice of a strong military man as prime minister brought a sharp reaction from the National Front. On June 27, 1950, when Razmara asked the Majlis for a vote of confidence, Mossadeq proclaimed that he could not vote for a man brought to power by foreigners who were bent on crushing the country's constitution and national sovereignty to achieve their own aims. Referring to Reza Shah's period, he stated that the country had suffered enough from military dictatorship and would not tolerate another dictator. Mossadeq and the other National Front deputies were in the minority, however, and the Majlis endorsed Razmara's premiership.[1]

On oil, Razmara promised both British ambassador Shepherd and AIOC that he would help get the Supplemental Agreement approved, but only if they helped him by improving its terms on a number of points, most of which had no financial implications. His demands were as follows: AIOC should devise a ten-year program to train Iranians for technical jobs so as to reduce British and Indian staff; Iran should be allowed to examine the company's books and to check its oil exports at ports to settle allegations that it was exporting more oil than it claimed; the Iranian government should be informed of the quantity and price of Iranian oil products sold to the British Admiralty and others at high discounts; and AIOC should make advance payments, on the basis of the draft Supplemental Agreement, to help implement Iran's development plan and to encourage the Majlis to ratify the agreement.[2]

Although Razmara came to power with British backing, in return for which he had undertaken to help obtain Majlis approval of the oil agreement, he did not get a positive response from the British on any of these issues. Dismayed, Razmara asked Henry Grady, the new U.S. ambassador to Iran, for help. An economist with extensive political experience and a record of successful missions to India and Greece, Grady had been sent to Iran on McGhee's recommendation to help solve the country's economic problems.[3]

On Grady's request, Acheson advised Bevin that Britain's failure to take positive action against AIOC's intransigence was "inappropriate to current internal Iran and world conditions." Grady felt that AIOC was "content to let matters slide," adding that "such an attitude can only be disrupting politically."[4] As we have seen, the position of AIOC's chairman Fraser was that he had offered Iran the most favorable terms he could and that if the Iranian government needed money, it should enact the agreement as it stood. AIOC's responsibility, he said, was not to subsidize governments but to ensure the interests of stockholders.[5] Although a number of Foreign Office officials did not agree with Fraser's arguments, as a whole the Foreign Office looked with awe on a company that had brought such spectacular gains to Britain. And it was generally felt that AIOC's performance was mainly due to Fraser's tight fist at the helm.

Fraser did not like to be told what to do by the government. He had contempt for civil servants and on occasion tried to intimidate them into doing what he wanted. His attitude toward American officials was no different. When Assistant Secretary of State George McGhee criticized his inflexibility, Fraser, "in his characteristically gruff Scottish voice," retorted: "The trouble with you, McGhee, is that you are operating on the basis of wrong information."[6] The feeling at the State Department was that AIOC dominated British policy in Iran and that the British government was in the company's bondage.[7]

Pending the solution of the oil problem, Grady suggested to Acheson that Iran be given $50 million in loans and grants.[8] The State Department decided to authorize an Eximbank loan of $25 million requested earlier by Iran. But Britain urged the United States to tie the loan to approval of the Supplemental Agreement; otherwise "Iranians might be less anxious to proceed with ratification." The British Treasury and AIOC, acting as if the good of Iran were their main concern, joined in saying that "any large scale loan or advance [to Iran] would probably be dissipated one way or another," adding further that it would have an "undesirable inflationary effect on Iran's economy."[9] Grady felt the British were wrong in thinking that Iran's need for funds would eventually force the Majlis to accept the oil agreement. He found AIOC's rigidity "incomprehensible." "It will not take great magnanimity on [the] part of the A.I.O.C. to make . . . some concessions," he said.[10]

The company had Iran in a stranglehold, and Razmara was embarrassed that he could not do any better than his predecessors. At this point the Soviets found it politically advantageous to make generous gestures to Razmara, and this upset the Americans. Charles Bohlen, the U.S. ambassador in Moscow, asked the State Department to press on with settling the oil dispute so that Razmara's hand would be strengthened "in resisting Soviet blandishments." He suggested that the United States should give financial assistance to Iran, adding, "If U.K. Government controlled A.I.O.C. is withholding badly needed 'advances' against Iranian concessions in final agreement, U.S. loan might convince British that bait has lost some of its efficacy."[11]

In September 1950, the State Department decided to hold serious discussions with Britain in the wider context of Anglo-American oil interests in the Near East. In preparation for these discussions, Richard Funkhouser, the State Department's petroleum adviser, drew up a report for McGhee. In it he said that the 50-50 profit-sharing agreement between Venezuela and Creole Oil was well-known in Tehran and thus Iran and other Middle East states could not be prevented from demanding the same terms. He stressed that Persian Gulf oil operations were "exceptionally profitable," particularly those of AIOC. "It is sophistry to suggest oil companies can't pay and do much more." He pointed out that the Arabian American Oil Company (Aramco) had recovered its total investments in five years of operation in Saudi Arabia and compared this performance with that of AIOC, which had been "operating for 40 years with production costs under 10¢ a barrel" and a sales price between $1 and $3. He advised McGhee to urge the Foreign Office to accept Razmara's demands before Aramco finalized its agreement with Saudi Arabia on a 50-50 basis.[12]

In another extensive paper on "Middle East Oil," Funkhouser emphasized the importance to the West of the region's annual production of 90 million tons of oil, 40 percent of it from Iran. He noted that because this vital area provided 75 percent of Europe's oil needs, every effort should be made to eliminate local dissatisfaction with foreign oil operations. Funkhouser contended that the appeal of communism in the Middle East was due to poverty and the Western powers' "lingering reputation for colonialism and imperialism." He added, "A.I.O.C. and the British are genuinely hated in Iran." To maintain the West's oil position in the area, he said, the people must be "clearly shown that the oil operations work to their direct benefit" and that the companies are genuinely interested in their progress. He deplored the tactics of those companies that refused to offer 50-50 contracts, saying that such tactics would threaten the life of their concessions.[13]

McGhee did not need convincing. On September 21, 1950, he and his aides met in London with Sir Michael Wright and Victor Butler, the Under Secretary of the Ministry of Fuel and Power, among others. McGhee told them that improving the terms of the oil agreement was essential to the survival of the Razmara government, "which both of us looked to as the one best suited to lead Iran out of the present crisis." He saw no chance for the Supplemental Agreement to be ratified unless AIOC agreed to the points specified by Razmara.

Butler was not prepared to accept any of Razmara's demands. As for Iran's checking AIOC's books, he said the company found it "impossible to concede" this right; it "could not divulge the nature of its world wide operations to Iran," which should be treated as "any other normal shareholder." He avoided making any commitment on training Iranian personnel for technical and executive jobs. His only comment about most of Razmara's other demands was that "the Iranians have never been very clear about them"—a common pretext for evading discussion. McGhee replied that he had talked about Razmara's demands with American oil companies operating in the Near East and had found that they considered the demands reasonable, saying "there were none they themselves could not meet." Giving Iran the right to check the company's accounts, in particular, made sense. Indeed, "Creole was obliged to present its accounts to the Venezuelan Government for examination," and Creole's operations in Venezuela, like AIOC's in Iran, were tied up with interests elsewhere in the world.[14]

In reply, the British argued that the general objectives of the United States and Britain in the Near East were identical and that they should not allow Iran to play one against the other. McGhee, unimpressed, insisted that AIOC enjoyed numerous advantages in Iran compared to oil companies elsewhere and was in a position to improve the terms it offered. "The advantage in negotiations today lay with the country where oil properties were located and about the best companies could do was to fight a graceful rearguard action." He referred to the new demands made by Saudi Arabia and stressed the urgency of coming to terms with Iran before the Saudi-Aramco agreement was finalized.

Acheson expected Britain to join the United States in supporting Iran's development plan, but Britain blocked even the $25 million requested by Iran from Eximbank, saying that they would not convert Iran's sterling balances into dollars for repayment of the loan. McGhee pointed out that "A.I.O.C. was the U.K.'s biggest overseas asset and had been a tremendous dollar earner for the British; by contrast Iran obtained very little." When his arguments failed to have the slightest impact, McGhee returned to the need to improve the terms AIOC offered Iran. Fraser's reply was, "One penny more and the Company goes broke." McGhee, well-informed of the company's huge profits, was stunned to hear such a disingenuous statement.[15]

When McGhee's London mission proved unsuccessful, Grady reported to Secretary of State Acheson: "It can only be concluded that the U.K. [is] bent on sabotaging our efforts to strengthen Iran [so as] to preserve its dubious supremacy and control there." He found such a British course "inconsistent with our mutual interest" and saw it as "jeopardizing the global position of Western democracies." He suggested that the United States should proceed independently. Acheson replied that economic concerns caused Britain "to place a different emphasis than we do on political and strategic necessities in Iran." Although the United States had repeatedly expressed to the British the necessity of getting AIOC to liberalize its terms, he added, the company was apparently convinced that no new concessions were needed. The "appointment of [Golam-Hossein] Foruhar who is known to be most friendly to UK, as Finance Minister, will probably stiffen their thinking in this direction."[16]

AIOC relied not only on Razmara and Foruhar but also on some members of the Majlis's Oil Committee. In July 1950 AIOC reported to its London office that of the eighteen committee members, only five, headed by Mossadeq, were against the oil agreement. The report gave details on the wealth, moral behavior, political inclinations, friends, and family connections of each member, contending that some of the remaining thirteen could be bribed to support the agreement.[17]

The company also had close contacts with several government officials, among them Bahram Shahrokh, Director of Radio and Propaganda. During World War II Shahrokh had directed the Persian section of Berlin Radio, which broadcast propaganda for the Nazis. Now he found it profitable to support AIOC's aims by arranging radio talks that favored the Supplemental Agreement. He did this with such ardor that the company, worried that his broadcasts might arouse resentments, cautioned him to tone them down. A number of newspapers, too, supported the company's aims for financial rewards.[18] As McGhee had observed, the British embassy and AIOC had great influence in the press and in the Majlis.[19] But both failed to notice the ever-growing influence of the nationalists among the educated and the masses and the great change in Iran's political orientation.

To silence opponents who called him a tool of the British and the Americans, Razmara concluded a trade agreement with the Soviet Union on November 4, 1950, and a week later banned the BBC and Voice of America relays on Radio Tehran. The British Foreign Office felt that "Razmara had played his hand with the Soviets rather well."[20] They considered the prime minister's moves a smokescreen to demonstrate his impartiality to his countrymen before proceeding with the approval of the oil agreement as promised to the British.

Although Razmara failed to obtain from AIOC the concessions he wanted, he told the Majlis that he was satisfied with the terms of the agreement. This angered the National Front deputies, and in mid-October 1950 they staged a debate in the Majlis on what they called a bill of indictment on behalf of the nation against AIOC. For four days four National Front deputies attacked the company's behavior on social, political, technical, and legal grounds. The British government, they claimed, dressed in the company's garb, had created a strong administration within the belly of Iran's weak administration, exerting power at whim and damaging the country's sovereignty and independence. British influence had infected the social and political structure of the country and had spread corruption. AIOC's power was such that it could stop the economic wheels of the state whenever such a move served its interests. AIOC was exploiting Iran's resources and making only trifling payments in return. The company was unwilling to let Iran check its accounts, or even to let Iranians hold technical jobs for fear they might learn oil operations.

It was Mossadeq who addressed the legal aspects of the situation. He considered the 1933 concession null and void, arguing that it was enacted during a dictatorship, a time when Majlis deputies, picked by the dictator, were not the real representatives of the people and the Cabinet had no authority. The aim of the Supplemental Agreement, he said, was to affirm and reinforce a basically invalid concession so that for the next forty-three years the nation would be subjected to its oppressive terms. Finally addressing Prime Minister Razmara, he said: "If you endorse this Agreement, you leave yourself with a disgrace which you will never be able to wash away."[21]

The view at the U.S. State Department was not much different. In a report to McGhee, William Rountree, Director of Greek, Turkish, and Iranian Affairs, noted:

> To me it seems crystal clear that the traditional British policy in Iran has not changed one iota despite the present world situation. They are still determined to let AIOC come first and to permit the Iranian internal situation to remain in a constant state of turmoil since that will . . . permit the AIOC to operate as it has in the past, bribing deputies and Government officials and being able to operate as it wishes in the absence of a strong Government. . . . At the moment it seems entirely clear that the AIOC dominates British policy in Iran and anything we can do to induce the British Government to escape its bondage is worth trying.[22]

Months of efforts by the Americans and Razmara to persuade AIOC to improve its terms proved futile. Within the Oil Committee, the five National Front members advocated the nationalization of oil; the remaining thirteen, headed by Jamal Emami, believed that fresh negotiations should take place. Since the terms of the agreement were unacceptable to both groups, they unanimously passed a resolution on November 25 stating that the agreement offered insufficient rights to Iran and thus the committee was opposed to it.

AIOC was unmoved by this development, feeling certain that Razmara and the pro-British and pro-court deputies would overrule the Oil Committee's resolution. The State Department, however, was not so optimistic. In a message to Bevin, Acheson repeated McGhee's request in the September meeting in London: persuade AIOC to make some compromise with Iran before the Aramco agreement was finalized.[23] Britain's Ambassador Shepherd conceded that "our task in getting the agreement ratified will be far more difficult if Aramco makes considerable financial concessions." He proposed that Bevin ask Acheson to delay the finalization of the Aramco agreement.[24]

At the Foreign Office, Geoffrey Furlonge, head of the Eastern Department, was greatly disturbed by the thought that Aramco might give Saudi Arabia 50 percent of its profits, since this would encourage all other oil-producing Gulf states to press for revisions of their existing agreements. "The harm which ARAMCO could do both to British and American oil interests in the Middle East by adopting an unnecessarily compliant attitude is therefore considerable."[25]

Razmara's government, unconcerned with Aramco developments, continued to press for approval of the Supplemental Agreement. On December 26, 1950, Finance Minister Foruhar made a long speech in the Majlis supporting the agreement and attacking those who advocated oil nationalization. He claimed that Mexico had nationalized her oil industry and later regretted it. He quoted figures showing that Mexico's oil exports had dropped since her nationalization. Hossein Makki shouted that Foruhar was a liar, that he was falsifying facts by quoting figures provided by AIOC, and that AIOC had given the same false figures to a number of newspapers, promising them payment for publication. Other members of the opposition joined Makki, calling Foruhar a traitor and a British tool. Faced with such attacks, Foruhar withdrew the bill on Supplemental Agreement.[26]

Razmara realized that his cavalier treatment of the Majlis had led him to an uneasy situation.[27] He confided to Ambassador Shepherd that since the Majlis was not cooperative, "the only course of action for him was to advise the Shah to dissolve the Majlis and to hold new elections." Shepherd supported such a course, but the Shah considered it awkward to dissolve the Parliament on the oil issue, on which public opinion was running high.[28]

Three days after Foruhar's antinationalization statements, National Front supporters and university students staged a large demonstration. Speakers sharply attacked Razmara's government for "its complicity with the A.I.O.C." and demanded the nationalization of the oil industry as the only way to end the company's exploitation of Iran. Shepherd reported these developments to Foreign Secretary Bevin on December 31, 1950; to calm the situation, he now suggested revising the agreement along the Venezuelan lines.[29]

There were good reasons for Shepherd's departure from his previous hard line. The day before, on December 30, Aramco had signed an agreement with Saudi Arabia calling for an equal division of profits. Not to fall behind, Bernard Burrows of the British embassy in Washington followed Shepherd in giving similar advice.[30] To past warnings from the Americans, particularly Acheson and McGhee, that the British would do well to settle Iran's oil agreement before the Aramco deal was concluded, the Foreign Office had responded that "they [the British] had long experience in dealing with Iranians, and that is that."[31] But now the Foreign Office took the line that "neither we nor the British oil companies in the Middle East were warned" about the Aramco deal.[32] Yet even after the Aramco agreement AIOC stood firm, saying that its proposed agreement to Iran was greatly preferable.

With the revelation of the terms of the Aramco agreement, Finance Minister Foruhar resigned and the Majlis, under public pressure, instructed the Oil Committee to formulate a policy that the government should pursue in securing Iran's oil rights. When the committee, in turn, invited suggestions from Majlis deputies, it received sixty-seven proposals ranging from reversion to the D'Arcy concession of 1901 (which was to end in 1961) to 50-50 sharing of gross profits along with a large measure of Iranian control. But it was the proposal of Mossadeq and his National Front colleagues on

January 11, 1951, which called for nationalization of Iran's oil industry, that set the future course of the Majlis and the government.[33]

Two weeks later, at the invitation of Ayatollah Abol-Qasem Kashani, some ten thousand people gathered at Masjid Shah, a large mosque in Tehran. After speeches by National Front members, the crowd passed a resolution calling for the nationalization of the oil industry. Seven leading Moslem clerics declared that it was the religious duty of every Iranian Moslem to support the nationalization movement. Ayatollah Mohammad Taki Khonsari issued a *fatwa* declaring that the Prophet Mohammad condemned a government that gave away the people's inheritance to foreigners and turned its own people into slaves.[34]

The British government and AIOC were undisturbed by these developments. At a meeting of officials from the Foreign Office, the Treasury, the Ministry of Fuel and Power, and AIOC, the view was that the company's situation was not critical. When E. G. D. Northcroft of AIOC was asked whether "the cry for nationalisation was very strong," he responded that he "did not attach much importance to it," especially since Razmara and the Shah himself considered the Supplemental Agreement "a good basis and did not want to destroy it." Northcroft's only concern was that since Foruhar was pushed out of office, Iranian newspapers no longer accepted prepared articles defending the company.[35]

Meanwhile the Oil Committee pressed Razmara for information about AIOC's sales of Iranian oil to the British Admiralty. When Ambassador Shepherd raised this question with London, he was instructed to tell Razmara that for "reasons of security the price and the quantity of fuel oil sold to the Admiralty were confidential."[36] The company expected Razmara to support its aims, yet left him unsupported when opposition confronted him on all sides. Some in the Foreign Office urged AIOC's chairman Fraser to propose 50-50 profit-sharing to Iran. He remained unwilling to take this step, but said that if the Iranians made such a proposal to Northcroft, the company would not refuse to discuss it. He expressed his irritation toward Americans, saying that they had not been helpful in Tehran.[37]

U.S. Ambassador Grady sympathized with the moderate nationalists in Iran and believed they could bring economic progress and genuine independence. Another American who sympathized with the nationalists was Max Thornburg, head of the Overseas Consultants mission to Iran, who advised the government on its development plan. Like Grady, Thornburg was openly critical of AIOC for not giving Iran a fair share in oil revenues, saying that the company was responsible for the economic instability and unrest in the country.[38]

These criticisms, along with those of U.S. Assistant Secretary of State George McGhee, led many in Iran to believe that they had United States support in their fight against the company. Since both McGhee and Thornburg were oilmen,[39] their views of AIOC added a new dimension to interpretations made in Iran and Britain. Some Iranian politicians argued that the American oil companies were prompting oil nationalization as a ploy to uproot AIOC in Iran and take its place. Though this was untrue, tempers rose among the British at the idea that the Americans were "poaching on their private reserves."[40] With these worries, AIOC suddenly became generous enough to make advance royalty payments to Iran. Razmara, anxious to avoid accusations that he had been bought, asked that these payments be kept secret.

Meanwhile, Mostafa Fateh, AIOC's assistant general manager, wrote a twenty-three-page private letter to E. H. O. Elkington, one of the company's directors, with whom he had been previously associated in Iran. The contents of this letter are of considerable interest. He began by saying that with the loyalty he had shown the company for thirty years he felt bound to give some frank advice. He urged AIOC management to show "breadth of vision, tolerance for other people's views and clear thinking to avoid disaster." He stressed that the company should understand the "awakening nationalism and political consciousness of the people of Asia," as well as Russia's active interest in exploiting such developments. He warned that pursuing "a Curzonian policy" was "disastrous, outdated and unpractical," nor was it in the long-term interest of the West to support "the corrupt ruling classes" and allow "leech-like bureaucracies to rule."

He pointed out that the Foreign Office had not given serious thought to Britain's long-term interests in Iran, preferring instead "to deal with the ruling clique which . . . has always proved to be subservient to British interests." He added that this "alliance with the ruling class . . . has alienated the liberal and progressive classes from Britain." As one who knew full well the company's relations with the Iranian governments of the previous thirty years, he considered the claim that it had not interfered in Iran's affairs to be pure hypocrisy. Finally, he expected AIOC, for its own sake, to respond to the rising tide of nationalism in Iran by dropping its alliance with corrupt officials and coming to the support of progressive elements in their drive for reforms.

On the oil problem, he wrote that the Majlis's Oil Committee would only negotiate on the basis of a 50-50 division of profits, Iranization of the company (replacing a majority of British personnel with Iranians), and shortening the period of the concession. He warned that if AIOC frustrated the committee by standing firm on these issues, the committee would press for nationalization. Fateh's advice had no effect whatever. The company showed no interest in following it, and at the Foreign Office one official noted that "Fateh is not to be trusted far."[41]

The U.S. State Department felt that the British were too slow in coming up with a positive plan to neutralize Iranian demands for nationalization and worried that Western interests in the Middle East would suffer. The U.S. chiefs of mission in the Middle East held a conference in February 1951 in Istanbul to discuss Anglo-American relations in the region. Chaired by McGhee, the conferees concluded that AIOC was "one of the greatest political liabilities affecting the United States/United Kingdom interests in the Middle Eastern area," that the company's policy was "a handicap in the control of communism in Iran," and that the "reactionary and outmoded policies" of British companies threatened stability. The conference recommended that the Foreign Office be vigorously urged to put pressure on British companies in the Middle East to conform to policies designed to promote stability.[42]

In spite of the State Department's remonstrations, neither AIOC nor the British government advised Iran that they were prepared to follow Aramco's lead. On February 11, 1951, Razmara asked Northcroft for the first time whether AIOC was prepared to consider 50-50 terms. Northcroft replied: "The Company would be willing to examine some similar arrangement. A British company would have to be formed for the operations in Persia. . . . It would take at least a year after the agreement had been reached before separation of the Company's activities within Persia from those outside it could be brought into action."[43]

Razmara showed no concern about the one-year delay. He responded that "it was essential to pay lip service to the idea of nationalisation if a 50/50 proposal was to be got through the [Oil] Commission." The Shah thought along the same lines.[44]

As demands for the nationalization of oil intensified, the Foreign Office proposed that the House of Commons stage a debate, with prepared questions and answers, conveying the British government's determined opposition to such a course. Ambassador Shepherd, who considered the Shah favorable to the British cause, consulted him on the particulars of such a debate. The Shah's reply was that the parliamentary debate, "to have any effect, . . . should indicate that an attempt to nationalise oil would lead to a delicate situation and have a bad effect on Anglo-Persian relations."[45]

The debate took place on February 21, 1951. When asked about the current state of oil negotiations, Foreign Under Secretary Ernest Davies said: "His Majesty's Government cannot be indifferent to the affairs of this important British interest." He went on to say that "the Company's present concession is valid until 1993" and should run its course.[46]

When the debate proved to have no impact in Iran, Shepherd suggested to the Foreign Office that the BBC should elaborate on it in its Persian transmission.[47] The Foreign Office dutifully prepared a draft for this purpose, which was "so cast to bring out that nationalisation is not, and cannot be, purely an internal Persian matter." The draft, after being cleared first with AIOC, was sent to the Treasury, which found its tone "stiff and official" and suggested that "to influence listeners favourably," some mention should be made of AIOC's willingness to discuss profit-sharing. Shepherd proposed that the program be broadcast on March 4 to reinforce the points Razmara was to make against nationalization at the Oil Committee meeting on March 3.[48]

The BBC polished the stiff text and broadcast it on March 4, calling it a news talk "written by our Diplomatic Correspondent." The script first sympathized with Iran's instinct to benefit from her natural wealth, but then declared that nationalization was an "arbitrary and unilateral" act that ignored "long-established international practices." It contended that Iran was able neither to pay adequate compensation to AIOC nor to provide the necessary technical skills to run the industry. "There is good reason to believe," it added, that the company would consider new financial terms based on the equal sharing of profits "in a spirit of utmost good will."[49] AIOC was not pleased. Northcroft considered the broadcast "too weak in tone, too ill arranged and insufficiently expressive." He was unhappy about "the apparent sympathy expressed for Iranian aspirations."[50]

The Iranian press was not impressed with the BBC talk either. It severely criticized AIOC and attacked Britain for leaving Iran in economic chaos after five years of occupation rather than giving a helping hand to Iran, whose oil, after all, was a major source of British enrichment. In response to American pressure and Iranian attacks, the Foreign Office finally advised Ambassador Shepherd to inform the Iranian government that AIOC was willing to agree to profit-sharing but not under the threat of nationalization.[51]

In a letter to Razmara, Shepherd responded to the attacks in the Iranian press. He stated that the United Kingdom had been responsive to Iran's economic needs in a number of ways. For example, Britain had provided postwar help to Iran by paying £8.25 million "for usage of the Iranian railway system"; and AIOC had "arranged for payment on account of royalties" a sum of £28.5 million during 1951 and had agreed to deposit £10 million with Bank Melli, Iran's national bank. He finally added that AIOC was "ready to examine an arrangement on 50-50 basis."[52]

For the British ambassador to describe oil royalties and payments for the use of Iranian railways as British assistance was ironic. His account of the £10 million that AIOC agreed to deposit in Bank Melli was also distorted. The fact was that in 1947 A. H. Ebtehaj, the governor of Bank Melli, complained to AIOC chairman Fraser that a company producing oil in Iran was not justified in depositing all its funds in British banks. Fraser reluctantly agreed to deposit £5 million, at the time a quarter of its cash balance, in Iran's national bank.[53]

Shepherd closed his letter on a haughty note. "It can scarcely be expected," he said, "that the British Government can countenance a campaign in favour of nationalisation of oil industry in defiance of the country's contractual obligations." Indeed, "a strong line of conduct should be adopted by the Iranian Government" in this regard. In conclusion, Shepherd resented "the apparent willingness of Iranians to permit themselves uninstructed criticism both of the Oil Company and of Great Britain" while taking no account of "the immense service to mankind of the British people in recent times."[54]

Razmara could hardly tell the angry public that the British were of "immense service to mankind." He confined himself to telling Shepherd that he could not control the press and the Majlis. In the end, he said, "there were only two courses open; one was to dissolve the Majlis and the other was to produce some formula for a draft resolution [for the Oil Committee] which while paying lip service to the principle of nationalisation . . . would in fact authorise the Government to negotiate with the Company on a 50-50 basis."[55]

Shepherd, under the illusion that Razmara would be able to push through for approval whatever draft resolution he proposed, prepared such a draft and sent it to the Foreign Office for comments, saying: "This would certainly be better than any draft which the Persians are likely to produce." The Foreign Office, in consultation with the Treasury, the Ministry of Fuel, and AIOC, then came up with a final draft resolution.[56] Speaking in the voice of the Oil Committee, this resolution said that because the concession could not be legally terminated, the Iranian government should negotiate with AIOC for equal sharing of profits. Shepherd was instructed to tell the prime minister that this was "what we want from him" and that "any resolution which does not refer to the illegality of nationalisation must be unacceptable to His Majesty's Government."[57]

Razmara preferred a different approach. His tactics were two-fold: to pay lip service to nationalization and to keep secret AIOC's readiness to discuss 50-50 terms. That way, if he succeeded in getting 50-50 profit-sharing, he would get the credit. He formed panels of experts whom he told to study the problems of nationalization and conclude that it would be catastrophic to nationalize. He passed on their reports to Ambassador Shepherd and AIOC's representative in Iran, Northcroft. With their guidance, he attacked nationalization at an Oil Committee meeting on March 3, 1951. According to the experts, he said, nationalization was not feasible owing to Iran's lack of skills, financial resources, and shipping facilities. He added that nationalization was not legally possible, nor was it wise to antagonize the British government. Shepherd boasted to the Foreign Office that Razmara gave the committee "the gist of my remarks."[58]

Razmara's report was broadcast that evening, and the public was infuriated. He seemed to be telling Iranians that they should stick with AIOC, whatever its faults, and continue to produce handicrafts rather than trying to run an oil industry. The company's British staff in Tehran harped on the same theme, spreading the word that if they left, no one would even be able to run the central heating in AIOC's offices.[59] As we shall see, the fact was that the Iranians had ample technical skills to run the oil industry, though at lower capacity.

The prime minister's report was considered humiliating and brought a backlash that strengthened support for nationalization. Four days later, on March 7, when Razmara was attending the mourning ceremonies for the death of a religious leader, he was shot dead. The assassin was identified as Khalil Tahmassebi, a young carpenter who was a member of the fanatical religious sect Fada'-iyané-Islam. There are claims, however, that Tahmassebi's shots missed and that it was in fact an army sergeant, acting on the Shah's instructions, who shot and killed Razmara in the mosque.[60]

From then on, events moved rapidly toward nationalization.

5

The Oil Nationalization Act

Razmara's assassination symbolized the magnitude of Iranian sentiments against AIOC and for nationalization. AIOC "had become the personification of the exploitative imperialism of the British Empire and the source of social and economic injustice." Moreover, the "oil question was one on which Iranians from different backgrounds could unite in protest against the old order."[1]

On the following day, March 8, 1951, the Oil Committee responded to public demand by unanimously approving a resolution recommending nationalization. The resolution asked the Majlis to give the committee two months to study how best to put nationalization into effect. On March 9, in response to Ayatollah Kashani's call, 15,000 people demonstrated in Tehran, urging the Majlis to endorse the committee's resolution. Even these developments did not awaken AIOC to the intensity of Iranian feeling against it. The company was still "under the illusion that the [oil] Concession is, in effect, a British Colony," and no one could touch it.[2] As for the Foreign Office, it "preferred to play the old game of politics, moving [Iranian] prime ministers and cabinets around like chessmen. It had worked in the past; why shouldn't it work now?" It believed that the people in Iran were helpless and could never influence politics.[3]

When the Shah appointed Hossein Ala as prime minister, Ambassador Shepherd began work on a scheme to replace him with someone more amenable to British desires. Meanwhile he reported to the Foreign Office: "We are doing all we can to arrange that there shall not be a quorum" when voting on nationalization takes place. To accomplish this, Lance Pyman, the embassy counselor, met Assadollah Alam, a confidant of the Shah, and suggested that the Shah "should use all his influence to persuade [Majlis] deputies under his control to keep away from the Majlis." He also made similar demands of two pro-British deputies. Pyman was given to understand that 43 of the Majlis's 131 deputies would stay away from the Majlis to avoid a quorum.[4]

In a meeting with the newly appointed prime minister, a British-educated aristocrat who had previously served as Iran's ambassador to Washington, Shepherd said that "the Company's operations cannot be legally terminated by an act such as nationalisation," but added that the 50-50 principle could be negotiated. "A fifty-fifty arrangement," Ala replied, "might have been accepted a little while ago but now something more would be required." Ala went on to say that "all Persians regard nationalisation as a desirable principle," that the idea "had penetrated far and wide," and that the people were "convinced that the welfare of the country depended on it." He stressed that the Iranians could not tolerate a concession imposed by the British to run until 1993.[5]

The futility of Shepherd's efforts was demonstrated on March 15 when the Majlis approved nationalization by unanimous vote of the ninety-five deputies present. Shepherd reported to the Foreign Office that even those whom the Shah personally told to stay away to prevent a quorum attended the Majlis and voted for nationalization. He contended that the Majlis was influenced by the "terrorist attitude of National Front and Kashani," and that their "threats to publish as traitors the names of deputies absenting themselves ensured a full house." But earlier on the same day he had sent a report presenting a different picture. In it he said that "the principle of nationalisation would have to be conceded. Recent events have bitten the idea so deeply into the public mind that no Government could afford to ignore it."[6] Shepherd had no comment on why the Senate, half of whose members were chosen by the Shah, unanimously approved the Majlis's nationalization bill on March 20.

The Foreign Office came up with an idea to stop the Nationalization Act. Since all parliamentary acts required the Shah's assent to become law, it asked Shepherd to suggest to the Shah "the possibility of withholding or delaying assent e.g. on the grounds of the doubtful legality of the resolution." Shepherd answered that this was not possible under the Iranian constitution.[7] On the other hand, "since His Majesty's Government own more than 50 per cent of the shares of Anglo-Iranian, the question arises whether one country can nationalise property of another."[8] The Foreign Office doubted that it could press this point.

On March 20 an extraordinary high-level meeting on the implications of Iran's oil nationalization was held at the Foreign Office. It was attended by, among others, Sir Donald Fergusson of the Ministry of Fuel and Power, Sir H. Brittain of the Treasury, Mr. C. E. Loombe of the Bank of England, Sir John Lang of the Admiralty, Sir H. Parker and Air Vice-Marshall G. H. Mills of the Ministry of Defence, and Lord Henderson and Sir William Strang of the Foreign Office. The consensus was that if oil was unavailable from Iran, it would cost Britain hundreds of millions of pounds to purchase it elsewhere. The Treasury was concerned about the resulting United Kingdom currency problems. Lang reminded the meeting that the Admiralty annually obtained two million tons, or 85 percent of its fuel oil needs, from AIOC at favorable prices. The Defence Ministry's concern was with the "West's ability to wage war successfully." All participants agreed on the need to intervene in AIOC's relations with Iran and to arrange for talks with the United States to build a united front to avoid Iran's oil nationalization.[9]

Unfortunately for both Great Britain and Iran, British Foreign Secretary Ernest Bevin, whose voice of moderation might have led to a solution, resigned in March 1951 owing to ill health. His replacement was Herbert Morrison, who lacked experience in foreign policy and whose jingoistic attitude intensified the crisis. Shortly after taking office, he proposed that British troops be sent near the area "ready if necessary to intervene in the Persian oil fields." The Defence Ministry undertook to consider such a move urgently.[10]

To keep developments in Iran under constant review, a Working Party on Persia was established, composed of representatives of the Foreign Office, the Ministry of Fuel and Power, the Admiralty, and the Bank of England, with the Defence Ministry to be kept in touch. The Foreign Office believed its immediate objective should be to install a government in Iran that Britain could negotiate with "reasonably." That meant getting rid of Hossein Ala and persuading the Shah to appoint Seyyed Zia ed-Din Tabataba'i, a pro-British politician, as prime minister. It also meant persuading the Shah to dissolve the Majlis, which, they believed, was "dominated by the extremist National Front."[11] To make sure that the United States would not interfere, the Foreign Office instructed Sir Oliver Franks, the British ambassador in Washington, to persuade the State Department to instruct the American ambassador in Tehran "at least not to indicate any disagreement or divergence from our point of view." Franks disliked the idea, saying that if he did so, "the State Department may get the impression that we are pushing."[12]

Philip Noel-Baker, Secretary of State for Commonwealth Relations, suggested that the Iranians be told that Britain would propose a new agreement for AIOC "only when Seyyid Zia comes to power," and that this appointment should be made "a prerequisite of negotiations."[13] The Foreign Office informed the Ministry of Defence that if the dissolution of the Majlis, which "might be the best solution from our point of view," failed, Britain might be obliged to consider the use of force.

Meanwhile in Iran, AIOC, in an apparent reaction to the nationalization law, cut the living allowances of workers in certain oil fields. This provoked a general strike, which soon spread to most oil areas. The U.S. State Department "found it hard to believe" that AIOC "had chosen this precise moment to reduce workers allowances" and wanted an explanation. Northcroft, the company's representative in Tehran, said that the strike was the work of "communist inspired" agitators.[14]

Although the Foreign Office conceded in private that the cause of the strikes was the reduction in allowances, the British government, using the strikes as an excuse, announced on March 28 that two frigates were being sent to Abadan "to safeguard British industries."[15] Later a third frigate and two cruisers were sent. The British show of force led to angry demonstrations in oil areas. The Iranian government instantly announced martial law to maintain order, but in Abadan fighting broke out between the strikers and the troops. Six Iranians were killed and many injured. Before the troops could restore order, the rioters killed two British oil workers and a British sailor. The Iranians firmly believed that AIOC's specific purpose in cutting the workers' allowances had been to ignite riots in order to justify British military intervention. The Foreign Office had advised Shepherd of its military plans "in the event of serious disturbances or threat of governmental action."[16] Under Foreign Office pressure, AIOC chairman Fraser reluctantly instructed that the payment of living allowances be resumed, though, he said, the payments were "to be regarded as intimidation pay [rather] than as strike pay."[17]

After Razmara's assassination, American concern about Iran had heightened. In March 1951, the State Department asked Assistant Secretary of State George McGhee to go to Iran and appraise the situation. On his arrival in Tehran on March 17, he was told by Shepherd that the "Aramco agreement had thrown a monkey wrench into Persian oil machinery." McGhee made "a spirited attack" on AIOC, saying that he had warned Fraser in September 1950 about the Aramco negotiations and their consequences. "The Company," he said, "had been too slow to acknowledge that a new situation had arisen for which new methods were required." He found fault with the Foreign Office for allowing Fraser to dictate its policies on oil in Iran. On a conciliatory note he pointed out that the United States opposed nationalization, adding, however, that "the history of oil concessions did not encourage reliance on the sanctity of contracts."[18]

To explain the U.S. position, McGhee visited the Shah and found that events in Iran had left him frustrated and fearful. When McGhee asked the Shah whether with U.S. support he could avert nationalization, which jeopardized American oil interests elsewhere, he replied that he could not do so and "pleaded that we not ask him to do so." McGhee asked whether a formula might work that paid lip service to nationalization but ended up in a 50-50 split of profits. But the Shah was "too much in shock from the . . . rise to power of the National Front, to consider such strategy."[19]

At the request of the Foreign Office, the State Department instructed McGhee to stop in London on his way back to Washington. There he had a high-level meeting on April 2 with the representatives of the Foreign Office, the Treasury, and the Ministry of Fuel and Power. Two days before this meeting Secretary of State Acheson had telegraphed the Foreign Office: "Since US recognizes right of sovereign state to nationalize, provided prompt and adequate payment made [the State] Department believes equitable solution must be predicated upon UK recognition that 'nationalization has become law' and 'what is done cannot be undone.' "[20] This set the scene for McGhee to suggest that AIOC not stand on its concession rights but instead put out a statement saying that it would not

oppose nationalization in principle and "would meet Persian aspirations." Emphasizing the political aspect of the problem, he observed
that "if we lost the day politically in Persia we would lose the oil
anyway." The British were in no mood to accept the principle of
nationalization. Some British participants suggested issuing a joint
statement supporting the principle of profit-sharing but even this
suggestion was rejected.[21]

McGhee then met Fraser, who he knew set both AIOC's and
Britain's policies with regard to Iranian oil. At a luncheon meeting
characterized by "tenseness" and "sparring comments," McGhee
tried to persuade Fraser to consider current realities in Iran and be
more forthcoming. Fraser was adamant, saying that McGhee's understanding of the situation was wrong and that there was no need
to give Iran any concessions. "Fifty-fifty is a fine slogan, but it seems
to be of dubious practicality," Fraser added. McGhee concluded
that Fraser "had not yet learned."[22]

To the new British foreign minister, Herbert Morrison, McGhee
reported his conclusions from his tour of the Middle East. "The old
discipline imposed by British Imperial power had been removed and
had not been replaced by stable national Governments. . . . The
struggle between Russia and the Western Powers and the growing
spirit of nationalism, provided further causes of unrest. . . . During
the next eighteen months we should be facing a critical situation in
the whole area, especially Persia."

McGhee criticized AIOC for "subordinat[ing] broader political
considerations to purely commercial interests," adding that the
British government "had failed to exercise sufficient control over the
Company's policy." He felt that Britain should come to an agreement with Iran. Morrison, who considered McGhee politically ignorant, stated: "We [Britain] had a long experience of the Middle
East and of the difficulties of dealing with . . . the area."[23]

To show his displeasure with McGhee's discussions in Iran, Morrison instructed Ambassador Franks in Washington "to convey
tactfully to Secretary of State that Mr. McGhee's approach to some
of our Middle East problems struck me as being light-hearted and
that . . . it was profoundly important that the United States officials
should not adumbrate policies in regard to the Middle East until we
had time to consult together." Franks, unaware that McGhee was a

close friend of Acheson and that the views of the two were similar, passed on Morrison's message. "Acheson listened . . . but made no comment."[24]

Next the Foreign Office, hoping to win over the United States, sent a delegation to Washington. Interestingly enough, the brief prepared for the delegation said nothing about possible solutions to the oil problem, concentrating instead on the need to maintain British power and prestige. The brief argued that the defeat of AIOC "would be widely regarded as a victory for the Russians." It maintained that the loss of control over Iran's oil "would cause a loss of £100 million per annum in the United Kingdom's balance of payments, thus seriously affecting our rearmament programme and our cost of living." Moreover, it would be difficult to replace Abadan's refined products while the "Royal Navy is dependent as to 85% of its furnace oil requirements on Abadan." In view of these problems, "substantial control of Persia's oil should remain in British hands." It called American cooperation "unsatisfactory" and complained that American economic assistance had been given to Iran "without previous consultation with us." The brief also emphasized the need to "secure the strongest possible Government in Persia, capable of dealing with terrorism and with the Majlis (not excluding dissolution of the latter)." The delegation was expected to induce the Americans to support Britain on the use of force and to announce in a joint public statement that "complete agreement exists" between the two governments.[25]

The Washington meeting began on April 9, 1951. Sir Oliver Franks headed the U.K. delegation, which consisted of the representatives from the Foreign Office, the Treasury, and the Ministry of Fuel and Power. The American team was headed by George McGhee and included Harold Linder, Assistant Secretary of State for Economic Affairs, and William Rountree, the State Department's Director of Greek, Turkish, and Iranian Affairs. Franks, using his Foreign Office brief, emphasized that AIOC was a vital asset for Britain "not only because of its magnitude as an element of our balance of payments . . . but also because of the power it gave us to control the movement of raw materials and as a bargaining weapon." He stressed the "importance of Persian oil to our common defence" and the effect of its loss on "our ability to rearm." Assuming the Americans to be ignorant of the company's past behavior in Iran, Franks argued that "the nationalisation movement had no solid grievances to feed on" and was insufficiently significant as a factor in the cold war to compel Britain to accept nationalization. He and his colleagues stressed that if Britain was to maintain her political, economic, and military muscle, Iranian oil must be under her full control until the concession terminated in 1993. Finally, he stated that the United States should support Britain in achieving this aim.[26]

McGhee was not convinced. From the U.S. point of view, he said, the main consideration was to maintain Iran's political stability. If Iran was lost to the Soviet Union, her oil would be lost too. The nationalization demand was a fact in spite of its "emotional and impractical character." The United States had been "forced to accept it as a bitter pill in Mexico," and Britain had to accept it in Iran—at least in principle and as a prelude to negotiations leading to 50-50 split of profits. As an experienced oilman, McGhee suggested that the United Kingdom offer Iran equity partnership without asking for compensation following nationalization. To him "nationalisation without compensation" was an attractive slogan. Assistant Secretary Harold Linder, as a lawyer, recapitulated this idea by suggesting that AIOC could turn over its assets in Iran to the government and then obtain a contract from the government permitting it to keep its control and get 50 percent of the profits.[27]

These meetings ended not with the British gaining U.S. support, but with the Americans pressing Britain to "bow to nationalization." Equally disturbing to the British was the fact that the American press advocated the same idea. On April 7, 1951, three important papers repeated the same theme. The *New York Times* wrote that nationalization "cannot be reversed and that British interests in Iran must adjust to an accomplished fact." The *Washington Post* reported that American officials were "convinced the Company must abandon the stiff-necked policies followed for many years by its president, Sir William Fraser." The *Wall Street Journal* said: "Acheson is going to twist the British lion's tail. His aim: to get reluctant Britain to give in to tiny Iran and agree to let her nationalize." It added that "the U.S. won't let Britain use force in Iran" and would insist that the British stop making "19th century threats."[28]

The British embassy in Washington strongly protested to the

State Department about these articles, which they felt were due to a briefing by McGhee. The British press and Parliament accused McGhee of having encouraged the Iranians to nationalize AIOC during his visit to Tehran so that American companies could take over. They ignored the fact that he had tried to convince the Shah to oppose nationalization. On June 21, 1951, in the House of Commons, Richard Crossman, a former lecturer of McGhee's at Oxford, characterized him as a "millionaire oil tycoon" who had deliberately given the Iranians the impression that "if the British were kicked out they could rely on somebody else and they might do a little better." Foreign Secretary Morrison added that "people, not of outstanding importance . . . associated with American oil industry . . . have said some foolish, unwise and perhaps dangerous things in the course of their travels through the Middle East."[29]

Ambassador Franks tried to convince Morrison that the problem was not confined to McGhee. He said: "We are thought by many Americans normally friendly to us to have acted in an old-fashioned imperialistic manner and be paying for exploitation of the Persians." He added that Acheson and the State Department wished to help but could not get "too far in front of public opinion."[30] Unpersuaded, Morrison continued his attacks on McGhee until the British embassy in Washington, finding such attacks counterproductive, advised him to "lay off." "We shall not procure [McGhee's] removal by these criticisms and we will merely render him much less amenable to our approach. . . . Unless we are to conduct our relations on a basis of cat and dog, I think we must try and spare his vanity."[31] Sir Roger Makins, Deputy Under Secretary at the Foreign Office, agreed, telling Morrison that "Mr. McGhee is not in any sense anti-British . . . [but] suffers to some extent from Irish ancestry and a Texas upbringing."[32] Morrison was finally persuaded to desist.

Meanwhile in Iran, the eight National Front papers published attacks on AIOC, accusing it of plundering Iran and spreading corruption. They contended that Iran could not be independent and corruption could not be uprooted as long as the company operated there. To them nationalization was of political rather than economic significance. They emphasized that the nationalist movement in Iran should not be ascribed to communist intrigues and urged the United States to help Iran in her fight for freedom and independence. The British embassy in Tehran tried to fight back by feeding some dailies with its own material, but found it "extremely difficult to secure any press publicity" and fell back on "lobbying . . . in conjunction with the Oil Company" to nullify nationalization. The embassy was happy that the British oil companies were "arranging for a series of broadcasts by the B.B.C. explaining the practical objections to nationalisation."[33]

Interestingly enough, it was AIOC's labor adviser, Sir Frederick Leggett, who was most critical of the company's shortsightedness. As early as February 1951, Leggett, a former associate of Ernest Bevin, told the Foreign Office that AIOC was still hoping to keep the concession alive "by offering a little money here and another sop there." He said that if the company did not adjust to the new realities it would lose its installations in Persia, adding that "even if the Russians did not come in, nationalisation might expropriate the Company." He considered the company's board "confused, hidebound, small minded, blind." At the Eastern Department of the Foreign Office, some agreed with this judgment.[34]

After nationalization, Leggett continued his fight to bring about a better understanding of the Iranian cause. He wrote to Sir William Strang, Permanent Under Secretary at the Foreign Office, that from his visits to Iran he knew that Iranians were "entirely friendly to this country." But since the British had ignored "Persian Rights" and had "failed to make a gesture of recognition of Persian national aspirations . . . we have lost the initiative and have reached the present deplorable position." Britain would be in a stronger position, he said, if she recognized the great change in national feelings in Iran. Otherwise there could be no hope of "suppressing of the monster which has been created."[35]

Earl Mountbatten, then Fourth Lord of the Admiralty, also criticized AIOC's policies. He wrote to Viscount Hall, First Sea Lord, that Iran's oil nationalization arose from a deep-seated and irreversible movement and that "economic and military threats could only make things worse." He suggested that the British government not be blinded by "considerations of prestige" but conduct negotiations with Iran based on the concept of nationalization without compensation; only this course would enable AIOC to operate as before. This was the same suggestion McGhee had offered earlier. When

Morrison, "the notoriously bellicose Foreign Secretary," opined that the Admiralty should send a fleet to the Persian Gulf "to cow these insolent natives," Mountbatten, considering such a course "disastrous," presented his proposal instead, adding that nationalization could not be stopped and "we should therefore have to steer it."

To do the steering, he and Viscount Hall suggested sending their colleague James Callaghan, Parliamentary and Financial Secretary to the Admiralty and later prime minister, to Iran.[36] When Ambassador Shepherd was consulted, he cabled back saying "I would not think there would be any advantage in a Junior Minister visiting Tehran." He apparently considered himself a better troubleshooter. Sir Donald Fergusson of the Ministry of Fuel and Power believed that a delegation should be sent to Tehran headed by "someone imaginative—'a Gulbenkian'" and not Fraser, who "still thinks he can get away without conceding anything like what we may find the situation demands."[37]

By late April 1951 no solid proposals had been made to Iran. The Foreign Office still hoped that Shepherd could persuade the Shah to install Seyyed Zia as prime minister. Shepherd lobbied with the Shah and some Majlis deputies to that end, hinting that otherwise Britain might take military action. Mossadeq was quick to turn Shepherd's activities to his own advantage. He told Prime Minister Ala that he "wished the oil question to be settled at once because there was a prospect of a change of Government or a coup d'etat."[38] Moreover, he warned the Majlis on April 26 that certain events might soon occur that would neutralize Iran's nationalization efforts. Pointing out that for every month AIOC stayed in Iran, millions of pounds belonging to the poverty-ridden people of the country were lost, Mossadeq urged the Oil Committee to lose no time finishing its job of establishing the framework within which nationalization would take place.

The Oil Committee met on the same day and, after a five-hour session, approved a nine-point draft resolution setting down procedures for the nationalization of oil industry. Mossadeq had actively participated in the preparation of this resolution. On the following day Shepherd held a press conference in which he protested against nationalization. At an earlier time some Majlis deputies would take their cue from the British ambassador in the belief that it would be dangerous to oppose British desires; but now, even the most pro-British deputies could not ignore public opinion. Shepherd's press conference was followed on April 28 by a letter from AIOC to the prime minister rejecting nationalization. But there was no prime minister. The day before, Ala, who in principle supported nationalization, had resigned as a result of not being consulted by the Oil Committee in the preparation of its resolution.

The Majlis's response to the British protests was utterly unexpected. On April 28, Jamal Emami, the Majlis speaker, proposed Mossadeq as prime minister, expecting that he would refuse. Instead Mossadeq surprised him by accepting, and the Majlis, overwhelmed by his popularity, voted 79 to 12 recommending his appointment to the Shah. Mossadeq, taking advantage of the opportunity, announced that he would accept the post with honor only when the Majlis approved the Oil Committee's resolution on nationalization. The Majlis responded on the same day by unanimously approving the resolution, and the Senate did the same two days later. The Shah, though dismayed with the Majlis and the Senate for making two such important decisions without prior consultation with him, had no alternative but to endorse both the choice of Mossadeq as prime minister and the Nationalization Procedures Act.

The act, which for the next twenty-eight months preoccupied the British and U.S. governments and the international oil corporations, had the following main provisions:

1. In order to implement nationalization of oil industry, a Joint Committee was to be formed composed of five senators, five Majlis deputies, and the finance minister or his deputy.

2. The government was required to dispossess AIOC at once under the supervision of the Joint Committee. The government was to deposit 25 percent of its net oil revenue in the national bank of Iran, to meet AIOC's claims.

3. The government was also required to examine Iran's claims as well as the rightful claims of AIOC under supervision of the Joint Committee and to submit its findings to the two houses for approval.

4. Inasmuch as after March 20, 1951, when the Senate approved nationalization, all oil revenues belonged to Iran, the government

was required to audit AIOC accounts under the supervision of the Joint Committee, which also was responsible for supervising the oil operations until the appointment of a board of management.

5. The Joint Committee was to prepare and present for approval of the two houses the statutes of the National Iranian Oil Company (NIOC), with provisions for a board of management and a supervisory board composed of experts.

6. In order to replace foreign experts gradually with Iranians, the Joint Committee was to draw up a program for sending students abroad to study in various fields connected with oil. The Ministry of Education was to be in charge of implementing this program.

7. All purchasers of oil from AIOC were hereafter to purchase oil from NIOC at current international prices.

8. The Joint Committee was required to complete its work within three months and submit a report of its activities to the Majlis.[39]

Britain, which had believed that she could manipulate the Iranian government and the Majlis as before, was thus faced with a crucial challenge to her most important economic outpost.

6

Forces at Work in Iran, Britain, and the United States

Iran's national movement, which led to oil nationalization, set in motion a politico-economic power game in which forces in Iran, Britain, the United States, and the Soviet Union, as well as the international oil companies and the media, exerted their influence in differing ways. The purpose of this chapter is to examine the forces that played a role in shaping events.

The nationalization of British oil interests in Iran had its roots in the constitutional revolution of 1905–9, when the nationalists tried to establish a parliamentary system that would limit the powers of autocratic rulers and invalidate the concessions that such rulers had, at their own whim, given to foreigners. Achieving the latter aim became even more important when a British oil company became a major political force in Iran, manipulating Cabinet ministers, government officials, and Majlis members for the purpose of increasing its own gains at the expense of Iran. The Iranians felt that constitutional rule could not develop as long as foreign domination fed local corruption. The nationalists had fought, off and on, a series of battles against these external and internal "evils," but with little success. With the end of World War II and the waning of British power, frustrated nationalists united behind Mossadeq to achieve their aims.

The National Front, which Mossadeq led, was a coalition of forces each of which had a powerful influence on public opinion. The twenty founding members comprised two law professors, seven lawyers, three journalists, two engineers, four civil servants, and two clerics. Eight of the twenty had been educated in France, three in Switzerland, eight in Iran, and one, a cleric, in Iraq. In terms of class origin, five, including Mossadeq, were from the landed aristocracy and the remaining fifteen from the urban middle class.[1]

In the founding group those besides Mossadeq who played a major role in nationalizing the oil industry were Hossein Fatemi, editor of the Tehran daily *Bakhtaré-Emruz*; Karim Sanjabi and Ali Shayegan, professors of law; Hossein Makki, civil servant; and Mozaffar Baqa'i, a lawyer. Mehdi Bazargan, a French-educated engineer, was also a major player.

What gave strength to this small group was that eight of its members were editors of papers with wide circulation, and that three others were backed by political parties and could mobilize their members in support of the Front. The main political parties of the National Front coalition were the Iran party, the Toilers' party, and the Nationalist Party of Iran. The Iran party, founded by Mehdi Bazargan, a French-educated engineer, consisted chiefly of members of the professional middle class, civil servants, university graduates, and college students. The party called for the elimination of foreign influence, autocracy, and corruption, and the establishment of genuine constitutional monarchy and social justice. The party's paper propagated Western ideas of freedom and called for strengthening the constitution by transforming the Shah into a ceremonial head of state. To this end it quoted Montesquieu's *Spirit of Laws* to argue that concentrating power in kings led to corruption and weakness in society.

The Toilers' party, established by Dr. Baqa'i, was composed of some college students, bazaar tradesmen, and shopkeepers. It had more or less the same goals as the Iran party, but was more to the left. This party identified with the socialist movements in Europe; its publications included ideas from André Gide and Bertrand Russell, among others.

The Nationalist Party of Iran was founded by Dariush Foruhar, a law student, with a membership composed mainly of high school and college students. The party was nationalistic in its aims while being both anticommunist and anticapitalist. It stressed that Iran's backwardness was due to corrupt royal courts and to the influence of foreign powers, reactionary mullahs, and greedy landlords.[2]

The National Front, a coalition of these and other groups, emerged as a major force in Iranian politics. Though the specific aims of its component groups differed to some extent, the Front as a whole had two common goals: to fight against foreign domination and to establish constitutional democracy. In their leader Mossadeq they saw the embodiment of these goals.

Closely associated with the National Front, but not formally a member of it, was a fourth party called the Society of Moslem Warriors led by Ayatollah Abol-Qassem Kashani, a religious figure who had a wide following in the bazaar and among seminary students. Kashani had been bitterly hostile toward the British ever since his father was killed in Mesopotamia after World War I by British occupying forces, against whom he and his followers had taken up arms. In 1941, when the British and the Russians occupied Iran, the British arrested young Kashani for leading a strong campaign against them. Upon his release at the end of the war, he resumed his attacks against the British and their oil company.[3]

His society, composed of seminary students, guild elders, and bazaar shopkeepers, called for strict adherence to Islamic law and Moslem unity against the West. Another religious group, associated with the society but not with the National Front, was Fada'iyane-Islam (Devotees of Islam). Members of this group were extremist fundamentalists who considered it right to assassinate anyone whom they considered highly irreligious.

The main rival of the National Front at this time was the Tudeh (communist) party. This party came into existence in 1941, when a group of Marxists imprisoned by Reza Shah were freed after his fall, and expanded during the war with Soviet backing when the Russians occupied northern Iran. Fanning discontent among the industrial labor force, including AIOC workers, Tudeh helped to create a leftist labor movement. In fact, Tudeh was the only well-organized party with an efficient structure and a nationwide network. In February 1949, when Tudeh was accused of an assassination attempt on the Shah, many of its leaders were arrested and the party was officially banned. In 1950, however, Prime Minister Razmara, in an effort to help the British, relaxed the controls over the Tudeh so as to undermine the National Front. The number of Tudeh party members at the time was estimated to be 14,000, one-third of whom were in Abadan. Most of the oil workers in AIOC's area of operation, however, supported the National Front.

The Tudeh party opposed nationalizing the oil industry throughout the country because such a step would make it impossible for

the Soviet Union to obtain oil concessions. It called only for nationalizing the British oil company. Distressed by the rising power
of the National Front, Tudeh virulently attacked it and Mossadeq,
calling him a "hireling of the Imperialists." Ironically, then, Tudeh
and the British had one goal in common: to undermine Mossadeq
and weaken his national movement.

Another force in Iranian politics was the Shah. He had the support of a major part of the army and some conservative landlords
and politicians, many of whom were pro-British. But he had two
major drawbacks politically. First, although he agreed in his heart
with the National Front's aim of curtailing the interference of foreign powers in Iran, he feared that any move against the British
might bring about his downfall. For this reason he had not joined
the National Front and the general public in their demands for oil
nationalization. Second, he was known to favor establishing autocratic rule whenever the opportunity afforded. Having shown himself at odds with the two fundamental aims of the public, he had lost
their support.

Another force to be reckoned with were the tribes, among whom
the Qashqais were "the biggest, strongest, best led homogeneous
group in Persia." Since Qashqai chiefs supported the National
Front, Sam Falle, then British acting consul in Shiraz, believed that
Britain should try to neutralize their efforts by establishing a coalition of tribal forces hostile to them.[4] These ideas never materialized.

Forces outside Iran, notably in Britain, the United States, and the
Soviet Union, influenced events in the country. The long-term objective of the Soviet Union was to bring Iran into her camp. In the
words of Edwin Bolland, Second Secretary at the British embassy in
Tehran and a man who had previously served in Moscow, the Soviet
policy was to work through the Tudeh party to "liberate" Iran from
the bonds of the "Imperialist" bloc and make her a communist state.
This would "enable Soviet power to exert a considerable influence
over Pakistan, India and other neighbouring countries in much the
same way as British power was able to dominate from India many
countries of the Far East and Middle East." Furthermore, it would
enable the Soviets to have Iran's oil and at the same time threaten
the oil supplies of the Western world.[5]

Despite these long-term plans, the Soviet Union took a low profile on the oil dispute, and her criticism of AIOC was minimal. Not so the United States, which was determined to support Iran as a first line of defense against what U.S. officials saw as Russian designs on Pakistan and Turkey. The Truman administration believed that nationalist movements would work as a barrier against communism. It was thus sympathetic to Iran's aspirations and considered Mossadeq "the embodiment of a surge of nationalist feeling . . . [whose] policy of ejecting the AIOC has the support of the vast majority of the people." Many in the State Department felt that any settlement, "however damaging to the AIOC's interests," was preferable to a situation that endangered Iran's economy and strengthened the communists.[6] They had no objection to the nationalization of Iranian oil as long as it did not challenge the 50-50 division of profits that was now standard with American oil companies throughout the world.

The British government was strongly opposed to the U.S. government's views on Iran. Although World War II had brought Britain's supremacy to an end, the imperial hangover was still there. As Corelli Barnett, a British historian, put it,

> [British] political leaders and the governing Establishment, conditioned as they had been from their Edwardian childhoods to take it for granted that Britain stood in the first rank of nation states, simply could not accept that British power had vanished amid the stupendous events of the Second World War, and that the era of imperial greatness . . . had now ineluctably closed. . . . They were resolved to restore and perpetuate Britain's traditional world role.[7]

Given this frame of mind, the British could not tolerate Mossadeq, who challenged their supremacy. Morrison in particular, with his persistent colonial outlook, considered it the right of the British to use Iran's oil wealth to remedy Britain's economic ills. During World War II Britain had lost about £7 billion, or a quarter of her entire national wealth. Furthermore, with the termination of the U.S. Lend-Lease Agreement late in 1945, Britain was faced with a critical financial situation that endangered her economic survival. To meet the crisis, John Maynard Keynes, the well-known British economist, obtained a long-term U.S. loan of $3.75 billion. But this loan was conditional on sterling convertibility, which put a heavy drain on Britain's gold and dollar reserves. Under these circumstances Iran's oil, which was a huge dollar earner for Britain, had added significance. In short, Iran was looked upon as a piece of real estate that should help Britain sustain her economy.

AIOC and the British government had complementary aims in Iran. The company's aim was to have the "monopoly of the take-off of Persian oil" and the "maximum possible share of the profits." The British government's aims were to provide the maximum possible benefit to Britain's balance of payments, to maintain the supply of sterling oil, and to secure satisfactory tax revenue for the Exchequer.[8] To achieve these aims, Britain sought ways of replacing Mossadeq's government with one more amenable to British aims. The British government was happy that the Soviets "have not intervened openly in the oil dispute," and was convinced that Mossadeq's "xenophobia" prevented him from doing business with the Russians unless faced with economic disaster.[9]

The British aims were thus diametrically opposed to the Iranian government's objective of eliminating foreign control over oil and securing higher revenues for itself. Mossadeq believed that no one could legally dispute nationalization, which was considered a sovereign right of every state. Britain had nationalized a number of her industries, and Mexico had taken over the property of American and British oil companies operating there. Mossadeq felt that Truman would accept Iran's nationalization of oil as Roosevelt had accepted Mexico's. After all, Roosevelt, on a visit to Mexico in April 1943, had proclaimed that "the day of the exploitation of the resources and the people of one country for the benefit of any group in another country is definitely over."[10]

Since the Iranian government contended that AIOC was the root cause of poverty and corruption in Iran, the British press began a campaign to demonstrate that the company had nothing to do with these evils. The London *Times* attributed Iran's "state of disequilibrium" to the "stupidity, greed, and lack of judgement of its ruling classes." In the struggle between the haves and have-nots, the corrupt and the reformist, the paper claimed, AIOC had become a scapegoat. The *Times* added that these ills could not be solved by oil nationalization, "as certain irresponsible Persian politicians claim."[11]

The *Economist,* following the same theme, wrote: "No Persian with any common sense really believes that the Anglo-Iranian Oil Company is responsible for the horrifying poverty of the masses." The Iranian nationalists, it said, by using this "monumental scapegoat" intend to seize an "enterprise in which over £350 million of British capital has been sunk."[12] One must question this figure of £350 million. As we shall see in the following chapter, the total worldwide assets of AIOC at the time were £286 million—of which only £28 million were in Iran.

Britain's main problem with regard to Iran was her difference in outlook with the United States. For Britain the oil dispute was simply a matter of British economic interests. For the United States the dispute had significant strategic implications in global confrontation with Russia at a time when the Americans were involved in the Korean war. The United States expected Britain to settle the oil dispute in such a way that Iran would not become another Korea. The Americans also stressed that the security of Iran and that of Western Europe were linked, since Iran provided so large a proportion of the oil used in Western Europe.

The British suspected that the United States was bent on grabbing their oil interests in the Middle East. Their suspicions were based on some precedents. In October 1943, James Byrnes, then director of the Office of War Mobilization, urged President Roosevelt to ask the British to transfer a third of their oil interests in Iran to the United States in compensation for the oil delivered to Britain under the Lend-Lease Agreement. Roosevelt did not take up the matter with the British. However, the American oil companies complained about having to provide 80 percent of the oil needs of the Allies from their own resources, as against only 8 percent from British-owned resources, in a war in which Britain's territorial and strategic interests were directly involved. Britain could not ignore these claims. Matters were settled after the war when AIOC satisfied the major American oil companies by offering interlocking arrangements in Kuwait and Iraq and deals on long-term oil contracts.[13] With these arrangements the American and British oil interests in the Middle East established a cozy partnership in the area.

On oil policy, however, Britain and the United States had different perceptions. Both countries supported their oil companies abroad in maintaining control over the oil resources allocated to them under their concessions. But the U.S. government's emphasis was on national security considerations, while the British emphasis was on maximum profits.

The U.S. State Department believed that Britain should settle the oil dispute to help ensure the security of Iran. The British replied, in effect, that if Iran's security was in danger, Mossadeq's government and the communists were to blame. The Americans were not impressed. At a Senate hearing on June 20, 1951, General Patrick Hurley, a former special representative of President Roosevelt in Iran, stated that Iran's oil nationalization, far from being communist-inspired, was simply a reaction to AIOC's "stubborn, unenlightened and greedy" conduct. The Iranians, he said, "see great wealth being produced from their own country, and they are not getting it." The Russians, he added, believed that without any effort on their part "Iran will fall into communist hands" because of Western greed. *U.S. News and World Report* reminded its readers that as early as 1944, Hurley had told President Roosevelt that Iran's development was hampered by the British, who "were milking the country dry."[14]

The *Washington Post* wrote that the Iranians viewed the company as "a thriving state within a stricken state—as a symbol of their poverty"; they considered oil nationalization their salvation.[15] The *New York Times* argued that if the United States did not give strong support to Mossadeq, American prestige in Iran and the entire Middle East would be in danger. It added that Mossadeq's following was nationwide and "his position in the country had been compared by one American official familiar with the country as not unlike that of Thomas Jefferson or Thomas Paine in the early United States."[16] It was no easy task for Britain to influence the press of a free country "brought up on a history which started with licking the British." P. H. Gore-Booth, who dealt with the press at the British embassy in Washington, was concerned about "the universal condemnation of the past policies of the AIOC," which added to "the natural 'anti-imperialism' of the Americans."[17]

Since the end of World War II, British relations with the United States had come under certain strains. The Americans, who fought the war to free nations from foreign rule, found that Britain, though she had consistently used the slogans of freedom and democracy during the war, had no intention of giving up her colonies unless forced to do so—as she was in India, Burma, and Palestine. Many Americans felt that the British looked upon the war as a short setback and were intent on restoring the era of imperial greatness. Moreover, they sensed that Britain wanted to pursue this aim at the expense of the United States. There were persistent British demands that America should share her wealth, power, and nuclear bomb technology with Britain—and all this under the pretext of the so-called "special relationship" between the two countries. The Americans considered these demands unwarranted. There was an outcry in the press that the U.S. government should in no way assist Britain in her colonial aims.

Faced with strong American criticism, Sir John Slessor, Marshal of the Royal Air Force, made a detailed study in the United States to see what could be done to improve Britain's image. He reported that "suspicion and dislike of the British is more deep and wide-spread than at any time in the past ten years," adding "it is no good saying that . . . twisting the lion's tail is a traditional American pastime." Considering Anglo-American unity extremely important, he advised the British government to influence U.S. public opinion by launching a large-scale public relations campaign, "even if [this should] cost a few thousand a year."[18]

The Foreign Office considered that a few thousand pounds a year could not help in dealing with "an emotional public opinion in this vast country and in the face of a largely hostile press." The task needed "a huge and fabulously costly organisation," which was difficult to finance. It chose to concentrate on "influencing key personalities all over the country, especially those who have a voice in native organs of public opinion." Following this line, British ambassador Sir Oliver Franks intensified his lobbying at "endless dinners in Georgetown," where he frequently met Dean Acheson and other State Department officials as well as leading American commentators. Gore-Booth of the embassy, too, stepped up his contacts, talking to a number of influential voices in the media, among them Edward R. Murrow and Elmer Davis.[19] These contacts bore fruit over time with respect to the British in general, but Franks felt compelled to inform the Foreign Office of AIOC's widespread unpopularity both within the U.S. administration and outside. "The real trouble with AIOC," he said, "is that they have not got far enough past the stage of western paternalism [which is] a bit out of fashion in this decade." J. V. Kelly, the British ambassador in Moscow, concerned that the Russians might exploit Britain's weak position in Iran, also noted that AIOC's board was still living in the world of 1910.[20]

The American oil companies in the Middle East, though harshly critical of Fraser's handling of the oil situation in Iran, were forced to cooperate with him because they had common interests in the area. If Iran succeeded in her nationalization drive, the U.S. oil companies could not remain unaffected.

Some people within AIOC itself, however, considered Fraser "a mean Scotsman who had no flexibility at all." Sir Frederic Leggett, the company's labor adviser, considered its management "blind," and unaware that "what was required was a fresh start, on the basis of equal partnership."[21] Within the British government, too, many were beginning to see Fraser and the company's board as the real problem behind the difficulties of Britain in Iran. They were shocked to learn from the British labor attaché in Tehran that many of the company's workers were housed in "cottages made of mud bricks, with no electricity, without outside water supply and sanitary arrangements . . . in other words, in veritable slums."[22] As it happened, the facts were even grimmer. The British minister in Tel Aviv sent the Foreign Office an article published in the *Jerusalem Post* by an Israeli who had worked for AIOC in Abadan since 1944. He wrote that the "unnamed" 60,000 skilled and unskilled workers were "the poorest of creatures on earth," having no living quarters.

They lived during the seven hot months of the year under the trees. . . . In winter times these masses moved into big halls, built by the Company, [each] housing up to 3,000–4,000 people without walls of partition between them. Each family occupied the space of a blanket. There were no lavatories. . . .

In debates with British colleagues we often tried to show them the mistake they were making in treating the Persians the way they did. The answer was usually: "We English have had hundreds of years of experience on how to treat the Natives.

Socialism is all right back home, but out here you have to be the master.

Sending this article to the Foreign Office, the British minister in Tel Aviv noted that "the Company . . . deserved what happened to them."[23]

It was thus not surprising to find the company's labor force heavily engaged in the nationalization movement. Months before nationalization, Philip Noel-Baker, Secretary of State for Commonwealth Relations, warned Foreign Secretary Ernest Bevin that something of the sort might happen: "the importance of Persian oil to the economy and defence of the United Kingdom and the Commonwealth is so great that we cannot afford to take the smallest chance of labour troubles and social unrest, the more so since the Company are making such large profits and have large reserves."[24]

AIOC chairman Fraser paid no heed to such warnings. Many found him a "second-rate intellect," with no notion of politics and "all the contempt of a Glasgow accountant for anything which cannot be shown on a balance sheet." When the Aramco agreement on equal division of profits was concluded, "Fraser did not immediately see the writing on the wall and resisted to go along with it."[25]

To avoid the wrath of AIOC shareholders on this last count, Fraser distorted the facts in the company's annual report for 1950. According to the report, "on hearing of the Saudi Arabian Agreement . . . the Company lost no time in communicating to General Ali Razmara, the then Prime Minister, its willingness to examine with the Iranian Government suggestions for a new agreement on similar lines. . . . There was no question of the Company being behindhand or less generous."[26] The records show that the reverse is true. Though Fraser was urged by the Americans as well as some Foreign Office officials to follow the Saudi agreement, he did not yield, saying he knew better how to deal with Iranians. As Assistant Secretary of State George McGhee put it, "The AIOC failure to act at this time can only be seen as a great tragedy."[27]

Clement Attlee's socialist government expected the company to have "a social conscience" and contribute to the welfare of its oil workers as well as the economic development of Iran. But such measures were bound to reduce the company's sizable contributions in the form of taxes to the British Treasury and dividends to the stockholders, a major one being the government itself. This difficulty prevented Attlee's government from pressing the claims of its social conscience in Iran. Iranians naturally concluded that no matter what type of government ruled Britain, AIOC would continue its unenlightened and oppressive exploitation of their country.

AIOC contributed enormously to Britain's balance of payments and the Treasury, thus partly compensating for the loss of the empire. As John Strachey, Secretary of State for War, put it, "This last empire, the empire of oil, has 'paid' better than any other."[28] The problem was Fraser's shortsightedness in running this empire, his blatant effort to squeeze out of Iran as much as he could. Within the labor government, some urged that Fraser be replaced by someone with "a broad outlook and statesmanlike qualities," and that his board be replaced as well.[29] The State Department's advice was that either Fraser should be removed or at least the Foreign Office should not allow him to dictate British policy.

The British government's policy for the time being was to crush Iran's nationalization before the idea spread to other British investments throughout the world. Burma's prime minister Thakin Nu warned that if AIOC were expelled from Iran, Britain would be humbled and extremists in Eastern countries would be strengthened, making it difficult for governments to withstand their pressure. In Southeast Asia, Britain had interests in the Burma Oil Company and the Burma Corporation in Burma, Royal Dutch Shell in Indonesia, and the Tin Syndicate in Siam.[30]

The major American oil companies backed AIOC, telling Secretary of State Acheson that Iran's nationalization would end the "sanctity of contracts," thus threatening U.S. oil and other investment agreements throughout the world. Many in the State Department, however, believed that associating the United States with AIOC's "colonial methods" would alienate Iran from the West and pave the way for Russian domination. The U.S. Joint Chiefs of Staff worried that if Iran was lost to the West, Turkey would be outflanked, leading to Soviet domination of the Middle East and all its oil resources.[31] The State Department's petroleum adviser, Richard Funkhouser, observed that if the USSR broke the flow of Middle East oil to its normal markets, such a rupture could affect "not only economic viability but also political stability and the defensive position of Western Europe."[32]

The United States was faced with an acute dilemma. She could ignore neither Britain, her close ally, nor Iran, a strategic country bordering the Soviet Union; yet the interests of the two were diametrically opposed. For eighteen months the Truman administration exerted all its efforts to find a middle ground that would satisfy both countries. But the divergent forces at work in Iran, the United States, and Britain made the task difficult. Furthermore the Russians, under Stalin, did not reveal their strategy, confining themselves to flirting with Iran's Tudeh party and Britain at the same time, while attacking "Western imperialism." It was the interplay of these forces that would determine the outcome.

7

Iran Takes Over the Company

AIOC responded sharply to Iran's enactment of nationalization procedures, proclaiming that Iran had shown plain ingratitude in nationalizing an industry built with British capital and knowhow. What the company did not say was that, in the words of Sir William Strang of the Foreign Office, it had "squeezed every pound it could get out of Persia"[1] to build its vast empire throughout the world. A study of AIOC's financial position at the time of nationalization is instructive.

According to the company's consolidated balance sheet dated December 31, 1950, AIOC's total assets, including its interests in subsidiary and allied companies throughout the world, amounted to £268.5 million. Of this amount only £32.8 million or 12.2 percent was financed by share capital; and even out of this total share capital, over one-third was provided by the conversion of part of the company's reserves to common stock given freely to shareholders. Thus one can safely say that by 1950 about £22 million of AIOC's worldwide assets were subscribed by shareholders to the company's share capital and the rest were attributable to the reinvestment of profits originating from Iranian oil.

Foreign Office and Treasury officials admitted among themselves that Britain could not refute Iran's claim that the company's worldwide business "had been built up on Persian oil," since "A.I.O.C. has raised no fresh money" since 1923. As explained earlier, the company expanded its operations at the cost of Iran by employing every possible device to reduce Iran's share in oil revenues.

AIOC had interests in refining companies in Britain, Australia, France, Italy, and Israel. It fully owned a tanker company, and tankers costing £21 million were on order. Furthermore, its investments in subsidiary and allied companies alone totaled £50 million.

It had a 50 percent share in the Kuwait Oil Company and 23.75 percent each in the Iraq Petroleum Company and Petroleum Development Ltd. in Qatar. The balance sheet value of AIOC's fixed assets in Iran, which it fully owned at the time, was £28 million, although the replacement value of these fixed assets was claimed to be £300 million.[2]

AIOC produced 51 percent of the Middle East's oil, three-quarters of it from Iran and the rest from its share of production in Iraq, Kuwait, and Qatar. Of the remaining 49 percent, 44.5 percent was produced by American companies and the rest by Dutch and French companies. AIOC in Iran was fully British, and Aramco in Saudi Arabia and Bahrain Petroleum Company were fully American (see Table 3). But in Iraq and Kuwait, AIOC had partnerships with American companies, which gave the two nations' companies a common interest.

At the time of nationalization, Iran was the leading oil producer in the Middle East and the fourth largest in the world, following the United States, Venezuela, and the USSR. Iran's annual production was 32 million tons or over one-third of the total 90-million-ton production of the Middle East. Moreover, Abadan was the largest refinery in the world, with a capacity of over 20 million tons.[3] Of the total requirements of Western Europe, Iran supplied 90 percent of crude, 40 percent of refined products, and 100 percent of bunkers. The U.S. Central Intelligence Agency (CIA) reported early in 1951 that the loss of Iranian oil and the Abadan refinery would have "an adverse effect upon Western European economic activity, and would impose severe financial losses particularly upon the British, who control all the oil production of the country." It estimated that supplying Western Europe's requirements from sources other than Iran "would involve an extra dollar expenditure of about $700,000,000" a year on the assumption that prices remained the same.[4]

It was to avoid such potential losses that the British were determined to block Iran's nationalization. However, AIOC's unfair treatment of Iran embarrassed even the Foreign Office. When it checked AIOC's accounts for 1950, it found that the company's gross profits for that year were over £100 million; taxes paid to the British government came to £50.7 million, allocations to reserves to £25 million, and payments to Iran to £16 million. Sir Roger

TABLE 3
Middle East Oil Holdings in 1950

Oil company	Country	How owned	Percentage
AIOC	Iran	*British*	
		British government	56
		Burma Oil Co.	22
		Private interests	22
Aramco	Saudi Arabia	*American*	
		Standard Oil of California	30
		Texas Co.	30
		Standard Oil of N.J.	30
		Socony-Vacuum	10
Bahrain Petroleum Co.	Bahrain	*American*	
		Standard Oil of California	50
		Texas Co.	50
Iraq, Mosul & Basra Petroleum Companies (IPC)	Iraq	*International*	
		AIOC	23¾
		Shell Group	23¾
		C.I.E. Française des Pétroles	23¾
		Standard Oil of N.J.	11⅞
		Socony-Vacuum	11⅞
		C. S. Gulbenkian	5
Petroleum Development Ltd.	Qatar	Same as IPC	
Kuwait Oil Co.	Kuwait	*Anglo-American*	
		AIOC	50
		Gulf Exploration Co.	50

Source: FO371/91522, Report by A. K. Rothnie, F.O., Feb. 6, 1951.

Makins, deputy under secretary at the Foreign Office, expected the company's statement to "cause a furore"; whereas "the gross profit and the deduction of the United Kingdom taxation have more than doubled in relation to the figures of 1949," Iran's royalties had increased from £13.5 million in 1949 to only £16 million.[5] Nevertheless the British government gave AIOC its full support.

To upset the Oil Nationalization Act, Britain took a series of different but parallel measures. These ranged from preparations for the possible occupation of Abadan[6] to efforts to undermine Mossadeq while at the same time negotiating with him within the framework of equal division of profits.

Meanwhile, Mossadeq presented his Cabinet to the Majlis. Eight of its members were sympathetic to the National Front; the remaining four were chosen by the Shah. British ambassador Shepherd lost no time in meeting the new prime minister to make strong objections to nationalization. Mossadeq tried to convince him that there was no ill will toward the British. "Britain," he said, "was a stabilising influence [against Russia] and Persia could not afford to break with her." However, a distinction must be made between the British government and AIOC, which was "responsible for nearly all the evils from which the country suffered today." According to Mossadeq, "he only wished to do in Persia what had already been done in Britain to carry out social reforms which would prevent and forestall communism. For this the country must control its important sources of wealth." In reply, Shepherd repeated his objection to the nationalization of the "most important British assets in Persia."[7]

On his second visit to Mossadeq, Shepherd passed on a message from Foreign Secretary Morrison warning Iran against taking any unilateral action. When Shepherd argued that Britain had been greatly helpful to Iran, Mossadeq asked him to give one example. Shepherd replied that Britain had paid £8.5 million for the use of Iranian railways during the war. Mossadeq retorted that according to his calculations "the damage to railways amounted to £72 million, far more than the amount paid by Britain."[8] Mossadeq's reply to Morrison's message was that "it is the sovereign right of every nation to nationalise its industries." He added that the "former" company would shortly be invited to help in the "implementation of the law."[9]

To sum up his understanding of Mossadeq after two weeks in power, Ambassador Shepherd wrote to Geoffrey Furlonge of the Foreign Office that the new prime minister had been "reasonably conciliatory" and "genuinely anxious to avoid anything in the nature of a break in relations." He added that Mossadeq "is obsessed by a single idea, the nationalisation of oil and the elimination of what he considers the maleficent influence of the Oil Company from Persia, and probably quite honestly believes that this result can still be achieved without a major row with His Majesty's Government provided the principle of compensation is observed." Shepherd concluded that "we must now assume a stiffer attitude" to make Mossadeq understand that there will in fact be a major row if Britain's wishes are ignored.[10]

In mid-May 1951 the Iranian government went ahead with nationalization by establishing an eleven-man Joint Committee as called for by the Nationalization Procedures Act. It consisted of Kazem Hassibi, under secretary of the finance ministry, and ten members of the Majlis and the Senate. Several committee members had been educated in the West and had previously held ministerial posts, and one was a professor of international law.[11] Shepherd, however, looked down on them and described them as "inexperienced and undistinguished"; he also considered them "extremists" or "fellow-travellers." But Professor Elwell-Sutton, who had served with the British embassy in Tehran, compared them favorably with the members of AIOC's board.[12]

On May 14, when the Joint Committee began its work, the British government announced that the Sixteenth Independent Parachute Brigade Group had been brought to a state of readiness, hinting that it might be used for military action in Abadan. A day earlier a communique issued by the Iranian embassy in Paris said that because of "plots against his life by agitators employed by Anglo-Iranian," the prime minister had decided "to facilitate security measures" by remaining within the Majlis premises. The Foreign Office protested.[13]

The Joint Committee appointed a three-man Provisional Board to manage the National Iranian Oil Company (NIOC). The board was headed by Mehdi Bazargan (founder of the Iran party), an engineering graduate from the Ecole Centrale of France, who was then Dean of the Technical College of Tehran University. Richard Seddon, AIOC's representative in Iran, was asked to join the board's discussions and told that if he did not do so, the Iranian government would proceed without his cooperation. The company's response was that Iran's action was a breach of the terms of the concession. The British government announced that it had lodged a complaint against Iran with the International Court of Justice (World Court) at The Hague.[14]

Iran advised the World Court that it did not have competence to deal with a dispute between the Iranian government and a foreign company. Furthermore, in a statement to the press, Mossadeq pointed out that it is the sovereign right of every state to nationalize and that Iran did not require permission from another government to do so, adding that the company's only remedy was to receive compensation as foreseen in the law.

The U.S. view on nationalization was the same as Iran's. The State Department expressed serious doubts about the company's basic legal position, saying that "no Government can deny itself the sovereign rights to nationalize an industry within its territory." Secretary of State Acheson told British ambassador Franks that the State Department's international lawyers found it difficult to go beyond the view that "breach of contract involved payment of damages or compensation." He suggested that Britain recognize the principle of nationalization and ask for negotiations.[15]

Clement Attlee, the British Labour prime minister, who had himself pioneered nationalization in Britain, could scarcely say that nationalization was right for his country but not for others. He felt Britain must accept the principle of nationalization. What he had in mind, however, was not genuine acceptance. Although accepting nationalization was like "granting a country independence" in his view, in the course of negotiations modifications could be introduced that would result in something a good deal less than independence. He added that the point was "to give Musaddiq an opportunity of saving face."[16]

Foreign Secretary Morrison, however, took a harder line. He could not tolerate allowing the prime minister of a weak Middle Eastern country to challenge British "rights." With Attlee's approval, he instructed Franks to tell Acheson that "Persian oil is of vital importance to our economy, and that we regard it as essential to do everything possible to prevent the Persians from getting away with a breach of their contractual obligations, in view of the probable repercussions in the Middle East and elsewhere to the United States no less than ourselves."

Further, "our experience of the Persian character" suggested that once Britain made it clear that British troops would be used, Iran would come to terms. If the Americans wanted Britain to refrain from the use of force, said Morrison, "their best course is surely to exert maximum pressure on Musaddiq to this end." He finally confided to Franks that "I am really rather annoyed at the American attitude of relative indifference to a situation which may be most grave to us all."[17]

In an effort to mediate the dispute, U.S. ambassador Grady invited Mossadeq and Shepherd to his residence for lunch to see if a basis for a negotiated settlement could be reached. Mossadeq told them there was nothing to be discussed except payment of compensation and arrangements to assure supplies to former purchasers. When Grady stated that it was impossible to replace British technicians, Mossadeq asked airily "whether the British were gods that others could not do what they could do." He added that he would use experts from neutral countries and that the British were not "supernatural."[18]

When Acheson made it clear that the United States had no intention of challenging Iran's sovereignty, Morrison complained, "It was almost as if American opinion did not approve of nationalisation, excepting when it damaged British interests." The matter came to a head on May 28, when Geoffrey Furlonge, head of the Eastern Department of the Foreign Office, reported to the Cabinet: "State Department are pressing us to declare categorically that we are willing to accept nationalisation in principle" and that Britain would send negotiators to Tehran.[19]

Under American pressure and Iran's unyielding stand, Britain finally agreed to make a conditional "bow to nationalisation." But Morrison stated in the House of Commons that he did not agree with "the right of any Government unilaterally, by itself . . . to sail over everybody's heads and merely pass Acts of Parliament."[20]

To smooth the way for a settlement, President Truman sent messages on May 31, 1951, to Attlee and Mossadeq advising both to negotiate. In his message to Mossadeq he said: "The United States is a close friend of both [countries]" and was anxious that a solution could be found through negotiations. In his message to Attlee, Truman warned of the inherent dangers in the "explosive situation" in Iran and urged him to reach a satisfactory solution.[21] By accident or design, Mossadeq received a copy of the message sent to Attlee, which the State Department claimed was simply sent for the U.S. ambassador's information. Although the United States apologized to the Foreign Office for "the unfortunate mistake," the British were upset that Mossadeq had discovered that the American president was pressing Britain to make concessions.[22]

Some American and Iranian papers did not think that the mix-up was a mistake. The *Wall Street Journal* asked, "Was it a blunder—or a highly diplomatic trick?" The Persian daily *Dad* wrote, "Such mistakes simply don't happen in modern diplomacy. What happened was one of the cleverest tricks in diplomatic history. Mr. Truman wanted premier Mossadeq to know that he was speaking more sharply to Mr. Attlee than to the Iranians."[23]

Ambassador Shepherd, with his imperial outlook, was unhappy that Truman's message to Mossadeq had not been cleared first with the British government. He exclaimed: "It seems to me deplorable that the Americans should keep butting in . . . without consulting us."[24] Attlee, however, sent a friendly reply to Truman complaining that the effect of Iran's action "on the economy of the United Kingdom would be most serious and might well affect our rearmament plans." He expressed the hope that when Britain sent a mission to Tehran, the United States would "exercise their influence" in her favor.[25] Mossadeq, too, sent a reply to the president saying that the Iranians considered the United States their sincere friend. He made it clear, however, that in his discussions with AIOC representatives the only topics on the table would be compensation and the sale and export of oil within the framework of the nationalization law.[26]

Britain planned to send a delegation headed by a high government official. But Mossadeq replied that Iran's dispute was with AIOC and that he would deal with the company only. The Foreign Office, resisting the idea, told Shepherd to impress upon Mossadeq that "His Majesty's Government have every right to intervene in the defence of this important British interest in Persia and moreover have a vital interest in the matter by reason of their majority share holding in the Company."[27]

When Mossadeq rejected this argument, Walter Levy, an American oil expert, suggested that he be appointed as an "honest broker" to talk to both sides. Britain did not want to lose her freedom of action by tying herself to a single broker. Furlonge, however, had the idea of planting Levy on the Iranian side of the table; that way, since Levy was thought to incline toward British views of the dispute, Britain might gain her ends by negotiating with him. It was thought likely that the Iranians would be pleased to have Levy as their "adviser" because he had helped Venezuela obtain higher royalties from oil companies.[28] Furlonge's idea was not pursued, however.

It was finally decided to send a delegation to Tehran headed by Basil Jackson, AIOC's deputy chairman. Jackson's delegation, which included Neville Gass, a member of the company's board, arrived in Tehran on June 11, 1951. On that same day the Iranians took over AIOC's central office in Khorramshahr so as to impress upon the British that they had no intention of reversing nationalization. Adding to Jackson's headaches was the published view of U.S. ambassador Grady: "since nationalization is an accomplished fact it would be wise for Britain to adopt a conciliatory attitude." Grady further stated that it was in the West's interest to keep Mossadeq's government in power. "Mossadeq's National Front Party," he said, "is the closest thing to a moderate and stable political element in the national parliament."[29]

Jackson met Mossadeq on June 13 and told him that the company was prepared to consider some form of nationalization. But Mossadeq made it clear that there was only one form—the real one—that would place the oil industry at the government's disposal. He went on to say that world peace would be possible only if the living standard of the deprived masses was improved, and that improving the living standard meant giving poor nations the political and economic freedom to make maximum use of their resources. He hoped that Britain could contribute to this good cause. In reply, Jackson urged Mossadeq to stop Iran's takeover of AIOC so that negotiations could proceed peacefully. Mossadeq made no such commitment.[30]

When AIOC's delegation met with the Iranian representatives, M. A. Varasteh, Iran's finance minister, made it clear that the purpose of discussions was not to change the law but to execute it. He said that the net proceeds of oil sales beginning on March 20, 1951, when oil was nationalized, would have to be paid to Iran. Of this, 25 percent was to be deposited in a mutually agreed bank to cover the company's claims for compensation. AIOC, he said, could purchase as much oil as it needed and ship it to world markets.

Mossadeq followed this up by asking Mostafa Fateh, AIOC's assistant general manager, to tell Jackson that if AIOC did not agree to the payment of oil proceeds to Iran, he had no alternative but to arrange for dispossession of the company. Fateh warned Mossadeq of the oil cartel's power, the importance of oil to the British economy, and the possibility that Britain would initiate an economic war that Iran, as the lesser power, would surely lose. The prime minister, however, sure of the validity of his position, discounted the power of the oil cartel.[31]

On June 19, when the two delegations met for the last time, Jackson presented a memorandum setting out the terms of AIOC's proposal. It said: "The Persian assets of the Company might be vested in a Persian National Oil Company and, in consideration of such vesting, the National Oil Company should grant the use of those assets to a new company to be established by the Anglo-Iranian Oil Company . . . [which] would operate on behalf of the Persian National Oil Company." To sweeten the deal, AIOC was prepared to pay Iran £10 million as an advance and £3 million a month from July onward until an agreement was reached.[32] Jackson thought that Iran's need for cash would attract her to this financial bait and would make her forget about genuine nationalization. The Iranian delegation considered the company's proposal an insult to their intelligence and rejected it.

Having failed to denationalize AIOC, the AIOC mission left Iran on June 30. On his return to London, Jackson announced that there was no hope of renewing negotiations while Mossadeq's government was in power.[33]

As we have seen, before the arrival of AIOC's delegation in Tehran the Iranian government had sent a mission to the southern oil fields to take over AIOC's operations there. British military threats, intended to cow the Iranians, had the opposite effect. Throughout May, a series of demonstrations demanded instant dispossession of the company. On June 10, when NIOC's Provisional Board and representatives of the Joint Committee arrived in Abadan, 50,000 oil workers and residents gave them a hearty welcome in spite of a raging sandstorm. On the following day they received another tumultuous welcome in Khorramshar, where they hoisted the Iranian flag over AIOC's central office, changed its nameplate to NIOC, and issued a statement saying that all Iranian and foreign employees of the "former" company would be considered employees of NIOC.[34]

British ambassador Shepherd, upset by the quick pace of events, reported to the Foreign Office: "I think the Government are prepared to use to the full the present wave of public opinion in favour of nationalisation." If disorders broke out, the "overwhelming body of opinion would be against the Company." He considered Mossadeq guilty of rousing public emotions and warned him: "Mass-hysteria was easy to arouse and difficult to control." Mossadeq argued, however, that public emotions were high owing to decades of selfishness by the company.[35]

The Joint Committee's representatives established themselves in the company's headquarters, and held a series of meetings with Eric Drake, the company's general manager, and his colleagues. They were told to produce copies of receipts of oil exported since March 20, 1951, to deposit the proceeds of such oil sales in the name of NIOC, and to permit two Iranian accountants to study AIOC's books.[36] NIOC's Provisional Board had in fact brought with them two British-educated chartered accountants: Mehdi Samii, later head of Iran's central bank, and Qassem Kheradju, later an executive of the World Bank and president of Iran's Industrial and Mining Development Bank.

Drake replied that he was responsible only to AIOC's board in London and would not accept any interference in the management of the company's affairs. The Iranians told him that since the enactment of the nationalization law, they did not consider the company's board to have any authority in Iranian operations. Further, they demanded that from then on tankers taking oil from Iran should give receipts to NIOC. In response, Fraser instructed Drake that no such receipts should be signed, adding that arrangements to the same end had been made by AIOC with Shell, Esso, Burma Oil Company, and Shwedagon tankers. To tighten AIOC's grip, the Foreign Office instructed Ambassador Franks in Washington to ask the State Department to persuade American oil companies to follow AIOC's lead. Franks cabled back saying that the American oil companies had agreed.[37]

In June 1951 the problem of receipts came to a climax. Tankers loaded with oil were not permitted to leave Abadan because they were not prepared to give receipts to NIOC. AIOC ordered its tanker captains to pump the oil back and leave the port. With this the export of Iranian oil came to a standstill.

The Iranian Cabinet believed that the job of dispossessing AIOC should be done speedily so as to leave no time for the British to work out schemes for neutralizing their work. On June 20, the Cabinet issued instructions for the takeover of the company's offices and installations and appointed certain Iranian officials to handle the takeover operation. It also instructed that checks and directives issued by AIOC executives should be considered null and void unless countersigned by a member of NIOC's Provisional Board. Mehdi Bazargan, head of the Provisional Board, was appointed managing director of NIOC.[38]

On June 21 the government submitted an antisabotage bill to the Majlis, which prescribed the death penalty or long jail sentences for those proved to be engaged in acts of sabotage in connection with the oil industry. Drake, who had advised tanker captains not to sign receipts in the name of NIOC and felt that the bill might include his acts, flew to Basra in Iraq. Before departure he sent a cable from H.M.S. *Wren*, in Abadan waters, asking the Foreign Office to inform Fraser that he would be carrying on his work from Basra.[39]

Meanwhile, U.S. ambassador Grady succeeded in persuading Mossadeq to drop the antisabotage bill. Mossadeq withdrew the bill unconditionally, though he argued that such laws were not uncommon and that a country like France had passed similar laws.[40]

On June 28 Mossadeq sent a message to all British and other foreign employees of AIOC saying that Iran was "anxious to benefit . . . from their services." If they desired to continue working in Iran, "our country will welcome you warmly"; moreover, they would have the same rights, benefits, and pensions as they had under their contracts with AIOC. Clearly, Mossadeq valued the skills of the foreign staff and hoped to retain them. AIOC, not wanting nationalization to succeed, instructed its employees to reject Mossadeq's offer, but Iran did not ask them to leave, hoping that in time they would transfer their contracts to NIOC. Back in May, Fraser had admitted that "if given a lead from London, a proportion at least of the British staff might be willing to stay on" under NIOC management. He acknowledged that without foreign technicians, oil fields could be kept going and the refinery could be run, though at reduced efficiency. But he was sure that the withdrawal of tankers by AIOC and other major companies would bring Iran's oil exports to a halt, thus making Iranian workers idle. "This in itself" he said, "would be fruitful material for stirring up trouble."[41]

Parallel with Iran's takeover of AIOC management in the south, measures were taken by NIOC to take over the company's management in Tehran. The occupation of AIOC's Information Office, where many sensitive documents were held, proved to be greatly embarrassing to the company. Shepherd reported that the company sent its confidential papers to the British embassy for safekeeping; but the Iranian government discovered that some documents had been transferred to the residence of Richard Seddon, AIOC's chief representative in Tehran, and ordered that his house be searched.

On June 30 Seddon's house was occupied by representatives of the justice ministry and the police. They found a vast array of files, some of which were being burned in the fireplace. Seddon was concerned that the Iranians might gain access to his safe, which contained the company's code books, ciphers, and sensitive files. He tried to remove it as personal property, but he was not allowed to do so and had to surrender the keys. The Foreign Office admitted that the "laws of all countries permit searching and seizure of private property."[42] Shepherd, however, was happy to report that "most of the important and compromising documents are now lodged in my archives." He was advised to send them in his confidential bag to London.[43]

In Abadan, Alick Mason, AIOC's deputy general manager, was cautious enough to move out important company papers in time. He conveyed them to Major C. F. Capper, British consul general in Khorramshar, who reported to the Foreign Office: "All current confidential and secret papers of Anglo-Iranian Oil Company are lodged in Consulate and secret archives have already been sent to Rafidain Oil Company in Basra."[44]

Telegraphic communications of a classified nature between the company in Iran and its London office became problematic once the Iranians had access to the code books and ciphers in Seddon's safe. Ambassador Shepherd advised the Foreign Office to allow the company's confidential telegrams to be sent "in our cypher over our channels," adding that Seddon would send someone to the embassy cipher room for the job.[45] Thus the British embassy and the Foreign Office placed themselves at the service of the company.

Drake also had communication difficulties in managing AIOC's activities in Iran from Basra. Thanks to the British Admiralty, his difficulties were overcome. Arrangements were made between the Foreign Office, the Admiralty, and AIOC for Drake to exchange all classified messages through the consul general at Khorramshar aboard H.M.S. *Mauritius* in the Persian Gulf.[46]

The company documents seized by the Iranians at Seddon's residence were examined on the spot. Photos were taken of the documents, and prints developed right there in Seddon's bathroom tub were handed over to a number of translators working in his vast living room. I was among the translators.[47]

These papers were a gold mine for the Iranian government and a mine field for the company. Although compromising documents had allegedly been removed, enough papers were left behind to make it easy for Mossadeq to prove that AIOC had interfered in all aspects of Iranian political life. The documents revealed that the company had influenced senators, Majlis deputies, and former Cabinet ministers, and that those who opposed it had been subtly forced out of office. Newspapers had been paid to publish prepared articles alleging that many of the National Front's leaders were actually paid stooges of AIOC. Interestingly enough, some leftist papers received financial support and newsprint to publish critical attacks on the United States so that the Americans would lose interest in supporting Iran.[48]

Among the documents was evidence that former prime minister Ali Mansur had begged AIOC to allow him to remain in office, promising in return to appoint a new finance minister more agreeable to the company. Another set of letters revealed that AIOC had helped Bahram Shahrokh to become director of Iran's Radio and Propaganda Department, and that on a trip to London he had been recruited to serve the company. There were also directives and reports on influencing guilds, through the mayor of Tehran, to rise against those in the bazaar who supported the National Front.[49]

Iranians also found interesting reading in a March 1951 report from E. G. D. Northcroft to AIOC's London office giving an overall picture of the company's nonbusiness activities in Iran. In the report Northcroft commented with pride on his private contacts with senators and Majlis deputies, and was pleased to say that he had prepared materials for the speeches made by Prime Minister Razmara and G. H. Foruhar in the Majlis supporting the Supplemental Agreement. His contacts with some newspapers, he wrote, had resulted in articles favorable to the company; he emphasized the need for funding certain newspapers on a regular basis. He wanted the BBC to dedicate its Persian-language broadcasts to promoting the company and offered to send the necessary materials.[50]

Mossadeq proclaimed that the documents showed beyond doubt AIOC's "sinister and inadmissible interventions." The publication of some of these papers was greeted with savage comments in the press and the Majlis. *Sheipuré-Mardé-Emruz* called the company's Information Office a branch of the British Intelligence and a hive of spying and corruption. It said: "Now that the curtain is lifted and the real identity of traitors impersonating themselves as newspaper men, Majlis deputies, governors and even prime ministers is laid bare, these men should be ridden with bullets and their carcasses thrown to the dogs."[51] In a series of heated debates in the Majlis, some deputies demanded that all the AIOC documents be published abroad officially so that the whole world would learn how a British oil company had interfered with every aspect of Iran's political and economic life. At the other extreme, those deputies who feared that they might be implicated proclaimed that the whole thing was a British plot. They argued that the company, knowing that its offices would be occupied, had planted the names of decent people in its files in order to defame them as collaborators.[52]

AIOC's London office, disturbed by these revelations, denied that the company had tried "to influence local opinion by improper means," adding that all activities shown in "recognisable" documents were "connected with the Company's normal and legitimate business." Ambassador Shepherd suggested that the BBC's Persian service should broadcast a talk questioning the authenticity of the documents published in Iran.[53]

Meanwhile in the House of Commons the British government was told by one Commander Maitland that the "events in Persia constitute the greatest opportunity and challenge the British Commonwealth of Nations has probably ever had," and that every opportunity should be taken to obtain the Commonwealth's assistance in resolving the problems that Britain faced in Iran.[54] But the Commonwealth hardly gave a helpful hand.

Although the leaders of India and Pakistan sent messages to

Mossadeq urging the need for peaceful negotiations, their sentiments lay with Iran. At a press conference on June 10, 1951, Prime
Minister Jawaharlal Nehru stated that India was "positively sympathetic" to Iran's policy on the nationalization of the oil industry.
About the 1933 concession, he said "there is no doubt about it that
all these agreements in the past with the Middle East Asian countries cannot possibly be called an agreement between equal parties."
Another Indian figure, Minister of Education Maulana Azad, made
public statements in Tehran "in fulsome praise of Musaddiq," saying that "Iran had a right to nationalise her own industries as Britain
had hers."[55] In a CBS broadcast, Howard K. Smith commented that
Britain had difficulty in finding supporters in her dispute with Iran.
"Iraq and Egypt on the one side, and Britain's own Dominion of
Pakistan on the other, have publicly taken Iran's side."[56]

Among those approached by Britain, King Abdullah of Jordan
obliged by writing a letter to "the Illustrious Minister, Dr. Muhammad Musaddaq, may God guide him in His Righteousness." In it he
advised Mossadeq to negotiate, saying that "God willing a person
with Your Excellency's wisdom, farsight [*sic*] and loyalty will steer
the country through the storm." He offered his "brotherly services"
for paving the way to conciliation. The letter was sent to Mossadeq
after being shown to the British minister in Amman, and was delivered the day after King Abdullah was assassinated in Jerusalem.[57]
For Dr. Baqa'i, an extremist in the National Front, the assassination
was good news: first Razmara, now another "great servant of the
British," had been assassinated. The day of reckoning had come, he
proclaimed, and "the hirelings of the British must be disposed of
one by one."[58]

Britain continued to urge the United States to support her, but
Fraser felt that no support from other countries was needed. He
believed that the Iranians would soon yield in desperation. The *New
York Herald Tribune* quoted him as saying: "When they need money
they will come crawling to us on their bellies."[59] Such vulgar remarks only increased the Iranians' determination to succeed in their
nationalization efforts.

The British government had set its hopes on a favorable ruling by
the World Court in response to its May 1951 complaint. The court,
needing time to decide whether it had jurisdiction in the case, issued

an interim ruling to the effect that while it considered the jurisdiction question the parties to the dispute should take no action to hinder oil operations. This meant that Iran should provisionally stop proceeding with nationalization. Mossadeq, who firmly believed that the court had no jurisdiction in a dispute between a government and a company, challenged the validity of the court's interim ruling (see Chapter 14). This led Britain to complain that Mossadeq had no regard for international law. The State Department was not impressed with this argument but was eager to find an equitable solution. It thus stepped up its activities to persuade both sides to settle the dispute through negotiations in which the United States would play a mediating role.

8

The Harriman and Stokes Missions

Although Secretary of State Acheson accepted Iran's right to nationalize her oil industry provided that fair compensation was paid, he considered the rigid attitudes taken by both Iran and Britain to be counterproductive and dangerous. "Britain," he said, "might drive Iran to a Communist *coup d'état*, or Iran might drive Britain out of the country." He believed that either development would be "a major disaster," and thought that "both sides were pressing their luck to the point of suicide in this game of Russian roulette."[1] To head off trouble, he felt that the United States should play a mediating role.

The opportunity to do so came when Mossadeq sent a message to President Truman saying that Iran was keen to maintain the flow of oil as before and to keep AIOC's foreign experts in the service of Iran's oil industry, leaving the company's organization untouched. Unfortunately, the company was not cooperating: by threatening Iran with the resignation en masse of the foreign staff and by refusing to let tankers give receipts to NIOC, it was apparently intent on stopping oil exports. Because the world regarded America as "the strong supporter of freedom and sovereignty of nations—a belief evidenced by the sacrifices of that great-hearted nation in the last two world wars," Iran expected U.S. support in achieving her national rights.

In reply, Acheson on the same day sent a message to Mossadeq suggesting a moratorium—"the adoption of interim arrangements for sixty days . . . without prejudice to the issues involved"—to permit oil operations to continue while permanent arrangements could be worked out. The draft of the message was first cleared with the British Cabinet.[2]

When Mossadeq did not agree to such an arrangement, which

would have meant a halt to nationalization, Acheson decided to send a negotiator to Tehran. A meeting was arranged on July 4, 1951, at the Washington home of Averell Harriman; present were Harriman, Acheson, George McGhee, Freeman Matthews, and Paul Nitze of the State Department and Sir Oliver Franks, the British ambassador. During the course of their discussions, "Sir Oliver left no doubt how seriously and angrily both the British Government and public viewed what they regarded as the insolent defiance of decency, legality, and reason by a group of wild men in Iran who proposed to despoil Britain."[3]

Since Britain was clearly contemplating the use of force, the Americans felt it necessary to inform Franks that in their opinion a British armed intervention in Iran would lead to Soviet intervention. Though "some in London might not be shocked at a partition of Iran into spheres of influence," in any such situation the United States, which had pressed to get the Russians out of Iran in 1946, "would end up at loggerheads with London." To stop a drift toward disaster, Acheson proposed that Averell Harriman be sent to Tehran as the president's special envoy and start meaningful negotiations. They all agreed that this was a good idea except Harriman, who appeared "a most reluctant bride." The next day, however, President Truman welcomed the idea, saying that he would send Harriman to Iran "in the interests of peace and stability to urge the resumption of direct talks" between the parties to the dispute.[4]

Harriman had worked closely with Roosevelt, Churchill, and Stalin during World War II and had served as ambassador to Moscow and to London, where he had developed friendly ties with both Churchill and Attlee. He had played a major role in missions of great importance during and after the war and had shown himself to be a cool, efficient negotiator. Acheson was sure that he could resolve the oil dispute to the satisfaction of both parties.

Acheson set the pace by telling Franks that whereas the Iranian "thesis on nationalization" should be accepted, a way should be found for AIOC to manage Iran's oil operations and obtain a reasonable share of profits as a management fee. Franks was not happy with any change that might loosen the company's control; the impression in London, he said, was that "Americans considered the British stake in Persian oil as in the end expendable." Acheson assured him that this was not so. Moreover, he pointed out that if the British went to the negotiating table and failed to get results, "the failure would greatly influence the American public opinion, which was not very favourable to the British case."[5]

In the British Cabinet there was no unanimity of views about Harriman's mission to Tehran. The hawks, Foreign Secretary Herbert Morrison and Minister of Defence Emanuel Shinwell, were against giving the United States a mediating role. But Prime Minister Attlee and Chancellor of the Exchequer Hugh Gaitskell, who were anxious to maintain friendly ties with Truman, believed that the president's suggestion should not be opposed. Indeed, Gaitskell felt that since Harriman was an anglophile his mission could be valuable to their cause.

Morrison, unconvinced, sent a message to Acheson saying that the main problem in Iran is a belief that "America in order to prevent Persia being lost to Russia, will be ready to help Persia out of any difficulties." In the circumstances "an approach by a representative of the President . . . would, I fear, merely encourage Dr. Musaddiq in this belief." He argued that no U.S. mediation was necessary; rather, what was needed was "a firm categorical statement by the United States" that Iran should follow the recommendations of the World Court.[6]

Acheson did not change his mind. At his suggestion, Truman sent a message on July 8, 1951, to Mossadeq saying that he would like to send Averell Harriman, "one of my closest advisers and one of our most eminent citizens . . . to talk over with you this immediate and pressing situation." In the same message Truman proposed that a "modus vivendi under which operations can continue" be worked out, as recommended by the World Court, while negotiations proceeded. In reply Mossadeq thanked the president for showing interest and for sending Harriman to Tehran, but stated that his government had already rejected the World Court's interim ruling and thus could only discuss matters within the terms of Iran's oil nationalization law.[7]

Shepherd, upset by the exchange between Truman and Mossadeq, gave a press conference in Tehran. Looking flushed and irritated, he told the press that he had learned "with astonishment and chagrin" that the U.S. president was sending his personal troubleshooter to Iran. "What is the use of Harriman flying here?" he asked, adding that "we are not inviting mediation in this matter." Since the British Cabinet had endorsed Harriman's mission, the Foreign Office was embarrassed by Shepherd's statement, which was widely quoted in the press, and told him to retract it. Shepherd did so.[8]

Morrison continued to take a hard line. He advised Acheson that Harriman should discuss a settlement on the basis of the offer already made by Basil Jackson, AIOC's deputy chairman; if such a settlement could not be achieved, Mossadeq should be removed.[9] Acheson, believing that Morrison "knew nothing of foreign affairs and had no feel for the situation beyond the sound of Bow bells," ignored his advice. So did Harriman, who said in a statement to the United Press: "In my opinion the British contention that the oil dispute cannot be solved as long as Dr. Musaddiq is in power is baseless. . . . Dr. Musaddiq is not the man the British have pictured in the *World*."[10]

Before his departure to Tehran, Harriman held a series of meetings with the State Department and with leading representatives of the American oil companies. The latter were unhappy with AIOC's handling of the whole affair, but they asked Harriman to take a "tough" line with the Iranians by sticking to the equal division of profits. If this principle were abandoned, they stressed unanimously, the industry would find itself without "the risk capital to undertake new expansion."[11] In other words they expected the oil-producing countries to provide them with this sort of capital. The State Department agreed that oil concessions elsewhere must not be upset. But Harriman was told that his first task was to ensure that Iran's ties with the West, shaken by the dispute, were reinforced.

Harriman left Washington on July 13, stopping in Paris overnight. Hugh Gaitskell, who happened to be in Paris, received a cable from Attlee asking him to tell Harriman to give his full support to Britain. When Gaitskell did so, Harriman replied that "he would not wish to push us along if only because the eyes of all American Oil Companies were on him." He added, however, that "the objective should be . . . to keep the oil in the South [of Persia] for ourselves and to deny it to the Russians."[12]

Harriman arrived in Tehran on July 15 accompanied by Colonel Vernon Walters, his interpreter; William Rountree, head of the State

Department's Near Eastern Division; and Walter Levy, the American oil expert. On the day of their arrival thousands of leftists held a demonstration, chanting anti-American and anti-British slogans. In a violent clash between the leftists and their opponents, fifteen were killed, including four policemen, and some two hundred wounded.

Some accused AIOC of organizing these demonstrations to weaken the Iranian government and to dissuade Harriman from helping Iran. The "evidence" offered was that the BBC, earlier the same day, had said that disturbances were expected on Harriman's arrival. On the following day, the BBC reported that the incident showed that Mossadeq could not control the situation in Iran, adding that without a British presence the communists would take over. Some newspapers blamed General F. Zahedi, the interior minister, for the demonstrations, arguing that he had known about the Tudeh's plans for demonstrating and had taken no precautions. There were also speculations that the Shah had collaborated with the company by permitting these demonstrations with the compliance of General Zahedi and the chief of police, whom the Shah had chosen for the post.[13]

Harriman wanted to discuss the oil dispute with Mossadeq in a friendly atmosphere free from British pressures. But the British thought that Iran could only be tamed under pressure. The day after Harriman's arrival in Tehran, the British Cabinet decided on certain economic sanctions against Iran. Moreover, Attlee told his Cabinet that steps were being taken to mount a military operation to occupy Abadan and continue operating the refinery there.[14] These moves were partly in response to parliamentary pressures on Attlee's government to hold on to Britain's sizable revenues from Iran's oil. During a debate in the House of Commons, Gaitskell was asked to what extent the loss of Persian oil "will weaken the sterling bloc or increase the cost of our imports," and would he not agree that "every family in this country would be poorer"? His answer was that "the burdens of this country will be increased, but not disastrously."[15]

In Tehran Harriman began his rounds by visiting the Shah to explore his views. The Shah suggested that for the moment he try to work out things with Mossadeq; "perhaps somebody else could then take over the Government and work up a long term decision."[16] Harriman knew that the Shah, uneasy with a prime minister who was not under his command, hoped someday to replace Mossadeq, but could not do so while Mossadeq enjoyed such widespread public support. Harriman and Vernon Walters next visited the prime minister at his home. What struck both was the sharp contrast between the lavishness of the Shah's palace and the unpretentious simplicity of Mossadeq's home.

Mossadeq poured out his feelings about the British, blaming them for Iran's misery. He told Harriman: "You don't know how crafty they are. You don't know how evil they are. You don't know how they sully the things they touch." Harriman stated that he knew the British well and they were not all that bad. He explained that the purpose of his mission was to provide a suitable atmosphere for direct negotiations between Iran and Great Britain. He warned Mossadeq about the difficulties of selling oil in international markets and the need for wisdom and foresight in considering the issues involved.[17]

Shepherd tried to cool Harriman toward Mossadeq by claiming that the prime minister did not enjoy the full support of the Iranian public and had firm opponents in the Majlis who wanted his downfall. Harriman's reply was that "Musaddiq was such a popular hero that his fall would create great excitement in the country."[18]

When Harriman met with the Iranian delegation,[19] he was given a paper on the oil question, prepared by the government, which emphasized that the idea of nationalization did not stem from a foreign source, such as Russia, but was a purely Iranian response to the necessity for defeating communism and blocking Russian demands for oil concessions in Iran. The paper warned that if nationalization was opposed and the West did not assist Iran in maintaining her oil operations, the economy would collapse and the poor, who made up 95 percent of the population, would seek refuge in communism.[20]

On the whole, the U.S. delegation was impressed with the Iranian delegation. Harriman told Shepherd that "he had been asked sensible and objective questions. . . . Persons concerned were anxious to get to the truth of the situation and weigh up the problem." However, he found Kazem Hassibi, an under secretary of the finance ministry, and a few others "completely intransigent." He told the Iranians that whatever they did within the country was their own affair, but "they had no control and no right to dictate what should happen outside it." He impressed upon them that if they interfered with AIOC's complex operations "they would be cutting their own throats," since they could not expect buyers simply to shift from AIOC to NIOC.[21]

Harriman suggested that the Iranians arrange for the efficient operation of the oil industry, and that to this end they had to come to terms with AIOC or a subsidiary created by it, as proposed by Basil Jackson. The Iranians rejected the idea of "a return to the same operating entity against which public opinion had been so much aroused." They said that they would accept an AIOC subsidiary only when it was part of a wider participation of other companies on Iranian terms. Harriman made it clear that "no American company would participate." He stressed that the best they could expect in a settlement was to secure arrangements comparable with those of other oil-producing countries in the Middle East. Finally he tried to convince them that they should not insist on the complete fulfillment of the nine-point Nationalization Act but instead base their discussions on the principle of nationalization alone.

According to Harriman, the Iranian delegation showed flexibility and goodwill, saying that they wanted friendly relations with Britain. They assured him that a satisfactory settlement could be reached if a British mission came to Iran with good will and with an understanding of the national sentiments of the Iranians. All they wanted was an arrangement that would free them from AIOC's control. Walter Levy assisted Harriman by "educating" the Iranian delegation and its technical team on the complexities of marketing oil. He told them that in his judgment Iran's best bet was to make an arrangement with an established "foreign" oil company.[22]

Reporting to the State Department, Harriman stressed "the very strong emotions . . . felt by all sections of the public" in Iran. "It is the opinion of all Americans in Persia and of responsible Persians that no Persian Government—whether Musaddiq's or any other—can run counter to this strong public feeling." Referring to "the deep and historic opposition in Persia against British officials," he pointed out that "the Persians are prepared to make great sacrifices of oil revenue" so as to rid themselves of "British Colonial practice." Walter Gifford, the U.S. ambassador in London, received a copy of Harriman's report and showed it to Sir William Strang of the Foreign Office in return for a promise that "its source would be kept confidential." The counselor at the American embassy in Tehran, too, though knowing that Harriman insisted on "playing his cards close to his chest," confided to his counterpart at the British embassy the details of Harriman's private discussions and evaluations as reported to the State Department.[23]

Iran's Cabinet specified the basis on which it was prepared to negotiate. The Iranian government, it said, would enter discussions with the British government's representatives, acting on behalf of AIOC, if Britain recognized in advance the nationalization of the oil industry in Iran as spelled out in the act of March 20, 1951, which stated that "All operations for exploration, extraction and exploitation shall be in the hands of the Government." It further stated that the discussions would be on the method of implementing the law insofar as it affects "British interests." The last point was added at Harriman's insistence, with the understanding that "British interests" meant the purchase of oil by Britain and the settlement of AIOC's claims.[24]

In response the British decided to send a mission to Tehran headed by Richard Rapier Stokes, Lord Privy Seal and Minister of Materials. But as a precondition Attlee's Cabinet wanted Iran not to proceed with nationalization, saying that "public opinion in this country would not tolerate the despatch of a minister of the Crown to Tehran . . . while the Company's operations were interfered with." Furthermore, the British expected the Iranian government not to ask Britain for prior acceptance of the nationalization law. Finally, Harriman was told that Jackson's "generous proposals" would, in substance, represent "the limit to which the Company and H.M.G. would be prepared to go."[25] In short, the British offered no concessions, expecting the Americans to do for them what they themselves were unable to achieve. In Washington, they continued to exert pressure on the State Department to make Iran amenable to their demands. McGhee, surprised and irritated, asked what did they expect. Did they want the Iranians "to repeal the Oil Law"?[26]

In a two-hour session in Tehran on July 27, Harriman tried to convince Shepherd of the impracticality of British preconditions, but Shepherd did not budge. After this meeting, Harriman "with fire in his eyes . . . protested vigorously against British tactics that have obstructed his attempt to bring about an early meeting of Iranian and British negotiators." He concluded that "the British were deliberately stalling, principally because they believe that the longer the Iranian Government is deprived of oil revenues, the more amenable it will be to settling on terms satisfactory to Britain."[27]

On that same day, Harriman decided to fly to London with Walter Levy and settle the problem with the appropriate British ministers. When the Foreign Office was so informed, it cabled Shepherd that Harriman's trip would not serve "a really useful purpose."[28] Harriman remained undeterred but was disappointed to find that Shepherd—whom he wanted to avoid—insisted on going with him to London.

On July 28, 1951, President Truman's envoy held a meeting with the British Cabinet. During a three-hour session, he told them that the nationalization movement in Iran was not only genuine but widely supported. Referring to their preconditions on sending a delegation to Tehran, he urged them "not to stand too much on ceremony, formality and technicalities but to get on with the discussions quickly" before a good opportunity was lost.[29] The ministers agreed to accept Iranian proposals for negotiations provided that the Iranian government recalled the delegation it had sent to the south to take over AIOC's operations there. Shepherd, who joined the Cabinet meeting on July 30, stressed that no ministerial mission should leave for Tehran before receiving such assurances from Iran. Some ministers argued that "if we missed this opportunity to resume negotiations, there was a great danger of antagonising the United States Government and world opinion generally." Others did not agree, insisting on firmness and expressing the hope that Harriman's mission would fail.[30]

Meanwhile Levy, who had "educated" the Iranians on the complexities of the oil industry and their inability to operate it alone, began "educating" the British about their problems in Iran. At a meeting with British government and AIOC officials, he told them that "AIOC had virtually no bargaining position" and that "the whole country would support National Front on the nationalisation issue." He was pleased to report that he had "succeeded in frightening the Persians" into agreeing to negotiations, and that he had obtained the Iranian delegation's consent to having a foreign-owned company operate as Iran's managing agent. Levy pointed out that it was not wise to present a settlement to Iran on a simple 50-50 basis; rather, the British should "so arrange it that the end result has a 50/50 split." Since AIOC could no longer operate in Iran alone, even under a new guise, he suggested that it be "diluted" by the inclusion of "neutral elements" and that the British government's share in the new company be eliminated or "heavily camouflaged." Levy concluded that the Iranians might let the oil industry stagnate or invite Russian technical aid rather than climb down and accept AIOC again. "Strong as is their antipathy to Russia their dislike of AIOC is stronger."[31]

Neville Gass, who represented AIOC at the meeting, lost no time in sending a paper to the Foreign Office rejecting Levy's proposals. Ignoring Iran's sentiments against AIOC, he argued that giving AIOC alone effective control of the oil industry would be to the best interests of the British Treasury, the Admiralty, the nation, and the company. He then spelled out the sizable benefits gained by each under such an arrangement and concluded that any delegation going to Iran should bear these benefits in mind before "diluting" AIOC.[32]

To make sure that AIOC's objectives would prevail, Fraser chose Gass to be the main AIOC representative in Stokes's delegation. Levy, upset by the choice of a man disliked in Iran, stated that "Stokes might as well not go to Tehran. For Gass to go to Persia would be like Mr. Levy, a Jew, going to Saudi Arabia." To get an unyielding Scot like Fraser to change his mind was not easy. Sir William Strang reported to Morrison that "it will take nothing less than the Prime Minister to bring him [Fraser] to drop Gass from the delegation." As to Levy's proposal that AIOC should drop the idea of maintaining its full control over Iran's industry, Strang thought that such a proposal would cause a major row with Fraser and the company's board, who are "very stubborn and not broad-minded people." He believed that Levy's proposal could not be accepted short of "a revolution in the management."[33]

Harriman finally succeeded in convincing Prime Minister Attlee to send a delegation to Tehran without setting preconditions. The British government thus agreed to start negotiations on the basis of the Iranian formula and announced her recognition of the principle of nationalization. It had taken the United States four months of persuasion to make Britain accept this principle. Her acceptance was not genuine, however, but simply a means of satisfying the Americans. The delegation arrived in Tehran in early August of 1951. In addition to Lord Stokes, its members included Sir Donald Fergusson, Permanent Secretary of the Ministry of Fuel and Power, and officials from the Treasury, the Foreign Office, and AIOC.[34] In the end, Neville Gass had been excluded.

In a series of meetings before leaving London, Stokes was told what he was expected to achieve. In a written guideline he was advised to insist on AIOC management and an equal division of profits along the lines of Saudi Arabia's deal with Aramco. Britain was concerned that Iran might also claim a share in the company's worldwide profits under the terms of the 1933 concession. The British felt that they could not argue against such a claim, especially because the company's expansion overseas was mainly financed by its profits from Persian oil.[35] To confine Iran to 50 percent of the profits arising out of local operations and to avoid problems with other producers, Stokes was told that if the Iranians insisted on their concessionary share of profits outside Iran, he should consider settling the matter by offering "a down payment to buy them off." Eric Berthoud, assistant under secretary at the Foreign Office, suggested that the best way to do so was for the British government to give Iran half its shareholdings in the company, a gesture that could be "coupled with [putting] Persian Government directors on the A.I.O.C. Board."[36] Outside of this issue, Stokes was advised to follow Jackson's proposal without mentioning it, but "to dress it up and present its main points in a different order together with trimmings or sweetenings as might be required."[37]

On the eve of the British mission's departure, the BBC announced in its Persian service broadcast that several major American oil companies, with the endorsement of the U.S. Defense Production Administration, had made plans to make up the oil shortfall created by the situation in Iran. The purpose of this broadcast was to tell the Iranians that the United States was on the British side, and that if they did not settle the dispute with Britain they risked being excluded from the world oil market.

On his arrival in Tehran, Stokes met Mossadeq, who told him

that "the state of poverty of present-day Persia was largely due to the machinations of the Company." Showing his concern about Soviet demands, Mossadeq said that any new arrangement with the company would become the basis for a Russian claim of reciprocity. He warned that if a fair settlement was not reached, many Iranians "would in despair become subject to extremist forces on the left." He added, "the Persian people wished to follow the pattern of British democracy in order to maintain liberty and the rights of the individual. . . . They were a religious people and preferred the democratic way to the Soviet."[38]

Mossadeq stressed that under the nationalization act the Iranian government had "divorced the Company" and that new arrangements must accordingly be made. Stokes retorted that "it was a curious arrangement for a man to divorce his wife and then attempt to starve her to the point where she is obliged to kill him." Mossadeq did not accept the analogy. He pointed out that there were only two problems to be discussed. One was retaining the services of British technicians and the other was compensating AIOC. On compensation he wished to follow the practice adopted by Britain in her nationalization of industries. As for the technical management of Iran's oil industry, Mossadeq's view was that NIOC could if necessary establish a "Conseil d'Administration" in which the majority of directors would be from such neutral countries as Sweden, Switzerland, and Holland.[39]

At a luncheon with the Shah, Stokes wondered if there might be some solution that did not involve the prime minister. The Shah did not think so, since "if he were to fall it might be said that a solution reached with a successor Government was due to pressure by the British. . . . Musaddiq should not be deprived of office in a manner which made him a martyr." Stokes warned the Shah that Iran might lose her markets to companies producing oil in other countries; indeed, "the power exercised by the international oil companies was rather frightening . . . they could kill the Persian oil business stone dead." The Shah responded by advising Stokes to talk to Mossadeq "more forcibly."[40]

Before starting substantive discussions, Stokes and Harriman, each with his own party, flew to Abadan. They were greeted at the airport by some members of the Joint Committee and NIOC's board. For some of the Iranians who were to take over AIOC operations, Stokes expressed a high regard. He described Bazargan, NIOC's chairman, as "a well educated engineer with French education . . . friendly and cooperative," and Ardalan as "an educated politician." Makki, by contrast, he considered "evidently uneducated, vain and unscrupulous." Angry at the arrogant behavior of the British toward Iranian oil workers, Makki had treated AIOC's British staff with a matching harshness and arrogance.[41]

One interesting demonstration of the British attitude in Iran involved Major Capper, the British consul general in Khorramshar. For all the world as if he were representing Britain in her imperial days, Capper held a press conference shortly before Stokes arrived, saying that the NIOC board "must leave Abadan" and that AIOC offices taken by Iran's nationalization teams "must be evacuated." A few days later he wrote to the governor of Khuzistan to protest "the manner in which certain Persian officials behaved" on Stokes's arrival. When driving away from the airport, his car had been immediately behind the one carrying Stokes; but then, he complained, two cars containing Persian officials had cut in front of his. He wanted the governor "to ensure that suitable instructions be given to officials . . . so that, in future, the representative of His Majesty's Government is not submitted to such indignities."[42]

In response, the Iranian foreign ministry demanded Capper's removal for his "inflamatory" remarks to the press and his "cavilling letter" to the governor. The Foreign Office's strong representations on Capper's behalf proved futile. Capper's reaction to his dismissal was to cable the Foreign Office offering his military services: "If I am compelled to leave the country but can still be of assistance in the event of a military operation [in Iran], I would suggest that I be held at Basra or some focal point in the vicinity."[43]

On his return to Tehran, Stokes held detailed discussions with the Iranian delegation. Reiterating that Iran had the oil but Britain had the technical skills and the means for running the industry and distributing oil worldwide, he concluded that Iran could not produce and sell oil without British cooperation.[44] He followed up this analysis by proposing to Mossadeq that the oil industry assets be recognized as belonging to Iran; that a British organization be formed to enter into long-term contracts with NIOC; and that this organization be given authority to take over the management of production, refining, and sales. Mossadeq responded that Stokes's proposals were no different from Jackson's, and that since the nationalization law did not allow Iran to delegate responsibility, oil operations must be conducted by Iran. When Stokes stated that such a measure would result in "Iran's bankruptcy and the advent of communism," Mossadeq replied: "If Persia was the mistress of her own destiny communism would not materialise. It was through the lack of independence that communism became a threat."[45]

Mossadeq wanted NIOC to have full control of operations under a management of twelve: four Iranian directors and eight experts from "neutral" countries, to satisfy the British staff. Stokes wanted the company to keep effective control. He reported to Morrison: "We have explored with Levy a number of devices by which this hard fact could be disguised but found nothing that was not either dangerous or too transparent for even the Persians to accept."[46] He stressed that his intention was to have an operating company that would be 100 percent "A.I.O.C. under a new name."

Harriman and Levy were not happy with such a scheme. Levy argued that since AIOC had a bad image in Iran, it should establish a consortium with Shell and the Burma oil companies to purchase oil from NIOC. He thought this would be acceptable to the Iranians because "the weakest point in the Persian armoury" is that they cannot transport and market oil themselves.[47]

Next Stokes and his team prepared an eight-point proposal, cleared it with London, and presented it in a memorandum to the Iranian delegation. As an introduction, Stokes told the Iranians that under his proposal the Nationalization Act of March 20, 1951, was recognized, "the A.I.O.C. will cease to exist in Iran," and the Iranian government would acquire full authority over oil operations.[48]

Contrary to Stokes's assertions, the proposal, in brief, was as follows: that AIOC transfer all its installations to NIOC; that compensation for this transfer be included in the future operating costs of the industry; that a purchasing organization be formed to enter into a long-term contract with NIOC for the purchase and worldwide distribution of Iranian oil; that this organization be authorized by NIOC to manage oil operations in Iran; and finally, that NIOC's terms of sale in no way be different from the terms currently prevalent elsewhere.[49]

In brief Stokes's proposal meant that effective control of the oil industry in Iran would be in the hands of AIOC, which would pay Iran 50 percent of the profits and would receive compensation for its enterprise in Iran. This meant that Iran would receive less than other oil-producing countries that had not nationalized and were receiving half of the profits from their oil without paying compensation.

The Iranian Cabinet rejected Stokes's proposals, but left the door open by saying that if the British delegation harmonized its proposals with Iran's basic framework for Anglo-Iranian negotiations, they would be prepared to extend the discussions. As if the problems could be solved with gifts, Shepherd cabled the Foreign Office that Lord Stokes "urgently requires . . . for eventual presentation to the Persians" a number of large silver photograph frames and a cigar box of "handsome appearance."[50]

As might be inferred from this cable, Stokes's approach to Iranian leaders was tactless, to say the least. At a meeting with Court Minister Hossein Ala, a British-educated statesman, he remarked that all Iranians were corrupt and incompetent; they could not run a business or even their own government. He made the same points to the Shah.[51] To Stokes it was plain that the oil industry should be run by the British no matter what the consequences for Iran.

That there was corruption in Iran was certain. In fact it was public exasperation with corrupt officials and their exploitation by British interests that had brought the National Front to power. But *all* Iranians corrupt and incompetent? Harriman was disturbed by Stokes's tactlessness, and so was Levy, who described Stokes as "an elephant in a china shop—breaking things unknowingly."[52]

One Iranian who got along well with Stokes was Seyyed Zia, however, who wanted the British to overthrow Mossadeq and install him in his place. Zia advised Stokes to make no concessions but instead make a sudden departure from Tehran to upset Mossadeq's government. He went on to say that the whole nationalization scheme was a plot by the Americans in favor of their companies and that Stokes should have a showdown with Harriman.

The Shah, too, told Stokes that he had been informed that the American embassy was working in favor of Socony Oil and Standard Oil of New Jersey. Stokes brought this up with Harriman, who dismissed it as nonsense, adding that he had made it clear to Iranians that no American oil company was interested in coming to Iran.[53] In fact, the U.S. oil companies formed a united front with AIOC to oppose Iran's nationalization, feeling that they would be cutting their own throats if they tried to exploit the situation in Iran.

Geoffrey Furlonge, of the Foreign Office, suggested that if Stokes's delegation had to leave Iran with no results, the British "might put it about that they would be prepared to return forthwith to negotiate with another government." He thought this would "strengthen the hand of Sayyid Zia in attempting to oust Musaddiq." Ayatollah Kashani did not think a change of prime minister would make any difference at all. He told Stokes that if Mossadeq himself, "who enjoys the unanimous support of the people," were to deviate from the nationalization law, he not only would risk the loss of his prestige but would suffer the fate of his predecessor Razmara.[54]

The Iranians complained that although Britain claimed to accept nationalization, the British delegation's only proposal was to establish a British entity with exclusive control of Iran's oil operations. In the words of Elwell-Sutton, "the British attitude was that, in return for their recognising the principle of nationalisation, the Persian Government should forgo its insistence on that principle."[55]

With negotiations at a deadlock, the Iranians handed Stokes a memorandum that made four main points. First, the British proposals did not conform to the principle of nationalization accepted by Britain and would only revive AIOC in a new form with full control of operations. Second, Iran was prepared to sell oil to Britain on the basis of commercial contracts and saw no justification in giving Britain a 50 percent discount. Third, the government was prepared to consider "fully and fairly the just claims" of the company to compensation, and to settle them after the claims of both parties had been established. Finally, the Iranian delegation would welcome negotiations on these points.[56]

Finding the disputants poles apart, Harriman held hurried meetings with the Shah and Mossadeq in a new search for a solution. He repeated his view that Iran would not be able to manage her oil industry and sell oil without the help of a worldwide marketing organization, and argued also that the country should not expect a higher income from its oil than other countries.[57] Peter Ramsbotham, who accompanied the British delegation, reported that since tabling its proposals the British delegation had concentrated on "screwing Harriman up" by getting him to support "publicly our proposals as conforming with the [nationalization] law."[58] There were, of course, other reasons for Harriman to support the British proposals, notably the desire to keep Iran from making any arrangements that would upset American oil concessions elsewhere. Nevertheless he disliked the fact that Stokes's proposals called in effect for full AIOC control.

Harriman and Stokes held further meetings with Mossadeq, who repeated that his government wished to reach an amicable solution with Britain but could not tolerate foreign control. Stokes reported Mossadeq as saying, "We should avoid the Chinese precedent, whereby we had driven the people into the arms of the Communists." Mossadeq also repeated his concern that if Iran were to accept anything like the British proposal, "Russia would demand similar treatment."

Mossadeq was willing to retain the company's British staff but with the NIOC board at the top. He complained that the British wanted "to interfere in the administration of a nationalised company."[59] When Stokes and Harriman insisted on their previous ideas, Mossadeq told them, "You are two statesmen who have come to Iran from two free countries of the world to settle the oil problem. One does not expect you to dictate things and to impose your will on us."[60]

Ramsbotham, who was present at these meetings, reported that he "was struck by the skill with which [Mossadeq] presented his ideas." He believed that if Mossadeq agreed to a settlement that ignored nationalization law, "he risks immediate loss of office." He was under pressure from both his supporters, who would accept nothing short of nationalization, and his opponents, who would use any deviation from the law to bring about his downfall. Ramsbotham concluded that the only way for the British to make progress with Mossadeq was to avoid demands for monopoly and control.[61] In fact, as we have seen, it was not fear of losing his office that compelled Mossadeq to pursue nationalization, but his deep-rooted belief that any other course would leave his country's sovereignty as shaky as before.

By now, Stokes had developed some sympathy with the Iranian

cause. He informed the Foreign Office that both he and Harriman believed that Mossadeq was genuinely ready to sign an agreement if enough concessions were made to enable him to persuade the Majlis that the agreement was in keeping with the law. The British Cabinet did not oblige. It instructed him to offer "no further concessions" and to return home at once. Although Harriman advised a soft approach to keep negotiations alive, Stokes sent an ultimatum to Mossadeq that he would be prepared to resume negotiations only if his proposals were accepted.[62]

On the following day, Mossadeq, who rarely left his home except for some Majlis sessions, went to Sahab-Gherania Palace, where Stokes and Harriman stayed, to see if a settlement might still be possible. When Stokes insisted on his own proposals, Mossadeq stated that he would put them before the Majlis for a vote but without recommendation. Stokes knew that without the prime minister's blessing his proposals would be rejected.[63]

Stokes left Tehran on August 23, 1951, and Harriman on the following day. The day before Stokes's departure, the British Cabinet approved a series of economic measures against Iran. It blocked Iran's sterling balances held in London and prohibited the export to Iran of such commodities as sugar and steel, which were then scarce. Ships already carrying these goods to Iran were instructed to change their destination. These measures were in addition to the oil boycott already in force. Furthermore, AIOC was directed to withdraw all its British staff from the oil fields and to reduce its personnel in Abadan to a "hard core" of some 340. Finally, the Cabinet stressed the need to organize a publicity campaign with the object of "rallying American support to the United Kingdom viewpoint" and "encouraging opposition to Musaddiq's Government."[64]

To gain U.S. support, Attlee sent Truman a message blaming the failure of the Stokes mission not on Britain's rejection of genuine nationalization but on the "blind intransigence of Dr. Musaddiq and his extremist followers." Playing to America's fears of communism, he told the president that Britain and the United States should join in not letting Iran fall under communist domination as a result of the disruption of her economy, adding that "under the present regime the Tudeh Party has made significant progress amongst the population." He contended that Mossadeq's regime had opponents who would emerge only when they saw Britain and the United States speak with one voice. He thus urged the president to make it plain that the United States fully supported Britain's position.[65]

Truman, like Acheson and McGhee, felt that if Britain was indeed interested in stemming communism in Iran, she should offer terms that would both meet Iran's sovereignty and strengthen her economy. Instead of supporting Britain, as Attlee had demanded, Truman simply issued a statement saying "I am confident that an arrangement can ultimately be worked out."[66]

The American press was critical of Britain's negotiating strategy, which it saw as based solely on the desire to exploit Iran. The *Washington Post* blamed Stokes for linking Harriman's name with British proposals, adding that these proposals did not have American backing. The paper chided Britain, saying that she had used all kinds of ploys to deceive the Iranians. It went on:

> Does the Stokes plan actually recognize nationalization or is it just a masquerade for the old system? If it does recognize nationalization, how explain the repeated insistence that company control must extend to the wells and pipelines covering the area one-sixth of the total size of Iran? . . . Does not maintenance of such control constitute an explicit denial of nationalization and an invitation to the political interference that the Iranians insist on shaking off? . . . If the present tactic is to force the Iranians to their knees, might they not bow to the Communists instead of to the company?

The paper described AIOC as "a State within a State" and an important political power in Iran.[67]

The *New York Times* conceded that Britain had treated Iran unfairly, but doubted that a weak country like Iran could face the British challenge, observing that Mossadeq and his associates had got "their ship in unchartered waters where almost anything could happen."[68]

To reverse the barrage of criticism against the company, the Foreign Office believed that Britain should try to convince the American public that Stokes "did everything humanly possible" to reach a settlement. Harriman and Levy thought such a deception would not work. On their way back to Washington, they stopped in

London, where Harriman told a meeting of British ministers that Britain should continue negotiations with Mossadeq, who was the only man who could steer an oil agreement through the Majlis. He advised them against putting pressure on Iran: "anything like economic sanctions or military pressure would stiffen the Persians." Harriman added that he considered Ambassador Shepherd ignorant and ill-fitted for the job of advising Britain on ways of settling the oil dispute.[69]

Levy reminded British officials that despite their desperate financial situation, the Iranians did not consider the monetary aspect of the oil dispute important. For them, he said, the main issue was sovereignty and the control of oil resources, adding that Fraser's insistence on the company's full control was the greatest obstacle to the solution of the problem. He believed not only that Fraser was completely out of touch with reality, but that he and many other directors of the company should be replaced if Britain was indeed interested in settling the dispute. Harriman shared his opinion, saying that Fraser and his men were trying to impose archaic policies on the British government.[70]

Eric Berthoud, assistant under secretary at the Foreign Office, reminded Morrison that AIOC should subordinate its interests to Britain's, adding that the two interests were not always synonymous. He pointed out that Stokes's proposals were far from compatible with nationalization and left intact AIOC's control.[71] Sir Donald Fergusson of the Ministry of Fuel and Power agreed: "We must not forget that the Persians are not far wrong when they say that our proposals are, in fact, merely dressing up A.I.O.C. control in other clothing. . . . [Moreover] under our . . . proposals the Persians will . . . be worse off than neighbouring countries because they will not only have to concede fifty percent of the profits but also have to pay compensation." Nevertheless, he said, Britain should not offer any concessions to Mossadeq but should wait until someone like Seyyed Zia, who "is known to be Anglophile," came to power and worked out a "reasonable" settlement that would keep AIOC in control.[72] Despite everything, it remained the opinion of most officials at the Foreign Office and the Ministry of Fuel and Power that all possible means should be employed to overthrow Mossadeq's government, even if this necessitated the use of force.

9

The Oil Cartel's Stranglehold

To crush Mossadeq's nationalization drive, Britain boycotted Iranian oil and urged all Western oil companies not to purchase oil from Iran and not to provide Iran with oil experts. All this required the cooperation of the international oil cartel. Furthermore, the cartel's assistance was needed to replace Iranian oil and provide AIOC with crude and refined products from other sources, enabling it to meet its customers' needs as before.

Before nationalization, AIOC's annual exports from Iran were 7.5 million tons in crude form and 22 million tons in refined products. For AIOC replacing Iranian crude was not difficult, but replacing the refined products was no easy task. The British oil companies could increase their refinery throughput outside Iran by only 6 million tons; the remaining 16 million tons had to be acquired from American oil companies. The Ministry of Fuel, which had rarely cared to remind AIOC to give a fair share of oil profits to Iran so as to avoid nationalization, now lamented that oil replacement costs would involve an annual additional amount of $350 million which, it said, "would have a serious effect upon the UK balance of payments." The problem at the time, however, was to acquire the assistance of the U.S. government so that major American oil companies, which were ready to meet AIOC requirements, would not be faced with U.S. antitrust laws for doing so.[1]

International oil companies based in the United States did not want Iran to succeed in nationalization lest other producers follow Iran's example and terminate their 50-50 arrangements with the companies. They watched the outcome of Iran's efforts "like a lynx"[2] and supported AIOC, but with a peculiar argument. They took the position that "in order to carry out the defense efforts of this country [the United States], it was necessary to grant [them] immunity from prosecution under the antitrust laws in order to relieve the 'tremendous world shortage' which resulted from the cessation of production in Iran."[3]

The U.S. administration bowed to this pressure from the American oil companies and provided them with antitrust immunity. Ironically, this was done in the name of U.S. national security interests, as if these were identical to those of AIOC. The outcome of such an arrangement was far-reaching, since it allowed full co-operation among nineteen oil companies in their overseas operations, "permitting the allocation of markets, the use of agreed upon supply schedules for the world outside the United States, the regulation of production of world oil in all foreign countries, the regulation of imports and exports in the United States . . . and any other mechanism which the world oil companies determined was necessary to offset the effect of the loss of Iranian production."[4]

The result was that world oil operations outside the communist bloc were controlled by a cartel that constituted an unprecedented concentration of economic power—a power "so vast as to invite its abuse."[5] And thus Iran, in her battle to implement nationalization, was faced not only with Great Britain but with the worldwide network of an economic giant.

In mid-1951 Iran announced that she would sell oil directly to customers who had previously bought their oil from AIOC. The company was not greatly concerned, since the bulk of AIOC sales were refined products, 94 percent of which went to the company's own subsidiaries, the Admiralty, and a number of major oil companies. The remaining 6 percent went to small distributing concerns in Italy, Switzerland, Sweden, and Turkey, to which AIOC provided tankers.[6]

The 7.5 million tons of crude that AIOC had previously exported from Iran did not arouse much concern either. The world's tankers were mostly under the control of major oil companies. In 1951 out of the total world tanker fleet of 1,500 T2 equivalents, 30.5 percent were under the British flag or chartered by British oil companies and 42.5 percent were under the U.S. flag or were American-controlled Panamanian tankers. This brought 73 percent of the total under the control of the international oil cartel. The British Ministry of Transport lamented that they could not corner the tanker market fully because the communist bloc and the Argentines owned most of the rest. They felt, however, that the independent tanker owners would not place tankers at Iran's disposal because they "will clearly be very wary of offending the oil companies who are their best customers."[7]

It was suggested at the Foreign Office that in case independent tankers broke the boycott and carried Iranian oil, the British Royal Navy should "intercept foreign tankers on the high seas on the grounds that they were carrying stolen oil from Persia." Sir Eric Beckett's legal advice was that such action was a breach of international law, and that Britain could use force at sea only if she were at war with Iran or had the backing of a U.N. Security Council Resolution. Otherwise, he felt, the interference of the Royal Navy might have "serious repercussions on our merchant shipping," and public opinion in the United States and elsewhere would become antagonistic to Britain. He advised the Foreign Office that if and when tankers carrying oil from Iran arrived at any port, AIOC should resort to an injunction.[8]

In September 1951, as a warning to potential purchasers of Iranian oil, AIOC made its case in an advertisement printed in the leading papers of thirty-three countries: "The Government of Iran in disregard of its solemn obligation to the Company ... attempts to sell oil derived from the area covered by the Convention of 29th April, 1933." Since the purchase of Iranian oil was accordingly "unlawful," AIOC would "take all such actions as may be necessary to protect its rights in any country."[9] The 1933 oil concession between Iran and AIOC was referred to as a "Convention" to imply that it was an agreement between two governments.

From then on, AIOC was on guard throughout the world to stop the purchase of Iranian oil. One step the company took was to intercept any telegrams sent to NIOC. As an example, in July 1951 Alick Mason, AIOC's deputy general manager stationed in Khorramshar, cabled Fraser that he had intercepted two telegrams from the Texas, Oklahoma, and Louisiana Oil Company to NIOC and gave their full text. In one cable this company had asked for a quotation for 10 million barrels of crude to be shipped over a year, saying that it would provide tankers. In the other cable the company's president had offered to provide NIOC with oil technicians. The Foreign Office instantly advised Franks in Washington to show the text of the intercepted telegrams to the State Department and ask them to "arrange for offers to be withdrawn." The State Department, though at the time unhappy with the British handling of the oil dispute, agreed to be helpful, feeling that if it went along with British demands, Britain would show greater flexibility in due course.[10]

AIOC also carried out a thorough monitoring effort through its marketing companies abroad. In a long report on what it called "known subversive attempts to dispose of Iranian oil," AIOC provided the Foreign Office in December 1951 with a detailed list of all firms that had communicated with Iran about purchasing oil and those to whom AIOC had sent warning letters. The report revealed that firms in twenty countries in Europe, America, Africa, Asia, and the Far East as well as America either had made offers to purchase Iranian oil or had made enquiries. Interestingly, Britain was among the eight countries in Western Europe whose firms had shown willingness to purchase Iranian oil.[11]

British embassies throughout the world concerted their efforts with AIOC and other members of the oil cartel to make sure that no deals with Iran took place. When Italian firms were found to be considering the purchase of Iranian oil, the British embassy in Rome lodged strong objections with the Italian government. Moreover, the Foreign Office told the Italian chargé d'affaires in London to restrain such firms, adding that Eden "feels strongly that there should be cooperation in this matter between us and other N.A.T.O. [North Atlantic Treaty Organization] powers." When Iran approached the Portuguese oil company Sacor with an offer to sell oil, the British told Sacor that any oil deal with Iran would invite "the hostility of big oil companies."[12]

As another expedient, Iran tried to include oil in her barter agreements with some countries. But here again the British government was closely on the watch. When it found that Iran intended to include oil in her trade agreement with India, the Foreign Office informed the U.K. High Commissioner there that "Persia has no right" to make such an arrangement. It pointed out that under the provisions of U.K. exchange control "all sterling payments into and out of Persia are subject to consent of U.K. Government whose present policy is to refuse such consent" on oil.[13]

When Iran signed a contract with a Turkish group to exchange oil for agricultural products, Rear Admiral Thomas Kelly of Socony Vacuum, which had storage and distribution facilities in Turkey, urged the State Department to advise the Turkish government not to interfere with its normal operations.[14] The result was that the deal never materialized.

Along with the boycott, the British government started a world-wide campaign to ensure that Iran would not get oil technicians, accountants, and international lawyers from anywhere. In July 1951 Britain learned that in response to Iran's advertisement West German technicians were applying for employment in the Iranian oil industry at the rate of twelve per day. Since Germany was still under the control of the Allies, the British resorted to a military government law "entitling the occupation authorities to prohibit any person from leaving Germany." The British High Commissioner there handed a memorandum to the German federal government asking it to instruct passport-issuing agencies "to refuse the grant of passports to German nationals intending to travel to Persia" for purposes connected with the oil industry. The British High Commission informed the Foreign Office that "in theory" it would be "legally possible for the Allies . . . to stop at the frontiers and ports of Western Germany all travellers holding visas for Persia who cannot establish that they are not oil experts." Such a measure proved unnecessary, however, as the German authorities cooperated in making sure that no German oil technicians would find their way to Iran.[15]

In Paris, the British embassy urged the governor of the Bank of France not to provide the accountants that Iran had requested. In Sweden, Austria, and Switzerland, too, where Iran was trying to recruit oil experts and accountants, the British stranglehold stopped all applicants. Britain did not want anyone connected with oil to make even a short visit to Iran. When Mossadeq asked an executive of the Italian national oil company (AGIP) to visit Tehran for consultations, the British agreed to his trip only when they were promised that he would report to them on the details of his discussions. The executive dutifully reported his discussions with Mossadeq to the Foreign Office.[16]

Interestingly enough, Britain had problems with some of her own nationals who wanted to serve Iran's national oil company. In November 1951 twenty members of the AIOC staff on leave in

England requested employment with NIOC. The methods used to dissuade these applicants were more subtle than those used in other countries. The Foreign Office informed them that there were no legal powers to prevent them from employment in a foreign territory with whom Britain was not at war. It added, however, that since Britain regarded Iran's nationalization as illegal, any British national employed by NIOC would not be allowed to convert his salary, paid in Iranian currency, into sterling for remittance to Britain.[17]

Iran tried to woo U.S. oil companies to provide her with oil experts. But the Foreign Office instantly advised the State Department that any such action would prejudice British negotiations for a settlement and would create an impression that American companies intended to replace AIOC in Iran. The State Department, which at that stage felt that the British were genuinely interested in settling the dispute through negotiations, replied by issuing a statement to the effect that there was a severe shortage of oil experts in the United States and elsewhere. But facts proved otherwise. The American press and radio reported on July 12, 1951, that Lee Factors, a Los Angeles engineering firm, had made an offer to the Iranian government "to recruit 2,500 American technicians to run the oil industry." The firm, however, had to withdraw its offer when it was described by the State Department as "contrary to British interests and embarrassing to the United States"—that is, to the department itself, with its allegation of severe shortages.[18]

In a separate move in Congress, Representative Owen Harris submitted a bill to authorize the Secretary of the Interior to ask representatives of the U.S. oil industry to provide Iran with oil technicians. The bill was referred to the House Foreign Affairs Committee, but soon the British embassy contacted two members of the committee and the bill was killed.[19]

Ambassador Shepherd's view was that in addition to the oil boycott and stopping foreign technicians from coming to Iran, the next best step would be to arrange the withdrawal of the company's British staff. He argued that such a move would have "maximum political effect" and would be a clear indication of Britain's firmness.[20] Lord Packenham of the Admiralty vigorously argued against withdrawing AIOC's British staff, saying that "unless we are prepared to revert to nineteenth century methods of annexation by armed force," Britain should give up resisting Iran in her nationalization drive and simply try to get adequate compensation.[21] Foreign Secretary Morrison disagreed, stressing that Mossadeq should be opposed by any and all means.

Shepherd agreed with Morrison and began an active campaign for the removal of Iran's prime minister. On September 6, 1951, Mossadeq, who saw that the British were more interested in removing him than in settling with him, severely criticized the British government's covert operations and the company's obstructive moves in a speech to the Senate. He stated that the Iranian government had reached the limit of its patience and could not be kept in a state of suspense any longer. He proposed asking the British to reopen negotiations and present their counterproposals; if they failed to do so within two weeks, he would cancel the work permits of the company's British staff.[22] For months Mossadeq had expressed his desire to keep the company's British technicians while the British government threatened their withdrawal, using their presence as a leverage to extract the type of agreement it wanted. Now Mossadeq had taken the sword out of British hands and turned it on Britain. It was a humiliating checkmate.

Shepherd advised the Foreign Office that Mossadeq's Senate speech should be "immediately countered by a . . . forthright official statement" rejecting further negotiations with him and his government. He provided the text of the statement to be issued, which, when broadcast, said that "His Majesty's Government declare that negotiations are . . . definitely broken off," and that the eviction of the company's employees "by force" would be contrary to the World Court's decision.[23]

Shepherd, concerned that this terse statement might expedite the expulsion of the company's staff, advised London to make it clear that Britain would respond with force to such a move. The Foreign Office concluded that it was not practicable to compel Iran to retain British employees "unless we are prepared . . . to take military action"; in the absence of a decision to this effect, it was felt that "the best method of reducing the blow to British prestige would be . . . to withdraw the residence permits ourselves."[24] The British government was upset that its reliance on Shepherd's advice had brought it to this mess. However, it did not want to lose face by changing course.

Mossadeq made one last effort to see if eviction could be avoided. He prepared a note containing his government's proposals on the solution of the oil problem and showed it to the Shah, who endorsed the proposals. This was Mossadeq's way of getting the Shah, who had oscillated between him and Shepherd, to support him in his nationalization efforts. The note, which was passed on to Shepherd, said that the Iranian government was making all efforts within the law to ensure that the oil nationalization did not harm the government and the people of Britain. It went on to say that full compensation would be paid based on mutual agreement, that large quantities of oil would be sold to Britain at international prices, and that oil operations in Iran would be managed by a foreign technical director, employed by Iran, who would act as liaison between the British staff and the executive board.[25]

In Washington, Assistant Secretary of State McGhee told British ambassador Franks that in his opinion Mossadeq's proposals were "not far from a basis for settlement except on the question of profit split." He handed Franks a paper on the State Department's views, which said that the Iranian approach offered new opportunities; it was "highly advisable for Britain to remain in a negotiating posture" and avoid summary rejection of Mossadeq's offer. William Rountree made much the same point to Franks: the State Department, he said, was disappointed that Britain was not making a constructive move. Franks reported to the Foreign Office that since a change of government in Iran did not seem imminent, "owing to the Shah's nervousness," and since it would be useful "to keep Americans firmly with us," it would be advisable to "leave the door open" to negotiations.[26]

On the same day, however, Ambassador Shepherd reported that he had received a message from the Shah saying that "he is convinced of the need of getting rid of Musaddiq and is now concerned as to how it can be done best." Shepherd went on to say that there was no need to consult the Americans at every step.[27]

Two other developments helped to toughen Britain's stance toward Mossadeq's proposals. One was the opinion of Ali Soheili, Iran's ambassador in London, who told Reginald Bowker, assistant under secretary of state at the Foreign Office, that "Dr. Mussadeq's Government could not last much longer." The other was the formation of an opposition group in the Majlis with the encouragement of the British embassy. This group was able to bring about a lack of quorum on some occasions when Mossadeq called for Majlis meetings.[28]

A further hopeful sign for Britain was the appointment, in September 1951, of Loy Henderson as U.S. ambassador to Tehran in the place of Henry Grady, who was sympathetic to Iranian nationalists and their aspirations. Because Henderson, who had preceded McGhee as Under Secretary of State and was later ambassador to India, viewed Britain more favorably than Grady, the Foreign Office hoped that he would in time change the U.S. attitude toward the Iranian oil dispute in favor of Britain.

The British Cabinet, encouraged by these developments, made its decision. Shepherd informed Court Minister Hossein Ala that his government could not regard the Iranian proposals as constituting a basis for resuming negotiations. To strengthen the opposition in Iran, the British embassy made it "perfectly clear that we are not prepared to do business with Musaddiq's Government."[29] At the Foreign Office, the Working Party on Persia, which met regularly during the oil crisis, prepared a paper entitled "Approach to a new Persian Government," in which it stressed the need to have a new prime minister in Iran who would "secure suspension of the [Nationalization] Laws."[30]

In response, Mossadeq finally decided to evict AIOC's British staff. He presented ample justification for such a measure. The company's British personnel were clearly not prepared to work for NIOC, he said, and AIOC had served notice that the Iranian staff's salaries would be stopped. Moreover, the company had withheld payment of oil royalties to Iran well before the oil embargo, and the Bank of England had frozen the country's sterling balances. Under these circumstances Mossadeq felt that British staff were part of the forces that were at war with him, and could in no way serve any useful purpose in his nationalization drive.

On September 25, 1951, the Iranian Cabinet approved the eviction of the British staff and informed staff members that they were to leave Iran before October 4. The government instructed NIOC's

Provisional Board that Iranian officials and others in Khuzistan "should extend utmost hospitality" to the British staff "and see them off with most friendly feelings."[31] The amicable tone of this directive was aimed at countering British propaganda to the effect that the evacuation of the staff might be blocked by Iranian armed forces. In fact, hundreds of British personnel had left Iran earlier on Prime Minister Attlee's instructions without any hindrance, and only about 400 remained.[32]

Mossadeq's decision to evict the remaining British personnel does not seem surprising in the circumstances, but the British government was evidently shocked by it. Attlee instantly cabled Shepherd to inform the Shah that the expulsion of the staff "will gravely affect relations between our two countries." The Shah's response was that a solution to the oil problem would be accelerated if the British staff left. "Once they were gone," he said, "it would be easier to demonstrate that the Government's oil policy had failed, and the fall of the Government would be hastened." This was what Shepherd had thought before, but things looked different when the party ordering the withdrawal of British personnel was Mossadeq himself. Shepherd impressed upon the Shah that "the expulsion of the British staff was an action which might be held to justify the use of force." But the Shah found himself powerless to take any action.[33]

Attlee cabled President Truman that submitting to eviction would have "the gravest consequences" for British and American interests in the Middle East. It would represent a blow to the "influence and prestige" of Britain and the West "in an area which . . . is weak in our containment wall [leaving] a vacuum in Persia which Russia, by the logic of events, would be bound to fill." He asked the president to instruct his ambassador in Tehran to join Shepherd in urging the Shah, "in the strongest terms," to prevent the expulsion of the staff.[34]

To make sure that Truman's reply would be favorable, Franks did some vigorous lobbying with Dean Acheson and Averell Harriman. Harriman did not agree with the British tactic of bringing pressure on Mossadeq, and let this become public knowledge. Whereas the British considered Iranian nationalism to be "superficial in character," Harriman saw it as "a real force and not just something whipped up and quickly allayed." Both he and Acheson thought that the Iranian people would not let the Shah get rid of Mossadeq unless he could "demonstrate that he could obtain something where Musaddiq had failed." Harriman stressed that "a negative attitude would not produce results."[35]

While Ambassador Franks was having a "friendly but difficult meeting" with Acheson and Harriman, his senior staff were appealing to Secretary of the Treasury John Snyder and General Omar Bradley to support Britain's stance. Snyder was told that the loss of Iranian oil would have serious consequences on Britain's "dollar costs." With Bradley the emphasis was put on "the strategic interests involved, especially at a time when we are trying to lay new foundations for a more durable system of defence in the Middle East." Both were asked to urge the president to support Britain in preventing the eviction of the company's British staff.[36] In spite of all this lobbying, Truman's reply to Attlee was that in order to secure a lifting of the expulsion order, the British government should take the initiative by coming forward with some suggestion that would provide a proper basis for negotiations.[37]

The Iranian press hailed the government's decision to evict the British staff. The independent newspaper *Keyhan* stated that Mossadeq's actions represented the people's will. The progovernment *Bakhtaré-Emruz* argued that since Britain rejected any settlement on the basis of nationalization, the eviction of the company's staff "might bring the British to their senses to abandon their imperialistic attitude."[38]

The company's hopes of keeping the staff in Iran were fading. But Foreign Minister Herbert Morrison, who for months had advocated the use of force, pressed the Cabinet to order the occupation of Abadan to enable the British staff to remain there. And thus British forces, already prepared for the occupation of Abadan, were "put at 24 hours notice."[39]

10

British Plans for the Occupation of Abadan

Military plans for the occupation of Abadan began soon after the Majlis enacted the nationalization of the oil industry. Beginning in May 1951 there were five months of hectic preparations for such an operation by the British Joint Chiefs of Staff and the commanders of the British Middle East Land Forces (MELF). However, the possibility of using force was first considered well before nationalization took place.

In October 1950, when oil negotiations with Iran bogged down, some British officials thought that instead of giving a higher share of oil revenues to Iran, Britain would be better off occupying the oil-producing areas. The problem was to persuade the Americans that such an occupation was to the benefit of the West as a whole. The occasion came in October 1950, when the two countries held their annual high-level political and military discussions in Washington on matters of mutual interest. The purpose of the discussions was to find ways to fight the expansion of communism.

On October 26, 1950, a number of high-ranking generals and civil envoys—among them General Omar Bradley, chairman of the U.S. Joint Chiefs of Staff; Philip Jessup, U.S. ambassador-at-large; Lord Arthur William Tedder, Marshal of the Royal Air Force; and British ambassador Sir Oliver Franks—met to discuss what should be done in case of a communist revolt in Iran.[1] Franks took advantage of the occasion to say that "in a case falling short of obvious U.N. concern, the U.K. felt that the dispatch of a small U.K. force to southern Iran would have a steadying and not a provocative influence [and] a small U.S. contribution to a force of this kind would be useful as a demonstration." This meant the occupation of Iran's southern oil fields and the refinery at Abadan by British forces, possibly with American support. There were then no signs of a communist revolt, but in order for Britain to justify such military action, a pseudo-communist uprising could be staged (as in fact happened three years later).

Ambassador Jessup rejected Franks's proposal, saying that short of the occupation of northern Iran by Russian forces or a communist seizure of power in Tehran, the dispatch of British forces to southern Iran would be provocative, giving the Soviets an excuse to send forces to Iran under their 1921 treaty with that country. He said that Britain and the United States must strengthen the position of the Iranian government in the cold war and stressed "the important contribution which a favorable A.I.O.C. settlement could make to this end." The American view was that troops should not be used in a cold war or in response to a local uprising. In a hot war, though, they favored the use of troops and the destruction of oil wells and refineries in Iran. The U.K. representatives stated that there were plans for demolition in case the area was overrun, and that these plans would be carried out "by civilian experts from the oil companies."[2] The British realized that if they wished to occupy Abadan, they would have to present the Americans with a more compelling pretext than the general threat of communism.

Early in March 1951, when the idea of oil nationalization was taking root in Iran, it was, strangely enough, the Bank of England that advised the use of force. Sir George Bolton, executive director of the bank, sent the Foreign Office a report by C. E. Loombe, his Middle East adviser, which said that "the political tempo [in Iran] is such that the possibility of direct intervention by taking over by force the [oil] fields and refinery must be considered."[3]

On March 20, the day Iran enacted oil nationalization, Geoffrey Furlonge, head of the Eastern Department at the Foreign Office, wrote to the Ministry of Defence that "the Shah is anxious to dissolve the present Majlis" so as to nullify nationalization. If this did not occur, he said, "we might be obliged to consider the use of actual force to prevent the Persian Government from seizing the oil installations." He asked the Chiefs of Staffs to make the necessary studies for a Cabinet decision on sending a force to Abadan Island.[4]

On the same day, as if by design, AIOC in Iran withdrew the "outstation" allowance of oil workers. This infuriated the work force and led to riots in which three British nationals were killed. The incident provided a good pretext for Foreign Secretary Morrison to declare in the House of Commons that Britain reserves the right "to act as we see fit to protect British lives and property." This declaration was followed by the British government's announcement on March 28 that the frigates *Flamingo* and *Wild Goose* were being sent to Abadan "to safeguard British industries." Shortly afterward two cruisers and four destroyers joined the naval force in the Persian Gulf.

Meanwhile preparations for a military operation proceeded. In May the Ministry of Defence advised the General Headquarters of the Middle East Land Forces (GHQ-MELF) to spell out the type and size of forces required to seize and secure Abadan so as to safeguard British lives and property and to resume the export of oil. GHQ-MELF was also asked to prepare an alternative plan for moving a force to Abadan to cover evacuation of AIOC's British staff and dependents "in the face of opposition by Persian forces."[5]

Soon after Mossadeq took over the prime ministership, the British Cabinet discussed different military options and the repercussions of each throughout the world. While such hawkish members of the Cabinet as Morrison and Defence Minister Emanuel Shinwell argued strongly in favor of occupying and securing Abadan, others believed that only the necessity of protecting British lives could justify military action. Chancellor of the Exchequer Hugh Gaitskell pointed out that intervention to protect AIOC's property not only would require the deployment of a large number of troops, but would have serious effects on Britain's image in the Commonwealth and would meet with strong disapproval from the United States and the U.N. Security Council. But Shinwell was adamant: he considered military action necessary "for the sake of preserving our prestige in the Middle East." At a meeting of the Joint Chiefs of Staff he declared, "if Persia was allowed to get away" with nationalization, others would be encouraged and "the next thing might be an attempt to nationalise the Suez Canal. . . . We must be prepared to show that our tail could not be twisted interminably."[6]

Both to intimidate Iran and to sound out U.S. reaction, the British government announced on May 14, 1951, that the Sixteenth Independent Parachute Brigade had been brought to "a state of readiness," and ten days later the brigade departed for Cyprus. The British press gave the issue maximum coverage, and Washington duly expressed dismay. Secretary of State Dean Acheson told Ambassador Franks that the president and the National Security Council strongly opposed "the use of force or the threat of the use of force" to solve the oil controversy. According to Acheson, the president was concerned that British military action might bring in the Russians and lead to a "wider conflict"; in particular, "the President stressed most strongly that no situation should be allowed to develop into an armed conflict between a body of British troops and the Persian forces of the existing administration."

Franks argued that British action would be solely for "protecting eight thousand British nationals," a highly exaggerated figure. Acheson's answer was still "No." Franks reported to Morrison that if Britain ignored U.S. advice and went ahead with the use of force, American "opposition to the British would probably become even more violent than it is at present."[7]

Morrison instructed Franks to tell Acheson that "Persian oil is of vital importance to our economy and that we regard it essential to do everything possible to prevent the Persians from getting away with a breach of their contractual obligations," which would endanger British and American investments throughout the world. Morrison tried his best to argue that the current situation would lead to a communist takeover. He contended that Mossadeq's government, though constitutional, was "embarking on a course of action which, if not stopped [will] produce such administrative and economic chaos as must inevitably facilitate the establishment of a communist-dominated regime."

As to American concerns over Russian intervention, he said that "the Russians do not at this stage desire a global war," and that any Russian intervention would accordingly be confined "to the northern provinces, in which case we should at least have preserved Persian oil." His idea boiled down to dividing Iran between Britain and Russia with American endorsement. Morrison told Franks "I am really rather annoyed by the American attitude of relative indifference to a situation which may be most grave to us all," and stressed that "we must reserve the right to take necessary measures" for the protection of British interests.[8]

There was an outcry in the United States against involving America in British "gunboat diplomacy." The *Wall Street Journal* wrote that Britain must stop making "nineteenth century threats" such as sending warships to Iran. The *Philadelphia Inquirer* said the United States must tell Britain that it would not support the use of force in Iran, a course that "risks a quick outbreak of World War III."[9] In the *Washington Post*, the well-known columnist Marcus Childs made a scathing attack on the British stand, which he considered both selfish and dangerous. He wrote:

> Teetering on the edge of the precipice in Iran, the British continue to bargain for their "rights" in Iranian oil as though they—and we—possessed all of eternity and the security that once was Gibraltar. It is one of the more interesting examples of fiddling while not only Rome but the whole Western World threatens to go up in flames. . . . Playing the ostrich in the face of facts has sent more than one civilization down the drain of history.[10]

In a CBS broadcast, Howard K. Smith commented that many countries in the Middle East and Asia fully supported Iran: "any forceful British action might thus stir all the Southern Asians to a rebellion against the Western foreigner and cause serious troubles for both Britain and the United States."[11]

Walter Levy, the American oil expert who had accompanied Averell Harriman to Tehran, told the Foreign Office that British military involvement in Iran would surely cause the Russians to intervene, which would bring in the Americans. He said he "could not imagine a worse issue on which to bring the Americans into a world war than in support of a British oil concession" that had been mismanaged owing to a "lamentable lack of statesmanship."[12]

American warnings against the use of force did not divert hawkish members of the British Cabinet from pressing on with war plans. At a Joint Chiefs of Staff committee meeting on May 23, 1951, AIOC chairman Fraser said that his company was "most willing" to assist the War Office and to provide information on transport and other facilities in Abadan. Asked about the chances of continuing oil operations under British military occupation, Fraser speculated that in such an event a fair proportion of low-grade Iranian labor might be willing to work for their livelihood; high-grade employees, by contrast, were unlikely to work because "their loyalty to their country would outweigh their cupidity." He was of the opinion that if Britain occupied southern Iran, Russia would occupy the northern parts of the country, in which event "the Persians would probably climb down" from their nationalization demands. Sir William Slim, Chief of the Imperial Staff, felt that oil operations under occupation, though difficult, could be managed. It was suggested that if the Iranian work force was not cooperative, "thousands of coloured men" might be brought in from East Africa.[13]

In May 1951 the Ministry of Defence and GHQ-MELF firmed up two plans code-named Plan Y and operation Midget. The objective of Plan Y was to "seize and secure Abadan Island and to protect the refinery and other installations so that the export of oil could be resumed as soon as oil is received from the oilfields." It contemplated the occupation not only of Abadan but also of the oil fields in a vast triangular area bounded by Abadan, Dezful, and Behbahan. The springboard for the attack was to be Bahrain, and jet fighters were to operate out of Sheiba in Iraq. The plan called for "a seaborne assault combined with the arrival of the maximum possible forces by air." The sizable naval, army, and air force requirements, including two companies of parachute troops, were spelled out. The land forces were to be those from MELF as well as from Britain. The execution of the plan required "a force of the order of 70,000," which necessitated "partial mobilisation of the army on a considerable scale, . . . raising of new units and the recall of [some] Reservists." Although the Chiefs of Staff considered Plan Y militarily unsound and the risks of failure excessive, Morrison and Shinwell did not give up and continued to press for military preparations along Plan Y lines.[14]

Operation Midget, later code-named Companion with some variations, envisaged the seizure of Abadan and its airfield long enough to evacuate AIOC British personnel; troops were to be withdrawn before they could be overwhelmed by Iranian forces. Since it was feared that the Iranians might hold the British staff in the oil fields as hostages, it was decided that all British personnel in the fields should be moved to Abadan. The necessary military force was to be conveyed by air to Abadan in successive lifts or, alternatively, flown to

Sheiba or Bahrain and then transported by road and sea to Abadan. Major Capper, the British consul in Khorramshar, who acted as the military liaison on the spot, reported that Abadan airport was unguarded and there were no Iranian forces within a mile. He therefore recommended "a direct fly-in to Abadan."[15]

Since the Chiefs of Staff considered Plan Y, which included the occupation of oil fields, to be hazardous, Sir Donald Fergusson, Permanent Secretary of the Ministry of Fuel and Power, suggested that the area of occupation be limited to Abadan so that crude could be brought in from Kuwait and refined there. Abadan was vital because its annual refinery throughput was over 20 million tons; even if it could not be held indefinitely, said Fergusson, the Chiefs of Staff should devise plans for a two-week occupation, during which time the stocks of refined oil in Abadan, amounting to one million tons, could be removed. He considered these stocks to be of "very great value" at a time when the Abadan refinery might be shut down completely.[16]

For weeks, opinions in Whitehall were divided over what type of military action Britain should take. Meanwhile the United States, as we have seen, had clearly expressed opposition to any type of military intervention. Former prime minister Winston Churchill, who strongly supported the use of force, told Attlee that he was "rather shocked at the attitude of the United States Government," which appeared not to realize that Iran "was much more important than Korea," where the Americans had involved themselves in war.

Churchill wanted Iranian oil to remain under British control and stressed "the importance of the balance of oil supplies as a factor in deterring the Russians from embarking on aggression."[17] But in a message to President Truman he argued that the planned British military intervention was not for the sake of oil but to prevent the takeover of Iran by communist forces. He said,

> The question of commercial oil is minor compared to the strategic and moral interests of our two countries and the United Nations. Short of an invasion of Western Europe I cannot think of any Soviet aggression more dangerous to our common cause than for the region between the Caspian Sea and the Persian Gulf to fall under Russian-stimulated Tudeh

Communist control. If this area fell behind the Iron Curtain it would be a serious blow to Turkey. . . . Iraq would inevitably follow suit and the whole Middle East, both towards Egypt and India, would degenerate.[18]

This did not impress Truman, who stood firm against the use of force. Some people, however, feared that Britain, which had skillfully brought an isolationist America into World War II, might do the same thing for military intervention in Iran. Ayatollah Kashani, who thought along these lines, told the American journalist Stewart Alsop that Britain might provoke a conflict between the United States and Russia solely for the purpose of saving her interests in Iran.

Some officials in the Foreign Office sought to obtain the backing of NATO member countries as a means of encouraging the United States to support Britain in her plans for military intervention in Iran. Geoffrey Furlonge, head of the Eastern Department, suggested making the argument that the "loss of Persian oil would gravely weaken the strategic potential of the NATO powers, quite apart from its effects on the economies of some of them (particularly, of course, our own)." But Sir Hoyer Millar, the British deputy at North Atlantic Council, pointed out that if the matter was raised, NATO member governments would simply say that Iran did not lie within the scope of the NATO Treaty.[19]

Britain's urge to use force found no support in the United States, among the NATO countries, or in the Commonwealth. In the end, however, Morrison felt that Britain should if necessary act alone. Mossadeq, "whose fanaticism bordered on the mental" and who had presumed to nationalize "our wells," should be stopped by any means; Britain should back her policies overseas by force and not be so "United Nationsy." Others talked in the same vein. Field Marshal Slim, Chief of the Imperial General Staff, stressed the need for "taking a strong line with the Persians" to maintain British "prestige." Lord Fraser, the First Lord of the Admiralty, said the British public was "tired of being pushed around by Persian pip-squeaks." To give "everyone a fillip and dispel the dumps and doldrums," his prescription was a large-scale military operation with all the might of the Home Fleet in the Mediterranean. All these pronouncements suggested, as Kenneth Morgan put it, "how the enduring call of empire exercised its siren effect on elements within the Labour government."[20]

Despite all the sound and fury, the chances of a successful military operation in Iran were small. The Chiefs of Staff admitted to the "military difficulty of mounting an operation in South West Persia" now that Britain had been "deprived of the use of the Indian army," which had been used in the assault on Iran in August 1941. Not to delay things, the attack was supposed to take place in the summer. But in that season the climate in southern Iran is so hot that the Chiefs of Staff believed "British troops of the Middle East Garrison would be ill-fitted to withstand it . . . without extremely severe casualties through sickness."[21] Nevertheless, Morrison pressed for military action, and on June 25, 1951, the Cabinet authorized Shinwell "to arrange for the immediate assembly in Egypt of the forces required for operation 'MIDGET.'"[22]

To try again to gain U.S. consent for the operation, Furlonge suggested that Morrison tell the Americans that Britain reserved the right to use force "without prior consultation with anyone if the lives of British nationals are in danger." Morrison advised Franks to use the same line of argument with Acheson.[23]

That this rationale was a pretext to occupy Abadan soon became clear to the Americans. Sir William Strang told Julius Holmes of the U.S. embassy that Abadan should be occupied to protect British property and to forestall a communist takeover. He considered it opportune to belabor the latter issue, but went on to lament the more direct effects of Iran's nationalization of oil: "It was an unfortunate fact that so many of the raw materials essential to Western industrial production were located in primitive or backward areas and if the kind of action which threatened us in Persia were to spread, Western industrial production might be placed in jeopardy."[24]

In Iran, British Ambassador Shepherd was advised that operation Midget was "being kept in instant readiness," that all British women and children were to be evacuated beforehand, and that the men in the oil fields were to be sent to Abadan. The forces required for the operation were made ready for action on short notice. The Middle East Land and Air Forces were strengthened, and twelve Hastings (Royal Air Force long-range transport planes), four destroyers, and a cruiser were placed at their disposal. The cruiser was "to convey the leading battalion from Bahrain to Abadan."[25]

British military threats did not intimidate the Iranian government, which continued to take over AIOC offices and oil installations. Baqer Kazemi, Iran's foreign minister, reminded Shepherd that the British government's majority shareholding in the company "does not give it the right to intervene in a matter which should be settled according to the regulations of municipal law." The British government, he said, was in the same position as other shareholders. He described Shepherd's statements concerning "the danger to the life and property of British subjects" as provocative, there being no such danger. E. H. O. Elkington, an AIOC director, agreed. He said that "the British staff in Abadan were completely safe" and that the Iranians, knowing that there were strong British forces in the neighborhood, would not give them any pretext for intervention.[26]

Eric Drake, the company's general manager in Iran, made the same observations on his return to London. On July 2, at a joint meeting of the Cabinet and the Chiefs of Staff, he opposed taking military action for evacuation of the British staff, saying that the Iranian government was determined to protect them. In fact, he believed that the British staff should remain in Iran, since "we should lose nothing by holding on."[27]

The Chiefs of Staff endorsed his evaluation. Nevertheless, they presented a paper showing how a large military operation might be mounted to seize Abadan and occupy it for an indefinite period. The First Lord of the Admiralty informed the Cabinet that much of the planning work had been done, but that legislation was required to authorize the selective retention of national servicemen and to call up some reservists. Morrison and Shinwell supported the plan; but Attlee, Gaitskell, Secretary of State for the Commonwealth Philip Noel-Baker, and Colonial Secretary James Griffiths urged caution on the ground that calling up reservists would be regarded in Britain as "implying preparation for a major war."[28]

It was generally agreed that occupying Abadan and securing it by force had two advantages. One was that the refinery could be used for refining oil from Kuwait. The other was that the British government would be in a strong negotiating position, since Iran would have oil but no means of refining it. On the other hand, the operation would "involve very grave political risks" given the opposition of the Commonwealth and the United States and the likelihood of a serious challenge at the United Nations, where it would be argued that Britain had taken "the law in its own hands."[29]

On July 5, 1951, when Iran rejected the World Court's interim ruling to the effect that all oil operations should provisionally proceed as before until the court decided whether it had jurisdiction in the case, Morrison again urged the United States to support British military action; but to no avail. Secretary of State Acheson told Ambassador Franks that in his view "an exchange of fire between British troops and the army of the Shah [would have] disastrous political consequences [leading] ultimately to the victory of Russia and the Tudeh Party." Both he and the president, he said, felt that the solution lay in meaningful negotiations. Franks advised Morrison to go along with Acheson lest Britain be seen to be acting in an "imperialist manner."[30]

On July 12 the Cabinet agreed that it could not oppose American advice in this matter. Attlee, who was at heart against the use of force, said that Britain could not fight Mossadeq, who had the support of his people, nor could she deny the right of Iran to nationalize. Not all Cabinet members agreed with him. Morrison argued that Iran's oil nationalization was illegal and that there was nothing in international law or the U.N. Charter to prevent a state from taking action to protect its vital interests. He went so far as to say that if the U.N. Security Council opposed British military action, Britain could use her veto.[31]

With the consistent persuasion of Morrison, Shinwell, and some members of the Chiefs of Staff, Attlee finally yielded. At a Cabinet meeting on July 19, he informed his ministers that "steps were being taken to put into execution at short notice the military operation for the protection of British lives at Abadan. The force available was now sufficiently large to hold the island for a time even against Iranian opposition, and the force sent in for the purpose of protecting British staff would thus be able, if desired, to protect the continuing operation of the refinery."[32]

Four days later, however, Attorney General Sir Frank Soskice told the Cabinet that breaking a contract with a foreign entity, especially when payment of compensation is indicated, is not of necessity an international wrong. He added that "the United Kingdom has no right at all in international law independently of any United Nations recommendation to intervene by force in Persia to prevent a wrong being committed against one of its nationals or indeed to prevent the implementation of the Persian proposals even if they constitute a wrong in international law." The Cabinet agreed to defer the use of force. Nevertheless, as a precautionary measure, three battalions of British troops were sent to Sheiba in Iraq on July 26.[33]

In the House of Commons, however, some members blamed Attlee for vacillation. On July 30 they pressed him to save British interests and prestige by military intervention. In reply, Attlee, repeating the views of Attorney General Soskice, stated that it was "quite incompatible with the acceptance of the United Nations organisation and the rule of law to think that we can go about the world in a kind of Palmerstonian fashion."

The British government decided that instead of using force it could put Iran under pressure by recalling the company's British staff, whom Mossadeq had initially urged to stay. Mossadeq's response and its aftermath are discussed in Chapter 9. On September 26, when Mossadeq announced that AIOC's British staff would have to leave Iran by October 4, the British troops assembled to occupy Abadan were put on "24 hours notice," and the British ambassador in Tehran and the British consul in Khorramshar were notified accordingly.[34] But the occupation of Abadan depended on U.S. consent—at a time when Britain could scarcely claim that the lives of her nationals were in danger or that British personnel could not leave without military intervention.

At a Cabinet meeting on September 27, 1951, Attlee informed his ministers that the U.S. government would not support the use of force for maintaining AIOC's British staff in Abadan and that the Americans expected Britain to present fresh proposals to Iran. To make it clear that he, too, was against military action, he said:

> An occupation of Abadan Island would not necessarily bring about a change in the Persian Government and might well unite the Persian people against this country, and neither the oil wells nor the refinery could be worked without the assis-

tance of Persian workers. If we attempted to find a solution by force we could not expect much support in the United Nations where the South American Governments would follow the lead of the United States and the Asiatic Governments would be hostile to us.

Morrison argued that if the staff were expelled and the British government's handling appeared "feeble and ineffective, the repercussions throughout the Middle East and elsewhere would be serious. Egypt might be emboldened . . . to end the military treaty [with Britain] and possibly bring the Suez Canal under Egyptian control." He pointed out that military preparedness was such that "operations could be mounted in twelve hours" and suggested that an occupation be authorized at once and at the same time a complaint be made to the U.N. Security Council. The Cabinet ruled that military action was contrary to the U.N. Charter, but approved a motion that the Security Council be asked to compel Iran to abide by the interim ruling of the World Court and not proceed with the expulsion of British staff.[35]

On the same day, Iranian troops occupied the Abadan refinery and prepared themselves for the safe eviction of the British staff. No British military operation was in fact needed for their "safe evacuation." The Iranians were under instructions not to hold them hostage but to facilitate their departure. The departure scene is well captured by Henry Longhurst:

> On the morning of October [3], 1951, the party assembled before the Gymkhana Club . . . to embark for Basra in the British cruiser *Mauritius*. . . . The hospital nurses and the indomitable Mrs. Flavell who . . . three days previously had intimidated a Persian tank commander with her parasol for driving over her lawn, were among the party. . . . There were a few jeers but little malice now, and, let it be said, a great sadness in many a Persian heart. . . . The cruiser *Mauritius* steamed slowly away up the river with the band playing, the assembled company lining the rails and roaring in unison the less printable version of "Colonel Bogey." . . . The greatest single overseas enterprise in the British commerce had ground to a standstill.[36]

On the following day all forces kept by Britain in a state of readiness for the occupation of Abadan were ordered to be "stood down completely."[37] Meanwhile the Iranian press, exalting over the departure of the company's staff, asserted that this signified the end of British colonial domination in Iran.

The eviction of the British staff dealt a humiliating blow to the British Labour government on the eve of general elections. The London *Times* wrote that "Labour statesmanship has never seemed to grasp the character of the power vacuum in the Middle East," creating "a problem in power politics that a statesman of average qualities in the Conservative tradition would readily perceive."[38] Perhaps so, but five years later, when Anthony Eden, a Conservative prime minister, resorted to force to take over the Suez Canal and depose President Nasser of Egypt, he failed badly and was forced to resign.

Attlee's perception of the limits of British power and Britain's dependence on the United States proved to be far better than Eden's.[39] Years later, Attlee reminisced that "if we had used force [in Iran] we would have raised the whole of Asia against us and a great deal of public opinion in the rest of the world too. And it would have been quite wrong morally and politically."[40] As for Morrison, who consistently pushed for military action with no regard to its consequences, Attlee called him the "worst appointment I ever made."[41]

11

The Oil Dispute Taken to the United Nations

After finally rejecting the military occupation of Abadan, Britain took her dispute with Iran to the United Nations Security Council. The idea had come up first in July 1951 when Iran rejected the interim ruling of the World Court that AIOC operations in Iran should continue while the court decided whether it had jurisdiction in the case. Some in the Foreign Office argued at the time that Britain should request the Security Council to make Iran abide by the court's ruling and at the same time attack Abadan, telling the Council that "as in the case of United States [military] action in Korea, we were coming to the Security Council immediately for authority and approval of our action." But others feared that if Britain did so, she might end up in getting no votes in her favor while being accused of indulging in "self-help."[1]

The matter remained dormant until late September, when Mossadeq announced Iran's decision to expel AIOC's British staff by October 4. Shortly after learning of this announcement the Foreign Office prepared a draft resolution for presentation to the Security Council. While expressing concern "at the threat to peace and security that may thereby be involved," the resolution called on the government of Iran to permit the continued residence of AIOC's British staff and to follow the World Court's recommendations.[2]

To obtain U.S. support for the British resolution, Morrison advised Ambassador Franks to tell the State Department that the establishment of "justice and respect for the obligations arising from the Treaties" was one of the basic aims of the United Nations under its charter. Portraying Iran's oil agreement with a British company as a treaty, he went on to say that if Iran disregarded her obligations, "a grave step will have been taken towards anarchy in international affairs."³ After discussions with the State Department, Franks informed Morrison that although the Americans desired to safeguard British interests, "they distinguish very sharply between the interests of Britain and the particular interests of AIOC. Here they have in mind the reality as they believe of the Persian nationalist reaction to the company."⁴

The State Department was against taking the matter to the Security Council, saying that the British draft resolution, as worded, would be vetoed by Russia, who would "claim to be acting in support of the rights of small powers." It prepared for Britain a new draft resolution calling on both parties to negotiate "according to the principles of the U.N. Charter." Morrison, upset by the mild language of the American draft, cabled Franks that this "could put us in the dock with the Persians, and represent a major victory for Musaddiq and force us to negotiate from a position of greatest possible weakness."⁵ Furthermore, he sent a message to Secretary Acheson saying: "America will surely not refuse to stand together with us in seeking to uphold through the United Nations the rule of law which has been our guiding principle in this issue."⁶

Acheson, who had developed a dislike for Morrison and his judgment in foreign policy, did not change his mind. Morrison then instructed Sir Gladwyn Jebb, the chief British delegate at the United Nations, to present an only slightly revised version of the original British draft resolution.

On October 1, 1951, when the Security Council began its debate on the British draft resolution, Semyon Tsarapkin of Russia objected to even considering it on the grounds that the question of nationalization in Iranian territory was wholly within Iran's domestic jurisdiction and that the United Nations was not authorized to intervene. Ting-fu Tsiang of Nationalist China joined in by asking why Britain considered the matter "a question of peace and security"; to him it was simply a matter of "property." The Security Council, however, placed the resolution on the agenda by nine votes to two, the two being the Soviet Union and Yugoslavia.⁷

Jebb, in presenting his government's case, stated that Iran had shut down AIOC's operations, "the proper functioning of which is of benefit not only to the United Kingdom and Iran but also to the whole free world. . . . Unless this process is promptly checked, the whole of the free world will be much poorer and weaker." What the Iranians wanted, said Jebb, was to extract more money from the foreigner; but "there comes a point at which the foreign goose will not lay any eggs at all."[8]

In reply, Ali-Qoli Ardalan, Iran's ambassador to the United Nations, stated that the British government had in fact recognized the principle of Iran's oil nationalization after the World Court's interim ruling. In his opinion, neither the World Court nor the Security Council had any jurisdiction in the matter. Iran was nevertheless prepared to present her case to the Council, but he requested that the debate be postponed for ten days to enable Iranian representatives to arrive in New York. Such a postponement upset the British plans to obtain a ruling before October 4, the deadline set by the Iranians for the eviction of AIOC's British staff. In spite of Jebb's stress on the urgency of the matter, the Security Council granted the requested postponement, and this made the British draft resolution redundant.

In Tehran British ambassador Shepherd reported, to Britain's dismay, that Mossadeq himself would lead the Iranian delegation to the Security Council, and that the effect of the British appeal to the United Nations had been to consolidate the Majlis, the Senate, and the press in his support. Court Minister Hossein Ala told Shepherd that Mossadeq was prepared to postpone expulsion of the company's staff "if there was some gesture of good will from the British side."[9] As we have seen, however, there was no such gesture, and Iran went ahead with the expulsion.

One thing that worried the British was that Mossadeq might produce in the Security Council documents showing AIOC's persistent efforts to corrupt Iranian politicians and the Iranian press. To dissuade Mossadeq from doing so, Richard Seddon, the company's representative in Iran, suggested in a cable to AIOC chairman Fraser that "it might be worthwhile to produce or threaten to produce, Keating-Musaddiq conversations last year." He thought that in those conversations, which took place in August 1950, Mossadeq had asked Geoffrey Keating, one of AIOC's assistant managers, for "British support in his campaign to oust Razmara." The idea looked very appealing to Fraser and the Foreign Office. But the record of the conversations proved disappointing. It turned out that Mossadeq had never asked for British favors but instead had complained about AIOC's inadequate payments to Iran and the company's failure to give its Iranian staff posts commensurate with their ability.[10]

AIOC's main concern was that Mossadeq might present documents to the Security Council indicating that former prime minister Razmara and his finance minister were provided written material by AIOC for inclusion in their speeches against nationalization. Seddon, however, assured his colleagues that the company's memoranda on these speeches were "typed on unwater-marked paper and . . . no covering letters were ever sent with them." That being so, Mossadeq would presumably be unable to prove that they came from the company.[11]

As a possible way of discrediting Mossadeq, Shepherd suggested publicizing the fact that the elderly prime minister had never visited Abadan. In response Lord Privy Seal Richard Stokes wrote to Morrison: "I warn you that I don't think that it is a very good point to make. . . . [Fraser] the Chairman of the Company has never been there either!!"[12] Indeed William D'Arcy, who obtained the original oil concession, never set foot in Iran.

Early in October 1951 Lazaro Cardenas, the former president of Mexico who had nationalized his country's oil industry in 1938, came to Iran's aid. In an interview with *Paz* magazine, he said that Iran, like Mexico, was fully justified in nationalizing her oil. He added that the United States should support Iran, and he called the British threats undemocratic and unwarranted. The same magazine published Cardenas's letter to Mossadeq congratulating him for nationalizing AIOC and for exercising Iran's sovereignty in the face of "imperialist" threats.[13]

Henry Grady, former U.S. ambassador to Tehran, believed that the British had made a "grave error" in taking the dispute to the Security Council. The Council, he said, would provide Mossadeq with "a great forum to tell the world how their [Britain's] oil company has oppressed the Iranian people and to show that Western capitalism is tending to control, and possibly destroy, other countries in the underdeveloped parts of the world."[14]

Besides complaining to the Security Council, Britain resumed her military threats against Iran. This brought a backlash from the press of some developing countries, particularly Turkey and India, both members of the Council. The Indian press considered British military threats against Iran as a "typical Palmerstonian technique of protecting British investments abroad." The Iranian press reacted by warning that if Britain resorted to military action, Abadan might end up in ashes.[15]

Jebb was concerned about the Security Council's reaction to British military threats. Worried that the Iranian delegation might plausibly describe the presence of British warships in the Persian Gulf as the area's only threat to peace and security, he suggested that the warships be withdrawn and the Persian Gulf squadron in Sheiba reduced before the Security Council reassembled for discussion. The British government accepted his advice and ordered the dispersion of naval forces in the Gulf, but kept three frigates and one cruiser on hand in case the Cabinet decided to intercept tankers taking oil from Iran.[16]

In a desperate effort to persuade the Americans to support Britain's case, Morrison sent a message to Acheson saying: "The unbridled and irresponsible nationalism which has overflowed in Persia and Egypt, and shows signs of doing so elsewhere, represents an even graver danger for the Western Powers. . . . Consequently, if it succeeds in ejecting foreign interests, a vacuum will be created which will provide an unequalled opportunity for Russian penetration."[17] When Acheson predictably replied that the British draft resolution would not be acceptable to the majority in the Security Council and that the best alternative was to resume negotiations with Iran, Morrison told Walter Gifford, the U.S. ambassador in London, that "we were tired of being lectured by the United States."[18]

Franks told the State Department that differences between Britain and the United States on the Iranian oil issue could lead to a strain in Anglo-American relations. He stressed that the only alternative to force was a recourse to "justice," complaining that the United States was not supporting Britain on this. Finally, after strenuous arguments, the two sides drew up a new draft resolution. After showing concern "at the dangers inherent in the dispute . . . and the threat to international peace and security," this resolution called for the resumption of negotiations.[19]

On October 8, 1951, Mossadeq and his party of fifteen, including three Cabinet ministers and a number of senators and Majlis deputies, arrived in New York for the Security Council debate.[20] At the airport, Mossadeq, addressing a large body of press correspondents, talked of British "colonial" exploitation in Iran. He reminded the Americans of their own fight for independence when their country was a British colony, and appealed for their support in freeing Iran from "the chains of British imperialism." His statement was well received by the American press, which took his side against Britain.

Mossadeq, whose health was poor, was taken to New York Hospital, where Assistant Secretary of State George McGhee and Ernest Gross, U.S. representative to the United Nations, went to see him. McGhee told him that President Truman and Secretary Acheson were looking forward to seeing him in Washington after the termination of the Security Council debate. Mossadeq, who hoped to achieve a negotiated "conciliation" prior to the Security Council's meeting, suggested that the debate be postponed. The British, he said, "were playing for time . . . so that economic pressures on Iran would make the latter more compliant." He wanted the Americans to help bring Britain to the negotiating table.[21]

Acheson, prompted by Mossadeq's eagerness to reach a settlement, urged Britain to allow the United States to negotiate with Iran's prime minister "in the role of honest brokers," while considering essential British interests. But Morrison was not forthcoming. He believed that such talks would strengthen Mossadeq's position in Iran. The Foreign Office made it clear to Franks, for his personal information, that "it is our objective to avoid giving Musaddiq any opportunity to claim that he has either extracted fresh concessions from His Majesty's Government or persuaded the Americans that such concessions are necessary." He was advised "to secure full American support in the Security Council."[22]

On October 15, the Security Council reassembled. Jebb stated that since Iran had already expelled AIOC's British staff, he was presenting a new draft resolution calling for a resumption of negotiations with due regard to the interim ruling of the World Court. He then appealed to Mossadeq "not to take up any aggressively nationalist attitude," but to show that "he too welcomes a constructive solution . . . that will redound to the benefit of the world as a whole."

Thus began a dramatic week in the annals of the Security Council, a week in which the representatives of two states, one powerful and the other weak, used the world forum to promote their diametrically opposed aims. Mossadeq spoke next. His strategy was to use Iran's weakness as a banner around which the virtuous and the oppressed should gather. The Security Council, he said, is "the ultimate refuge of weak and oppressed nations." If great powers did not respect the principles that the Council was created to embody, it "would become an instrument of interference in the internal affairs" of the weak. He added:

> The Second World War changed the map of the world. In the neighbourhood of my country, hundreds of millions of Asian people, after centuries of colonial exploitation, have now gained their independence and freedom. It is gratifying to see that the European powers have respected the legitimate aspirations of the people of India, Pakistan and Indonesia, and others who have struggled for the right to enter the family of nations on terms of freedom and complete equality. . . . Iran demands just that right.

Mossadeq maintained that nationalization was the unquestionable right of every sovereign state, and that the British sought to trample upon this right. Britain had "sought to incite internal dissension, . . . to intimidate us by stationing warships . . . and by sending its land and air forces to the vicinity of Iran," and had tried to use the World Court to further her "illegal aims." He urged the Security Council to give "protection to the rights of all nations, the little as well as the big," adding that this may be "still a vision of the future" because the "great and the powerful still lord it over the world."

He went on to say that the oil agreement between the government of Iran and a British company did not confer any "rights, standing or competence" on the British government. Furthermore, he added, nothing in international law put aliens in a favored position over the nationals of a country. If governments had sovereignty in internal affairs only over their own nationals and "not in respect of foreigners who have the support of powerful Governments," this meant that the foreigners enjoyed special "capitulatory" rights.

But such an arrangement was "incompatible with the equality of rights. . . . No independent state would . . . subject itself to such degradation and slavery." He reasoned that since the oil agreement was not with the British government, neither that government nor any international organization had the right to interfere in the matter.

As for the draft resolution's warning about dangers to peace, Mossadeq said, if nationalization endangered peace, then Britain, which had nationalized so many industries, should be brought before the Council "for having sapped . . . the pillars of peace." It required "a deficient sense of humour to suggest that a nation as weak as Iran can endanger world peace. . . . Whatever danger to peace there may be lies in actions of the United Kingdom Government," which had stationed warships and paratroops close to Abadan. "Iran has stationed no gunboats in the Thames."

Reflecting on Iran's recent history, Mossadeq told the Council that the 1921 military coup d'etat that brought Reza Shah to power had taken place "with British connivance" for "the establishment of a dictatorial regime." Its purpose was to extinguish democratic freedoms and to impose on the Iranian people the 1933 oil agreement, which extended the period of the concession to 1993. Notwithstanding its commercial garb, he said, AIOC was "a latter day parallel of the former East India Company which brought the great sub-continent of India under its sway." It had "a hand in the Majlis elections and the formation of Cabinets . . . for the sake of securing the highest possible income," had encouraged corruption, and had "in reality created an *imperium in imperio*" that undermined Iran's independence. It was for these reasons that Iran had decided to end AIOC's usurpations by nationalizing the oil industry. The company's record, he observed, was one of covetous exploitation. It had contributed hardly anything to the economy of Iran, as might be inferred from the fact that Iranian oil workers lived in hovels.

In conclusion, he expressed his "sincere desire" for friendly relations with Britain if an atmosphere of good will and sincere mutual confidence could be created. But "under pressure, we will not . . . engage in negotiations affecting our internal affairs. To do so would not only constitute an admission that we are not a sovereign and equal nation, but would eventually be fatal to our independence."[23]

On the following day, October 16, Mossadeq concentrated on the revised British draft resolution. He stated that since Britain had been unable to persuade world public opinion that "the lamb has eaten the wolf," she had brought the matter to the Security Council to make a case that she needed help to open negotiations with Iran. No such help was needed. The Iranian government had waited for five months for Britain "to make proposals on principles of law but, instead, we have been subjected to a steady application of the rule of force." The only question that remained to be settled was the matter of compensation, which Iran had stressed all along that she was prepared to pay.[24]

In reply to Mossadeq, Jebb stated that the prime minister's speech was "a profitless . . . interpretation of past events," which amounted to "wild accusations." He rejected Iran's argument that neither the British government nor the Security Council had any legal jurisdiction over the Iranian action, which, in his opinion, aimed at "expropriating a billion dollar concern." He maintained that the expropriation of foreign property is a matter "governed by definite rules of international law" and is not one of domestic jurisdiction. Mossadeq, he claimed, was bent on carrying out his "precipitate," "suicidal" action by "arbitrary" means, and had created a distressing situation in Iran "entirely owing to his own folly and that of his . . . misguided supporters." Moreover, Mossadeq's "allegations and imputations . . . are manifestly inaccurate, not to say willfully distorted": in fact, Britain and AIOC had made great contributions to the Iranian economy. In particular, Mossadeq's allegation that Iranian oil workers were living in hovels was false. By way of proof, Jebb passed around an album of photographs of the company's housing and other facilities, which he described as "the most eloquent proof of the work of the Company."[25] The Iranian delegation pointed out that the pictures in the album were of the housing of AIOC's British and Iranian executives, not its workers.

In a statement that Jebb found "full of sarcasm and irony," Majlis deputy Allahyar Saleh responded that the British representative's portrayal of AIOC "has all the quality of a commercial puff in a stock-company prospectus. . . . It is phrased in those pseudo-sociological terms which we have come to expect from educated stock-brokers." After all, he said, Jebb "speaks as the representative of the principal stockholder of the Company." He read a passage from a report of the International Labor Organization (ILO) in which "the great majority" of oil workers were said to "live in the older overcrowded sections of the municipal district" or in "mudhouses" or "tents" put up by AIOC. He added: "I shall not . . . ask what proportion of the social benefits presently enjoyed in the British Isles are paid for by the revenues from our oil. . . . The fact is that there is no advanced country in the world in which a commercial enterprise could have taken so much and given so little."

Jebb, who could not contest the validity of the ILO report, stated that "in the light of experience, earlier conditions, both economic and social, come to be regarded with the passage of time as outmoded." He argued that AIOC's financial policies had been far-sighted since, in a sense, the company "has had to act as trustee for the Iranian people" until the termination of the oil agreement in 1993.

Interpreting this last remark as a hint that the Iranians could not manage things themselves and needed a trustee, Saleh described it as "not only a gratuitous offence" but "instinct with that smug superiority which has always marked the attitude of the former Company" and Britain toward Iran. He added that if the company had in fact been a trustee, its financial dealings with Iran could only be described as "embezzlement and theft." To prove his point about AIOC's interference in the affairs of Iran, he read documents from the company's offices indicating that AIOC had manipulated Iran's Cabinet ministers and the Director of Radio and Propaganda to achieve its aims.

Jebb for his part considered all the company's dealings in Iran to have been "quite open and normal." Moreover, he said, if the company had not developed the oil resources, the people of Iran as well as the whole world "would have been poorer than they are today." On the oil dispute itself, he said that his government "has repeatedly declared its willingness to recognise the principle of nationalisation in Iran and to negotiate a settlement" compatible with nationalization while taking into account the interests of all parties. In an effort to impress the Security Council with Britain's altruism, Jebb said:

I appeal . . . to the Prime Minister of Iran to look beyond the narrow bounds of nationalism to the wider common interests of the world community. We are united in a common purpose: to raise the standard of living of people throughout the world. . . . If civilization is to survive, we must find the means of working together towards common aims. There is no place for national selfishness. . . . Material resources cannot be used selfishly.

The Council, many of whose members were more or less familiar with British colonial history, was unimpressed by this appeal. Nor was Jebb's defense of AIOC convincing to a body numbering many members from developing countries that had experienced similar problems with foreign investment.

Saleh reminded the Council that Jebb had described Iran's actions as "insensate," "precipitate," "arbitrary," "intolerable," "intransigent," and "hustling"; Iran's grievances as "wild accusations"; and the Iranians as "ridiculous" and "intemperate," committed to "illusory" goals and "suicidal" tactics. In contrast, he said, Jebb painted a glowing picture of his country and AIOC, the former to be admired for her social contributions to Iran and the latter a model to be copied by the rest of the world. But those acquainted with conditions of life in Iran, he stated, did not view the company's activities "with quite the same wide-eyed wonder as Sir Gladwyn Jebb." Indeed, "as the vision of Utopia which he [Jebb] conjured up fades away into the never-never land which is the abode of all fantasies and fables, the harsh facts that cannot be spirited away abide with us."

The truth was, said Saleh, that all the company did in Iran for half a century was to accumulate exorbitant profits at Iran's expense, enabling it "to self-finance a host of other profitable companies." By way of example, "The profits of the Company in the year 1950 alone, after deducting the share paid to Iran, amounted to more than the entire sum of £114 million cited by the representative of the United Kingdom as the total sum paid to Iran in royalties in the course of the past half century." What Iran had earned from her oil was no more than "crumbs . . . from the Company's table." Giving figures on the company's profits, dividends to shareholders, and taxes to the British Treasury, he challenged Jebb to contest his figures. He concluded that Iran would under no circumstances turn over the control of her oil again to the AIOC. "We are not prepared . . . to finance other people's dreams of empire from our resources."

Jebb, realizing that his aggressive stance had been counterproductive, tried to make amends. The only accusation that had wounded him, he said, was that he was smug. "In crossing swords with so eminent and respected and admittedly high-minded an antagonist as the Prime Minister of Iran, that is the last impression that I should wish to create and, if I have created it, I am very sorry."[26]

The Soviet representative considered the whole debate futile, reiterating that the matter was domestic and had nothing to do with the Security Council. Sir Bengal Rau of India agreed, as did Dr. Antonio Quevedo of Equador, who feared that a Security Council vote on the British draft resolution "might open new avenues for foreign intervention in the domestic affairs of weaker countries to which all the countries of Latin America have long declared their opposition." Tsiang of China doubted whether Britain's acceptance of Iran's oil nationalization was genuine. He observed that "the day has passed when the control of the Iranian oil industry can be shared with foreign companies or foreign Governments."

Ernest Gross of the United States, while supporting the British draft resolution, stated that the U.S. attitude toward the issue "is grounded upon the unalterable friendship of the United States for both the people of Iran and the people of the United Kingdom and is motivated solely by the desire to see . . . [a] constructive solution." The Americans were reluctant to support Britain's case and had withheld using their leverage in her favor. All along they had been against bringing the issue before the Security Council and had advised negotiations. Reporting to the Foreign Office, Jebb found it "lamentable" that the U.S. representative did not give him full support and implied that the whole U.S. attitude was "based on the desire to show maximum friendship to both parties." Jebb considered U.S. policy in the matter to be "one of appeasement at any price."[27]

Mossadeq and his aides clearly won the debate. As Grady had anticipated, the British complaint had provided the old prime minister, a lawyer by training, with an international forum to make his case to the world. The American media were all behind him because, as Acheson put it, he did his job "with great skill and drama. . . . Overnight he became a television star, quite outshining the British representative, Gladwyn Jebb."[28]

With few friends on the Security Council, Jebb found himself in an awkward situation. The Dutch promised to support him "out of self-interest": they feared that "the same thing may happen to their oil interests in Indonesia" and expected "equal support" from Britain. The French had similar concerns.[29] Finally on October 19, when Jebb had lost all hope of passing his watered-down draft resolution, Francis Lacoste of France proposed a graceful way out: since the World Court had not yet determined whether the case fell within its jurisdiction, the Security Council should adjourn its debate until that determination was made. Jebb seconded a motion to this effect, though he expressed indignation at "a clear imputation" by some that "my Government was perhaps at fault in bringing this matter before the Security Council at all." Britain, he said, had sought legal remedies for an injustice and had failed to obtain them because the Council had "declined to act." He added that "if the rule of law is rejected, [the tendency] can only be towards a rule of anarchy. . . . But the Council as a whole seems to ignore these dangers."

Many Security Council members objected to Jebb's remarks. Sir Bengal Rau stated that the Council had performed its duties under the U.N. Charter, which under Article 2 says: "Nothing contained in the present Charter shall authorise the United Nations to intervene in such matters which are essentially within the domestic jurisdiction of any state." Rau saw no danger to peace that would justify invoking any article of the charter. Moreover, if Britain in fact accepted Iran's oil nationalization, as she had claimed, there were no grounds for dispute.

In reply, Jebb declared "there is nothing in the various offers we have made . . . which can be regarded as in any way inconsistent with full and complete nationalisation." But compensation was necessary, and Iran could not pay it because she could not run the oil industry. Not so, said Rau: Iran's prime minister had explicitly informed the Security Council that his government was ready to sell ten million tons of oil each year to Britain at half price, the other half to be applied to redeeming compensation claims. As to Iran's ability to run the oil industry, he stated, Prime Minister Mossadeq had made it clear that his government would seek the services of qualified technical personnel. Jebb could make no reply.

The French motion for adjournment of the debate was approved by a vote of 8 to 1, with the United Kingdom and Yugoslavia abstaining. The Soviet Union voted against the motion, once again arguing that the Council had no business discussing the issue in the first place.[30]

The debate ended in a humiliating defeat for the British government while making Mossadeq a national hero. Jebb feared that the outcome might lead Iran to define the issue as purely a "domestic affair between her and the Company," but Ambassador Shepherd remained hopeful. "We should let the oil question simmer for a while," he advised the Foreign Office, "and meantime encourage, so far as we properly can, a change of Government [in Iran] in the near future." He considered the Americans to be the real villains. Not only would the company's disappearance be "a considerable blow to our prestige," but there would be "a further blow if we indicated our subservience to the Americans in this matter" and appeared to be "completely under the Americans' thumbs."[31] Shepherd seemed to feel that Britain could, as in her imperial days, impose her will with no regard to the judgment of other powers.

The Iranian press was jubilant about the outcome of the Security Council debate and praised Mossadeq for what it called his brave, uncompromising fight against colonialism. The British press, conversely, expressed its frustration by blaming the Labour government for its inability to handle the situation. The *Financial Times* wrote that Morrison "has shown himself utterly incapable of dealing with the Persian Prime Minister, who has won a succession of resounding diplomatic victories."[32] In America *Time* magazine chose Mossadeq as "Man of the Year" for 1951.

12

Mossadeq's Discussions
in the United States

On October 26, 1951, when Churchill's Conservative government came to power, Mossadeq had already expelled the British staff of AIOC and had frustrated British attempts at the U.N. Security Council to give an aura of legality to their contentions in the oil dispute. Churchill blamed Attlee's Labour government for these failures and considered himself better suited for the task. At the opening of Parliament on November 6, the king's speech, prepared by the new government, promised "to repair the injuries our rights and interests have suffered in Persia."[1]

Churchill had no illusions that Britain could singlehandedly resolve the oil dispute and the other international problems she faced after World War II. He considered American support vital in overcoming these problems. In the course of a speech at Guildhall on November 9, he stressed the importance of relations between Britain and the United States, which, he said, had "risen to the leadership of the world," though adding that Britain had every right to receive the fullest consideration of her views.[2]

The Americans were quite willing to help settle the oil dispute, the more so since Mossadeq had told Assistant Secretary of State George McGhee that he was extremely eager to settle the dispute through American mediation. McGhee and Mossadeq held a number of discussions between October 8 and October 22, while Mossadeq was in New York for the Security Council debate. Throughout these discussions, McGhee found Mossadeq quite cooperative, "basically pro-Western," and "extremely agreeable in conversation," with a marked ability to stick to his points while having "an unpredictable sense of humour." They reached agreement on a number of points, which McGhee enumerated in a memorandum to Dean Acheson.[3]

The main points of disagreement were the price of oil and the employment of British technicians, which Mossadeq categorically rejected. When McGhee pointed out that a refinery was too complex to be operated by hired technicians, Mossadeq replied that "the refinery hasn't been nationalized." McGhee, "dumbfounded," considered this to be a real breakthrough, feeling that "Mossadeq had given back, via *me*, the largest refinery in the world." But his elation was short-lived when Mossadeq told him later that the Abadan refinery was in fact included in the nationalized oil industry. Still McGhee felt that if all other problems were settled, he could persuade Mossadeq to exclude the refinery from nationalization.[4]

Mossadeq stressed that it would be easiest if the matter could be finalized "by the Presidency of the United States," adding that "the British were always acting with the interest of their own pocket in mind, whereas the United States was a disinterested party." This prompted Acheson, who was to see Mossadeq in Washington, to tell the British to crystallize their ideas, "reduce matters to a piece of paper," and let the Americans settle things with Mossadeq.[5]

Meanwhile Henry Morgenthau, former Secretary of the Treasury under Franklin D. Roosevelt, proposed to Trygve Lie, the U.N. Secretary General, that the United Nations create an authority to purchase the British government's 51 percent interest in AIOC by issuing special bonds and to use the profits to help finance U.N. activities. He told Lie that if this were done and a similar method were used in dealing with the Suez Canal problem, it would "demonstrate to the nations of the world that the United Nations could meet any situation arising in the world economic field."[6] Morgenthau's imaginative approach had no chance of success. Under no circumstances was Britain prepared to give up her stock in such a lucrative business as Iranian oil, let alone to open the way for giving up the Suez Canal.

Mossadeq left New York for Washington on October 22, 1951. On the way he stopped in Philadelphia, where he told some two hundred people in Independence Square that Iran's oil nationalization was inspired by the same spirit of idealism that had prompted the United States to break the shackles of British colonial rule in 1776. This speech, like every other move of Mossadeq's, made headlines in Washington, London, and Tehran.[7]

Acheson welcomed Mossadeq at Washington's Union Station, and on the following day they and Colonel Vernon Walters, who served as interpreter, had lunch with President Truman at Blair House. Truman told Mossadeq that the United States was a friend to both Iran and Britain and had "no national or private interest in the matter other than achieving a fair settlement" of the oil dispute. The president added that "Russia was sitting like a vulture on a fence waiting to pounce on the oil. That is why we were so anxious to get these problems solved. . . . If the Russians secured this oil, they would then be in a position to wage a world war."

Mossadeq agreed: if Iran continued to remain under British economic pressure, he told the president, the country's independence would be gravely endangered by communism.[8] In Acheson's view, Mossadeq's chief concern was that British operation of the oil industry in Iran was coupled with interference in the country's internal affairs, something he could not accept. Acheson emphasized, however, that the matter should be settled "on a basis that could not destroy the whole fabric of oil agreements around the world."[9]

On October 24 Acheson met Mossadeq at Walter Reed Hospital, where he was staying at the presidential suite during the course of a medical checkup. Also present were George McGhee and Paul Nitze, Director of Policy Planning at the State Department, who later played an active role in an American effort to settle the oil dispute. Acheson asked Mossadeq to clarify his position precisely so that a proposal could be worked out and discussed with British Foreign Secretary Eden in Paris, where Acheson intended to go for a U.N. General Assembly meeting on the following day. Mossadeq stated that he wanted an agreement based on genuine nationalization; if Britain did not cooperate and blocked Iranian oil exports, Iran's economy would collapse and only the communists would benefit, with disastrous consequences for world peace. "The United States," he said, "would then have to fight a war in Iran like the war in Korea, equally without result." Mossadeq stated that AIOC and the British oil technicians would not be allowed to return to Iran. The National Iranian Oil Company (NIOC), with a mixed board of Iranian and foreign nationals, would manage oil operations and would sell oil to previous customers at the Persian Gulf oil price of $1.75 per barrel.[10]

Acheson told Mossadeq that Iran should sell her oil at $1.10 a barrel, the price at which Middle East producers sold it to distributing companies. Mossadeq disagreed. Companies like Aramco and AIOC operating in the Middle East obtained oil at a low price from the producing countries and sold it at a high price to bulk purchasers. Acheson's proposed price would have denied Iran the fruits of her nationalization because it was the price that producing companies paid to host governments where oil was not nationalized.[11] At this price, which Acheson had been given by American oil companies who followed the 50-50 division of profits, Iran would net only 65 cents a barrel after allowing 45 cents for production and investment costs, which were hers to bear.[12] Clearly Acheson, though wanting to be helpful to Mossadeq, was not prepared to upset what he called "the whole fabric of oil agreements" elsewhere.

When Mossadeq stated that he could not tell his people why their oil should be sold at such a low price, Acheson replied that "one of the geniuses of the late President Roosevelt was his ability to present matters to the people in such a way as to make them acceptable," adding he "felt sure that Dr. Mossadeq possessed the same genius." Mossadeq admitted that he did not, nor did he want to impose on his people what he did not believe in. McGhee insisted that if Mossadeq set a price higher than $1.10, Iran would lose her markets and the American public's favorable opinion. Mossadeq "laughingly asserted that he was not running Iran for the entertainment of American public opinion."[13] Apart from the matter of price, McGhee felt that Mossadeq's demands were quite reasonable.

A State Department memorandum to the British government on the matter began by saying that the U.S. government, motivated by "mutuality of interest" with Britain and by recognition of probable effects upon oil investments elsewhere, had tried to obtain maximum concessions from Mossadeq. Stressing that the return of AIOC to Iran in any form would not be possible, the memorandum stated that in the department's opinion a settlement could be reached on the basis of the following U.S. proposals:

1. AIOC would sell the refinery to a non-British firm. Under such an arrangement, the problem of compensation would be eliminated, and AIOC could arrange to purchase the refinery's products in sterling.

2. NIOC would be directly responsible for crude production and the Kermanshah refinery. To assure efficient management, its board would consist of three Iranians and four members from neutral countries employed by NIOC, which would retain a large oil company (possibly Dutch) as a consultant and for access to modern technology, research, and management.

3. AIOC would establish a purchasing organization to purchase from NIOC as much as 30 million tons of oil per year at $1.10 per barrel, which "would not destroy the principle of 50-50" because Iran would have to cover the cost of production, including capital investment. The Iranians had not yet agreed to this price, but the United States considered it vital to keep the price at this level.

The State Department pressed the British government to give the matter their "most urgent consideration" and to send a negotiating team to Washington. They stressed that it was "in British interest and in the interest of the entire free world not to lose this opportunity." Finally, the Department pointed out that the U.S. government did not wish American firms or technicians to have any part in this plan.[14]

At the Foreign Office, the British Working Party on Persia considered the American proposals disastrous for Britain in the Middle East, particularly because British nationals were excluded from Iranian oil operations. Neville Gass stressed that the refinery should be left as "an AIOC holding disguised in some other British company," and that NIOC should employ consultants from "a company controlled by AIOC." In short, said Gass, whatever the Americans or others might suggest, AIOC would not accept anything other than full control in one way or another. Gass even rejected the American-proposed price of $1.10 per barrel, saying that it was too high.[15]

Sir William Strang, Permanent Under Secretary at the Foreign Office, saw the American proposals as formally ratifying "expropriation at the expense of British interests." Surely any new agreement would not last its term, but Britain should "hope that enough hay could be made while the sun continues to shine." The Iranian oil issue became so important for Britain that Churchill approved the formation of an informal Ministerial Committee under Eden's chairmanship to address it, with the help of an informal Official

Committee headed by Sir Roger Makins, deputy under secretary of state at the Foreign Office.[16]

In the first meeting of the Ministerial Committee, Chancellor of the Exchequer R. A. Butler opposed accepting the U.S. proposals because "our own economic viability was at stake which was much more important than Persia's." Sir Leslie Rowan opposed negotiating with Mossadeq; instead he proposed that a scheme be prepared for getting rid of him. Eden, however, questioned whether AIOC could return to Persia in any form "except by the use of force."

In a brief prepared by the Foreign Office, Eden was advised to tell Acheson that AIOC did not consider the U.S. plan a sound commercial proposition; in particular, the price of $1.10 per barrel would give Iran "excessive remuneration" at AIOC's expense. Moreover, it said, "the position of sterling depends to an extent . . . upon our invisible earnings. The [Iranian] oil industry accounts for a very large proportion of these earnings." It stressed that in any settlement Iran should not only pay compensation but also be restricted to 50 percent of the profits.[17]

Some members of Parliament criticized the Americans for being helpful to the Iranians at Britain's expense. Sir Herbert Williams told the Foreign Office that "the Yankees behaved very badly over the Persian oil and that in fact they inspired Persia without realising the adverse effects it would have." It was thought at the Foreign Office that Mossadeq had frightened the Americans with the prospect of a possible Tudeh coup in Iran. Some argued that every effort should be made to prevent the Americans from giving any assistance to Mossadeq. If he left Washington empty-handed, it was felt, he would fall within a short period.[18]

On the other side of the Atlantic an editorial in the *New York Times* blamed Eden for his "distinct lack of interest" in the American formula. It compared Mossadeq to those brave men in America who had fought against Britain to gain freedom. It concluded by saying that if the United States did not give Mossadeq strong support, "the result will be a severe blow to American prestige in Persia and the entire Middle East."[19]

On November 4, 1951, Eden left for Paris, where he had five long sessions on Iran with Acheson, who was accompanied by Averell Harriman and Walter Gifford, the U.S. ambassador to London. Acheson, who had a poor opinion of Morrison, considered Eden "a great and signal improvement, except for Iran," on which subject he "continued to take advice from the same sources which had . . . poisoned the judgement of the Labour Party." These sources were people in AIOC, the Ministry of Fuel and Power, and the Treasury, "where Sir Leslie Rowan played the part of St. Michael, the avenging angel, [who] decreed that Mossadeq, leading the attack on foreign investment, had to fail, to be crushed and punished."[20] In fact Rowan, along with Lord Leathers, Secretary of State for Coordination of Transport, Fuel and Power, and Sir Donald Fergusson, had flown to Paris at Eden's request.

On November 5, when the two foreign ministers met, Eden belittled Mossadeq and his nationalist movement. He did not agree with the American argument that "the only alternative to Musaddiq was a Communist regime"; another alternative was a more tractable prime minister. But Acheson thought otherwise, saying that there was little prospect of Mossadeq's fall and that if he should fall the alternative would be chaotic. "It seemed a reckless policy," he said, to sit back and watch Iran go to pieces, "as it would if Mussadiq were left without any help." He added that the U.S. Chiefs of Staff were "deeply concerned at the accretion to Soviet war potential which would result from their acquiring Persian oil." Acheson pointed out that American proposals met fundamental British interests apart from the matter of prestige, "which he dismissed somewhat airily." He thought that the oil embargo would crack and that the only way for the British to stop Iranian oil from leaving the country would be a naval blockade, which was out of the question. He stressed that under the U.S. proposals Iranian oil was subject to British control in distribution. "The one point," according to Acheson, "on which it was beyond the powers of the United States to help us was allowing the AIOC to operate again in Persia."[21]

Eden stated that it would be impossible for him to defend in the House of Commons the exclusion of Britain and British technicians from Iran. He considered Mossadeq a hazard to Western interests, and contended that the best way forward was to engineer his removal. When Acheson disagreed, Churchill, who was following the Paris discussions, cabled Eden encouraging him to stand firm. He said, "I think we should be stubborn even if the temperature rises somewhat for a while."[22]

Next the British Cabinet, in an effort to win U.S. support, proposed the participation of American oil companies with AIOC in Iran. With Churchill's approval, Eden was directed to tell Acheson that "American participation would be in accordance with the general strategic policy which both Governments are pursuing in the Middle East and we should like to see . . . a general policy of combined operations by British and American companies throughout the Middle East." In return for American participation, however, the British government expected the Americans to give AIOC a share in Saudi Arabian oil.[23]

Acheson rejected the proposal, which he told Eden would make it appear "that the whole object of the American intervention had been to secure commercial interests for themselves." He insisted on the U.S. proposals. In a "tough" three-hour meeting, Eden raised objections to the American proposals and continued to criticize Mossadeq. Why was Mossadeq in Washington anyway, he asked. Since no solution could be reached for the time being, there was no reason why he should stay there.[24]

On November 8 McGhee, Nitze, and several other American officials closely involved in the oil negotiations were in the State Department's communications room anxiously awaiting a call from Acheson to tell them whether or not Eden had accepted the U.S. proposals. Acheson finally called and told them that "Eden wouldn't buy it." To McGhee "it was almost the end of the world." He had attached "so much importance to the agreement and honestly thought [that the United States] had provided the British a basis for one."

McGhee informed Mossadeq, who "accepted the result quietly with no recriminations." He pointed out, however, that Iran's independence required economic stability and asked if the United States might be willing either to help Iran run her oil industry or lend her $120 million to buy time to work out a solution not imposed by the British. McGhee made it clear that American oil companies were reluctant to replace AIOC but suggested that the prime minister write President Truman requesting a loan.[25] Mossadeq did so, but Truman, not wanting to antagonize Britain, rejected the request.

American money was, however, forthcoming in the form of increased development aid under Point IV of the 1947 Truman Doctrine, which was designed to assist countries in danger of communist domination. On November 8, 1951, William Warne was sworn in as director of the U.S. Technical Assistance Program in Iran. On the following day, he visited Mossadeq and informed him that for the fiscal year ending June 1952 the United States had appropriated $23 million for Iranian development projects. Mossadeq expressed the hope that the money would be spent in a useful manner and not fall into the hands of "charlatans" as had happened in China.[26]

On November 10 Robert L. Garner, vice-president of the International Bank for Reconstruction and Development (World Bank), met Mossadeq and told him that the bank was prepared to run Iran's oil industry until a settlement was reached (see Chapter 13). Mossadeq showed willingness to explore the possibilities once Britain accepted the idea.

In Paris, Acheson and Eden had their last meeting on Iran on November 13. Acheson argued that the British were "too rigid," insisting on points that were "unrealistic in the sense that no Persian Government would accept them." He stressed that the United States had "to pay to keep the regime afloat in Persia," and that Mossadeq's fall would be succeeded by communism—a prospect to which the British response was "incredibly light-hearted." Eden felt that if Mossadeq fell he would be replaced by "a more reasonable government" with which "a satisfactory agreement" could be reached. To make sure that the American proposals would not be revived, Eden spoke favorably of the World Bank proposal.[27]

On November 14 Mossadeq made a long speech at the National Press Club in Washington. He reviewed the history of AIOC's misconduct in Iran and of British colonial policy in a country that was not a British colony.[28] On the following day McGhee brought Mossadeq the president's negative response to his request for a U.S. loan. The news was expected: Mossadeq knew as well as Truman that a U.S. loan to Iran would have angered the British. He pointed out that he abhorred the communist system and conceded that Iran had to stick to the West. But he expressed his disappointment that the West, in its dealing with Iran, was not keen to uphold the values it prized so dearly for itself.[29]

By this time McGhee had been appointed as U.S. ambassador to Turkey, at his own request, and had to leave Washington in a matter of weeks. However, because he ardently wished to make a settlement of the oil dispute one of his major accomplishments as assistant secretary, he made one last effort before departing. He and Nitze held a meeting with Mossadeq and told him that a settlement could be reached if Iran accepted British staff and agreed to sell oil at a discount of 45 percent. McGhee advised Mossadeq to be realistic, to ask "what was the best deal Iran could get?" Failing a realistic settlement, "History would say that the Prime Minister had won a great victory but had been unwilling to harvest its fruits for his country."

Mossadeq's reply was that his conscience would not allow him to put his country again at the mercy of the British. He emphasized that for Iran the dispute was political rather than economic, and that the main issue was one of assuring independence. The British, he said, had no rightful claim to return to Iran but were only entitled to receive compensation. Deputy finance minister Kazem Hassibi, who joined the discussions on the last day along with some members of Iran's Oil Committee, stated that compensation to AIOC could not possibly exceed £100 million. He said this was equivalent to 21 million tons of oil, a quantity that could be turned over to the company in no time. He went on to say that Iran would be satisfied to produce and sell one-fifth as much oil as had been produced before rather than bring back AIOC and sell oil to it at bargain prices.

McGhee responded that if congressmen asked why Iran needed financial assistance in spite of her oil wealth, he was compelled to say that it was because "the Iranians wanted to discriminate against the British" and also because they expected to obtain a higher price for their oil than other countries. Mossadeq remarked that what the British wanted was not a settlement with him but a favorable deal with Ahmad Qavam, after overthrowing him.[30] On the very same day in Tehran, Qavam sent a letter to the British chargé d'affaires saying that he would solve the oil problem in Britain's favor if he came to power (see Chapter 16).

Although McGhee's goodwill was plain, he was too optimistic in assuming that if Mossadeq agreed on price and British participation, the British would settle with him—a nationalist leader who had pioneered the nationalization of foreign concerns in the Middle East. Britain had vast interests in the area and was in no way prepared to deal with someone whose outlook and ideology challenged those interests.

Mossadeq left Washington on November 18, 1951. He stopped for three days in Cairo, where he was given a tumultuous welcome. He arrived at a time when the rising tide of Egyptian nationalism had led to the annulment of the Anglo-Egyptian Treaty of 1936 and the Condominium Agreement of 1899, which established dual control over the Sudan. Mossadeq's defiance of the British had encouraged the Egyptians to abrogate these agreements unilaterally.

The Egyptian press called him a nationalist hero who had "conquered history," and placards reading "Long Live Mossadeq" appeared throughout Cairo and Alexandria. *Al-Ahram* wrote that "Mossadeq won freedom and dignity for his country" and that "Iran and Egypt have taken up the sacred duty of cleansing themselves from colonialism." Mossadeq met King Farouk, attended a state dinner given in his honor by Egyptian prime minister Nahas Pasha, received leading ministers and politicians, and accepted an honorary doctorate at Fouad University. In a message to the press he maintained that the Suez Canal belonged to Egypt just as Abadan belonged to Iran, and that no one could claim the possession of either on the basis of treaties or agreements signed under duress.[31]

The British embassy in Cairo reported to Eden that speeches by Mossadeq and Egyptian leaders presented "a picture of two small but gallant countries struggling to free themselves from the shackles of blood-sucking imperialism."[32] Mossadeq's enthusiastic reception in Cairo hardened the British stand against him. If he succeeded in nationalizing Iran's oil industry, they felt, Suez would be next.

On his arrival in Tehran, Mossadeq was met at the airport by a crowd numbering tens of thousands. *Shahed* wrote, "This political genius not only precipitated Iran's bid for independence but also advanced anti-colonial policy in the Middle East."[33] Although he returned from the United States empty-handed, he received an overwhelming vote of confidence on his oil policy from both houses of Parliament. This gesture was due partly to his popularity at home and partly to his victory at the U.N. Security Council. Yet serious problems remained. As the opposition would soon point out, Mossadeq had neither achieved a settlement of the oil dispute nor obtained American financial assistance; and little could be done without one or the other.

13

Britain Manipulates the World Bank

The World Bank's proposal that it be authorized to run Iran's oil industry pending a settlement was prompted by Habibollah Isfahani, the Pakistani ambassador to Washington, who believed that the bank should play an active role in helping its member countries. With his government's support and the personal backing of Yagub Shah, Pakistan's representative on the bank's board, Isfahani urged Robert Garner, vice-president of the bank, to visit Mossadeq while he was in Washington and present him with a plan by which the bank could step in to resolve the dispute.[1]

Garner and Isfahani met Mossadeq on November 10, 1951, and discussed an interim plan to get the oil flowing while Britain and Iran worked out a settlement. Mossadeq expressed his willingness to consider the plan once it was spelled out in detail, provided it was compatible with Iran's Nationalization Act and did not call for the employment of British personnel.[2]

Although the British discouraged Garner from visiting London to discuss his plan, he went anyway. His goal, he told Cabinet ministers, was to provide AIOC with a unique position by making it the bulk purchaser and distributer of Iranian oil. The ministers supported his plan in principle but advised him not to go to Tehran for discussions until after the Iranian elections.[3] The reasons for the delay are explained by Foreign Secretary Eden in a cable to Ambassador Franks: "We do not want a premature approach [by the bank] to reinforce Musaddiq's position [in the elections]. On the other hand we do not through overlong delay want to let the pot go off the boil and give a chance to the Persians or the Americans to do something silly."[4]

The pot began to go off the boil when Mossadeq, having heard no word from Garner for weeks, sent a message to him saying that a number of firms had approached Iran for the immediate purchase of oil. If Garner or his representative did not come to Tehran by December 16, the Iranian government would conclude sales agreements with them. Still another possibility was raised by *Shahed*, a Tehran daily, which wrote that since Britain and her allies were boycotting Iranian oil, the government had no choice but to try to sell oil to Russia and the Eastern bloc.[5]

Garner asked AIOC to send a person of authority to Washington to help him finalize the bank's proposals. When the company declined, Eugene Black, president of the World Bank, flew to London and met with Eden, who subsequently persuaded AIOC to send two of its directors, Neville Gass and H. E. Snow, to Washington. Except on this issue, Black's extensive discussions with British officials brought no conclusive results.[6]

In mid-December, Iran pressed the bank again to send its representatives to Tehran. Eden saw Mossadeq's appeal to the bank as "transparent blackmail," designed "to help himself surmount his political difficulties, particularly during the elections." He advised Sir Oliver Franks, Britain's ambassador to the United States, to dissuade Garner from sending anyone to Tehran for negotiations.[7]

Garner and Black told Franks that the trip was necessary; otherwise the Iranians could reasonably blame them for traveling to London for discussions with the British government while consistently ignoring their invitations to visit Iran. Black stressed that the bank, as an international organization, must avoid openly favoring one party to a dispute. He promised, however, to do his best to meet Britain's aims and also to clear beforehand with London any letter or proposal sent to Mossadeq. In conformance to this promise the bank sent Eden for clearance a letter informing Mossadeq that Torkild Rieber, an oil consultant, was being sent to Iran to visit oil installations and advise the bank on restoring operations. Eden replied to Black that Rieber should wait for Gass to arrive from London and consult him before going to Tehran. He also told Black that Mossadeq was in political trouble and urged that he be left with his difficulties for a few weeks because "his continuation in office is undesirable."[8]

George Middleton, the British chargé d'affaires in Tehran, hoped that the bank would end up not sending anyone to Tehran. "Silence and apparent indifference to the fate of Persian oil are at present our best weapons," he told the Foreign Office. But Loy Henderson, Grady's replacement in Tehran, advised the State Department that the bank should send a representative with full powers at once, failing which Mossadeq might feel that he had no alternative but to sell oil to the Soviet bloc. In rebuttal, the Foreign Office cited Reuters news agency, to the effect that there was no commercial reason for Eastern Europe to purchase Iranian oil since Rumania had surplus oil and had offered to sell it to the West.[9]

The World Bank finally sent Torkild Rieber and Hector Prudhomme of its Loan Department to Tehran with a letter from Garner to Mossadeq formulating the general principles on which the bank was prepared to take over oil operations in Iran. Although this letter was prepared in close consultation with Gass of AIOC, some in the Foreign Office argued that the bank should not correspond with Mossadeq at all. Sir Roger Makins, however, observed that since the bank had "consulted us and the Oil Company in a very detailed fashion," it would be unreasonable to try to prevent Garner and other bank officials from communicating with the Iranian government.[10]

On their way to Tehran, Rieber and Prudhomme stopped in London for last-minute consultations with the British government and AIOC. There Basil Jackson, the company's deputy chairman, did his best to "steer Rieber in the right direction."[11] The two bank envoys arrived in Tehran on the last day of 1951. Shortly afterward they handed Mossadeq Garner's letter, which said that the World Bank was prepared to assist in restoring oil operations in Iran on the following terms:

1. The oil operations would be conducted "under the management of a neutral top executive group to be selected by the Bank," which would be free to engage non-Iranian nationals. "All management, staff and other personnel would be responsible to the Bank [which] would be given all authority necessary . . . to provide efficient operations."

2. "The Bank's services would be rendered as an interim measure . . . without prejudice to the legal rights of the interested parties."

3. The bank would make a bulk export contract for the sale of oil "through established distribution channels." The sale proceeds, after allowing for costs, would be allocated as follows: "one part to Iran, one part to the bulk buyer and the remainder to be held by the Bank in trust." Details on the price of oil and the percentage distribution of the proceeds would be embodied in the bank's detailed proposal.

4. Before submitting a detailed proposal, the bank wanted to know if the above terms were acceptable to the Iranian government. The bank was asking for a similar assurance from Britain.[12]

It was disingenuous of the bank to say it was asking for similar assurances from Britain on the contents of a letter every detail of which had been worked out in cooperation with AIOC and the Foreign Office. Indeed, Prudhomme had had to make some changes in the wording of Garner's letter when U.S. embassy officials in Tehran described its tone as "too British." Mossadeq also found the contents of the letter too British, telling Henderson he did not understand why a portion of the proceeds should go to the bulk buyer "unless it simply meant that the International Bank were acting as agents of the A.I.O.C. and trying to restore the concessionary regime."[13]

Britain thought that Mossadeq would keep the bank's proposals secret from the public until some favorable solution was reached. Instead he published the full text of Garner's letter, along with his own reply, to demonstrate that he did not intend to make deals behind closed doors.

In his reply, Mossadeq told Garner that his proposals were not in keeping with their discussions in Washington. He raised a number of questions. What was meant by "neutral" executives, and what would be the nationality of the non-Iranian staff to be employed? Who would be the bulk buyer, and why would any purchaser who had no partnership with Iran be given a portion of the sale proceeds? With regard to the bank's demand for full authority, he reminded Garner that under Iran's nationalization law the ultimate authority was the Iranian government. Thus, he said, the bank could act only within the framework of a delegation of authority from Iran and could not be an agent of both Britain and Iran. He pointed out that the World Bank could charge a commission in return for services rendered to Iran. With regard to the bank's idea that its services would be rendered "without prejudice to the legal rights of the interested parties," he noted that the Iranian government was "free to reject any proposal which prejudices its legal rights."[14]

At the Foreign Office, Peter Ramsbotham of the Economic Relations Department noted that Mossadeq had asked pertinent questions and that any attempt by the World Bank to answer them "could undoubtedly reveal the [British] intention to restore A.I.O.C. to its former position as a monopoly purchaser" and the recipient of a portion of the profits. "I think it would be unwise," he said, "for the Bank to lay too much stress on the return to *status quo ante*."[15] But Eden ignored the advice and instructed Franks to tell the bank that it should not modify "any of the basic principles in an attempt to meet Musaddiq's objections."[16] Eden was concerned that the Americans might respond to Mossadeq's demands by modifying the bank's proposals, which were actually his.

Meanwhile Churchill decided to go to the United States to obtain American support for Britain's position on the Iranian oil dispute and other major issues. The repayment of heavy American and Canadian loans had begun, and there was an "imminent prospect of economic breakdown . . . national bankruptcy and the break-up of the sterling area."[17] On the last day of 1951, Churchill set sail for the United States with Eden and General Lord Ismay, Secretary of State for the Commonwealth, among others.

On January 5, 1952, Truman gave a dinner on the presidential yacht for Churchill and his party, which was attended by Secretary of State Acheson, the Secretary of Defense, the Secretary of the Treasury, the Chairman of the Joint Chiefs of Staff, Averell Harriman, and others. After dinner Churchill asked Acheson if he felt "that around that table this evening there was gathered the governance of the world—not to dominate it, mind you—but to save it." When private discussions began between Truman and Churchill and their foreign secretaries, Churchill, elaborating on the same theme, stressed the need for the two countries to show unity of purpose in world affairs and to demonstrate firmness in particular toward the Middle East. He stressed that American support for

Britain in the oil dispute with Iran benefited the United States and the whole Western world, adding that "if we [Americans] could stand solidly with the British, the Iranians would come to terms in short order."[18]

Finding Truman unwilling to give any such promise, Churchill harped on the same theme the following evening with Acheson and General Omar Bradley. He began by criticizing Attlee's government, which, he said, "had scuttled and run away from Abadan when a splutter of musketry would have ended the matter." He added: "The British had been kicked out of Abadan in a most humiliating manner. If he had been in office, it would not have occurred. . . . While the oil companies may have made mistakes, that was past and was not a reason for weakness in the face of Mossadeq's impossible conduct." Acheson's response was that they "could not dismiss the past quite as easily as Mr. Churchill has done." The problem in Iran, he said, arose from the unsatisfactory nature of AIOC's dealings with that country. This had "precipitated a national position in Iran which was far more serious and permanent than the mere personality of Mr. Mossadeq."[19]

Unable to bring Acheson to their side, Churchill and Eden turned to the World Bank for achieving their aims. At a luncheon at the bank with Black and Garner, Eden obtained Black's assurance that he would stick to the bank's proposals. Black promised to neutralize the State Department's objection that the proposals were too favorable to Britain. Furthermore he promised to consult Neville Gass of AIOC whenever the bank intended to reply to Mossadeq's questions.[20]

At a high-level meeting on January 9, attended by Acheson, Eden, and their aides, Acheson said that in view of Iran's economic plight it was no longer justifiable to delay a requested loan of $25 million from the U.S. Export-Import Bank. Eden opposed such a loan. He had clear instructions from Churchill that "Americans should be told that we mean to bring economic pressure to bear on Persia" for the settlement of the dispute. William Rountree of the U.S. State Department stressed that without U.S. economic assistance Iran "would be tempted to sell [oil] to Russia or to the Satellites," and this would drive the country to the Soviet bloc. Eden again objected to U.S. assistance, saying that the Iranians should not be given the impression that the policies of the United States and Britain on Iran were at odds.

Acheson turned to the World Bank's proposals, saying that he considered them unfair to Iran. He wanted Britain to agree to a lasting solution by accepting compensation in oil and money and letting the Iranians run the industry. Franks's reply was outspoken: "what we wanted was to keep our hands on the oil." Eden stressed that he "much preferred the Bank's present proposals to an alternative which would leave Persia in sole control." He reasoned that Iran could not operate her oil industry without help, and "this might . . . play into the hands of the communists."[21]

For purposes of American consumption Eden had repeatedly raised the possibility of a communist takeover as a result of bad management by the Iranians. Taking him at his word, Acheson suggested that a long-term solution could be reached if the problem of compensation could be settled and efficient management guaranteed. He proposed a scheme that called for the World Bank to assess the amount of compensation against which Iran would give a portion of her oil to AIOC free of charge for five years while selling the rest to the company at a discount. The bank would manage the oil operations and gradually withdraw, leaving the management to the Iranians once they proved to be doing the job efficiently. This plan, he said, would meet Mossadeq's repeated argument that the first thing to do was agree on compensation.[22]

Eden found it difficult to reject Acheson's scheme and responded that he and his aides had to study the matter. What he had in mind, however, was to expedite Mossadeq's fall. The Majlis, where Mossadeq's strength lay, was near the end of its term and elections for the new Majlis took months. In the absence of the Majlis, the British thought, the prime minister could be removed through their leverage with the Shah.[23]

On his return to London, Eden cabled Franks that Acheson's scheme was "quite unrealistic" and "unacceptable." Franks should tell the State Department that the British government views "with utmost misgiving any proposal for a settlement with Persia which would put a premium on confiscation . . . [and] put at risk all United Kingdom foreign investments on which we so largely depend." He added that the Iranians could not manage the industry efficiently and thus no long-term purchase contracts could be made with them.[24]

Eden's argument on this point collapsed when Rieber's report on his visit to Abadan praised the good condition of the installations and the high standard of the maintenance work carried out by the Iranians. It seemed clear to Rieber that Iranian personnel, without the help of foreign technicians, could "produce between 15 and 20 million tons of oil annually, and up to 6 million tons of refined products." With such capability, he was convinced that the bank's plan stood no chance of winning Iran's approval. Rieber's report revived Acheson's alternative scheme for involving the World Bank, and Paul Nitze told Black that it was the only practical alternative. Black instantly reported this to Makins, advising him that "if we [the British] were going to turn down [the scheme] . . . we should do it very loudly and clearly, otherwise . . . they [the Americans] would never leave it alone."[25]

Opposed to Acheson's plan as offering too little to Britain, the bank told the State Department that it was reluctant to enter into an operation that would take longer than originally planned. But this did not lessen the department's pressure on Britain. Acheson sent a message to Eden saying, "I am most concerned that the Bank may proceed with the [original] proposal which will not have sufficient flexibility"; moreover, the bank's demand for full managerial control was unacceptable to the Iranians. Nitze, elaborating on the same theme, stressed that "ultimate responsibility must rest with the Persians." He suggested that the bank come up with alternative plans that would bring about a permanent solution. To solve Iran's immediate financial problem, Nitze proposed that Garner be authorized to purchase oil products already stored at Abadan at 50 percent discount and sell them to AIOC. He argued that this would stave off Iran's economic collapse and "remove stocks which might otherwise be sold to the Iron Curtain." As a further encouragement for the British, he pointed out that "some stocks could be used to meet heavy United States Service requirements in the Pacific."[26]

Eden rejected these proposals. "It is an extraordinary proposition," he wrote, "that the A.I.O.C. should be called upon to buy their own oil" at a time when the British government and the company had warned prospective buyers against the purchase of "stolen oil." Eden wanted the bank to stick to its original proposals and not waste time on alternative schemes. (Yet he added, "I do not want to tie the hands of their representatives.") He stated that the Americans "in their nervousness at what they believe to be the imminent collapse of Persia and the advance of communism . . . are producing scheme after scheme." He finally noted:

> I . . . think the time has come to place the issue squarely before the State Department, stressing the danger to our whole economic position if we allow arrangements with Persia to prejudice our foreign investments throughout the world. None of the State Department's suggestions are acceptable to us or the Company. . . . If they continue to press us to accept arrangements which endanger our vital interests, they will be confronting the choice between having an effective British ally and risking Persia going over to communism (a risk which we believe they exaggerate).[27]

Here Eden ignored the fact that he himself had repeatedly warned Acheson of the danger of communism in Iran.

Bernard Burrows, of the British embassy in Washington, relayed Eden's message to Nitze, adding the familiar complaint that the United States was not paying sufficient attention to the importance of protecting British interests. Nitze's response was that he "fully realised that U.S. interests correspond more closely to our [British] own than to Musaddiq's" and that the United States was keenly interested in protecting Britain's overseas investments to keep the British economy strong. Nitze, however, did not agree to Burrows's request that the American ambassador in Tehran be instructed to tell Mossadeq that the United States supported the bank's interim plan without reservations.[28]

Meanwhile Garner, along with Rieber and Prudhomme, who had returned to Washington, left for Tehran to discuss the details of the bank's contract with Iran. Interestingly enough, it was AIOC's Neville Gass who prepared a "draft contract between the International Bank and the Persian Government," to be used by Garner as a basis for discussions in Tehran.[29]

Indeed Eden had succeeded in turning the World Bank into a vehicle for furthering the aims of Britain and AIOC in Iran. Garner, in his high position at this international financial agency, did things for the British that they could not do for themselves. One was to obtain assurances of Acheson and Secretary of the Treasury Snyder that the United States would not give any financial assistance to Mossadeq during the course of the bank's negotiations. Another was to step in when Eden was unable to reject Acheson's long-term scheme for the bank to operate Iran's oil industry. Black and Garner solved this problem by telling the State Department that the bank was only interested in short-term plans while advising the British to make loud noises against the American plan.[30] The situation was ideal for the British, who were happy that "the Bank's initiative . . . had an appearance of being completely independent." Franks reported that Black is "fully conscious of our point of view . . . and anxious to do everything he can to meet us."[31]

The World Bank gave its full support to Britain for a number of reasons. Secretary of the Treasury Snyder, who was influential in the financing of the bank, favored a solution in Iran that would not disturb American oil companies, who identified their interest with AIOC's. When Black, the bank's president, sounded out the chairman of Standard Oil of New Jersey to see whether his company along with Texaco and Gulf would assist the bank in operating Iran's oil industry, the chairman's "tepid reaction" was that "the American oil companies did not want to be accused of trespassing on other people's preserves." Influence in Britain's favor was also exerted by a number of the bank's British officials, many of them formerly employed in the colonies or British foreign service, who were instrumental in its decision-making process. Among them was William Iliff, a former counselor at the British embassy in Tehran, who was the head of the bank's Loan Department. Iliff, who was next in rank to Vice President Garner and was regularly consulted on the oil issue, used to say that the bank was mainly financed with American money but was run by the British.[32] Finally, Britain's ambassador in Washington, Sir Oliver Franks, a former professor of moral philosophy who had developed a close friendship with Black, had a share in smoothing the way in favor of his country.[33] A small country like Iran could in no way match the British clout at the World Bank.

Under these circumstances Black and Garner both felt that it would be more propitious to back Britain than to be impartial. But their backing went too far. When the World Bank wanted to employ Rieber, an oil consultant, to work on its oil project in Iran, Black checked with Sir Roger Makins of the Foreign Office "whether this appointment was agreeable to the British side." Only when the British cleared the appointment was Rieber employed. Furthermore, the bank's plan was hardly any different from what Gass of AIOC had outlined. Although Mossadeq did not know about what was taking place secretly in London and Washington, he suspected. He told a Majlis deputy that the British "were pushing the World Bank" to get a "disguised concession" in favor of AIOC, but he would not give it to them.[34]

The British were concerned that the State Department might press the World Bank further to change its proposals. To avoid this, Paul Nitze was invited to London for a series of meetings at the Foreign Office. Nitze and U.S. Assistant Secretary of State Harold Linder were told that it would be advisable to keep the bank's proposals intact and that Mossadeq should not be led to think that if he rejected them, more attractive proposals would be forthcoming. The British contended that they had "seriously and positively . . . tried to find a satisfactory solution" to the oil problem, but had had no success with Mossadeq, whom they portrayed as hostile to the West and whose policies would lead to communism in Iran. In an effort to influence the bank's plan through Nitze and Linder, the British encouraged both to stay in London until Garner returned from Iran.[35]

Meanwhile in Tehran, Garner held a series of meetings with Mossadeq and his aides, telling them that the bank proposed to operate Iran's oil industry on behalf of both parties to the dispute. To do this it needed to have a free hand in employing managerial and technical staff of whatever nationality it chose, and it had to sell oil to AIOC at a high discount. When the Iranians raised their earlier questions on these issues and asked for clear written answers, Garner tried to answer them verbally. Black had advised him not to put his answers on paper lest such a document provide Mossadeq with grounds for accusing the bank of acting as an agent of the company.[36]

Mossadeq contended that since Iran's oil industry was nationalized, the bank should only represent Iranian interests. Furthermore, he wanted no British nationals to be employed, saying that the purpose of Iran's nationalization was to get rid of them. Garner did not accept either condition.[37] As to the sale proceeds of crude oil, Garner stated that the bank intended to give the bulk buyer a discount of 33⅓ percent on the Persian Gulf posted price of $1.75 per barrel and to keep 21⅛ percent in trust until the compensation question was settled. This left Iran, which would pay 30 cents for production and investment costs, with 50 cents per barrel or about 28.4 percent of the posted price. On refined products, the bank expected Iran to give the bulk buyer a discount of 45 percent on the Mexican Gulf price. The Iranians proposed to sell crude oil to the bulk buyer at a discount of 20 percent and refined products at a discount of 25 percent on the above price bases.[38] Garner lost no time in rejecting these proposals.

The fact was that the British, in cooperation with the oil cartel and the bank, wanted to punish Iran for having nationalized her oil so that no other country would follow Iran's lead. Garner was so eager to achieve Britain's aims that even George Middleton of the British Embassy in Tehran considered him to be "too rigid" with the Iranians, and U.S. ambassador Loy Henderson was also "critical of him for this reason." Henderson reported to the State Department that the Iranians were "not inflexible" and were anxious to get results; in Garner's words, "no one jumped out of the window" in response to his proposal.[39] When negotiations reached a deadlock, an Iranian Senate delegation headed by Ahmad Matin-Daftari tried to find a compromise. But the bank did not budge from its original stand.

The bank mission left Tehran for London on February 21, 1952, to meet with Eden. When informed that Eden was in Lisbon for a NATO meeting and would not be back until February 28, Garner said that he would wait.[40] Meanwhile the Foreign Office tried to impress upon Nitze that even an "impartial" institution like the World Bank could not reach a "reasonable" agreement with the "intractable" Mossadeq. Garner had two meetings with Eden, giving a full report of his mission and the difficulty of persuading the Americans to endorse his rigid approach. He promised, however, "to use all his influence to ensure that the State Department firmly supported Her Majesty's Government and gave the Persians no reason to hope that they could play off the Americans against the British."[41]

Garner and Prudhomme were lectured by the Foreign Office on

what was expected of them. Prudhomme was advised to return to Tehran and was given a memorandum on the British views to use as his "guideline." Since Mossadeq was against having the bank act on behalf of both parties, it was suggested to Prudhomme that different wording be used in the bank's agreements with the Iranians and the British. The Iranian agreement could say that the bank would be acting on Iran's account, the British agreement that it would be "acting on behalf of the British interests" concerned. As it happened, however, the bank's legal adviser considered it unacceptable to have two different texts telling each party that the bank acted on its behalf alone. On Iran's objection to British technicians, Prudhomme was advised by the Foreign Office to declare that the bank was against discrimination. To remove Iran's suspicion of the British, he was told that Britain was ready to offer a "Treaty of Friendship" with a clause "disclaiming any desire on the part of either signatory to interfere in the internal affairs or to undermine the economic and political independence of the other."[42] In other words, Britain wanted to say that she would stop such interference in Iran.

On his return to Tehran, Prudhomme had a number of meetings with Mossadeq and the Joint Oil Committee during which he presented the bank's old proposals along with the new British arguments. The Iranians, however, stood firm. A new element entered the discussions: Iran wanted the freedom to sell 30 percent of her total exports to customers other than the bulk purchaser at the same price offered to the latter. The bank did not favor such an arrangement, which would loosen AIOC's monopoly and bring Iran into the international market. Prudhomme cabled AIOC officials in London to inform them about Iran's position. AIOC replied that no agreement could be reached unless Iran accepted the employment of British staff and World Bank management for both sides.[43] But for the Iranians these two issues were not negotiable.

When the Shah pressed Mossadeq to find some sort of compromise, Mossadeq replied that none was possible: the only formula acceptable to the bank was to return AIOC to Iran under a new guise. If the Shah insisted on accepting the bank's proposals, Mossadeq said, a draft agreement with the bank could be submitted to the Majlis, but "he himself would resign before the matter came up for discussion."[44]

Meanwhile, certain developments heartened the British. Middleton reported to the Foreign Office that Iran was faced with financial crisis, and that in the Shah's opinion Mossadeq had "lost a great deal of prestige over the elections" because fewer National Front deputies than before were voted into the new Majlis. Moreover, the Shah had told Middleton that "he might, if necessary, have to make a change of Prime Ministers" and bring in "a strong Government [that] could control the next Majlis." Thus Middleton advised "taking a firm line" regarding the bank's negotiations with Mossadeq.[45]

The British received additional encouragement from Ali Soheili, Iran's ambassador in London, who hoped to replace Mossadeq as prime minister with British support. Soheili told Eden that Mossadeq's position had deteriorated and that "most Persians were sick and tired of the present situation." He then offered to help "in any way he could."[46] The British government, happy with these assessments of Mossadeq's position, showed more interest in expediting his removal than in reaching a compromise settlement of the oil dispute. And thus the World Bank's negotiations with Iran broke down.

The Iranian government believed, rightly, that Britain's stand on Persian oil had not changed one iota since nationalization, and that the British were determined to bring AIOC and the British staff back to Iran under the World Bank's umbrella. At a social gathering of the newly elected Majlis members, Mossadeq observed that the arrangement proposed by the World Bank, if executed, would have led Iran down the road to hell and would have deprived her of her national sovereignty.[47]

Britain at this point seemed to be in a strong position whether or not Mossadeq accepted the bank's conditions. If he accepted them, the bank would operate Iran's oil industry with British managerial and technical staff to produce and sell oil at a high discount to AIOC, which would also receive compensation. If he did not accept them, the British could rally world support for their cause by portraying him as a stubborn and intransigent character with whom even an "unbiased and impartial body" like the World Bank could not settle a dispute.[48]

14

Judgment at the World Court

With the collapse of the World Bank negotiations, both Britain and Iran anxiously awaited the judgment of the World Court. As we have seen, in May 1951, when the British government was making military preparations to occupy Abadan, it felt that it should first try instituting legal proceedings against Iran at the World Court, based on the right of diplomatic protection of a British company.

To counter Britain's contention that Iran's Nationalization Act violated the terms of the 1933 concession and was thus illegal, Mossadeq prepared a memorandum, with the help of a number of Iranian lawyers, arguing that the court could only deal with disputes concerning treaties and conventions between governments. He then commissioned two of the coauthors of the memorandum to take it to The Hague and explain Iran's position. But performing this mission was no easy task. Flights between Tehran and European capitals were infrequent, and there was no time to be lost. The two lawyers eventually found an old twin-engine plane that was flying to Paris for a complete overhaul and was not supposed to take passengers. Although the trip took over two days, with the flight from Paris to Amsterdam and the drive from there to The Hague, they arrived at the court in time. Furthermore, the trip generated rewarding publicity because a large number of press correspondents turned out to greet the representatives of a weak country that was ready to stand up against a strong power.[1]

The court proved unable, on such short notice, to decide whether it had jurisdiction in the case. Pending a decision one way or the other, it issued, on July 5, as we have seen, an interim ruling that Britain and Iran should avoid taking measures that might hinder industrial and commercial exploitation of Iranian oil.[2] In effect, this ruling meant that Iran should provisionally stop nationalization.

Foreign Secretary Herbert Morrison was delighted with the

court's ruling, but his euphoria did not last long. On July 9, the Iranian government, in a message to U.N. Secretary General Trygve Lie, stated that the World Court had no jurisdiction in the matter and that the British government, which "animated" the company, had no right to bring such a case to the court "as Iran has concluded no treaty with Britain in this regard." The message made it clear that under her 1932 Declaration Iran would recognize the court's jurisdiction if such a treaty existed, but denied its jurisdiction over contracts between Iran and foreign companies.[3] Britain's former Attorney General Sir Frank Soskice found Iran's position persuasive. As he had pointed out, "The [Oil] Concession Agreement is almost certainly not a treaty. . . . [Thus] it will be next to impossible to establish that jurisdiction exists."[4]

Nonetheless, Britain deposited a memorandum with the court arguing that it had jurisdiction in the case.[5] The court set hearings to begin June 9, 1952. Britain was alarmed when Mossadeq himself decided to present Iran's case at the court. To avoid a duplication of his performance at the U.N. Security Council, Britain decided to publicize her case through the BBC while "the British Government filled the press of Britain, America and Europe with justification of its case and distortions of its opponents."[6] One such distortion was that in an effort to portray the 1933 oil agreement between Iran and AIOC as an international commitment, the British in their publicity had referred to it as the "1933 Convention."

Aware of the weakness of its case, the British government chose some of Britain's foremost legal authorities for its delegation to The Hague. Sir Lionel Heald, the new U.K. attorney general, was assisted by Sir Eric Beckett, the Foreign Office legal adviser, and C. H. M. Waldock, professor of international law at Oxford University, and others from the English bar, the Foreign Office, and AIOC.

The Iranian delegation, headed by Mossadeq, included M. H. Aliabadi, professor of law at Tehran University, and three other legal experts: Ali Shayegan, Allahyar Saleh, and Mozaffar Baqa'i. Mossadeq himself had studied law. Adding weight to the delegation was Henri Rolin, professor of international law at Brussels University and formerly president of the Belgian Senate, and Marcel Sluszny of the Brussels bar, whom Mossadeq had employed for the occasion.

Sir Neville Butler, the British ambassador at The Hague, reported to Eden that Mossadeq's visit was arousing considerable interest. On June 9, 1952, when he arrived at the Peace Palace, where the court held its hearings, he was "assailed by the expected barrage of press photographers."[7] In addition, a large group of Iranians from around Europe, Dutch citizens, and foreign press correspondents had crowded the halls to see for themselves this man from Iran, rendered frail by years of political struggle and imprisonment, who had challenged almighty Britain.

The court's president was Sir Arnold McNair of Britain; but since he was a national of one of the parties to the dispute he transferred the presidency, as was the custom, to the vice president, eighty-year-old Jose Gustavo Guerrero of El Salvador. The attending judges were nationals of fourteen countries.[8]

When the hearings began, Mossadeq made a short speech on the moral and political background against which, he said, the legal issues should be considered. He stated that long years of political and economic oppression by a foreign power had inevitably culminated in the nationalization of the oil industry, there being no other way to free the Iranian people from tyranny and exploitation. He accused Britain of interfering in Iran's internal affairs and AIOC of treating Iranian employees "like animals" while manipulating Iranian governments in order to have a free hand in "plundering" Iran.[9]

Butler reported to Eden that "Dr. Musaddiq in his speech did not try only for dramatic effects. . . . [He] spoke in measured tones and with some dignity." Butler added that, in talking to foreign journalists and Dutch friends, he found that Mossadeq's "tactics have produced considerable effect" in his favor. After his opening appearance, Mossadeq kept to his hotel room and did not appear in the court again. It was left to Professor Rolin to present the legal arguments on behalf of Iran.[10]

The basic arguments that the British presented to the court were as follows. First, the Iranian government had accepted the compulsory jurisdiction of the court in all disputes relating to the application of conventions or treaties. Second, by nationalizing the oil industry, Iran had violated her obligations toward Britain under the treaties of 1857 and 1903, which had promised most-favored-nation treatment to British nationals in that country. Third, the

1933 oil concession "Convention" had been concluded through the mediation of the Council of the League of Nations, and Iran had violated the "treaty stipulation" arising out of the involvement of this world body. Finally, since according to international law the dispute did not fall exclusively within the jurisdiction of Iran, the court was the right institution to deal with it.

In a submission full of legal references to the court's statute, the charter of the United Nations, and various other international conventions, Rolin rejected the British claims of the court's jurisdiction. He reminded the court that Iran's Declaration of October 2, 1930, ratified on September 19, 1932, recognized its jurisdiction in any dispute concerning "the application of treaties or conventions accepted by Persia" with the exception of, among other things, "disputes with regard to questions which, by international law, fall exclusively within the jurisdiction of Persia"; and also that "Persia reserves the right to require that the proceedings in the Court shall be suspended in respect of any dispute which has been submitted to the Council of the League of Nations."

The mere fact that the League of Nations had put the oil dispute on its agenda, said Rolin, did not make the 1933 oil contract between Iran and a foreign company a treaty or convention; Britain, after all, was not a signatory of that contract, which she falsely called a "Convention." He added that, on the basis of the U.N. Charter and international law, Iran's oil nationalization laws and any disputes arising out of them fell within that country's domestic jurisdiction. He stressed that no government could deny itself the sovereign right of nationalization within its territory by signing a contract with a foreign national, and that all AIOC could legally claim was fair and adequate compensation for nationalization, which Iran, as a supporter of law and justice, had undertaken to pay. He pointed out that the British government had announced its acceptance of Iran's oil nationalization after its application to the court, as a result of which the application had lost its meaning. Rolin concluded that Iran had not violated any treaties or conventions, that British claims were inadmissible, and that the court should declare that it had no jurisdiction in the case.[11]

Rolin's defense ran on for three days, from June 9 to June 11. He was a man of great ability in international legal matters, one who had been consulted on other issues by his British counterparts. Beckett considered him "an able man and personally a very friendly one."[12]

For the next four days the court heard Heald and Beckett on behalf of the United Kingdom opposing Rolin's arguments. They contended that after the ratification of her 1930 Declaration Iran had signed treaties with Denmark, Switzerland, and Turkey that contained most-favored-nation clauses based on the Anglo-Persian Treaty of 1857 and the Commercial Convention of 1903; thus Britain should be treated the same as the former three. Moreover, they argued that since the mediation of the Council of the League of Nations had led to the signing of the 1933 oil agreement, the agreement had a "double character," being not only a concessionary contract between Iran and AIOC but also a treaty between the two governments. Thus, they claimed, it should be considered within the meaning of a treaty or convention.

The British also contended that since Iran had unequivocally undertaken not to cancel the 1933 oil "Convention" unilaterally, she was in no position to cancel it by an act of nationalization without the consent of the other party. As for Iran's claim that Britain had accepted Iran's oil nationalization, Beckett stated that this was ill-founded; the British government had accepted the claim in principle for negotiating purposes, but when negotiations failed, the acceptance was null and void. Iran's claim on this point, he said, "looks rather like the claim of a party who thinks that he has laid a trap and that his opponent has been caught in it." Finally, Beckett argued that the very fact that Iran had agreed to present her case to the court meant that she had conferred jurisdiction upon it on the basis of *forum prorogatum*.[13]

On June 23 the acting president closed the hearings, advising the disputants that the court would announce its decision in due course. By that time, however, both sides knew what the court's judgment would be. Beckett reported to the Foreign Office that with regard to "our prospects of success . . . I am the least optimistic of anybody . . . [though] our tactics were better than those of our opponents." He went on to say: "If we go down, I am convinced that it is because we had a weak case. . . . As a conscientious lawyer, I could not blame the Court if it decided against us. I shall simply hate to be the British judge sitting on the Bench at the present moment."[14]

Thirteen months earlier Sir Frank Soskice, then U.K. attorney general, had warned Morrison that "it is not of necessity an international wrong for a Government to break any contract with an individual of another country."[15] The British government, however, had felt that if it lobbied with member governments of the court, their judges would vote in its favor.

On June 23, before his departure to Tehran, Mossadeq gave a press conference in which he fully exploited the British seizure at Aden on June 18 of a tanker carrying Iranian oil. Since the incident had occurred at a time when the court was dealing with the dispute, he said, it was clear that Britain would rather perform "an arbitrary act" in her own interest than take the court seriously and wait for its judgment. He called the incident "a vivid example of the way Britain is endeavouring to strangle us." The British had first prompted the oil cartel to boycott Iranian oil and then resorted to the court, in both cases merely playing for time; they were awaiting the "fall of my Government" while "refusing to come to a fair and just settlement based on realities of the case." Reporting this press conference, Butler informed Eden: "I fear Dr. Musiddiq has managed to leave behind him in The Hague a generally favourable impression."[16]

A month later, on July 22, 1952, the court's ruling was issued. After a detailed analysis of the contentions of both sides, the court rejected the British arguments. Iran's submission to the compulsory jurisdiction of the court, it said, "is limited to the disputes relating to the application of treaties or conventions accepted by Iran after ratification of the Declaration" in 1932. Contrary to the British government's view that the involvement of the Council of the League of Nations in the 1932 dispute between Iran and the British company made the concession a treaty between Iran and Britain, the agreement "is nothing but a concessionary contract between a government and a foreign corporation, [and the] United Kingdom Government is not a party to the contract." The court did not agree with the British contention that Iran, by agreeing to present her case at The Hague, had conferred jurisdiction on the court on the principle of *forum prorogatum*. In a word, the court had "no jurisdiction to deal with the case" and the provisional measures indicated by its order of July 5, 1951, were accordingly no longer operative.[17]

Nine judges concurred with this finding and five dissented, the dissenters being from the United States, Canada, France, Chile, and

Brazil. One would have expected the British judge to be among the dissenters, but he was not. In the words of Sir Eric Beckett, "Sir Arnold McNair has made history by voting against us." Beckett, who had firmly argued the British case, went on to say, "if I had personally been a judge on that Court, my opinion would have been exactly the same as that of Sir Arnold McNair."[18]

15

British Attempts to Overthrow Mossadeq

Since the end of World War II, Mossadeq had led the forces of nationalism against foreign exploitation in Iran. The British, under the illusion of their past imperial power, had considered themselves immune from any challenge to their interests. When Mossadeq proved otherwise, they regarded him as a dangerous enemy. Their two main goals in Iran became to remove him from office and to reverse his nationalization of Iran's oil.

British efforts to remove Mossadeq from the political scene began well before he became prime minister because of his consistent opposition to the 1933 oil concession. In March 1951, as we have seen, British ambassador Sir Francis Shepherd schemed to get rid of Mossadeq and his supporters in the Majlis by urging the Shah to dissolve that body and install as prime minister Seyyed Zia or Ahmad Qavam, with either of whom—in the absence of a Parliament—he felt he could "strike a bargain" and settle the oil dispute in Britain's favor. But to dissolve the Majlis at a time when national feelings were highly roused against Britain would have made the Shah an obvious collaborator of a foreign power. Thus the Shah rejected Shepherd's proposal.[1]

Shepherd's next scheme was for Seyyed Zia, a politician with close contacts with the British, to be voted into the prime ministership. When Ala's Cabinet resigned in April 1951, the Shah, with Shepherd's prompting, told the Majlis speaker to ensure that Zia would get enough votes to form a government. But when the vote took place, Zia obtained only one vote and Mossadeq was elected prime minister with the votes of 79 of the 100 deputies present. In the Senate, too, despite emphatic instructions by the Shah and the fact that half of its members were nominated by him, Mossadeq's prime ministership was endorsed by the majority.[2]

The news shocked the Foreign Office. Geoffrey Furlonge, head of the Eastern Department, suggested to Foreign Secretary Morrison, that as "an essential first step" Mossadeq be given "a stern warning" against proceeding with oil nationalization.[3] Shepherd, who continued to believe that the choice of Iran's prime minister required British endorsement, told the Shah that "His Majesty's Government would not have confidence in Musaddiq." When the Shah proved unable to install the kind of prime minister Shepherd wanted, he reported to Morrison that "the Shah is no longer, or at least not for the moment, a force in politics."[4]

Disenchanted with the Shah, the Foreign Office sought to loosen Mossadeq's grip by strengthening the opposition in Iran. To this end Assistant Under Secretary Eric Berthoud consulted Ann Lambton, lecturer in Persian at the London School of Oriental Studies, who had previously served in the embassy in Tehran. Considered an expert on Iran who "knows the language and the mentality of its people better than anyone else in this country," Miss Lambton had little use for Mossadeq. She suggested that "covert means" should be used to undermine him and to give encouragement to "Persian friends we still have who are unlikely to show their faces and risk being called traitors without some support."

Miss Lambton proposed that Dr. Robin Zaehner, lecturer in Persian at Christchurch, Oxford University, who had been successful in covert propaganda in Iran during the war, be sent to Tehran to start a campaign against Mossadeq and try to influence the choice of a successor favorable to Britain. Her first choice for the job was Seyyed Zia; her second choice was Ahmad Qavam or Ali Soheili, Iran's ambassador in London. She later added Abbas Eskandari, a Tudeh party leader, who, she said, when given a good government job had left the communist party. She considered Eskandari "a complete opportunist but able. . . . He would do most things for money."[5]

Reviewing the list of candidates suggested by Miss Lambton, Furlonge had reservations about all four. He felt that although Seyyed Zia was Britain's best choice, his "chances seem problematic since he is regarded as very pro-British and we could hardly expect too quickly a swing of the pendulum in our favour." Qavam was old and ill. He added General Fazlollah Zahedi, Mossadeq's former interior minister, to the list, then ruled him out, saying that he was involved during the war with "pro-German intrigues," though adding that he "bears no malice" against the British for having imprisoned him then.[6]

Many officials at the Foreign Office believed that there was no nationalist movement in Iran, only a small band of extremists who had intimidated the Majlis into approving the oil nationalization bill. Shepherd, who was responsible for this mistaken view, believed that genuine nationalism in a backward country was possible only if that country had been a Western colony for some time and had had the experience of being developed by "a virile and civilised nation." Because Iran was not a Western colony, she had sunk to "Asiatic decadence" and was "now paying heavily for her immunity from tutelage."[7]

Shepherd's reports about the National Front were contradictory. In a report to Morrison in mid-March 1951, he conceded that the Front had been successful because its members were "free from the taint of having amassed wealth and influence through the improper use of official positions. . . . They can therefore attack the majority deputies [in the Majlis], few of whom are in the same happy position, without fear of dangerous counter attacks." He concluded that the National Front "have established themselves as the only active and legal party . . . [and] have shown considerable tenacity of purpose, [being] able to exploit the feeling of resentment against the Company among the educated and semi-educated."[8] But when Mossadeq and his National Front came to power, he reported to Morrison in July 1951 that the Front had "gained prominence as a result of the efforts of a few demagogues . . . with a talent for organisation of intimidation." He contended that the group as a whole was "obnoxious to the general body of politicians" in Iran and that Mossadeq did not have "the reasoned support of influential opinion," though he did enjoy public support.[9]

Putting these two reports together, one cannot fail to equate "the general body of politicians" who disliked the National Front with those who, because they had "amassed wealth and influence through the improper use of official positions," feared a noncorrupt "active and legal party" and opposed it. It is also clear that Shepherd relied on the opinion of such an opposition group.

In Dean Acheson's opinion Shepherd was an "unimaginative disciple of the 'whiff of grapeshot' school of diplomacy," a man whose "erroneous appraisal of the situation in Iran" had misled Morrison and all those in the Foreign Office who had to deal with Mossadeq.[10] To Shepherd, the nationalization of a British oil concession was an unforgivable act for which Mossadeq had to be crushed. He proposed that Britain threaten the Iranians with force and put them under economic pressure until they yielded. He had no notion of the Iranian mentality, which called for a soft, sympathetic approach to the solution of problems. Court Minister Hossein Ala considered him a cold, gray figure not suited to Iran, a country of poetry, emotion, and imagination.[11] Most Iranians who knew Shepherd found him smug and arrogant.

Shepherd's views, though distorted, "made a persuasive case . . . to those who took pride in the British Empire." More nostalgic than factual, his reports resembled those written by colonial administrators at the turn of the century stressing the power of the gun to tame the natives.[12] Acheson's view was exactly right.

While admitting that Mossadeq had great popularity, Shepherd attributed this to his "demagoguery." Furthermore, he dismissed Mossadeq's occasional faintings, which according to his physicians were due to his having been harshly treated in Reza Shah's jails, as "bogus." He called the prime minister a "lunatic" and referred to his aides as "thugs." Like Churchill, Mossadeq sometimes conducted the affairs of state from his bed; Shepherd mocked him for doing so. Once, when lectured by Shepherd for not being "reasonable," Mossadeq reacted with humor. He was having a blood transfusion for his anemia, he said, and the blood came from America. Did the ambassador think that "a little American blood would make him more reasonable?"[13]

Shepherd hated Mossadeq. Like a child who hates another and imputes to him all possible faults, he described Mossadeq in these words: "He is rather tall but has short bandy legs so that he shambles like a bear. . . . He looks rather like a cab horse and is slightly deaf so that he listens with a rather strained but otherwise expressionless look on his face. He conducts his conversation at a distance of about six inches at which he diffuses a slight reek of opium."[14]

George McGhee had quite a different impression:

> My recollections of Musaddiq come from liking him as a man . . . admiring his patriotism and courage in standing up for what he believed best for his country . . .
>
> . . . He was tall, gaunt, balding, with a long thin face and an oversized beak nose. His face was very highly mobile, the variety of poses giving him an almost comical aspect. And yet, underneath his lugubrious exterior there was evidence of a deep firmness, determination, and clarity of purpose.[15]

Mossadeq did not in fact smoke opium, as Shepherd tried to imply, but Robin Zaehner, the Oxford don sent to Tehran to dislodge him, was a longtime opium smoker. When he was appointed to the embassy staff in Tehran as a cover for his operations, he urged other embassy officials to join him in enjoying the pleasures of opium.[16]

A few weeks after Zaehner's arrival in Tehran, Christopher Woodhouse of the British Foreign Intelligence (MI6) joined him, and the two began their activities in cooperation with Geoffrey Wheeler and Lancelot Pyman of the embassy. Their job was to initiate a psychological war against Mossadeq and to encourage opposition leaders in the Majlis and the Senate to defy him by assuring them of British support.[17] Shepherd coordinated their activities while pressing the Shah for a change of government.

As we have seen, there were reasons for the British ambassador to feel that the Shah would be responsive to British pressure. His father had been forced into abdication by the British and the Russians in 1941, and he himself had been picked by them for the throne. He felt that if he tried to show independence he might suffer his father's fate.

Shepherd repeatedly urged the Shah to oust Mossadeq. But the Shah, though unhappy with Mossadeq for having reduced his status to that of a constitutional monarch, was unable to comply. As Sir William Strang of the Foreign Office put it, he was perhaps waiting to have "a manifest excuse for action without appearing to be pulling British chestnuts out of the fire."[18] In August 1951, when the Stokes mission failed to settle the oil dispute, Reginald Bowker, assistant under secretary of state at the Foreign Office, instructed Shepherd "to tell the Shah in firm language that he must dismiss Musaddiq." Shepherd did so, urging that the Shah replace Mossadeq with Seyyed Zia. The Shah replied that although he had encouraged Zia and Qavam to organize their parties, Zia, as a known anglophile, was not quite right for the job.[19]

Shepherd, who had an exaggerated view of his own importance, suggested that the Foreign Office summon him to London for consultation, while giving "a hint that I shall not return until there is a new Prime Minister." The Foreign Office, having no such illusions, replied that his withdrawal "might well prove ineffective with Musaddiq."[20]

Zaehner had served in Iran as British press attaché during 1943–47 and knew many Iranian politicians. He was soon in touch with various people whose vested interests were threatened by Mossadeq, old-guard politicians who thought that Iran should get along with Britain at any price, and opportunists who expected a reward from Britain if they opposed Mossadeq. There were also those who played a double game, among them Senator Reza Hekmat, known as Sardar Fakher, who gave Mossadeq superficial support while urging the British to have him assassinated.[21]

Pyman, finding Hekmat cooperative, asked him to tell "his friends in the Senate to interpellate the Government"[22] while encouraging Mossadeq's opponents to urge Taqizadeh, the president of the Senate, to cultivate an opposition group. Taqizadeh refused and told Shepherd that a foreign ambassador had no right to ask the Shah to change his government. The Shah, for his part, was confused. Although Shepherd had repeatedly asked him to replace Mossadeq, he privately assured his courtiers that the British were in collusion with Mossadeq and wanted to keep him in office. He did not see how the prime minister could have remained in power without British support.[23]

Meanwhile, some opportunists came up with plans for overthrowing Mossadeq. Ali Shafia, an Iranian timber merchant, told the Foreign Office that if he was provided with a sizable amount of money he could remove the prime minister by influencing Majlis deputies and Senators and by instigating the tribes against the government (see Chapter 16). Horace Emery, a businessman with wide experience in Iran, suggested a similar scheme; "with the support of the Shah and the distribution of a certain amount of money," a sufficiently powerful opposition could be built to oust Mossadeq.[24]

Haig Galustian, an Armenian merchant then stationed in Iran, added a new dimension. On a visit to London he told Donald Logan of the Foreign Office that the extremists in the National Front should be separated from Mossadeq to reduce his power base. He suggested that he could possibly buy out Hossein Makki and Mozaffar Baqa'i, two vociferous National Front figures, for about £100,000 each. Logan was impressed by the offer, since this merchant, he said, had previously been "very successful in 'buying' [Iranian] officials able to influence the award of contracts in favour of British firms."

Galustian's suggestion, though not considered by the Foreign Office at the time, was reserved for later use if all else failed. There would be no difficulty in financing any of these schemes, it was felt, since AIOC had withheld millions of pounds of royalties due to Iran.[25]

There was at least one other scheme. An Austrian economist approached Bernard Burrows of the British embassy in Washington saying that he represented Prince Salar-ed Dowleh Qajar, who claimed to be the head of the former reigning dynasty in Iran. He said that if Britain assisted the prince in gaining possession of the throne, he would settle the oil dispute in Britain's favor.[26] The scheme looked too problematic and uncertain to succeed.

It seemed more practical to put pressure on the Shah to replace the government than to replace the Shah himself. When Mossadeq announced his decision to expel AIOC's British staff, Shepherd was instructed to tell the Shah that "we were anxious to do anything possible which would assist him in getting rid of Musaddiq." Shepherd met the Shah and "devoted some time on debunking Musaddiq's popularity and the alleged dangers of a change in Government." But the Shah told him that according to the Majlis speaker there were not yet enough votes to remove the prime minister.[27]

George Middleton, the embassy official second in rank after Shepherd, felt as Shepherd did that Britain ultimately called the shots. Middleton believed it should be made "perfectly clear" to Iranian politicians that "we are not prepared to do business with Musaddiq's Government." As long as "we stick to this simple issue, the opposition is encouraged to continue its efforts to bring about a change of Government."[28]

Lord Stokes, who in the course of his abortive mission to Tehran had advised the Shah to get rid of Mossadeq and "jail all agitators," now had second thoughts. He believed that Mossadeq had "tremendous influence in the country and the more we go for him the stronger he gets." He felt that Britain should compromise with him. "It would be stupid for the Ambassador to press a change of Government"; as for saying "we can't negotiate with Musaddiq," this is nothing more than "a silly slogan."[29]

Elwell-Sutton, who had earlier served at the British embassy in Tehran as press attaché, offered this appraisal to the Foreign Office:

> At the moment our policy . . . is aimed at bringing down Mosaddeq's Government by a combination of economic sanctions, international pressure, intimidation and propaganda. It is questionable whether it will work. . . . All the evidence shows that Mosaddeq's uncompromising line is welcomed in Persia, and that the only opposition comes from those who think he is not moving fast enough. Mosaddeq's Government and the National Front group in the Majlis are more representative of Persian public opinion than any other political grouping. . . . There can be no disputing the fact that this [oil nationalization] was done by constitutional methods.[30]

Even within AIOC there were a few who reasoned that the problem was not with Mossadeq but with the company's way of doing business in Iran. Sir Frederick Leggett, AIOC's labor adviser, urged his country to give "greater recognition to Persian national dignity." It was time for the Foreign Office, he said, "to give the Persians a better status than that of a Concession." At the Foreign Office itself, L. A. C. Fry and some other members of the Eastern Department were of the same opinion.[31]

Prime Minister Clement Attlee thought along the same lines. At a Cabinet meeting on July 12, 1951, he said:

> Dr. Musaddiq had been able to form his Government owing to the support of Persians who were dissatisfied with former rule by a corrupt clique. We could not safely assume that if we succeeded in upsetting the present Government their successors would be less unsatisfactory, and we should risk identifying ourselves with support of an equally undemocratic regime. . . .

We must not alienate genuine nationalist feelings in Persia by clinging to the old technique of obtaining concessions.[32]

As we have seen, this view was opposed by Foreign Secretary Herbert Morrison, who viewed Mossadeq as a serious danger to British interests in the Middle East and elsewhere. Supported by the Ministers of Defence, the Treasury, and Fuel and Power, Morrison won the day and pressed on with efforts to remove Mossadeq while urging the United States to join in.

Obtaining U.S. support proved difficult. Henry Grady, the U.S. ambassador in Tehran, admired the prime minister and believed that "Mossadeq's National Front party is the closest thing to a moderate and stable element in the national parliament."[33] Grady compared the national movement in Iran to the anticolonial movement in India, which had led to that country's independence, and warned that if the movement in Iran was not supported the United States would be discredited and the communists strengthened. Public opinion in the United States was with Grady. The British embassy in Washington warned the Foreign Office of "the natural 'anti-imperialism' of the Americans and the almost universal criticism of the past policy" of AIOC; though U.S. oil companies gave AIOC effective assistance, the State Department was not prepared to help Britain.[34]

Shepherd was instructed to develop friendly relations with the American embassy staff in Tehran, but he did not consider the effort worthwhile. The Americans, he wrote, "are certainly ambitious of increasing American influence in this country and regard us as their chief rival." Citing as an example Averell Harriman, who considered Mossadeq a great popular hero, Shepherd decried the American "suspicion of the colonialist and imperialist attributes of British policy in all parts of the East," and contended that with this mentality the Americans "are quite prepared to sacrifice [AIOC]."[35] Shepherd disliked and distrusted Grady, whom he considered "a vain man . . . desperately anxious to be the saviour of Persia in the same way he believes himself to have been the saviour of Greece and . . . India." As to Grady's staff, Shepherd considered them "rather mediocre" and "individually anti-British."[36]

Undeterred, Morrison instructed Ambassador Franks in Washington to get the State Department's support for a joint approach to the Shah either to dissolve the Majlis and rule by the army or to oust Mossadeq. Assistant Secretary of State George McGhee opposed both courses. Not only was the Shah not strong enough to dissolve the Majlis, but for the Shah to dismiss Mossadeq would be "to set himself against his Government, the Iranian Parliament, and the Iranian public opinion." McGhee complained that the British government "had never taken United States advice—or, if they had, had taken too little too late"—and that they were now committed to an impossible cause.[37] U.S. Under Secretary of State Freeman Matthews supported McGhee, pointing out that national feelings in Iran were widespread and could not be bridled by the removal of Mossadeq.[38]

In September 1951 a paper handed to Franks by the State Department maintained that it was impossible for the Shah to install a new government until there was a change in Iran's political atmosphere. If Mossadeq's government was changed prematurely, the paper said, "there is great danger that the Shah himself would be overthrown in which case the last element in Iran which the Western World can rely on would be lost."[39] Franks's efforts to sway Acheson and Harriman also failed.[40]

Shepherd argued against consulting the Americans at every step. It would be a "blow to our prestige," he told the Foreign Office, "if we indicated our subservience to the Americans" in the matter of the oil dispute and were perceived as being completely "under the American thumb." The Foreign Office disagreed; in any move to oust Mossadeq, it replied, "it is essential that the Americans act with us."[41] When it became clear that the Truman administration could not be persuaded to help overthrow a popular noncommunist government for the sake of Britain, the Foreign Office came up with a scheme for ruining Mossadeq's popularity in Iran. Assistant Under Secretary Eric Berthoud suggested an all-out effort by the BBC Persian program to convince the Iranians that their misery was due to "their corrupt and inefficient administration" and that the "first requisite for a satisfactory settlement [of the oil dispute] is therefore a proper Persian Government."[42]

As to the upheaval that might follow the overthrow of a popular government at the instigation of a foreign power, Berthoud was not worried: "if there is a breakdown of the Persian Administration and Russian intervention in the North [of Iran], we can if need be set up a British sphere of influence in the South on the lines of past history."[43] Britain did not mind if Iran lost her sovereignty or disintegrated, as long as the country's oil fields and the area along the Persian Gulf remained under British sway.

Shepherd, too, urged the use of the BBC. The opposition in Iran, he wrote, felt that "the chances of Musaddiq being thrown out in the near future" would be strengthened by a BBC statement that there was no hope of reaching a "reasonable" settlement with the present government.[44] Shepherd not only provided the Foreign Office with the line of attack to be adopted, but sent directives to the BBC. Because of Mossadeq's popularity, he should not be attacked personally for the time being. Instead, said Shepherd, the Iranians should be told that their government's nationalization policy would alienate Britain, without whose support Iran would relapse into anarchy and communism, and that the company's offers to Iran had been very generous.[45]

Furlonge informed Shepherd that "we meet the organisers of the Persian Service of the B.B.C. every fortnight when we attempt to indicate the line which that Service might follow." He added that the BBC "were very glad to have an indication from you of what was likely to be most effective and will arrange their programme accordingly." He went on to say that the Persian Service broadcast would portray the present Iranian government as "stupid and obstinate" while playing on the "Persian fear of Russia . . . possibly encouraging speculation as to where Russia may strike next" after a cease-fire in Korea. He added, "We shall . . . avoid direct attacks on the 'ruling classes' since it seems probable that we may want to deal with a government drawn from those classes should Musaddiq fall."[46] Shepherd, encouraged by the Foreign Office, continued to provide guidelines as well as material for the BBC.

Middleton suggested two contradictory alternatives for the BBC campaign. One possibility, because Mossadeq was genuinely popular and was moderate compared to those around him, was to assail "sinister elements" who prevented Mossadeq from settling the dispute. The other was to discredit Mossadeq by the "suggestion that he had done a private deal with us."[47]

Geoffrey Wheeler of the embassy staff in Tehran, who had done effective publicity work for AIOC some years earlier, had another idea. While in London he suggested, with Assistant Under Secretary Bowker's blessing, that he and Ann Lambton furnish the BBC Persian Service with "letters purporting to come from British residents in Persia," containing ideas that the Foreign Office wished to propagate. But the suggestion was rejected by the BBC, which felt that Iranian listeners might find such letters suspicious and discover the truth.[48]

When Mossadeq announced on September 6, 1951, in the Senate that AIOC's British staff would be expelled, Shepherd not only prepared the text of the BBC's statement on the expulsion but also dictated its timing. He cabled the Foreign Office on the day of Mossadeq's announcement to urge that the prime minister's Senate speech be "immediately countered by a brief and forth-right official statement . . . quoted in full in B.B.C. Persian Service this evening and repeated in to-morrow's transmissions." The BBC obliged by broadcasting Shepherd's text, which said that further negotiations with the present government could not produce results.[49]

As Mossadeq's pressure on AIOC grew, the British dropped their inhibitions against direct attacks on him and prompted the opposition press in Iran to mount a fierce campaign against him. *Tolu*, a Tehran daily, wrote that Mossadeq had no plans for the settlement of the oil dispute, that his government was doomed to failure, and that he should resign. *Dad*, another daily, wrote: "It is indeed unfortunate that the country is placed in the hands of a sick man subject to emotional excitement and that we allow him to play with the nation's destiny."[50]

Other newspapers supported the government. *Shahed* contended that some members of the press as well as certain groups in the Majlis and the Senate were acting as British proxies. It called on Mossadeq to purge "imperialistic agents" to expedite "the death of British imperialism" in Iran. The independent *Keyhan* accused Britain of fomenting opposition to Mossadeq's government on the pretext that under Mossadeq Iran was doomed to be the victim of communism. "If Britain really wished to forestall communist threat," said the paper, "she should fight people's poverty and not the people themselves."[51]

Meanwhile Ambassador Franks and his men, along with American-owned international oil companies, achieved some success in reversing the pro-Mossadeq tendency in the American press. The *Washington Post* and the *Christian Science Monitor* both said, in effect, that Mossadeq's asking price for Iranian oil was out of line, thus putting Iran at odds with the world oil leasing and marketing system. Of Mossadeq's request for American aid, the *New York Times* asked, "Is it really conceivable that the United States should reward Iran for breaking her oil contract? . . . Who is our greatest ally in the defense of the West, Britain or Iran?" *Life* magazine said that to maintain order in the Middle East "our best allies are Kings and 'strong men.' . . . We must also align our policies with those fading and hated colonial powers, Britain and France, especially when basic order is at stake." In the *New York Herald Tribune*, Joseph Alsop talked of the "feebleness and folly" of people like George McGhee, "who take out honorary citizenships in the regions of their specialties" and enter a sort of "Middle East popularity contest."[52]

In a further effort to muddy American relations with Mossadeq's government, AIOC directed the opposition press in Iran to attack the United States. Mossadeq, who was very sensitive to American opinion, told the *U.S. News and World Report* that "a large part of such attacks on America are provoked by foreign elements, and it must be said openly that the former oil company [AIOC] has a great share in these provocations."[53]

The BBC and press propaganda, along with the activities of Zaehner and Woodhouse in organizing an opposition, had their impact. In the Majlis a group of fourteen deputies, headed by Jamal Emami, began attacking Mossadeq for his failure to settle the oil dispute. On September 6, 1951, when the Majlis assembled for a speech by the prime minister, too few members were present to constitute a quorum.

When the Majlis reconvened on September 9 under public pressure, Mossadeq said the British government, intent on protecting the interests of AIOC, had employed agents everywhere—in the Majlis and the Senate, in the government and the royal court, in the community and society at large. He went on to attack also those Iranians who took their lead from the left, meaning Russia; Iran's destiny, he said, should be determined by the will of the nation and not by the whim of foreign powers. He then read parts of some broadcasts of the BBC's Persian Service, which he described as a propaganda machine used by Britain for exercising her influence abroad. Clearly, he concluded, the British government planned to install a government in Iran that would accept the type of oil agreement Britain wanted, but he would fight on.

Reporting the prime minister's speech to the Foreign Office, the ineffable Shepherd complained of Mossadeq's "disbelief in the honesty of purpose of the British Government." Clearly "agreements between Governments must rest on the basis of mutual confidence and Dr. Musaddiq has now made it clear that this confidence does not exist."[54] Astonishingly enough, Shepherd viewed Britain's effort to overthrow Iran's elected government and replace it with her own men as acceptable practice within the norms of international conduct. He could not see why Iranians should doubt Britain's "honesty of purpose."

Mossadeq's speech, which was a reaction to the British covert operations, strengthened his government at the expense of the opposition, which could not come out in favor of Britain. As the *New York Times* wrote:

> The clever old politician has successfully contrived to get himself recognized by the countless little people—shopkeepers, artisans, frustrated literates, and even parts of the inarticulate multitude—as their champion against foreign "imperialists" and their domestic hirelings among the landed gentry and the venal bureaucracy. Dr. Mossadeq is the repository of obscure hopes and aspirations. He is the protection against the plunderers of every stripe. . . . Therefore let the Old Guard beware.[55]

The British Labour Government's last important meeting on the question of overthrowing Mossadeq took place on October 23, 1951. At this meeting, the Treasury's Permanent Secretary, Sir Edward Bridges, urged the removal as well of another principal in the dispute, Sir William Fraser, AIOC's chairman, whose narrow-mindedness and lack of political insight had in Bridges's judgment led to the Iranian oil crisis. Sir Leslie Rowan of the Treasury raised the central question: in case Britain was determined not to negotiate with Mossadeq, "were we ready to take steps to engineer his downfall?"[56] Two days later Attlee's Labour government narrowly lost the elections. The Conservatives, led by Churchill, took over the government and with it the task of engineering Mossadeq's downfall.

Months before, Churchill's Foreign Secretary, Anthony Eden, had suggested that Britain and the United States "make a joint approach to the Shah . . . trying to bring about a *coup d'etat* in Persia."[57] On taking office, Eden received a letter from Sir Frederick Leggett, AIOC's labor adviser, advising him that the way to undermine Mossadeq was to show open sympathy with those in Iran who wanted reforms, who were sick of seeing Britain support corrupt governments in power, and who asked, "Where is Britain's will to defend moral principles?" Leggett's views were rejected out of hand.[58]

Five days after taking office, Eden arranged a high-level meeting on the Iranian oil crisis. At this meeting Rowan maintained that Mossadeq was playing the Americans against the British, believing that "Americans would in the last resort never allow the Persian economy to be shattered." Shepherd, who had come to London to advise the new government, remained certain that the movement led by Mossadeq "is not based on any genuine national sentiment," and that the inherent political forces at work in Iran would bring about his downfall, leading to AIOC's return to that country. Eden did not agree, saying that AIOC could not return to Iran in any form "except by the use of force."[59]

Ann Lambton advised patience: "if only we keep steady nerves Dr. Musaddiq will fall" and AIOC could return to Iran. In her opinion Mossadeq and his supporters lacked the "stature to maintain so strong a stand without outside support." She suspected that Kashani had received "large sums of money from somewhere," probably not from the Russians but possibly from "an American source, not of course, State Department, but perhaps the U.S. brand of S.O.E. [Special Operations Executive] who may for some time have been supporting Dr. Musaddiq and Mr. Kashani as their answer to Communism." (There is no evidence for this view.) Lambton rejected the American assessment of Mossadeq's strength, saying that the Americans "have not the experience or the psychological insight" of the British in matters concerning Iran.[60]

Britain's sources of information on Iran, as the Foreign Office records show, were primarily politicians in and out of the country who were more interested in promoting their personal interests than in giving impartial advice. Seyyed Zia, who with British backing became prime minister in 1921, wanted their renewed support for an attempt on his part to occupy that position again. Assadollah Alam, a landed aristocrat and a confidant of the Shah, saw the fulfillment of his ambitions in collaborating with the British. He willingly agreed to contact some Majlis deputies on behalf of Shepherd and encourage them to oppose Mossadeq. Furthermore he acted as liaison between Shepherd and the Shah to coordinate their efforts to bring about Mossadeq's downfall.

The main British contacts in the Majlis, according to Foreign Office documents, were E'ezaz Nikpey, Hadi Taheri, and Manuchehr Teymurtash, all of whom believed that Iran could accomplish nothing against the wishes of the British.[61] In the bazaar were the Rashidian brothers, who felt that their business interests would best be served by helping the British.

Outside Iran, the British drew on the advice of old guard politicians. Ali Mansur, who in 1950 lost the prime ministership and became Iran's ambassador to Rome, longed to be prime minister again, to which end he sought to strengthen his ties with Britain. To please his British counterpart in Rome, he told him that "Mossadegh was a lunatic and a disaster."[62] In London Iran's ambassador Ali Soheili had similar ambitions and a similar strategy. When his press secretary, A. Hamzavi, was obliged to deliver an Iranian government note that was critical of AIOC, he told Geoffrey Furlonge of the Foreign Office that he and his ambassador were "embarrassed" to deliver such a communication. Furthermore, he offered Furlonge advice designed to further British policy in Iran: the British, he said, must make it clear to the Iranian government that the United States was solidly behind them.[63] Soheili himself, as we have seen, offered Eden his personal assistance.

A. H. Ebtehaj, then Iran's ambassador in Paris, was not a member of the old guard but was critical of Mossadeq owing to clashes between the two when Ebtehaj was heading Iran's national bank.[64] According to Sir Oliver Harvey, the British ambassador in Paris, Ebtehaj believed that the oil crisis could not be settled unless Mosaddeq resigned and that the British should hold out at Abadan.[65]

To promote their aims, the British cultivated relations with Iranians critical of their government, but they stopped short of sounding out a true cross section of the society. As Elwell-Sutton put it: "Britain's greatest failure in her dealings with foreign peoples has been the inability of her diplomats . . . to 'get inside' the people with whom they have to deal. They have been content to remain ensconced behind their embassy compound walls. . . . Of the people of the country, of their hopes, fears and aspirations, even of the way they live, they know and care nothing."[66]

Meanwhile, the British government intensified its efforts to convince the Americans that Mossadeq's remaining in power would harm Western interests and that the United States should refrain from giving him any political or economic support. Roderick Sarell of the Foreign Office suggested that the following argument might be used to allay U.S. concern about the danger of a communist takeover if Iran's economy collapsed: "A primitive agricultural community such as Persia where 80% of the population are estimated to live off the land at bare subsistence level does not 'collapse' economically. It sags, and no doubt more of the population will die of starvation than usual. We do not believe in the imminence of the catastrophic phenomenon forecast by the State Department."[67] In other words, Sarell did not mind if more people "than usual" died of starvation to achieve British aims, and he considered it quite proper to make this view of his known to the Americans.

Not only did the State Department oppose subjecting Iran to financial starvation for the sake of overthrowing Mossadeq, but it believed that Mossadeq's government should be kept afloat. With British and American purposes at odds, the Foreign Office invited Paul Nitze, director of Policy Planning at the State Department, to London in February 1952 to try to convert him to their views. As we have seen, this effort was not at first successful. Nitze maintained that Mossadeq was basically anticommunist and eager to fight corruption and institute reforms along Western lines. He added that "the result of the last two years' events in Persia had been to change the character of the political scene," culminating in a "new political consciousness [that] went along with Dr. Musaddiq's programme."[68]

Since the views of the two sides were far apart, it was decided to consult British and American embassies in Tehran, asking them to reply to specific questions such as "If Mossadeq fell from office, what sort of person would succeed him?" Another important question was: "What is the present loyalty of the Army to the Shah and what are the chances of the Army being able to stage a successful coup if called upon by the Shah? In such an event where would the political leadership . . . come from, and of what type and how effective would the opposition be?"[69]

Despite the serious differences in the two sides' views, the very fact that the Americans were prepared to put these particular questions to Loy Henderson, their ambassador in Tehran, proved that the British had succeeded to some extent in bringing them around to their way of thinking. This development helped pave the way for the coup against Mossadeq in August 1953.

Two days after receiving these questions, George Middleton of the British embassy sent his answers. If Mossadeq could not find a solution to Iran's financial problems, he wrote, "particularly in view of the unhelpful attitude at present displayed by the Iron Curtain countries," and if he found the Shah and the army against him, he would resign, stating that he could not carry on "in the face of the interference from Court and Army," but he would not abandon "his role as leading protagonist of Persian nationalism." His replacement would be one in whom the Shah has confidence, but such a person would not last long. The Tudeh party could not take over unless there was financial chaos and the army did not get paid. The army was loyal to the Shah and did not like to be subordinate to the political aims of the National Front. "We do not believe [however] that . . . the Shah is likely to call upon the Army to carry out a coup nor do we believe that just now there are in sight any political leaders for such a coup."[70] Henderson sent almost identical answers to Nitze.

Middleton's reply did not describe Mossadeq as expendable, as he had earlier, because the Foreign Office had instructed him to concert his reply with his colleague. The new British strategy was to change U.S. views cautiously step by step. Donald Logan of the Foreign Office, who was sent to Washington to convert the State Department to the British cause, had directed the Foreign Office that "cold water should not be turned too soon on Nitze and his ideas."[71]

The British ministers did their utmost to persuade Nitze that Britain wanted to help the third world, that the two countries were in the same boat regarding the rise of nationalism, and that Britain was undertaking studies "to turn it to good ends or to mitigate its adverse impact upon our interests." Thus they impressed upon him that the two governments must present a common front to the Persians. These talks, characterized by a show of flexibility and an appeal to enlightened self-interest, had their impact. The Foreign Office informed Franks that "Nitze is now more sympathetic with us."[72] But this did mean that the United States was ready to cooperate with them on the removal of Iran's prime minister.

For one whole year the British made every effort to overthrow Mossadeq's government without success. Moreover, they had not found a candidate for prime ministership with the ability to tame the rising tide of anti-British sentiments in Iran. If they were to have any chance of persuading the Americans, the Shah, and the opposition to remove Mossadeq, they had to find such a person first.

16

Qavam's Prime Ministership and the Communist Threat

In June 1951, just two months after Mossadeq took over as prime minister, an Iranian timber merchant named Ali Shafia told George Rodgers, chairman of London Group of Labour members of Parliament, that Ahmad Qavam-ul-Saltaneh would be a much better successor to Mossadeq than Zia, whom the British were promoting. Shafia claimed that in order to pave the way for the eighty-year-old Qavam, he was in a position to destabilize the situation by influencing twenty Majlis deputies and fifteen senators to oppose Mossadeq and by encouraging Arab tribes in southern Iran to demand secession. All this, he said, required money on the order of £1 million.[1]

When word of Shafia's scheme reached Churchill, then the leader of the opposition party, he arranged for three Conservative members of Parliament with an intelligence background to meet with Reginald Bowker, under secretary at the Foreign Office in charge of the Middle East, to see if the matter was worth following up. At this meeting Qavam was ruled out because, as Alan Rothnie of the Foreign Office put it, "we have put our money on another horse"— Seyyed Zia.[2]

When Churchill took over the government in October 1951, Shafia praised him for "his knowledge and savoir-faire" in foreign affairs and tried again to promote Qavam as the only person capable of toppling Mossadeq. This time, however, he asked for £2 million, for "distribution among Persians in and outside the Majlis, and among 'tribesmen' . . . who would produce the necessary popular demonstrations in Qavam's favour." He reasoned that such an amount was small compared to what Britain would gain in oil if she recovered her position. The British government was skeptical, believing that Qavam did not have a considerable following in Iran and that Shafia was an opportunist who hoped to convert his close relationship with Qavam into financial gain.[3]

In Tehran, however, Dr. Robin Zaehner, whose appointed task was to unseat Mossadeq, thought that Qavam was the right man. He was impressed by Qavam's friend Abbas Eskandari, who had told him that Qavam wanted "to preserve [Britain's] legitimate interests in Persia without jeopardising Persia's political and economic independence." Eskandari had added that Qavam "greatly preferred that British influence should be exercised in Persia, rather than that of the Americans (who were foolish and without experience), or of the Russians who were Persia's enemies."[4] These arguments did not convince Under Secretary Bowker that Qavam should be supported.

In November 1951, Qavam gave up using intermediaries and wrote directly to Middleton: "I am prepared to accept office at this critical moment . . . in the conviction that I will be sincerely assisted by His Majesty's Government in laying the foundations of . . . real friendship between the British people and the people of Persia who today call me to office."[5] Meanwhile, *Khabar*, a Tehran daily financed by Qavam, began attacking Mossadeq as unfit to be prime minister. The paper said that "Qavam would not refuse to serve if called upon by the nation."[6]

Although Donald Logan of the Foreign Office wondered why Qavam assumed that the Iranians would call him to office, he felt that Qavam's coming to power would be to Britain's benefit.[7] After much deliberation, the Foreign Office advised Middleton to tell Qavam that "if he were to become Prime Minister he would have the encouragement of H.M. Government in reaching a satisfactory solution [on oil]." In late December 1951, the embassy passed this message to Qavam, who mysteriously replied that there was nothing he wished to discuss and soon afterward left for Europe. Qavam's words confused the Foreign Office, which concluded that he might be reluctant to discuss matters of critical importance with officials at the embassy level.

However, Middleton noted that if Qavam, "a master of the double-cross," was supported by Britain in coming to power, "he would do his best to seek a settlement with us."[8]

Nothing was heard from Qavam until February 7, 1952, when he sent a message from Monte Carlo to Julian Amery, a Conservative member of Parliament, saying that he would like Amery to meet with him there. Amery informed Eden about this message and asked what he should do. After two weeks' hesitation and consultation with Ann Lambton, Amery was told to go to Monte Carlo and see what Qavam had in mind, but without giving him the impression that he was acting on behalf of the British government.[9]

The reason for giving Amery the go-ahead was that a week earlier Kenneth de Courcy had met Qavam in the south of France and had been impressed by him. A Conservative figure who had an intelligence background and was the publisher of the *Intelligence Digest* and other journals, de Courcy reported to Anthony Nutting, Parliamentary Secretary at the Foreign Office, that Qavam was fully convinced "he could easily take power into his hands" but would need British support to remain in office. Since Qavam wanted the assurances of the Foreign Secretary, it would be essential for Eden himself to meet him in Paris; otherwise "we shall lose our best chance of a favourable solution." He noted that Qavam had made it clear that on taking office he would be at first obliged to appear anti-British, but that Britain should understand the situation and "abide by a secret agreement with him," awaiting results.[10]

Qavam wanted to make sure that once he took power the British would not be "selling him down the river by some sort of compromise with Russia," by which he meant a scheme that would allocate the oil in southern Iran to Britain and any oil in the north to Russia. De Courcy stressed that Qavam should be supported for the prime ministership, but warned that "if we supported him but failed to see him through, I would not put it past him to make terms with Russia himself." He added, however: "By interest and inclination Qavam is anti-Russian and pro-British."[11]

Following de Courcy's visit, Amery went to see Qavam, who was then in Paris. The two met over dinner in a private room in Qavam's hotel with Prince Hamid Qajar, pretender to Iran's throne (alias Captain David Drummond, a British subject). When Amery assured Qavam that the British would "regard his return to power as a change for the better," he replied that as prime minister he could settle the oil dispute within the terms of Iran's nationalization law by providing the British with a settlement that would not prejudice their oil agreements elsewhere.[12]

Qavam told Amery that he did not trust the Shah and had in the past "suffered from his intrigues." He considered it necessary to remove the Shah and install his guest, Prince Hamid, on the throne. This came as a great surprise to Hamid, to whom Qavam had not previously mentioned this idea. When Qavam asked Amery what the British reaction would be to such a proposal, Amery replied that "we had been rather disappointed by the present Shah and that it would be a matter of complete indifference to us whether he stayed or went."

When the prince left them alone, Qavam contended that Hamid was much preferable to the present Shah because of his English education and his connections in London. Amery's impression was that Qavam wanted "a Shah who would be dependent upon him . . . and who might provide a useful link with London."[13] It is interesting to note that ten years earlier, in September 1941, Julian Amery's father, Leopold, and Anthony Eden were involved in a scheme to put the very same prince or his father on Iran's throne following the forced abdication of Reza Shah (see Chapter 2).

Eden was not sure that Qavam could be easily handled once he came to power. He asked the views of Archibald Ross, head of the Eastern Department, who responded: "He [Qavam] is by far the cleverest of the Persian politicians and his methods are anything but straight. . . . However just because of his cleverness he may be the man to negotiate an oil settlement on terms which are satisfactory to us and which give the Persians at least the outward appearance of satisfying their national aspirations."

On the other hand, Ross saw no virtue in Qavam's strained relations with the Shah and his plan to replace him with a prince from a preceding dynasty. He doubted whether the present "Shah has ceased to be a helpful factor so far as the British interests are concerned," and in any event felt sure that any attempt to replace him would "immeasurably" complicate an already difficult situation. It would be "the height of folly," he said, to give Qavam the impression that he had British support for his scheme "to set up a puppet King," and he suggested that Qavam should instead be advised to improve his relations with the Shah.[14] Eden was persuaded by

Ross's argument that Amery was wrong in not opposing the return of the Qajars to the throne. He noted that the "Amerys of this world can be dangerous, though they are well intentioned busybodies."[15]

Qavam returned to Tehran in mid-April 1952 and began to cultivate the support of Mossadeq's opponents. Among them was the Queen Mother, Tajol Moluk, who provided funds for Qavam's campaign without knowing that the old politician was scheming to dethrone her son. Meanwhile, Bowker at the Foreign Office informed Middleton in Tehran of Amery's discussion with Qavam and advised him to tell Qavam that he should "do his best to support the Shah."[16] When Qavam proved reluctant to do so, the British became more hesitant about offering him their support. The only other candidate at the time was Javad Bushehri, Mossadeq's Minister of Roads, who had secretly informed U.S. ambassador Loy Henderson of his readiness to take over the government, promising to exhibit flexibility over the settlement of the oil issue. No one considered Bushehri a serious candidate for prime minister.[17]

Sam Falle, who under the cover of his title as Oriental Counselor was charged to assist Zaehner in removing Mossadeq, thought that Qavam would be the right man to replace him. Falle believed that "if Qavam comes to power he will try to act as a dictator—dissolve the Majlis and arrest dissident elements, among them probably Musaddiq and Kashani." But he was concerned that the Shah did not favor a strong figure like Qavam and was "determined that the new Prime Minister be a weak man."[18]

Early in May 1952, Sir Francis Shepherd, British ambassador to Tehran, was posted to Warsaw. Thus it was up to George Middleton, who had taken over as British chargé d'affaires, to sort out things with the Shah. Middleton hesitated to recommend Qavam to the Shah until Qavam overcame his reluctance to make himself acceptable to the sovereign. Meanwhile, to gain American support for Qavam the British embassy arranged for him to meet Ambassador Henderson, who was impressed by the elderly politician.[19] This meeting disturbed the Shah, who told Zia, "I gather that he [Qavam] has managed to fool these idiotic Americans."[20]

The Shah, though conceding that Mossadeq's oil nationalization had "served a useful purpose in reviving Persian self-respect," told Middleton that Mossadeq should be replaced by a prime minister who could settle the oil problem and restore friendly relations with Britain. Middleton happily reported to the Foreign Office that "this represents the first glimmer of hope that the Shah may now intervene in a positive manner."[21] But Middleton's hopes were dashed when U.S. Under Secretary of State Henry Byroade gave him quite a different impression of the Shah's thoughts. Byroade, who had replaced McGhee, was in Tehran briefly in May and met the Shah, who, he reported, had made no decision to dislodge his prime minister and "seemed quite content to let events take their course."[22]

During his visit Byroade met Mossadeq and asked whether he could not facilitate a resolution of the oil dispute by offering to accept a limited number of British nationals as oil technicians. With his dry humor, Mossadeq replied that in Moslem religion wine is forbidden whether one drop is taken or one gallon. To the Iranian people, he said, the use of British nationals in the oil industry, whether in small or large numbers, was equally an unforgivable sin. Byroade realized that as long as Mossadeq was in power, the British had no chance of reaching an agreement with Iran.[23]

Middleton advised the Foreign Office that the Shah's vacillation on Mossadeq's removal could be overcome if a joint Anglo-American approach was made to him with "considerable pressure."[24] Ross endorsed this approach and urged Eden to discuss it with U.S. Secretary of State Acheson on his visit to London in June 1952. He argued that "Mussadiq will not fall unless the Shah pushes him and the Shah will not take the necessary action except under pressure from outside . . . applied jointly by the US and ourselves . . . accompanied by threats."[25] Eden raised the matter with Acheson but obtained no results.

Britain's main hope of unseating Mossadeq lay with the Majlis elections in June, for which the British embassy was actively engaged in promoting pro-British and anti-Mossadeq candidates. Moreover, by harping on the Shah's suspicion that Mossadeq was against monarchy, the embassy succeeded in convincing the monarch to use his influence in supporting British-sponsored as well as royalist candidates. The National Front thus found itself hemmed in by a combination of conservative landowners and opposition politicians supported by the royal court, the army, and the British embassy, while at the same time it had to fight against communist candidates.[26]

To influence the industrial labor force, which was mostly pro-Mossadeq, W. E. Thomas, the labor attaché at the British embassy, succeeded in persuading some trade union representatives to oppose the National Front's campaign. Embassy officials at first decided to provide union representatives with "a printing press at present stored in the Embassy compound and also the payment of 20,000 Rials per month for publicity purposes." In the end the printing press was not offered; it was arranged to give the unions "a helping hand less obtrusively" and to assist them in publishing a weekly called *Kargar-i-Azad* (Free Worker). At the Foreign Office, F. C. Mason of the Eastern Department felt that these measures were "indeed dangerous and somewhat unorthodox," but hoped that the whole relationship would remain secret.[27]

When the elections finally took place, the National Front won all seats in Tehran and some in major cities. But in most provincial constituencies, particularly the rural areas, the majority of winners were candidates supported by the court and the British. Mossadeq had foreseen this outcome months earlier, telling McGhee that AIOC had set its hopes on influencing the elections through the landlords, who would herd illiterate rural workers to the ballot boxes.[28] In some areas, however, things did not go smoothly; there were bloody clashes among voters, which led the government to stop the voting and impose martial law.

The elections ended with seventy-nine deputies elected, of whom only twenty-nine belonged to or identified themselves with the National Front. However, when Mossadeq resigned on July 5, 1952, in accordance with parliamentary tradition, the Majlis, not daring to confront public opinion, reelected him prime minister with a large majority while giving his rival Qavam only two votes. In the Senate, all votes were in Mossadeq's favor except one for General Fazlollah Zahedi. Even so, the Shah told Henderson that the new Majlis "could not be cowed" by Mossadeq.[29]

After the elections the British embassy expected the opposition to intensify its campaign against Mossadeq but was reluctant to finance its efforts. Sam Falle noted that "the opposition, in particular the Imam Jum'ih, wants money from us to form gangs and to make propaganda against the Government." He rejected this demand, saying that if the wealthy and influential were opposed to Mossadeq they should use their own funds.[30]

On July 14, Mossadeq introduced to the Shah the members of his Cabinet, most of them technocrats who supported his aims. He had reserved the war ministry for himself to ensure that the Shah would be unable to oppose him in affairs of state with the backing of the army. Under the Constitution the prime minister was entitled to choose all his Cabinet members, but the Shah, who had the ceremonial title of Commander-in-Chief of the Armed Forces, had in all previous Cabinets appointed the war minister as well as the chiefs of staff and the army commanders.

The Shah was shocked by Mossadeq's initiative and rejected it at once. Knowing that he could not succeed in his fight on the foreign front if the Shah used the Majlis, the Senate, and the army to weaken him on the home front, Mossadeq promptly submitted his resignation.

The British were delighted. For fourteen months they had exerted constant pressure on the Shah to remove Mossadeq, and now he had himself chosen to resign. As his replacement Qavam best suited their purpose. At first the Shah's hostility toward him presented a serious problem,[31] but British persuasion and the lack of opposition by the Americans finally worked in Qavam's favor. The Shah was led to believe that Qavam was the only man able to deal with whatever crisis might erupt after Mossadeq's departure.

On July 17, 1952, at a Majlis meeting lacking a quorum, forty deputies supported Qavam's appointment. The deputies not in this group argued that under parliamentary rules, voting on such an important issue should take place at an official session of the Majlis with a quorum present. The Shah ignored their objections and appointed Qavam prime minister. Qavam, suspicious of the Shah and concerned about Mossadeq's supporters in the Majlis, was bent on dissolving the Majlis, but the Shah refused, feeling that such a move would stir up the public and increase Qavam's power at his own expense. Next, in an effort to win over Ayatollah Kashani, Qavam offered him the choice of six of his Cabinet positions. When Kashani rejected his offer, Qavam secretly planned to arrest him despite his parliamentary immunity. On learning of this scheme, which was not carried out, Khashani joined forces with the National Front members of the Majlis in challenging Qavam's prime ministership.[32]

Whitehall greeted the choice of Qavam with joy. At last, it was thought, a settlement of the oil dispute was within easy reach.

AIOC's chairman Sir William Fraser felt that since the new government needed money, "the best chance of negotiating something which would be of any value to the shareholders of the Company would be by the Company itself negotiating some new and quick bargain," without discussing it with the Americans. He wanted to conduct negotiations in Iran without making any financial advances before a settlement, causing Eden to comment that "Fraser is in cloud-cuckoo land."[33] Sir Roger Makins believed a friendly Iranian like Ambassador Ali Soheili should be used for negotiations, but Eden ultimately chose Minister of State Selwyn Lloyd.[34]

As to whether any funds should be advanced to Qavam in order to make "a quick bargain," Sir Donald Fergusson, Permanent Under Secretary of the Ministry of Fuel and Power, noted: "If Americans are ready to give Qavam immediately a limited sum of money to tide him over a period of negotiation there is no reason for us to object, though I should hope that the sum would be limited so as to encourage Qavam to feel the need for a settlement."[35] It is ironic that British officials did not care to ask AIOC, which had withheld millions of pounds of Iran's oil royalties, to assist a government committed to serving British interests in the oil dispute, and that all they cared to do was signal approval of American financial aid to Qavam. The Americans obligingly agreed to pay him $26 million.

Between July 18 and July 21, while Britain prepared to send a delegation to Tehran, Iran rose up against Qavam's prime ministership. On July 18, when Qavam took over, he issued a blunt statement saying that the oil issue had set the country on fire owing to Mossadeq's mishandling of the problem. Anticipating trouble, he stressed that he would severely punish those who disturbed the peace or disobeyed government orders.[36]

His threats were ignored. Twenty-nine Majlis deputies issued a statement calling on people all over the country not to go to work on July 21 "so as to demonstrate to the world that our national movement cannot be blown out." Ayatollah Kashani, too, issued a statement saying the imperial powers who for centuries had imposed their proxies on Iran had now overthrown Mossadeq's government, the greatest barrier to their misdeeds, and replaced it with their own mercenaries. He called upon all Moslems in the country to engage in a "holy war against the imperialists."[37]

Qavam responded by ordering the army to show its presence in Tehran with tanks and armored cars. But this did not intimidate the public. On July 21, a national strike affected all the major cities in the country. In Tehran a huge demonstration was staged by people from all walks of life, including civil servants. The Tudeh party, which had all along attacked Mossadeq, joined the demonstrations because they hated Qavam for having double-crossed Moscow when he was prime minister in 1947 (see Chapter 3). To disperse the demonstrators the army used live bullets, killing scores of people. Soon, however, signs of disobedience appeared among the soldiers. Shaken, the Shah instructed the army and the police to withdraw, and Qavam's resignation soon followed. Jubilant demonstrators converged on Mossadeq's residence. He appeared at the door and spoke briefly, saying, "Iran's sovereignty had been lost, but you regained it with your courage."[38]

Despite months of secret discussions between the British and the Shah about overthrowing him, Mossadeq managed to turn his resignation into a major victory. The very same Majlis in which forty deputies had supported Qavam five days earlier voted Mossadeq back to power on July 22 by an overwhelming majority. This radical reversal revealed the true source of power in Iran: public opinion. The Shah and the British had succeeded in electing a majority of their own men to the Majlis, but had failed to debunk Mossadeq in the eyes of the people.

Mossadeq followed up his victory by taking over the war ministry, which the Shah had denied him earlier. Also the president of the Majlis, a favorite of the Shah, resigned, and Kashani was elected to replace him. Finally, on the same day Mossadeq returned to power, the World Court announced its ruling that it had no jurisdiction over the Iranian oil dispute (see Chapter 14).

Immediately after the fall of Qavam, the British and American embassies in Tehran began pondering their next move. Middleton reported to the Foreign Office that the Shah, fearful of a strong prime minister like Qavam, was "busily intriguing against the latter almost as soon as he called him to power." He blamed the Shah for bowing to public opinion out of cowardice and betraying Qavam by ordering the withdrawal of the troops that had been brought in to disperse the demonstrators. As for the present situation, "Temporarily he [Mossadeq] is riding on the crest of a wave of popular feeling and success. There are no rival candidates in the field, the Shah has been reduced to impotence and the army and the morale of its senior officers has been severely shaken."

Middleton went on to observe that the events of July 21 "may well prove a turning point in Persian history, [because] for the first time the small ruling class found itself impotent in the face of a well organised mob, and, in future, consent of that mob may be a decisive factor for any future Government."[39] This lesson had been well learned by August 1953, when the British and the Americans used hired mobs to overthrow Mossadeq.

In another report, on July 27, Middleton observed that the army, unhappy with the current situation, was disposed to stage a coup if a suitable leader could be found. On the following day, he reported that General Zahedi might be prepared to lead a coup, but Middleton was not sure of his ability. Archibald Ross suggested that the Foreign Office authorize Middleton to contact "personalities whom he thinks may emerge as leaders of a coup d'etat" and tell them of the type of oil settlement Britain expects from them. To strengthen the British in their discussion with the Americans on the removal of Mossadeq, Middleton sent yet another cable to the Foreign Office, one that seems to have been specifically worded for presentation to the State Department. In it he maintained that "as matters are developing a Coup d'Etat may be the only hope of saving Persia from communism."[40]

U.S. Ambassador Henderson's evaluation of the situation in Iran was much like Middleton's, but his proposed line of action was quite different. He reported to the State Department that the prestige of Mossadeq and Kashani was higher than ever before, and that the two had convinced the public that "Qavam was an agent of Western imperialism." He felt that National Front opponents such as the royal court and the landowners could not do much. He rightly pointed out, however, that the "varied political views and personal ambitions of National Front leaders bode trouble for its future." In particular, the ambitious Kashani was trying to undermine Mossadeq and all other rivals and to make himself "complete master" of Iran. As for relations between the United States and the National Front, Henderson reported that they were deteriorating owing to America's support for Britain's basic demands and willingness to deal with Qavam.

To reverse this trend, he suggested that the United States give Mossadeq significant financial assistance before it was too late for him to concentrate his energies on "saving Iran from International Communism." Henderson stressed the urgency of the matter, since "there is no guarantee that he [Mossadeq] might not at any time become incapacitated by illness or assassination." He worried that the elimination of Mossadeq might give Tudeh a chance to strengthen itself, but he thought a military coup unlikely because the Shah "would probably take fright at the very idea of a coup."[41]

Edwin Bolland of the British embassy in Tehran believed that the Tudeh party was determined to take over the government in Iran with Soviet backing. He reported that the National Front leaders, aware of Tudeh's aims, had dissociated themselves from that party, calling its members "hirelings of the Cominform." He expected Tudeh to try to undermine Mossadeq by branding him and his supporters as "traitors intent on handing the country to American imperialism."[42]

In fact, Mossadeq, during his first term in office, had been the object of constant abuse by the Soviet bloc and Tudeh press as well as by the British media. Because the media attacks of both sides were aimed at destabilizing Mossadeq's position, there were speculations that Tudeh was in fact cooperating with the British. *Shahed* wrote that Britain was "using the Tudeh Party to neutralise Mossadeq's successes." The paper contended that Britain had used "not only the corrupt ruling class—satellites of the Oil Company—but also the Tudeh party, to push her proxies into the Majlis."[43] The Iranian press based such allegations on the documents seized from the residence of Richard Seddon, AIOC's representative in Iran, which proved that AIOC had in some instances assisted the Tudeh press (see Chapter 7).

Mossadeq was of two minds about the nature of Tudeh's connections with AIOC. Sometimes he suspected that the company had hired mobs to attack American installations in Tudeh's name, so that the Americans would think that Mossadeq could not control communism. At other times he thought that some of Tudeh's leaders were in AIOC's pay.

There is no doubt, however, that the Russians were unhappy with Mossadeq's national movement and his oil nationalization, the very same things the British disliked. Ehsan Tabari, a leading figure in the Tudeh party at the time, contended some thirty-five years later that there was collusion between the Soviet and the British governments against Mossadeq during the latter part of his prime ministership.[44]

Qavam, too, as we have seen, believed that Britain, in her efforts to regain her oil interests in Iran, might elect to "appease Russia" and divide Iran between the two countries. In his discussions with Kenneth de Courcy, Qavam contended that Churchill and Stalin were making just such a deal.[45] These suspicions were not completely unfounded. In June 1951, Eric Berthoud of the Foreign Office suggested the division of Iran between Britain and the Soviet Union in such a way as to create "a British sphere of influence in the South on the lines of past history."[46] This is indeed what Britain and Russia did under the Anglo-Russian Convention of 1907. However, there is no conclusive evidence concerning Anglo-Soviet negotiations on this issue in the early 1950s. This is because the documentation is sparse. Some British documents relating to the 1950s will not be available to the public until the 2050s. Thus facts on this issue might remain in the dark for decades to come.

Whatever the truth of these speculations, the Americans continued to worry about the possible expansion of communism. Acheson told British ambassador Franks that Mossadeq was the only chance of preventing the spread of communism and the loss of Iran to the West, pointing out that "if Mossadeq collapsed and affairs in Persia became chaotic, American public opinion would want to know what we had been doing to stop this." He believed there was no alternative but to secure Mossadeq's position by removing his financial difficulties and by reaching an oil settlement with him.[47]

Mossadeq started his second term in office in a difficult political atmosphere. Although he still enjoyed great mass support, the centers of power stood against him. In the Majlis the opposition was in the majority, and the Shah had turned against him. To strengthen his position, Mossadeq obtained legislative powers from the Majlis for a period of six months. In addition, in his capacity as Minister of War, he set up two committees to purge the army of corrupt officers who had misused government funds in the purchase of arms and of officers who had shown communist tendencies. This resulted in the voluntary and forced retirement of 136 officers, including 15 generals. Most claimed that the only reason they were purged was that they had supported the Shah.[48]

To reduce tension between the government and the royal court, Mossadeq established a parliamentary committee to define the powers of the Cabinet and the Shah within the Constitution.[49] But on July 23, by way of assurance that he did not seek to alter Iran's constitutional monarchy, he sent the Shah a copy of the Koran with this message on the flyleaf:

> Consider me an enemy of the Koran if I take any action against the Constitution, or if I accept the presidency in case others nullify the Constitution and change the form of the country's regime.[50]

17

Churchill's Games with Truman

In beginning his second term, Mossadeq felt that his bargaining position against the British was strong. He had defeated Britain at the World Court and had returned to power on a wave of popular support. Soon after taking over from Qavam, he demanded that Britain free Iran's sterling balances in London and that AIOC hand over the sum of £49 million, which he claimed it owed to Iran.[1]

Mossadeq admitted to Middleton that his financial difficulties were such that his government could not afford to pay the country's armed forces and civil servants. He feared that if the situation continued, "revolution was around the corner" and the beneficiaries would be the communists. As to the oil dispute, he stated that it was time for Britain to abandon her hostile policy and come to terms with him within the framework of Iran's nationalization law. All AIOC could claim, he said, was compensation—the amount of which could be determined by international arbitration.[2]

Pleased that Mossadeq had agreed to international arbitration, Acheson proposed that the United States grant Iran a sum of $10 million, ask Mossadeq to refer the question of compensation to arbitration, and start negotiations for a permanent arrangement for the sale of oil.[3] Since Eden wanted AIOC to control Iran's oil industry, he was leery of international arbitration. If compensation was in fact referred to arbitration, he said, "the terms of reference should be sufficiently wide to include the question of the validity of the Persian Nationalisation Law and its compatibility with the A.I.O.C.'s concession." Moreover, the arbitrators should be empowered to decide not only the extent of the damages the company had suffered, but also the future conduct of the Iranian oil industry.[4]

In his continued efforts to discredit Mossadeq, Eden overplayed his hand by implying that U.S. ambassador Loy Henderson shared

British chargé d'affaires Middleton's "serious doubts" about "Musaddiq's value as a barrier against communism." Actually, Henderson had advised Acheson that the best way to avoid communism in
Iran was by supporting Mossadeq. Acheson was irritated by Eden's
behavior, and especially by his suggesting terms for arbitration that
he "knew from the outset were impossible." The State Department
prepared a stiff message to Eden, which said that the United States
could not accept the British position and felt free to act independently. But Ambassador Franks intervened and asked Acheson not
to send the message.

Franks subsequently advised Eden that "it is of the greatest importance that we should not have a major split with the Americans."
He reported indications that "the American Administration had
reached the conclusion that they could not act jointly with us about
Persia or any other Middle Eastern problems and would have to go
it alone." Acheson eventually toned down his reply to Eden, stating
that he did not think the British terms would be acceptable to
Mossadeq or to anyone succeeding him.[5] It is worth noting that
Acheson and Eden were often at odds and had numerous clashes.
Franks played a mediating role between the two to smooth their
relations.[6]

Eden next asked Middleton to sound out Mossadeq on his proposal. Mossadeq responded with a four-point proposal of his own.
First, the two governments would ask the World Court to settle the
question of compensation. Second, the British government would
make some funds immediately available to Iran from the sums due
by AIOC. Third, Iran would sell the bulk of her oil to AIOC
provided a satisfactory agreement was reached on the price of oil.
Finally, any compensation awarded by the court would be paid by
Iran either in free oil deliveries or by a reduction in the sale price
of oil.[7]

When Britain rejected these proposals, which the U.S. State Department considered reasonable and fair, the U.S. government once
again began looking for a solution of its own. An opportunity arose
in mid-August 1952, when Alton Jones, president of the Cities
Service Company, an American oil independent, informed President
Truman that he intended to accept an invitation from Mossadeq to
go to Iran to help in the operation of the oil industry. The president

endorsed his intention, and this disturbed the Foreign Office. Eden was ill at the time, so Churchill took up the matter himself. He sent a message to Truman saying:

> I am concerned about the Alton Jones's visit to Mossadeq. . . . If it came about that American oil interests were working to take our place in the Persian Gulf oil fields . . . this might well raise serious controversy in this country. We are doing our utmost to bear the heavy load . . . helping all we can in Korea. No country is running voluntarily the risks which we are, should atomic warfare be started by Soviet Russia. I hope you will do your best to prevent American help for Mossadeq . . . from becoming a powerful argument in the mouths of those who care little for the great forward steps towards Anglo-American unity.[8]

In brief, Churchill hoped that in exchange for British support of the United States in the Korean war, Truman would help Britain regain her oil interests in Iran. Truman, who felt that Britain was the oppressive party in the dispute, urged Churchill to come to a fair settlement, which he said required the solution of only two problems: an agreement on the amount of compensation and the creation of conditions that would enable Iran to pay this amount out of her oil revenues. Jones, he said, would help Iran resume production and refining so that there would be oil for AIOC to buy and for Iran to use to pay compensation. He added that the Americans "have not the slightest wish to profit by your present difficulties."

In addition, Truman urged Churchill to accept Iran's oil nationalization law, which, he said, "seems to have become as sacred in Iran's eyes as [the] Koran." He pointed out that "if Iran goes down the communist drain," the West would gradually lose the Middle East and its oil resources to the Soviets. "Such disaster to the free world," he said, "would undoubtedly also place a strain on general Anglo-American relations."[9] Truman thus made it clear that relations between the two countries did not rest on a simple quid pro quo basis.

In replying, Churchill resorted to a new political game of trying to involve Truman personally in the dispute with Iran so that the two could establish a common front against Mossadeq. He sent him an innocent-looking message saying: "why do we not send a joint telegram personal and secret to Mossadeq? . . . It might be a help to our common interests. . . . Shall I try my hand at a draft or will you?" Mossadeq, he said, was admirable in a way: "We are dealing with a man at the very edge of bankruptcy, revolution and death but still I think a man." He finally added, "Our combined approach might convince him"; otherwise the United States would be "infinitely blackmailed by Persia to the detriment of her greatest friend."[10]

Churchill next cabled Truman a draft of the proposed joint message. It called on Iran and Britain to submit to the World Court "the question of compensation to be paid in respect of the nationalisation of the [AIOC] enterprise in Persia and the termination of the 1933 Concession Agreement." Once this was done, the draft said, AIOC would negotiate on arrangements for the flow of oil to world markets, the United Kingdom would relax trade and monetary restrictions on Iran, and the United States would make a grant of $10 million. Churchill noted that the terms of reference for arbitration should not prevent Britain from "maintaining the validity of the 1933 Concession and claiming damages for its unilateral abrogation."[11] In brief, he wanted to make sure that AIOC would obtain full compensation for the loss of profits until 1993, the termination date of the concession, and at the same time return to Iran and control the country's oil industry.

Churchill's draft was discussed at a high-level meeting attended by President Truman, Secretary Acheson, Secretary of Defense Robert Lovett, Averell Harriman, and others. The consensus was that the wisest course of action would be to send separate but parallel messages rather than a joint one, which might give the impression of "ganging up" on Mossadeq.[12]

Truman was "extremely reluctant" to take a joint approach, he told Churchill, and he thought Britain should join the United States in giving financial assistance to Iran. To make sure that Britain's ultimate intention was not to manage and control Iran's oil industry, he stressed that "it is not any longer a matter for discussion as to whether AIOC would produce oil or operate the Abadan Refinery." Regarding arbitration on compensation, Truman did not like any specific mention of damages resulting from the "termination of the 1933 Concession."[13]

In the hope of overcoming Truman's resistance to a joint approach, Churchill replied ingratiatingly: "I thought that it might do good if we had a gallop together as I often had with F. D. R. [Roosevelt] . . . Our 'physical separation' did not prevent such methods in the war. . . . I do not myself see why two good men asking only what is right and just should not gang up against a third who is doing wrong." Churchill rejected the idea that Britain should extend financial assistance to Iran, saying that the U.S. grant of $10 million would suffice and that Iran should not get the impression that "blackmail pays."[14] Truman finally agreed to a joint approach.

On August 27, 1952, the U.S. and British representatives in Tehran called on Mossadeq and presented him with the joint Truman-Churchill message, which proposed that the World Court deal with "the question of compensation to be paid in respect of the nationalisation of the enterprise of the AIOC in Iran, having regard to the legal position of the parties existing immediately prior to nationalisation." The two leaders' message went on to suggest that negotiations take place between Iran and AIOC regarding the flow of oil to world markets once agreement was reached on price. It finally referred to Britain's removal of trade and financial restrictions on Iran and the U.S. offer of a $10 million grant.[15]

Mossadeq expressed his utter disappointment with the proposals. If the court was to base its decision on "the legal position of the parties . . . prior to nationalisation," he said, it meant reopening the question of the legality of nationalization. As to the U.S. offer of a grant of $10 million, the amount was insignificant and "smacked of charity," which he did not want. What he wanted was £49 million, which he claimed the company owed Iran. He expected the proposals to be revised in a fair and equitable manner.[16]

Truman agreed with Mossadeq that the "validity of the Nationalisation Law [should] not be brought into question," and he wanted the joint message to reflect this point.[17] But Churchill was strongly against any changes. The message was thus officially delivered and published in Washington and London, giving the impression—as Churchill wanted—that Britain and the United States were in agreement on the Iranian oil dispute. The joint proposals were rejected by Mossadeq, and the Iranian press blamed the United States for abandoning impartiality.

The British intensified their propaganda campaign against Mossadeq's government, saying that it had no respect for international law and no intention of paying compensation. This was too much for Lord Stokes, a former member of Attlee's Cabinet who had been personally involved in negotiations with Mossadeq the year before. In a letter to the London *Times* he argued that "the Persian case has never been properly stated in England." He asked whether the British general public knew that in 1950, according to AIOC's published accounts, "whilst the British Treasury took £50 million in tax [on Iranian oil] the Persians received under their agreement approximately £16 million. . . . The Persians were within their democratic rights in nationalising their oil." Moreover, the Iranians "recognise the principle of adequate and fair compensation." The joint proposals, he said, even fell short of what he had suggested to Iran the year before. It was not true that the Iranians hated the British; "a great store of good-will remains in Persia towards individual Englishmen." In Stokes's experience, "The Persians are a sympathetic people, chivalrous to their friends and reasonable in their individual business relations."[18]

In reporting on the joint proposals to the Majlis, Mossadeq said that he had expected the British government, after its defeat at the U.N. Security Council and the World Court, to show more respect for the law. Instead, Britain's declaration that it would lift its economic blockade only when Iran accepts its "oppressive terms" showed that it was still committed to the rule of force. There was no reason for Iran's poverty-stricken people to continue giving their resources and the fruits of their labor to Britain, which "for centuries has been accustomed to plundering weak nations." Instead, it was high time for the British government to change its world outlook. Indeed, such a change was in Britain's own interest, since "abiding by law and respecting the rights of the weak not only would not diminish, but would greatly enhance the position and prestige of the strong."[19]

He said the Iranian government was prepared to accept the judgment of the World Court on the amount of compensation "based on any law carried out by any country nationalising its industries in similar instances." Also to be determined, he added, was the amount of compensation payable to Iran for damages resulting from the

British oil embargo and the economic blockade. The Majlis and the Senate overwhelmingly approved his proposals, and Mossadeq forwarded them to Churchill and Truman on September 24, 1952.[20]

To make sure that Truman would not be influenced by Mossadeq's counterproposals, Churchill sent the president a message:

> Britain has suffered by Persian depredations losses which I am told may amount to £60 million sterling a year. . . . We cannot I am sure go further at this critical time in our struggle for solvency than the proposals which you agreed were fair and just. [Furthermore] it would be a hard prospect for the American taxpayer to have to bribe Persians (and how many others?) not to become communists. . . . Mosadeq will come to reasonable terms on being confronted with a continued Truman-Churchill accord.[21]

Understandably, Churchill's main concern was his country's financial difficulties. In effect, however, he was proposing that Britain remain solvent at the expense of Iran.

Both Henderson and the State Department advised against a joint reply to Mossadeq, as Churchill proposed. They argued that the United States should "avoid being locked into a position with the British by which our future relations are tied irrevocably to this [joint] proposal." It was decided that Acheson and Eden should send separate but parallel messages to Mossadeq. They did so on October 5, saying that the Truman-Churchill proposals should not be read as failing to recognize nationalization. Mossadeq promptly sent messages to Acheson and Eden proposing that AIOC representatives come to Iran within a week for discussions within the framework of his counterproposals. But first, he said, the company should pay Iran, as a token of its goodwill, £20 million of the £49 million it owed.[22]

Eden stood firm on the Anglo-American proposals, calling Mossadeq a "megalomanic" and his proposals "blackmail." On October 14 he sent Mossadeq an uncompromising note saying that his counterproposals were unacceptable and that AIOC could not debar itself from claiming compensation for the unilateral termination of the 1933 agreement. As for Iran's claim for damages arising out of the British oil embargo, Britain "cannot admit that Persia has any claim. . . . The AIOC have merely exercised their legal rights in regard to oil they regard as theirs and have the full support of the British Government in defending their rights throughout the world." Eden further rejected the payment of £20 million, and characterized Iran's claim of £49 million as incorrect.[23]

Eden was encouraged to take this tone by a note from Middleton to the effect that the opposition in Iran was growing stronger and that General Zahedi has attracted support as the only alternative to Mossadeq.[24] With Middleton's encouragement, Zahedi, then a Shah-appointed senator, had gathered around him a coalition of forces with the aim of overthrowing Mossadeq.

Reacting to Eden's provocative note and the British plots against him, Mossadeq made a bold move. In a radio broadcast on October 16, he announced his government's intention to break off diplomatic relations with Britain. He accused the British government, in its urge to exploit Iran, of threatening the country with military intervention, applying economic and financial pressures, instigating riots to overthrow the government, and resorting to intensive propaganda schemes to misrepresent Iran's lawful action in nationalizing her oil. Political relations between governments, he added, are for fostering mutual friendship and cooperation, not for promoting unilateral interests by devious means.

The Shah tried to dissuade Mossadeq, but failed to change his mind. Henderson, too, made a last-minute attempt, saying that the United States was actively engaged in finding ways to break the deadlock; in response, Mossadeq agreed to postpone action until October 22. When nothing was achieved by that date, he told Henderson that he would go ahead with breaking off relations. It was clear, he added, that "hard times lay ahead and that there would no doubt be internal disorders" instigated by the British, but if they remained in Iran "they would only aggravate trouble by their intrigues."[25]

On October 22, Hossein Fatemi, Iran's Foreign Minister, sent a note to Middleton advising him of the break in diplomatic relations but expressing the hope that the British government would "eventually appreciate the nature and reality of Iran's national movement and the aspirations of the people."[26] By the end of October, the British embassy staff had left Tehran and the Iranian embassy staff had left London. Before his departure, Middleton reported to Eden: "If the idea that the Americans are working against us and are supporting Dr. Musaddiq and the National Front could be eradicated from the Iranian mind, this would be the greatest single blow that could be dealt to Dr. Musaddiq."[27]

The closing of the British embassy in Tehran was the culmination of a series of actions taken by the Iranian government to combat British covert and overt operations against it. In September 1951 Iran prohibited the British Bank of Iran and the Middle East from foreign exchange transactions. In January 1952 Iran demanded the closing of nine British consulates throughout the country, claiming that they were used for intelligence purposes and for creating disturbances. At the same time the government made it known that it would not accept British diplomatic officials who had previously served in Iran or in the British colonies, saying that such officials would have difficulty in adapting themselves to an Iran that could no longer be treated as a British colony. Because of this policy the Iranian government refused to accept R. M. A. Hankey as the British ambassador to replace Shepherd. Hankey, who had previously served in Iran and knew Persian, had in fact advised Britain to cooperate with the nationalists.

Aware that Zahedi and some other senators were plotting against the government, the National Front deputies in the Majlis found a way to deprive them of parliamentary immunity. Since the Iranian Constitution called for simultaneous and equal terms for both houses, and since the Majlis term was two years, the Senate's decision that senators should serve six-year terms was unconstitutional. On the strength of this argument, the Majlis voted on October 23, 1952, to end the Senate's current term, which had run over two years. When the Shah reluctantly endorsed this vote, turning it into law, Zahedi, having lost his parliamentary immunity, went into hiding.

No solution seemed to be in sight for the oil dispute. Eden continued to believe that Mossadeq would eventually yield under the economic pressures of Britain and the oil cartel, but not many agreed with him. The *Frankfurter Neue Press* believed "Dr. Moussadek would rather be fried in Persian oil than make the slightest concession to the British."[28]

Meanwhile the U.S. presidential elections were drawing close, and Truman wanted to settle the oil dispute before his term ended on January 20, 1953. Acheson felt that the best chance was for the two parties to reach a general agreement on compensation so that Iran could be free to run her oil industry. Since the two parties could not agree on the components of compensation, Acheson came up with the idea of a lump-sum payment without spelling out the components. Such an arrangement, he argued, had the advantage of allowing "each side to make a good case for itself at home."[29]

To Acheson, settling the problem would both save Iran from potential catastrophe and bring credit to Truman's administration. But reaching an equitable solution with the British was no easy task. As he put it: "Within our government . . . [many] had come to the conclusion that the British were so obstructive and determined on a rule-or-ruin policy in Iran that we must strike out an independent policy or run the risk of having Iran disappear behind the Iron Curtain. . . . Their sense of exasperation was easily understandable." The British opposition to a fair settlement had to be overcome, even at the risk of creating "damaging ill will."[30]

At a meeting on October 8, 1952, with Secretary of Defense Robert Lovett, Secretary of the Treasury John Snyder, Attorney General James McGranery, and General Omar Bradley, chairman of the Joint Chiefs of Staff, Acheson outlined his idea of a possible solution. First, Iran should make a lump-sum settlement with AIOC, with payment preferably to be made in oil. Second, Mossadeq should be given prompt financial assistance in the form of a loan against future oil deliveries. Third, an international oil-distributing company should be formed with the participation of major American, British, and Dutch oil concerns to purchase Iranian oil and sell it to AIOC and others. Bradley and Snyder agreed with his proposals, but McGranery felt that the scheme violated U.S. antitrust laws. It was up to the president to propose a way of dealing with this difficulty.[31] But it was President Truman himself who had initiated action through the Justice Department to put a stop to oil companies' monopolistic control over oil production, prices, and markets.[32]

The National Security Council (NSC) prepared a guideline for the president, which said: "Because of its [Iran's] strategic position, its petroleum resources, its vulnerability to intervention . . . by the U.S.S.R.," the United States should assist Iran "in every practical way" and help to start her oil industry. The United States should "not permit the U.K. to veto any United States actions," though "sacrificing legitimate United Kingdom interests" should be avoided. However the president might view the antitrust problem, "the major United States policy objective with respect to Iran is to prevent the country from coming under communist control . . . [and we should] pursue the policies that would be most effective in accomplishing this objective."[33]

To restart Iran's oil industry, the NSC advised the president to "approve voluntary agreements and programs" under the Defense Production Act.[34] On November 20, 1952, the president, using his authority, advised Acheson that he would go along with a voluntary agreement under which one or more U.S. companies together with AIOC purchased and marketed Iranian oil. Acheson was directed to hold urgent discussions for this purpose with the oil companies in consultation with the Attorney General.[35]

The British had no interest in such an arrangement. Instead they proposed that an export company—to be a 100 percent subsidiary of AIOC—be formed to conclude commercial contracts with Iran for the purchase of 7.5 to 10 million tons of oil at a price "not to risk undesirable repercussions" in other oil-producing areas of the Middle East. As to compensation, they rejected a lump-sum payment, saying that the question should be left to the World Court's arbitration.[36]

The feeling at the State Department, in the words of Charles Bohlen, U.S. Ambassador to Moscow, was that Britain would "rather see Persia go communist" than sign an agreement that did not fully satisfy British interests. At a meeting in New York, Acheson told Eden that "Iran was on the verge of an explosion." If Mossadeq concluded that the United States could not assist in settling the dispute, he would break off relations with the United States as well, thus reaching "the point of no return." "For the past 18 months," said Acheson, "the United States has utilised its greatest efforts to put forth ideas which could lead to a mutually acceptable solution," but to no avail. He warned Eden that if a solution acceptable to the British could not be found, "the U.S. Government may have no alternative but to move forward in a manner best designed in its opinion to save Iran." Eden, whose intention was to wait out an outgoing administration that supported Mossadeq's views, told Acheson that these matters required extensive study and proposed that Nitze be sent to London for this purpose. Acheson agreed provided that deliberations would not go on for an indefinite period.[37]

At the Foreign Office, the Persia (Official) Committee, a group of high-level officials that had replaced the Working Party on Persia, believed that Britain should reject Acheson's proposals, but expressed concern about Henderson's advice to the State Department that "it would be fatal to American influence in Persia for the U.S. Government to 'stand solid' with the British on the oil question." If Britain "cannot restrain the Americans from taking some unilateral action," said the committee, it would be necessary to decide "whether we should acquiesce in order to preserve the common front or, by standing firm on our proposals, allow that front to be manifestly broken." It finally gave the opinion that "we should aim to keep the Americans in play as long as possible . . . at least until we can gauge the attitude of the new administration to the Persian problem."[38]

When General Dwight D. Eisenhower won the U.S. presidential elections in November 1952, the British were uncertain what to think. His attitude toward the oil dispute was unknown, but both Churchill and Eden disliked John Foster Dulles, who was to be his Secretary of State. Even before Eisenhower was elected, Eden had expressed to him "the hope that I might appoint someone other than Dulles," with whom, he said, he could not work.[39]

At a White House meeting on November 18, Truman and Acheson familiarized Eisenhower with the main problems facing America. Among international issues, Acheson told him that the Iranian oil problem was most pressing, and that they had been trying hard to find a fair solution to no avail. He said that the British were determined to hold on to the Iranian oil, and that "the Iranians were more concerned with freeing the oil from British control than they were in the economic benefits . . . from the oil industry." Acheson warned of the dangers of unrest and chaos in Iran as a result of British economic pressure. He stated that the United States should start taking unilateral action so that "some degree of British cooperation might be stimulated," though this might be accompanied with "considerable bitterness."[40]

With Eisenhower's blessing, Acheson pressed ahead with his plans. His first move was to tell the British that their blockade of Iranian oil no longer had U.S. backing. There followed a statement, released on December 6, 1952, which said: "This [U.S.] government believes the decision whether or not . . . purchases of oil from Iran should be made must be left to such individuals or firms as may be considering them, and be determined upon their judgment."[41]

The British government countered by announcing that it regarded the products of Iran's oil industry as the property of AIOC. In response, the Iranian government instantly issued a statement saying there were no legal risks involved in the purchase of Iranian oil. In support of this contention, it cited not only the ruling of the World Court but the failure of foreign companies operating in Mexico to win lawsuits against purchasers of Mexican oil after nationalization.

On December 4 and 9, Acheson and his aides held discussions with representatives of five major U.S. oil companies asking for their participation in moving Iranian oil. To Acheson, meeting these oil men was "like approaching the shyest of wild creatures." They were relieved at being given assurances that they would be immune from antitrust laws, but they did not like "the appearance of hovering like vultures over the carcass" of AIOC in Iran. Moreover, they did not need additional oil, since their sources of supply were adequate.[42] Stressing that the Joint Chiefs of Staff considered Iran important to the security of the United States, Acheson asked for the oil companies' cooperation in buying 10 million tons of Iranian oil, hoping that AIOC would take an equivalent amount. The companies agreed to cooperate provided that AIOC and the British government reached an agreement with Iran on compensation and that the price set for Iranian oil did not violate the 50-50 principle.[43]

At a meeting with Foreign Office officials and AIOC representatives in London, Nitze spelled out the State Department's plan to no effect. Acheson followed up the matter in Paris, where he and Eden had gone for a NATO meeting in December 1952. Acheson's view was that as compensation Mossadeq should be urged to make a lump-sum payment of $500 million, which, he said, "might well be larger than any sum an arbitral tribunal would award." Eden rejected this idea.[44]

To stimulate the British to show some flexibility, the State Department made it known that the Eximbank of the United States was considering a loan of $25 million to Iran. Eden cabled the British embassy in Washington "to speak in the strongest terms" to the State Department that such a loan "would place a very severe strain on Anglo-American relations." After once again urging the British to find some constructive way to settle the oil dispute, Acheson agreed not to extend the Eximbank credit "in the interest of general overall relations with our ally." Earlier Eugene Black, the World Bank's president, had helped Britain by rejecting American suggestions that his bank extend a loan to Iran. Franks, pleased with his response, recommended to the Foreign Office that whenever Black visited London "it would be worth taking some trouble to confirm and develop the alliance [with him] which may well prove very useful to us here."[45]

Convinced that Britain was intentionally stalling until the Eisenhower administration took over, Acheson and his colleagues found a way to make the British realize that the new administration's approach would be no different from theirs. In what seemed to be a leak by the State Department, both the Associated Press and the United Press ran stories to the effect that a plan proposed by Acheson to Eden for settling the Anglo-Iranian oil dispute had the full support of Eisenhower and Dulles, who both believed that "Iran may go under to Communism soon unless drastic effort is made to settle her oil dispute with Britain." According to the press reports, the Acheson plan called on Britain to agree to payment of compensation by Iran on a lump-sum basis with money provided by a World Bank loan.[46]

The British retaliated instantly. A series of articles emanating from London and appearing in American papers, including the *New York Times* and *Herald Tribune*, argued that Loy Henderson, the U.S. ambassador to Iran, should not be allowed to discuss with Iran any proposals on compensation outside the World Court's arbitration, and that Mossadeq should be given an ultimatum to accept British proposals or lose world markets. Under Secretary of State Henry Byroade complained to the British embassy in Washington that these articles were damaging and that the unanimity of their contents suggested official inspiration. The British embassy reported to the Foreign Office that the State Department was seriously upset on this matter, particularly at a time when it had agreed to British demands that the United States withhold credit to Iran.[47]

The United States finally yielded to Britain and agreed to direct Henderson not to suggest a lump-sum settlement to Mossadeq but to urge him to settle the compensation issue through international arbitration. To make this course attractive to Mossadeq, Henderson was to promise him that once agreement on this matter was reached, the U.S. Defense Materials Production Department (DMPA) would make a $100 million advance to Iran against future oil deliveries and that arrangements would be made for the sale of oil to others. In response, Mossadeq agreed to arbitration by the World Court provided that the determination of the amount of compensation "be based on any law carried out by any country for nationalising any of its industries which might be agreed to by Anglo-Iranian Oil Company."[48]

When Henderson stated that the British Coal Nationalisation Act provided compensation to private owners for loss of future profits, Mossadeq responded that if so, and if the court confirmed that Iran should make such a payment, he would abide by the court's decision. On the commercial sale of oil, Mossadeq stated that once the problem of compensation was settled, Iran should be free to sell oil to anyone. He did not want U.S. advances to be tied to the conclusion of long-term contracts with AIOC, but he was prepared to negotiate long-term contracts with an international company in which AIOC was a participant.[49]

The State Department considered Mossadeq's response encouraging and "a real basis for discussion." It prepared two draft agreements, one on compensation and the other on the sale of oil, and sent them to the Foreign Office with a memorandum saying that once an understanding was reached on the question of compensation, Iran should be able to sell oil to anyone "free and clear of any and all claims or liens by the A.I.O.C." As to the U.S. dollar advance, the State Department felt that it should be made when DMPA and the National Iranian Oil Company (NIOC) reached agreement on future oil deliveries. The proposed price was to be the standard Persian Gulf rate less a discount of 35 percent.[50]

In rejecting these proposals, Archibald Ross of the Foreign Office asserted that although, after arrangements for compensation had been determined by arbitration, Iran would be free to sell oil to all comers, this did not mean that "we were indifferent as to whether A.I.O.C. should be a customer." Eden was concerned that once Mossadeq received DMPA funds, he might avoid selling oil to AIOC. He wanted the questions of arbitration and oil sale contracts to AIOC to be tied to the U.S. advance payment to Iran. "We cannot agree to refer to arbitration," he said, "without some assurance that there will be genuine arrangements for marketing Persian oil [by] A.I.O.C. or its subsidiary or to an international company in which A.I.O.C. participates."[51] If the Iranians felt that once they settled the question of compensation they would be free from the company's bonds, they were wrong.

Henderson considered the British conditions "fatal," since Iran would surely view such an arrangement as a scheme to bring back AIOC. He advised Byroade to urge the British to show flexibility at a time when "there is within our grasp the elements of a settlement more fair to the United Kingdom than any which [it] is likely to get in future."[52] Byroade tried but failed.

Once again the State Department yielded to the British. Against Henderson's repeated pleadings, it agreed to make U.S. advance payments to Iran "conditional on progress with negotiations on commercial sales" to an international company in which AIOC was envisaged to be a major partner. As to the terms of reference for the World Court in determining compensation, the British originally thought of following the terms of the British Coal Nationalisation Act, which included compensation for the loss of both physical assets and future earnings. But was the AIOC concession part of the company's assets? In the view of G. G. Fitzmaurice, the Foreign Office legal adviser, the Iranians might well argue that since the concession had been "extinguished" by their nationalization law, "there would have been no future earnings anyhow and therefore no compensation should be awarded in respect of such earnings." He believed there is "no way of preventing the Persians from arguing that the Concession was invalid *ab initio.*"

Another difficulty was that Britain could not determine the value of the AIOC enterprise on the basis of what a willing buyer would offer; since "the Concession was by nature non-transferrable," such a basis could not be used. Given these problems, it was suggested that the terms of reference for the World Court should only call for determining "the sum required to provide fair compensation to the A.I.O.C. in respect of assets owned by the Company in Iran immediately prior to the passing of the Iranian Oil Nationalisation Laws." This sum should be based on "the net annual revenue which the Company might reasonably have been expected to earn in the future" if the above laws had not been passed. Although Ross felt that "we could probably get away with this formula," others doubted whether Mossadeq would accept it.[53]

The Americans did not like the proposed terms. Henderson stressed that "Mossadeq has said again and again that he would agree to permitting the AIOC to designate a British law [as a basis for determining compensation] even though that law might provide for future profits"; but "Public opinion will not permit Mossadeq to . . . state in so many words that Iran is willing that the question of [AIOC] future profits should be considered" by the tribunal.[54] The British remained adamant, but finally agreed to substitute the expression "loss of the Company's enterprise in Iran."[55]

Henderson, who wanted to see the agreements approved before January 20, 1953, while Truman was still in office, met Mossadeq on January 12. He told him that the draft agreements would reach Tehran on January 15 and asked him whether he could obtain Majlis approval quickly. Mossadeq stated that he could do so without any problem. The two went so far as to discuss the timing of publicity in Washington and London.[56]

The assumption in London was that Iran would sign the agreements and that all the British had to do was send someone to Tehran to sign them on behalf of the British government. Harold Beeley, the British counselor in Bagdad, was the chosen emissary, and Eden prepared a letter to Mossadeq introducing him. In the concluding paragraph of this letter, Eden said "I look forward with confidence to the new era which the conclusion of the agreement will open in relations between our two countries."[57]

As a precautionary measure against other oil-producing countries that might contemplate following Iran's lead in oil nationalization, the Foreign Office sent cables to its chief representatives in many countries advising them to tell government leaders that the settlement agreement with Iran, if achieved, should not be interpreted as a victory for Mossadeq. Because the agreement called for a price discount and the payment of compensation, the outcome was not "more favourable to Persia than would have been the case under the 50/50 principle."[58]

Eden cabled Churchill, who was then in Jamaica, informing him that the proposed agreements, if accepted by Mossadeq, would "give us a satisfactory outcome both financially and politically on this long and troublesome business." Outside this business, Eden added, "Do hope you are not in fog as we are in London."[59] What was also foggy, had he known it, was the outcome of negotiations on the draft agreements with Mossadeq, which categorically differed from what the prime minister and Henderson had discussed earlier.

On January 15 Henderson gave Mossadeq two sets of draft documents, one concerning methods for the settlement of compensation and the other concerning the sale of oil. The first one specified the terms of reference the World Court tribunal would use to determine the amount of compensation to be paid to AIOC "for the loss of its enterprise in Iran as the result of the Iranian Oil Nationalisation Laws." To meet compensation payments, the draft said that 25 percent of the gross proceeds of Iranian oil sales would be set aside and that interest had to be paid on the unpaid balance.[60]

As Henderson had anticipated, Mossadeq objected that the tribunal's proposed terms of reference were quite different from what he and Henderson had agreed upon. He wanted the word "enterprise" deleted, and proposed that compensation be determined for "losses caused the Oil Company as a result of the laws nationalising Iranian oil . . . in accordance with one of the laws, to be selected by the Oil Company, nationalising industries in the U.K., enacted and enforced prior to the laws nationalising A.I.O.C." The other significant change he suggested was that funds set aside for paying compensation be 25 percent of net proceeds, not gross proceeds, to conform with Iran's nationalization laws.

The second draft agreement, concerning the sale of oil, said that on the conclusion of the arbitration agreement DMPA would sign a contract with Iran for the purchase of $133 million worth of oil. Of this total, $33 million would be placed in escrow for compensation,

$50 million would be advanced to Iran, and the remaining $50 million would be paid to Iran in monthly installments of $10 million. The agreement also called for Iran to conclude long-term commercial contracts with an international company at Persian Gulf prices less a discount of 35 percent.

These arrangements were also different from what Mossadeq expected. He had been promised a lump-sum advance of $100 million, but on British urging it was now proposed that half of this sum would be paid in installments so as to force him to conclude commercial contracts. Mossadeq modified this draft by decreasing the sale of oil to the United States from $133 million to $65 million and requiring an immediate advance of $50 million. He agreed on price and other details, including the commitment to enter into negotiations for long-term contracts "with an international company registered outside Iran and the United Kingdom," in which AIOC could be included.[61]

The State Department, finding the terms of reference for arbitration to be the main problem, urged the Foreign Office to delete the word "enterprise," saying that the omission of this word would not prejudice their position with regard to compensation as they perceived it. The British, however, opposed any changes in the draft agreements. To make sure that no agreement was reached before Eisenhower took over, they asked the State Department to advise Henderson not to seek any further meetings with Mossadeq.[62]

In spite of eighteen months of consistent efforts by President Truman and Secretary Acheson to settle the oil dispute, no solution was reached before their departure from office. The reason was simply that Britain expected the United States to give her undivided support to British interests at the expense of Iran. This the two Americans could not bring themselves to do. As statesmen who believed in certain moral values and aspired to maintain the credibility of the United States as the leader of the free world, they could not accept victimizing the weak for the sake of the strong.

18

Iran's Oil-less Economy

"To prevent nationalisation," writes George Stocking, the British "brought into play all the diplomatic, business and economic strategies at their command."[1] What hurt Iran most was the oil boycott, which endangered the country's economy and political stability. From the start of the oil boycott in mid-1951, Iran made consistent attempts to sell oil directly to the outside world at an appealingly low price, only to be frustrated by the overwhelming power of Britain and the oil cartel. In time, however, she made a nick in the boycott and brought panic to the cartel.

In February 1952, NIOC signed a contract to supply 400,000 tons of oil to EPIM, an Italian oil company. EPIM, which had previously broken the Mexican oil blockade, tested the waters by sending the *Rose Mary*, a small tanker, to Bandar Mashur, where it took a cargo of 1,000 tons of oil and sailed toward Italy. On June 18, 1952, Royal Air Force planes circled low over the ship at the southern coast of Arabia, diverting it to Aden, a British protectorate.

AIOC submitted a brief to the Aden Supreme Court claiming that the cargo was stolen property belonging to the company. Presenting the case for Britain was no less a figure than Sir Hartley Shawcross, a former Attorney General. In court Shawcross stated that the Iranian oil fields "rightfully belonged to the AIOC under the Concession," that the cargo was from these oil fields, and that "courts in a place where stolen property was located must necessarily have jurisdiction over the property." The charterers denied the court's jurisdiction on the grounds that the ship had been forced into Aden, that Iran's oil nationalization was the act of a sovereign state upheld by the International Court of Justice, and that no foreign court was competent to adjudicate on the legality of the Iranian government's action. On January 9, 1953, the Aden Supreme Court ruled that the cargo of oil belonged to AIOC and had to be surrendered forthwith. Iran did not expect a different ruling from the court of a small British protectorate.[2]

At about the same time another Italian oil company, Supor, signed an oil contract with NIOC and sent the tanker *Miriella* to Abadan, where it took 4,600 tons of oil. Avoiding British-influenced ports, the *Miriella* reached Venice in mid-February 1953. When AIOC brought proceedings against Supor and the tanker owners, the Venice court ruled that Iran's nationalization was legal and that no Italian court could refuse to honor Iranian laws. Supor continued to ship oil from Iran.[3]

Meanwhile, the chairman of Lloyds Insurance informed the British Treasury that the *Miriella* was partially insured by them. The policy being up for renewal, arrangements were made with the underwriters to insert a clause "excluding claims from British capture or seizure in respect of present and/or similar voyages."[4]

The British were angry that their blockade had been broken. Sir Pierson Dixon, Deputy Under Secretary of State at the Foreign Office, noted that "we have been pressing the Italian Government hard to make a clear statement . . . disapproving of any trade in 'stolen' Persian oil" with no result. He considered the Italian oil deals "the most immediate threat to our 'oil embargo.' "[5] In June 1953 the Italian Foreign Ministry offered a solution to the Foreign Office. It suggested that Italian firms buying Iranian oil pay an agreed sum per ton to AIOC to satisfy the British and to avoid legal harassment. The Foreign Office rejected the proposal, saying that "Anglo-Italian economic relations would be affected" by any such deal.[6]

Italy's indifference to British claims, Churchill lamented, "shows what paltry friends and allies the Italians are." Fearing that a big oil trade might develop between Iran and Italy, doing "great harm" to AIOC interests, he suggested "buying the oil contract from the Italian company, even at a heavy price, and then cancelling it."[7] AIOC, for its part, suggested that Britain complain to the World Court about countries whose courts refused to uphold the embargo. But Fitzmaurice ruled against such a course, because Britain would have difficulty proving that Iran's nationalization law was wrongful.[8]

Finding the British blockade broken, the Japanese company Idemitsu Kosan negotiated an open-ended deal for Iranian oil at a 50 percent discount from the Persian Gulf price. In mid-April 1953, the company's tanker *Nissho Maru* loaded at Abadan. The British embassy in Tokyo protested to the Japanese foreign ministry, warning that Japan's other suppliers, "whether American or British, were not likely to look kindly upon deals in [Persian] oil." The Japanese authorities took no action: all the ministers were away campaigning for election, they reported, and no one else could decide on the British request. Lawsuits brought by AIOC in Japanese courts were unsuccessful.[9]

These successes in breaking the blockade encouraged Argentina, which had tankers of her own, to send a mission to Tehran for the purchase of large quantities of oil. The Argentine negotiators demanded a discount of 40 percent, but Iran, believing the blockade broken, would not go beyond a discount of 30 percent and negotiations were suspended.[10] Earlier NIOC had received an offer for the purchase of substantial quantities of oil from the Chinese communist government, but Henderson had warned Mossadeq that such a deal "could do incalculable harm to Persia's position in the free world." Although Mossadeq complained that it was extremely unfair for the West to embargo Iranian oil while telling him not to sell oil to the communist bloc, he said he had no intention of selling oil to China.[11]

Iran's sale of oil at large discounts in the spring of 1953 coincided with a 40 percent drop in tanker rates owing to increased competition and other factors. Thus blockade runners were in a position to sell oil at rates much cheaper than the cartel. This prompted U.S. independents to press the State Department to allow them to purchase Iranian oil. The department warned Britain that even without Iran's large discounts, "at the new low tanker rates Persian oil could still be sold in any United States Market including West Coast at a profit." It suggested that before the British bargaining position with Iran worsened further, Britain should come to a settlement on compensation to be paid by Iran in oil, which could be bought at a cheap price. The Foreign Office disagreed, saying that "pirate" firms could not do much because major oil companies were in a position to deny them their distribution and refining facilities.[12]

Behind this cool facade, however, the British were in a state of panic because the Americans, concerned that a collapse of Iran's economy might lead to communist political gains, were no longer cooperating fully in the blockade. Dixon, who wanted "to let Musaddiq stew in his own oil," advised the State Department that "there is no evidence of any Communist advances." He directed Sir Roger Makins, who had replaced Sir Oliver Franks as British ambassador in Washington, "to keep the Americans in play" lest they get "restless."[13] Peter Ramsbotham, of the Economic Relations Department of the Foreign Office, suggested involving the Americans in drawing up a long-term oil policy that could not be characterized simply as "an instance of an obstinate and negative British policy."[14]

What worried the oil cartel was that Iran's continued sale of cheap oil could result in a "significant fall in the price of Middle East oil." Shell suggested that British and American oil companies cooperate in stabilizing oil prices by cutting back production.[15] Such cooperative measures, however, had to wait until a way could be found around the U.S. antitrust laws.

The Iranian government, for its part, remained concerned that it might not prevail against the power of the cartel. NIOC had sold only 118,000 tons of oil in eighteen months since the beginning of 1952, which compared poorly with AIOC's export of 31 million tons in 1950. But Kazem Hassibi, who advised Mossadeq on oil, was confident that Iran's large discounts would eventually break the cartel's blockade, enabling Iran to export large quantities of oil. He argued that if Iran could sell 5 million tons of crude and 3 million tons of refined products annually, she would earn $70 million, twice what the country had received from AIOC before nationalization for the export of 31 million tons. According to American intelligence reports, however, since production in some oil-producing countries had increased to replace Iranian oil, the quantity of oil that Iran could sell was no more than 3.5 million tons.[16]

As part of Britain's effort to paralyze Iran economically, the government directed the Bank of England to make it practically impossible for Iran to convert her sterling balances. When Iran protested that Britain's actions ran against the principles governing normal banking and trade relations, the answer was that the Iranian "Government action (which has deprived British interests of Iranian oil) had left Her Majesty's Government no alternative but to with-draw . . . facilities hitherto granted to Iran by virtue of the impor-tance of Iranian oil to the economy of the United Kingdom." Under these circumstances Mossadeq feared that Britain might go further by confiscating seventy tons of gold in Iranian government ac-counts, most of it held by banks in Ottawa and Pretoria. He consid-ered transferring the gold to the custody of the Federal Reserve Bank of New York, but ultimately decided not to.[17]

To make sure that Iran remained short of foreign funds, Britain consistently stopped the United States from giving the country any financial assistance. In response to British economic pressures to crush his government, Mossadeq declared on June 29, 1952, that he would not compromise Iran's sovereignty for the sake of oil reve-nues. He said: "If the Iranian nation . . . aspires to regain the status and position it deserves, it must not shrink from deprivation, self-sacrifice and loyalty to its homeland. . . . We must not tolerate living under conditions devoid of freedom and independence."[18]

Mossadeq repeated this message to the Majlis in December 1952, saying that those who degraded Iran's "holy struggle" by measuring her achievements in economic terms and equated the country's independence with a few million pounds were making a serious blunder.[19] Iran's freedom and sovereignty were not for sale. To meet the British challenge, his advice was perseverance and his prescrip-tion an austerity program based on an "oil-less economy." An economic council was established to study ways of achieving this aim.

Commendable as these sentiments were, Iran relied heavily on oil revenues for budgetary and trade purposes. Direct revenues from oil dropped from £16 million in 1950 to £8.3 million in 1951 and to practically nil in 1952. In fiscal 1949–50, oil revenue contributed over 11 percent to the government's budget, and the share of oil in Iran's visible exports was 73 percent. Making up for the loss of oil revenue was no easy task. In November 1952, Mossadeq invited a U.N. financial advisory group headed by Camille Gutt, a former Belgian finance minister, to Iran to give him its advice. Gutt's mis-sion proposed increased taxes, foreign exchange savings, and for-eign borrowing of $36 million.[20] By this time, however, the U.S. government and its financial institutions, which had been a source of foreign finance, were under British pressure not to assist Iran. Thus Mossadeq's government prepared an austerity program without foreign borrowing.

In foreign trade, the government concluded barter agreements with West Germany, Italy, France, Poland, Hungary, and Czechoslovakia. To reduce the drain on foreign currency, Iran imposed import quotas, increased import duties, and provided financial inducement to exporters by allowing them to sell their foreign currency earnings through the national bank to importers at rates well above the official rate of Rls. 32.25 to the dollar. These policies resulted in a growth in exports and a degree of import substitution. In fact, Mossadeq's period was called "the period of industrial recovery."

The balance-of-payments figures for the years 1949–53, as shown in Table 4, demonstrate the outcome of the government's economic policies.[21] The net contribution of the oil sector, which was Rls. 4,024 million in 1949–50, fell to zero in 1952–53. Non-oil exports during the same period, however, rose from Rls. 1,244 million to Rls. 2,807 million. Thus, after including services, the current account deficit over this period fell from Rls. 1,982 million to Rls. 1,122 million. Since there was a range of different foreign exchange rates for various imports and exports, those rates have been used to calculate the corresponding figures given in the table rather than using a single rate. The deficit in the overall balance of payments fell from Rls. 1,096 million to Rls. 657 million in this period. To meet part of its balance-of-payments deficits, the government made two drawings from the International Monetary Fund totaling $8.8 million.

The budget for public finance, in addition to the loss of oil revenues, was saddled with the oil industry's annual expenditures of Rls. 2 billion, mainly for wages and salaries. The government overcame these difficulties by raising domestic revenues and by keeping annual expenditures virtually constant at about Rls. 10 billion. It raised revenues chiefly by increasing excise taxes and customs duties. It lowered expenditures by a number of devices, which included abolishing state subsidies and making transfers from the royal court and military budgets to those of health and education. During its twenty-seven months in office, Mossadeq's government had to finance a deficit of over Rls. 4 billion. This was done by raising

TABLE 4
Balance of Payments of Iran, 1949–54 (in million rials)

Year[a]	1949–50	1950–51	1951–52	1952–53	1953–54
Oil sector					
Net balance	4,024	3,902	1,026	—	—
Non-oil sector					
Exports	1,244	2,110	2,710	2,807	3,075
Imports	−6,831	−6,427	−5,686	−3,829	−5,666
Services (net)	−419	−169	−175	−100	149
Balance	−6,006	−4,486	−3,151	−1,122	−2,442
Current account balance	−1,982	−584	−2,125	−1,122	−2,442
Capital account[b]	886	739	−327	465	3,439
Overall balance	−1,096	155	−2,452	−657	997

Source: IMF, *International Financial Statistics,* Vol. VIII, Number 1, Jan. 1955, p. 155.
[a]Years begin March 21.
[b]Includes errors and omissions, private and official grants.

Rls. 500 million through the sale of public bonds and by borrowing Rls. 3.6 billion from Bank Melli.

Based on IMF figures, the average annual rise in the cost of living index between 1950 and 1953 was only 6.3 percent.[22] However, during the last year of Mossadeq's government, there were shortages of foreign goods and their prices rose sharply. Despite its financial difficulties, the government did not ignore the implementation of Iran's development plan, which proceeded, though at a slower pace. Official gross national product figures for Iran are not available for the years prior to 1959. However, other economic indicators make it clear that in spite of the disruption created by the absence of oil revenue, the economy did not perform too badly.[23] Even so, it seems clear that Iran could not sustain a fast pace of development without oil revenues.

Mossadeq's austerity program could not have been implemented without popular support. However, not everyone supported him. In particular, the rich and the privileged elite were against his reforms, which reduced both their income and their influence. But Mossadeq believed that reforms were necessary to bring about social justice and lay the foundations of democratic institutions. In the absence of such reforms, not only would the majority suffer at the hands of a few, but the communists would find fertile ground for an effort to take over the government.

Iran at the time had a population of over 18 million, of whom 13 million lived in rural areas. The majority of rural inhabitants were landless peasants living in distressful conditions. To improve their lot, Mossadeq passed bills that abolished feudal dues and at the same time deducted 20 percent from landlords' share of the income from agricultural products, half of which went to the peasants and the other half to local development funds for pest control, training, education, health, and housing. Furthermore, he approved a social security bill that entitled workers in business and industry to receive health and insurance benefits from their employers.

To build democratic institutions, bills were approved for the establishment of elected local councils in villages and towns, each charged with governing its own area. As to the Majlis elections, Mossadeq, who had observed for decades how landlords and the military herded illiterate peasants and workers to the ballot boxes, introduced an innovative bill under which only those who could write were eligible to vote, among them, for the first time, women. The Majlis, however, opposed this bill.

To make the government responsive to the public rather than leaving it at the mercy of the royal court and the privileged elite, Mossadeq approved a series of bills that provided independent institutions for uprooting corruption in the judiciary, for ensuring democratic elections of chambers of commerce, for granting financial independence to universities, for encouraging scholarship, and for promoting the integrity and freedom of the press. So keen was Mossadeq on freedom of the press that he advised the judiciary authorities not to prosecute anyone for derogatory statements against him.[24]

Mossadeq's effort to establish democratic institutions with public participation was anathema to the privileged elite. The general public, however, was impressed when Mossadeq, himself a landed aristocrat, initiated bills that were not to his own advantage or that of his class. It was even more impressed when Mossadeq, first as a Majlis deputy and later as prime minister, donated his entire salary to charities. Even British ambassador Shepherd, who hated him, never disputed his incorruptibility or that of his Cabinet colleagues.

Despite Mossadeq's record and his widespread support, the opposition, with British backing, conducted an intensive psychological campaign against him, hammering home the idea that he could not win in his economic battle against the might of Britain and the oil cartel and that he should be replaced. Like Britain's political and economic attrition, this campaign met with little success. But Britain remained determined to bring about Mossadeq's overthrow if and when the U. S. Republican administration could be induced to help.

19

Eden's Games with Eisenhower

The British government felt confident that the new Republican administration would be more supportive of its aims in the oil dispute than the outgoing Democratic administration. The Eisenhower Cabinet was one of big business with George Humphrey, a Cleveland banker and president of a far-flung conglomerate, as Secretary of the Treasury; Charles Wilson, the president of General Motors, as Secretary of Defense; Joseph Dodge, president of the Detroit Bank, as Director of the Bureau of the Budget; and John Foster Dulles, a senior partner in Sullivan and Cromwell—a law firm that represented many great American corporations, including some in the oil business—as the Secretary of State. An administration with such men at the helm was not likely to do anything to threaten the contractual arrangements of U.S. oil companies with the producing countries; and presumably they knew that if they sided with Iran in her oil nationalization, there was the danger that other producers might challenge American oil interests. On the other hand, the U.S. concern about the expansion of communism in Iran argued against moving categorically to Britain's side.

Prime Minister Winston Churchill was not sure what the Eisenhower administration's approach to Britain's problems in Iran, Egypt, and elsewhere would be, particularly because Dulles (whom Churchill considered "a stupid man and could not stand the sight of him") would be in charge of U.S. foreign policy. To ease his doubts, he decided to confer with Eisenhower before he took office. Early in January 1953, under the pretext of wanting to visit his old friend Bernard Baruch, Churchill left for New York, where the president-elect was staying.

In his meeting with Eisenhower on January 6, 1953, Churchill invoked the days of World War II, when he and Roosevelt "were sitting on some rather Olympian platform with respect to the rest of the world and directing world affairs from that point of vantage." He expected a similar partnership with the new president; this time he and Eisenhower would sit on their mountaintops and rule the world. But Eisenhower had no interest in banding together with Britain to tell other countries what to do. He considered Churchill's approach "paternalistic"; moreover, with "the present international complexities, any hope of establishing such a relationship is completely fatuous." When Churchill raised the question of the oil dispute with Iran, Eisenhower criticized Britain for putting forward her own proposals as a joint Truman-Churchill proposition. "All that did," he said, "was to get Mossadegh to accuse us of being a partner in browbeating a weak nation."[1]

Churchill had little success with Eisenhower on the Iranian oil problem. Foreign Secretary Anthony Eden, however, felt sure that the Republican administration would eventually prove sympathetic to the British cause. He thus decided to discontinue even the semblance of flexibility he had shown to Truman and Acheson on this issue. On January 20, 1953, the day Eisenhower took office, Eden cabled Sir Roger Makins, the new British ambassador to Washington, "to do your best" to obtain an assurance from Dulles that the new administration would not take any action on Dean Acheson's suggestions. Dulles should know, he said, that Britain's approach to the oil dispute was based on four principles: "Persia must not obtain better terms than other Middle East countries . . . nor must she be seen to benefit by her wrongful action;" AIOC must receive fair compensation; Iran's oil industry must be run efficiently to enable her to pay such compensation; and there must be no discrimination against the British in Iran's oil industry.[2] Simply translated, these principles meant that in order to ensure the payment of compensation to AIOC, the British should return to Iran to run the industry efficiently while paying Iran 50 percent of the profits.

The State Department, which still contained many people who had served under Acheson, was irritated at this new indication that the British were determined to dictate their own terms. It sent a memorandum to the Foreign Office saying, "the Department does not consider . . . that the documents prepared in London have a sanctity in themselves." It hoped that the British would make changes in their proposals of January 15 "to meet Mossadeq's view," adding that most of the modifications he had suggested did not harm British interests. The Foreign Office remained adamant, considering it against Eden's four "principles" to make any changes "except on points of presentation" so as to make the proposals look "more innocent from the point of view of Musaddiq's public relations."[3] Archibald Ross of the Foreign Office told Joseph Palmer, Counselor of the U.S. embassy in London, that the proposals "were a joint offer in the fullest sense of the word" put to Mossadeq by "Mr. Henderson as the United States Ambassador and the spokesman of the British Government." Palmer's reply was that the proposals were not "a final definite offer."[4]

The most significant point in dispute was setting the terms of reference for the World Court to determine the amount of compensation. In the judgment of Fitzmaurice, the Foreign Office legal adviser, Britain could properly argue that no matter whether the concession was extinguished by Iran's nationalization law or transferred to Iranian public ownership, AIOC was deprived of it and thus should be compensated for its loss.[5] Mossadeq disagreed. Referring to the British nationalization of coal, he argued that whereas in Britain owners of mines had title to them, in Iran AIOC did not own the land or subsoil minerals. He therefore suggested that the World Court be directed to determine only the value of "the property and installations" of AIOC in Iran, the determination to be based on any law concerning nationalization of industries that was acceptable to the company.

Alternatively, he proposed that AIOC specify the amount of compensation it desired and the number of years Iran would be given to complete payment. Mossadeq made it clear to Henderson that if the sum claimed by AIOC, whether or not it included future profits, was not large, he would give it full consideration. He pointed out that because public opinion would not accept "a formula which indicated Iran's willingness to compensate for loss of future profits," it would be best to reach agreement on a lump-sum payment.[6]

Kazem Hassibi, one of Mossadeq's advisers on oil, proclaimed that it was beyond his comprehension that AIOC, which had "looted" Iran for forty years, should be unashamedly claiming compensation on future profits for the next forty years. He believed that the company's capital invested in Iran had been recovered a hundredfold, since it had set up numerous companies throughout the world with its "unjustified" gains in Iran. Hassibi concluded that even if AIOC had obtained the 1933 concession by honest means and had not "hoodwinked" Iran for decades, it could not claim compensation for future profits since the concession was extinguished by nationalization.[7]

It is interesting to note that seventeen months earlier, Richard Stokes, the British Minister of Materials, who was involved at the time in oil negotiations with Iran (see Chapter 8), had told Prime Minister Attlee that AIOC was not entitled to claim compensation from Iran for its capital investments in that country. He said: "The 1949 balance sheet of A.I.O.C. showed £53 million [depreciation] written off £81 million" capital expenditures relating to refinery, tank installations, pipelines, land, and buildings. In other words, over a number of years the company had set aside accumulated depreciation totaling £53 million, thus leaving the refinery and other property at a book value of £28 million. By doing so, the company had charged Iran for capital investments by reducing the profits by £53 million, thus reducing substantially Iran's royalties and other payments owed to her. With this and other write-offs elaborated in his letter, Stokes stressed that "in our asking compensation they [the Iranians] are being asked to pay twice."[8]

In February 1953 Camille Gutt of Belgium, who had visited Iran as the head of a U.N. financial advisory mission late in 1952, told the Foreign Office that Mossadeq could never accept a claim for loss of future profits and that pressing such claims would make him "more irreconcilable."[9]

The State Department urged Britain to go along with Mossadeq's suggestion that AIOC specify a reasonable sum for compensation and recommended a twenty-year period for its payment. Otherwise Mossadeq could maintain that "the British had refused to accept any type of settlement which did not imply that Iran might be required to pay indefinitely and in amounts beyond her capacity." Meanwhile Mossadeq told Henderson that if no solution was reached by February 21, 1953, he would ask Majlis approval to sell oil at any price to anyone—including the Soviets—to remedy Iran's deteriorating financial situation.[10]

Eden rejected the idea of a lump-sum arrangement for compensation but agreed with limiting the period of payment to twenty years for the sake of "maintaining the common Anglo-American front." He then, through Makins, offered a lesson in diplomacy to the Americans. He noted that Mossadeq should not be told anything about the period and methods of payment before he was confronted firmly on the previous proposals. "It is surely a normal exercise in diplomacy, to see that the other side do not break off negotiations before the full hand is played. You should therefore urge the State Department to instruct Henderson accordingly."[11]

The Foreign Office revised the draft agreements of January 15 only on points of presentation, paying no regard to the modifications demanded by Mossadeq and supported by the Americans. The terms of reference set for the World Court remained the same in essence, and the U.S. oil purchases and payments remained conditional on Iran's acceptance of concluding a long-term contract on the sale of oil.[12]

The Foreign Office advised Makins to tell the State Department that the proposals were fair and equitable, and that Britain in her eagerness to reach a settlement had made every possible concession. Makins did so, and the new top men at the State Department, who were unfamiliar with the facts, went along with the British argument. Makins was pleased to report that both Dulles and Under Secretary of State General Walter Bedell Smith supported the British proposals and "regarded this as the last round," pointing out that if Mossadeq did not accept them "Henderson would disengage."[13]

In presenting the revised draft agreements to Mossadeq, Henderson stated that the proposals came from the British, who had done "their utmost" to meet his demands and "were not able to go further."[14] At the Foreign Office, Sir Pierson Dixon was irritated to find that Henderson had told Mossadeq that the proposals came from the British. He observed that the U.S. ambassador has been "maddeningly 'neutral'" and that "he had no right to be." As if Henderson was a British civil servant who had to be reprimanded, he noted: "Another irritating feature is Henderson's omission to stress the fairness and advantageousness of the proposals. . . . No harm in letting the U.S. Embassy know how we feel about this." The Foreign Office expressed his criticism of Henderson to the U.S. embassy in London, saying that he should "stand firmly by us and not somewhere between us and Musaddiq."[15]

In his discussions with Henderson, Mossadeq reiterated that the terms of reference for the World Court were unacceptable to him and that the court should be told "to determine the sum required to provide compensation to the Company as a result of Iranian oil nationalisation laws." He said that the terms of the sale agreement nullified the very purpose of nationalization because they robbed Iran of her freedom to sell oil to anyone who offered better terms. Henderson made it clear that his instructions were not to accept any substantial change in the proposed texts. He observed that the United States, while wishing to uphold the security and independence of Iran, wanted to preserve the sanctity of international agreements. Mossadeq asked whether the United States intended to uphold the sanctity of an oil contract concluded between a British company and "a tyrannical Government which did not represent the people of Iran." If so, he said, the United States considered the United Nations principles "fraudulent and farcical."[16]

In an effort to gain the support of the new U.S. administration in dealing with Britain's economic and political problems, particularly in Iran and Egypt, Eden flew to Washington on March 4, 1953, along with Richard Butler, Chancellor of the Exchequer. On Iranian oil, Eden's task was not only to ensure that the United States would stick to the proposals submitted to Mossadeq but to prevent Alton Jones, the president of Cities Service and a personal friend of Eisenhower, from sending oil technicians to Abadan, a move that would be perceived by Mossadeq as indicating the end of Anglo-American solidarity in the oil dispute.

In August 1952 Jones had visited Abadan with Truman's blessing and had expressed his company's readiness to assist Iran in her oil operations. Churchill had been unable to persuade Truman not to endorse Jones's trip, nor had he been able to persuade Eisenhower not to allow Jones to send the oil technicians requested by Iran. Eisenhower had made it clear that he would not reject Iran's "moderate" request for technical assistance, since he "did not wish to appear small in the eyes of the Middle Eastern countries."[17]

The highlight of Eden's trip to Washington was his meetings with Eisenhower at the White House. At their first meeting, on March 6, which was attended by Dulles and Ambassador Makins, among others, the president praised Alton Jones, saying that if Mossadeq rejected the present proposals he intended to send Jones to Iran with "authority to make the best arrangement he could to get the oil flowing again." Moreover, he wanted Jones to send technicians to Iran for a lubricating plant. Eden exerted himself to dissuade the president, saying that "if it became known that the Americans had at this juncture sent technicians to Persia, there might easily be a major storm in the British press and there would certainly be a serious injury to Anglo-American relations." He said he "could not believe that the importance of sending these technicians was greater than the desirability of avoiding such an event." Dulles, who had talked with Eden earlier that day, agreed with him on this point. He felt the matter "was not worth the risk of upsetting Anglo-American relations."[18]

The president's main concern was that the oil dispute might provide a fertile ground for Soviet schemes in Iran. He said that "if the Russians secured control of Persia it might mean mobilisation in the United States." To avoid a military confrontation with Russia, Eisenhower appealed to Eden and Dulles to come up with an "imaginative approach" to solve the oil problem and thus keep Iran in the Western orbit. Eden thought it unlikely that Mossadeq would link himself either with the West or with Russia. "Persia wished to stay in the middle," he said. "This had been Persia's policy for two thousand years and he did not think it was likely to change now."

Eisenhower, however, considered the "extension of Russian control of Iran . . . a distinct possibility," saying that this would lead either to "the loss of the Middle East oil supplies or the threat of another world war." As if he did not mind seeing Iran fall behind the Iron Curtain if she did not yield to British demands, Eden stated that "Russian control of Iran, if it was ever achieved, would not necessarily involve the control of other Middle Eastern oil supplies." Moreover, even if the Russians took over Iran "they could not benefit from Iranian oil resources" because there was no means of transporting Iranian oil to their country. All they could do, he said, was to deny those resources to the West. The president did not accept Eden's argument. U.S. experts, he said, believed the Russians could build a pipeline from Abadan to the Caucasus within a couple of years. Moreover, he considered Mossadeq as "the only hope for the West in Iran" and was greatly concerned about the communist takeover of Iran if Mossadeq's government was faced with economic chaos. "I would like to give the guy 10 million bucks," he said, though he was aware that keeping Mossadeq afloat was a much more expensive operation.[19]

In his second meeting with the president, Eden tried to discredit Mossadeq by arguing that his remaining in power would seriously harm the economic and strategic interests of the West. He stressed that "we should be better occupied looking for alternatives to Musaddiq rather than trying to buy him off." While he was urging this course on the president, the MI6 men who had accompanied him to Washington were trying to convince Allen Dulles, head of the Central Intelligence Agency (CIA), that it was necessary to get rid of Mossadeq if communism in Iran was to be avoided (see Chapter 20).[20]

As a result of Eden's discussions in Washington the United States agreed to stand firm on the February 20, 1953, proposals until a decision was reached on the fate of Mossadeq himself. On March 6, the State Department issued a statement that "In the opinion of the United States Government these proposals are reasonable and fair to both parties." This was followed on March 7 by a joint communiqué on political talks between Dulles and Eden. According to this document, Eden told Dulles that the British government was determined not to alter its proposals, under which, he claimed, "Iran would retain control of its own oil industry and of its own oil policies" while selling its oil "at competitive commercial prices in world markets."[21] These pronouncements were merely an exercise in public relations and did not reflect the actual contents of the proposals.

The Iranian government found that whereas the Truman administration had played a more or less impartial role in the oil dispute, the Eisenhower administration had squarely sided with Britain. The Iranian press reacted to this change of attitude in different ways. *Dad* wrote that the U.S. government had unmasked its policy by supporting British colonialism. *Jebhé Azadi* accused the United States of overgenerous support of Britain in the oil dispute and urged Mossadeq's government to close down the U.S. military and economic institutions in Iran, which, it said, promoted British imperial aims. The opposition press, prompted by the British, expressed the view that since Mossadeq had lost American backing he should resign.[22]

Despite U.S. proclamations of support for Britain, Mossadeq still looked to the Americans as being in the best position to facilitate a solution. He asked Henderson on March 9 whether the United States could urge Britain to "immediately indicate the amount of compensation they planned to request from the [World] Court" so that he might gauge "the extent of the burden." Furthermore, he wanted to know whether the United States was prepared to help Iran by purchasing oil, or by encouraging U.S. companies to do so, or by giving Iran a loan to be repaid in oil. Henderson's response was that the prime minister should accept the proposals of February 20. Mossadeq remarked it was regrettable that the United States was unwilling to help Iran free herself from British slavery, and that the new administration "allowed the United Kingdom to formulate United States policies concerning Iran." In his view the British objective was "to get the Americans out of Iran and the whole Middle East," and Britain had "never wanted an oil settlement which would be reached with the assistance of the United States."[23]

Mossadeq, whose protracted negotiations had proved futile, next played the Soviet card. He told Henderson that he was prepared to sell oil to U.S. oil companies at a 40 percent discount, failing which he would be compelled to deal with the Soviet bloc. Henderson's response was that as long as the problem of compensation was not settled, no major American company was likely to purchase Iranian oil, and that sales to Iron Curtain countries would do "the greatest damage to Persia's international reputation." Aware that Mossadeq viewed Russia as Iran's worst enemy, Henderson knew that the prime minister would under no circumstances commit Iran's oil to the Eastern bloc. Mossadeq remarked that "it would create an unfortunate impression if the United States were seen to be 'ganging up' with the United Kingdom and forcing Persia, by economic pressure, to accept an oil settlement."[24]

It was clear to Mossadeq that the United States had closed all doors on him. To inform the public of the policy of the United States and Britain toward Iran he drafted a speech to be broadcast on March 20, and several days earlier he asked Henderson to comment on his draft. Finding the text critical of the United States and Britain, Henderson expressed his disagreement with Mossadeq's position. Meanwhile, he communicated the text of the draft to the State Department, which in turn transmitted it to the Foreign Office, where officials instantly prepared a response to be made through the BBC. Perhaps even the British found it difficult to justify the February 20 proposals. At all events, the Foreign Office withheld them from publication while directing its News Department to say that they provided the basis for "a fair and equitable settlement" despite Mossadeq's "quite fallacious interpretation."[25]

In a long broadcast on March 20, the eve of the Iranian new year, Mossadeq stated that the proposals presented to him during the last two years, though different in wording, had all been aimed at bringing AIOC back to Iran under a new guise, while forcing Iran to pay compensation and at the same time accept an equal division of profits. To achieve her aims, he said, Britain had used all possible means to install a puppet government that would impose her imperial terms on Iran. He expressed the hope that the British government would come to understand that such behavior was incompatible with the awakening of nations.

Mossadeq went on to say that in August 1951 the British government had announced its acceptance of the principle of oil nationalization in Iran. Since "this acceptance automatically acknowledges the abrogation of the imposed 1933 Concession and the invalidity of any claims for the loss of future profits," compensation should be confined to the value of AIOC's property and installations in Iran. The problem, he said, was that the company, which with the British government's support had plundered Iran's major source of wealth for decades, paying only hush money to puppet governments, expected Iran to compensate it for the loss of future plunder. He stressed that Iran was prepared to settle the problem of compensation either through the World Court or through bilateral negotiations.[26]

Although Mossadeq could not accept the February 20 proposals, he was still prepared, he told Henderson, to submit the question of compensation to the World Court, provided that Britain would indicate the amount she desired and that this amount was within reason. As an alternative, he said, he was willing to have the dispute settled by an arbiter whom both Iran and Britain could trust. He suggested for this purpose President Eisenhower himself.[27]

Eden, who received all communications between the U.S. embassy in Tehran and the State Department through the U.S. embassy in London, instantly advised the State Department that he expected the United States to remain united with Britain on the February 20 proposals and that no new ideas should be entertained.[28]

Despite continued demands of this sort for U.S. support, Britain did not care to admit openly that she needed such assistance. When AIOC sent to the Foreign Office for required "amendments" the draft of its annual statement, which contained references to American views, the company was advised "not [to] quote the opinion of the U.S. Government as if it means so much to us."[29]

Although the Eisenhower administration supported Britain on the oil dispute, it was open to new ideas to break the deadlock. One such idea—to form a consortium to purchase AIOC interests in Iran—came from several different persons, among them Jean Henri Clos of the American Charter Company. Clos wrote to General Walter Bedell Smith, U.S. Under Secretary of State, to propose that a consortium of leading American, French, and Dutch oil companies be formed to purchase AIOC interests by giving the company twenty-year 5 percent debentures equal to the net cost of its installations, being $94 million as given in its 1951 statements, and by also paying AIOC a royalty of 3 cents per barrel for forty years. The consortium would take over the company's Iranian operations and purchase oil from Iran. He calculated that under such an agreement, if the Persian Gulf oil price remained $1.75 per barrel and daily production remained at 700,000 barrels as before, Iran would gross $440 million per year compared to the $45 million per year she had received from AIOC.[30]

Continental Oil presented a plan by which a group of American oil companies with no interest in the Middle East would purchase AIOC interests in Iran.[31] Dulles and treasury secretary Humphrey, who strongly favored such a plan, discussed the idea at length with the representatives of some American oil companies. But Richard Butler, Britain's Chancellor of the Exchequer, lost no time in telling Humphrey that his country would view such an arrangement as "evidence of American attempts to reduce our influence in the Middle East."[32] The Chancellor's Cabinet colleagues were equally opposed to what they sarcastically called American "bright ideas." Butler wrote to Humphrey saying "we should face great political criticism in London if we appeared to be surrendering important British interests in the Middle East to American companies."[33]

Since Humphrey was a key figure in the U.S. administration, Dixon suggested that "we should not seem to rebuff him or give him the impression that Her Majesty's Government are pursuing a purely negative and inflexible policy in the Middle East." Some more subtle way must be found to forestall Humphrey's scheme. Peter Ramsbotham of the Foreign Office suggested getting the Americans involved in a review of the Middle East oil problem as a whole; this would keep them from focusing on Iran alone, "where they tend to lose a sense of proportion, from their fear of communism in that area."[34]

The French government, unaware that Britain was determined not to settle the dispute with Mossadeq, expressed its willingness to assist Britain in the solution of the problem. But the French were told that their help was not needed. Always suspicious, the British believed that "the French motive is to assert their position as a great power in the Middle East."[35]

Meanwhile the U.S. Petroleum Administration for Defense (PAD) wrote to the State Department that the United States should not envisage "the re-entry of Iranian crude and products into world commerce on a basis that would upset world markets or sources of supply." Otherwise, it said, the effect would be to "restrict the expansion of petroleum supplies in the United States and other Western Hemisphere countries which are of extreme importance to National Defense."[36]

PAD's views were not shared by those in the State Department who feared that if Iran's economy collapsed owing to lack of adequate oil revenues, communism would follow. Mossadeq, though unaware of PAD's views, began to wonder whether the oil cartel, in its eagerness to control prices, was reluctant to let Persian oil reenter world markets. He asked Henderson about the U.S. government's view on this matter. Furthermore he wanted to know whether "it is the intention of the U.S. Government . . . that Iran must accept such conditions as the British Government may prescribe." If so, he said, he would "resign rather than stay on and see Iran ruined as a result of being taken over by the British or by the Russians or by both." Henderson's reply was that the United States had no such intentions.[37]

Henderson knew that Britain's aim was not only to obtain a huge compensation but also to control Iran's oil industry. Though telling the State Department that Britain's intentions were unfair, Henderson warned that "our world-wide relations with the British are so important that we should think very carefully before we jeopardize them." He said, "An attempt to settle the oil problem along lines not satisfactory to the British would never be successful." Nevertheless he added that "it would be foolish for us to try to solve the compensation problem along lines which would not be acceptable to the Iranian public."[38] This in itself showed the dilemma that faced the United States. With this divided thinking, Henderson let himself flow with the stream.

Mossadeq, frustrated with American mediation, told the Swiss minister in Tehran that he preferred to conduct negotiations with Britain through the Swiss, "a completely disinterested party."[39] When the Swiss showed no desire to serve as mediators, he approached the Berliner Handelsgesellschaft Bank through an intermediary and proposed that a consortium of German banks form a purchasing and distribution organization to handle Iranian oil. He maintained that he had "only one enemy—Russia," and that if he could not settle the matter with the West "Iran will fall to the Russians." The bank was interested, but West German chancellor Konrad Adenauer advised it to seek U.S. opinion first. The State Department, at a time when the possibility of forming an American oil consortium was being discussed, discouraged Bonn from proceeding with the scheme.[40]

The British strategy was "to sit tight" awaiting the fall of Mossadeq, which was expected to occur as pro-Mossadeq sentiments in the United States abated. Despite British efforts, there were still influential voices in the United States who supported Iran's position. As an example, Robert Louis Taylor, a friend of Eisenhower, wrote him that "we should drop the moral support given British imperialism . . . and firmly urge acceptance of the decision by the Iranian Courts as to both nationalization and compensation both by Iran for property legally seized and by Britain for oil illegally stolen." Mossadeq, unable to reach a solution with the British on the question of compensation, was in fact contemplating filing suit against AIOC in Iranian courts to settle the question on the basis of Iranian laws.[41]

Lyndon B. Johnson, then U.S. Senate Democratic leader, sent the

State Department for "serious consideration" a letter from H. P. Nichols of the East Texas Oil Association. According to Nichols, when Mexico expropriated the oil interests of aliens "no effort was made by British owned companies, nor those owned by U.S. citizens to intimidate or harass Mexico"; all that happened was that the companies were paid a reasonable sum for expropriated properties. But when Iran "saw fit to cancel a unilateral contract with the British, the British began howling and have since tried to make it impossible for Iran to dispose" of her oil. The British, he said, "did not send war craft to prevent Mexico from disposing of its oil," yet they used every possible threat against Iran. He wanted the State Department to explain the difference between these two expropriations. He received a reply to the effect that the department was not at fault.[42]

Walter Levy, the American oil expert who had accompanied Averell Harriman to Iran in 1951, believed that Iran's nationalization of her oil industry should be treated the same way as Mexico's. He advised the State Department that both Iran and Britain would benefit by following Mexico's example in the matter of compensation. The agreement reached in 1947 between Mexico and the British concerns called for payment of $85 million in compensation. Comparing the reserves and the crude and refined annual production of British concerns in Mexico with those of AIOC in Iran, he suggested that Iran should pay AIOC $800 million in compensation. He felt that Mossadeq could be persuaded to follow the Mexican example and pay off this debt in 15–20 years. As to the British public, he felt they should be told that $800 million represented fourteen to fifteen times the 1950 rate of AIOC profits from operations in Iran after taxes; for comparison purposes, the nationalized British coal mining companies had obtained eleven to twelve times their prenationalization profits as compensation. He pointed out that the sum of $800 million would, "on a per-share basis, provide considerably more than the highest stock exchange quotation ever registered by the . . . Company," and it would cover the replacement cost of production and refining facilities elsewhere. Levy's proposal was fair in every respect. Even if it failed, he said, it would be "of some political and psychological value" as showing which side was not in favor of "justice and equity."[43]

Soon afterward Levy met Allahyar Saleh, Iran's ambassador to Washington, and told him about his proposed settlement. Saleh passed the word along, and Mossadeq invited Levy to Tehran for consultations. But there the matter ended. The State Department told Levy that the political situation in Iran was "too turbulent at the moment to make it advisable for him to accept Dr. Mossadeq's invitation."[44] What Levy did not know was that an Anglo-American plot to overthrow Mossadeq had already been set in motion.

Britain and the United States had finally formed a common front, leaving Mossadeq helpless. In a last-ditch attempt to prompt Eisenhower to assist him, Mossadeq wrote him on May 8, 1953, declaring his readiness to pay compensation along the lines suggested to Henderson. He said that as a result of British schemes the Iranians were facing acute economic difficulties, which might have serious international consequences. "If prompt and effective aid is not given to this country now," he said, "any steps that might be taken tomorrow to compensate for the negligence of today might well be too late." He concluded by inviting the president's "sympathetic and responsive attention to the present dangerous situation in Iran."[45]

The British used Mossadeq's letter against him, arguing that the "dangerous situation in Iran" and the threat of communism were the result of his own inept policies. Shortly after the dispatch of this letter, Henderson left for Washington for consultations on what proved to be the scheme for a coup in Iran. Before his departure, he sent the State Department a proposed draft of Eisenhower's reply to Mossadeq, which was discussed at a meeting held soon after his arrival in Washington. The general view was that "keeping Mossadeq afloat will serve only to perpetuate the present frustrating situation." It was felt that Eisenhower should politely refuse his request for aid and refrain from giving him "any ammunition which would strengthen his political position."[46]

After being deliberately delayed for five weeks, Eisenhower's reply to Mossadeq was delivered by Henderson on his return to Tehran on July 3, 1953. In it Eisenhower said: "It would not be fair to the American taxpayer for the United States to extend . . . aid to Iran so long as Iran has access to funds derived from the sale of its oil . . . [as it would] if a reasonable agreement were reached with regard to compensation. . . . The Government of the United States is not presently in a position to extend more aid to Iran or to purchase Iranian oil." Eisenhower went on to say that a settlement with AIOC on the basis of its physical assets alone was not considered reasonable, and that the most practical way to settle the problem was to refer the matter to an international body.[47] As we have seen, Mossadeq was prepared to accept international arbitration, but not on the terms of reference that Britain had prepared for presentation to the World Court.

When the exchange of messages was published by both sides, it became clear that Mossadeq had lost the support of the United States and that Britain had finally won the full backing of the U.S. administration.

Some argue that it was the extremists who prevented Mossadeq from reaching a compromise settlement of the oil dispute. But those who knew Mossadeq personally or were associated with him during his prime ministership did not believe that he was influenced by the extremists, though he was somewhat constrained by them. In fact what eventually separated Kashani, Makki, and Baqa'i from Mossadeq was that they could not influence his decisions. True, Kashani and Hassibi made his job difficult by insisting that AIOC was not entitled to any compensation at all; but Mossadeq ruled out this argument, considering it to be against legal principles. Mossadeq never made decisions for the sake of satisfying friends or silencing opponents. He based his decisions on what he considered to be legally and morally right.[48]

There are also those who argue that the main problem with Mossadeq in the oil dispute was that he had no notion of the complex financial, technical, and commercial factors involved in the international oil business; if he had had a clearer grasp of such matters, it is argued, he would have come to terms with AIOC. But how well he understood the oil business is a secondary question. He had repeatedly stressed that the oil problem was political rather than economic. His first priority was not gaining more profits for Iran but removing the British-backed AIOC, which he believed was the single biggest obstacle to genuine independence for his country.

20

The Coup

For Britain Mossadeq's overthrow was "objective number one" for over two years, but in spite of all her economic and political pressures on Iran this objective had not been achieved. The covert activities of Christopher Woodhouse of British Intelligence (MI6), and Robin Zaehner of Oxford University, who had been sent to Tehran to destabilize his regime, had also fallen short, though before the closing of the British embassy the two men had managed to reestablish their contacts with the three anglophile Rashidian brothers[1] and to recruit several new agents—among them Ernest Perron, the Shah's Swiss companion, and Shapur Reporter, an Indian Parsee who was Queen Soraya's English teacher. Also their search for a man who could lead the opposition to Mossadeq had turned up General Fazlollah Zahedi, a retired army officer who was trying to build up a coalition of anti-Mossadeq forces.

The "keystone" of British subversive activities, however, was the Rashidian brothers, who were wealthy businessmen with wide contacts among people of their own profession as well as old-guard politicians who were used to working with the British. Before departing from Iran, Woodhouse consolidated the MI6 network and arranged with some British nationals there to carry out covert operations with the Rashidians, who were provided with a radio transmitter to communicate with MI6 in Cyprus. The CIA representative in Tehran, with whom Woodhouse had developed friendly relations, was used as another channel of communication.[2]

On their return to London, Woodhouse and Zaehner reported their activities to Foreign Secretary Eden. Zaehner believed that Britain could not do much to dislodge Mossadeq. Eden, convinced that the job required American cooperation, sent a team of Foreign Office and MI6 officials, including Woodhouse and Sam Falle, to

Washington in mid-November 1952 to arrange a joint plot with the CIA for Mossadeq's removal. To convince the Americans of the need for such action, Woodhouse and his colleagues invoked the communist threat. But their American counterparts responded that the best way to remove such a threat was to support a noncommunist figure like Mossadeq. When the British insisted that Mossadeq was the problem, General Walter Bedell Smith, who then headed the CIA, told them, "You may be able to throw out Musaddiq, but you will never get your own man to stick in his place."[3]

Woodhouse, nevertheless, presented a plan for engineering a revolt against Mossadeq. As possible replacements for the prime minister he offered a list of fifteen names provided by the Foreign Office. The State Department, expressing scepticism toward the operation, decided to appoint an academic to examine the situation and report to the CIA.

In fact, two academics were advising the CIA. One was Donald Wilber, a former agent of the Office of Strategic Services (OSS) who had operated undercover in Iran during World War II. He had joined the CIA in 1947 as a consultant.[4] The other was Richard Cottam, who had worked at Tehran University in 1951–52 and later became a leading expert on Iran. According to Cottam, the British, knowing "the extent of paranoia in the United States concerning Communism," were adept at exploiting it to serve their own aims. At a time when Senator Joseph McCarthy was making widely publicized speeches about the communist menace, "the British consciously played on that fear in order to help persuade us to involve ourselves in the coup."[5] The British team, however, left Washington with no tangible results.

It was AIOC that set the coup in motion. In November 1952, when Kermit Roosevelt, the head of CIA operations in the Middle East, stopped in London on his way back home from a visit to Tehran, AIOC officials, with British authorization, intercepted him and presented him with a plan for a coup. Roosevelt told them that he had no authorization to discuss American support for such an effort. Furthermore he disapproved of their scheme, which looked too much "like a military plan." On his return to Washington, he informed Allen Dulles, then the CIA's deputy director, of the proposed coup. This was in November, just after Eisenhower's election.

Dulles instructed Roosevelt to keep the plan secret from Truman and Acheson, who were sympathetic to Mossadeq, and wait until late January, at which time Dulles would become the CIA director and his brother would take over as Secretary of State.[6]

The British could not wait. During the same month their embassy in Washington held discussions with the State Department on the coup scheme, which was code-named "Operation Boot." But the department ruled out any action against Mossadeq, "dreaded the outcome of his downfall," and preferred to negotiate with him. The British almost concluded that they should abandon their scheme and discontinue their monthly payments of £10,000 to the Rashidians, who had already received a total of £1.5 million. Finally, however, they decided to wait until Eisenhower's men took over.[7]

Meanwhile the British intensified their harassment of Mossadeq. In January 1953, the opposition against him, fanned by Zahedi and the Rashidians, grew in the Majlis. To strengthen his position, Mossadeq asked for a year's extension of his emergency powers. A number of deputies opposed this extension, including Ayatollah Kashani, the Majlis speaker, but after extensive demonstrations in support of Mossadeq the Majlis voted in his favor. This was a blow to Kashani and his supporters, who began to separate themselves from Mossadeq.

In fact Kashani and such vociferous National Front members as Makki and Baqa'i had cooled toward Mossadeq earlier. As a reward for their support, they had expected to be given a say in the appointment of his Cabinet ministers and in his government's policies as well as personal favors, but they had been disappointed on all counts. Kashani, like Ayatollah Ruhollah Khomeini twenty-five years later, insisted on initiating fundamental social change along religious lines. Furthermore, to launch himself as a leading Islamic figure, Kashani intended to arrange an international Islamic conference in Tehran and expected the government to finance it. When Mossadeq was told that it would be politically expedient to accept Kashani's demand for funds, he replied: "I am seventy-four years old and I have not so far paid hush-money to anyone."[8] Makki and Baqa'i fared no better. Mossadeq maintained that he had come to power for a cause, and that those who chose to follow him should believe in that cause without expecting favors.

Zahedi and MI6 Iranian agents exploited the differences between Mossadeq and his supporters and incited some of the disaffected to join the opposition. They also encouraged the Shah to stand firm against Mossadeq. And in February 1953 they instigated the Bakhtiari tribal leaders to rise against the government. The tribesmen, armed by MI6 and by officers supporting the Shah, occupied gendarmerie posts in their area and issued anti-Mossadeq and pro-Shah statements. The government crushed the Bakhtiaris, jailing their leader and arresting Zahedi and several others.[9]

Mossadeq, seeing the Shah's hand in the plot, warned him against such subversive activities. The warning caused the Shah to lose face, and he decided to go on a European trip for two months. But the Shah's departure would have confirmed Mossadeq's victory. Kashani and Mohammad Behbahani, another leading clergyman, supported by retired army officers, organized a crowd that marched to the palace on February 28, asking the Shah not to leave the country. The crowd then marched on to Mossadeq's home, where he was, as usual, working in bed. The crowd tried to break in and shouted that they had come to kill him. Mossadeq in his pajamas climbed over his back wall and went straight to the Majlis, where he told deputies that members of the Shah's court had attempted to assassinate him.[10] To deal with the threat he appointed General Taqi Riahi, on whom he relied, as Chief of Staff of the Armed Forces.

Eden was informed that the "popular clamor" in favor of the Shah "was certainly organised by Kashani and was not a spontaneous expression of a loyalty deep-seated or significant enough to stiffen the Shah."[11] The British did not consider the Shah strong enough to stand against Mossadeq. Moreover, the Shah himself, finding that it was the prime minister who enjoyed mass support, felt isolated and rejected. During his meetings with Middleton in 1952, his general theme was that "nobody loves me." Indeed, he sometimes felt disposed to abdicate and might have done so if Mossadeq had not dissuaded him.[12] The fact remained, however, that the two could not get along and had continual clashes.

The root cause of these clashes was that each party believed the other was operating beyond the limits assigned him by the Constitution. To settle the differences between the two, the Majlis set up a committee to examine the scope of powers of each; and this committee came to the conclusion that under the Constitution the Cabinet, not the Shah, had full responsibility over Iran's civil and military affairs. But when Mossadeq asked the Majlis to put the committee's resolution to a vote, the opposition, led by Jamal Emami, blocked it.

On March 1, 1953, the day after Mossadeq's home was attacked, the CIA reported to Eisenhower that "the elimination of Mossadeq by assassination or otherwise might dissipate decisive events except in the unlikely alternative that the Shah should regain courage and decisiveness." Although Kashani was a serious contender to replace Mossadeq, the latter was stronger and had a broader base of support than any of his opponents, including Zahedi, whose success the CIA deemed "unlikely."[13]

Determined to pursue the coup scheme in Washington, the British sent a team there soon after Eisenhower took over the presidency. To encourage American participation and get the CIA fully involved, they suggested that any operation for Mossadeq's overthrow should be headed by Kermit Roosevelt. As the grandson of President Theodore Roosevelt, he had "a very prominent family name"; moreover, they said, he was known to the Shah.[14]

To keep up the pressure, Eden went to Washington in March 1953 with a team of Foreign Office and MI6 officials. While he tried to convince Eisenhower that Mossadeq was threatening Anglo-American interests in the Middle East, the MI6 men met with the CIA and played on American fears of communism in Iran. Allen Dulles, the CIA director, Frank Wisner, head of CIA covert operations, and Roosevelt favored a coup against Mossadeq. But many others, including the CIA station chief in Tehran, were against such a move, which they thought smacked of colonialism.[15] Before reaching an agreement on the coup, Eden wanted to reach an understanding with the Americans on Mossadeq's replacement. Kashani appealed to him because he had turned against Mossadeq, had sided with the Shah, and possessed "the street machine"—meaning access to mobs. He told Henry Byroade and Walter Bedell Smith, the new Under Secretary of State, that Kashani had "less history behind him in the oil dispute and might for that reason perhaps be easier to conclude a deal with."[16]

George Middleton of the British embassy in Tehran had earlier noted that Kashani was a reactionary and difficult to work with. He classified Makki and Fatemi as reformists and felt that Makki "appeared to have the best chance of eventually being accepted as the national leader," adding that the British would "find it possible to do business with him."[17] But Alan Rothnie of the Foreign Office had little use for Makki as a leader, saying that "it has frequently been reported that he was willing to abandon the National Front if we would pay him."[18] The British choice narrowed down to Kashani and Zahedi. The Foreign Office finally concluded that Kashani would be a change for the worse and that Britain and the United States would do better with Zahedi.[19]

Shortly after his return to London, Eden became seriously ill with gallbladder problems. In the course of surgery "the knife slipped" and his bile duct was accidentally cut. He was compelled to undergo two further operations and could not return to active duty for some seven months.[20] He had activated the coup operation in Washington, however, and Churchill was pleased to follow it up.

Immediately after the Washington discussions of March 1953 the CIA sent Roosevelt to Tehran, where he explored the possibilities of executing the coup with MI6 agents there. Until then the CIA's work in Iran had been mainly concerned with monitoring Tudeh and Soviet activities, with funding newspapers, right-wing organizations, and some religious leaders to denounce Tudeh, and with trying to influence people like Baqa'i and Makki to break ranks with Mossadeq, thus lessening extremist pressure on him and making it easier for him to accept a compromise settlement of the oil dispute.[21]

Following Roosevelt's trip to Iran, the CIA studied "Operation Boot," which had been originally initiated by AIOC and MI6, and found it too rigid and regimented for a clandestine operation. Donald Wilber was given authority to prepare a more flexible plan, which he did, renaming it "Operation Ajax." Wilber met Roosevelt in Beirut and they went over the plan with other agents. The plan was then taken to London, where it was finalized with MI6 in mid-June 1953. Churchill, who enjoyed dramatic operations and had shown active personal interest in the scheme, gave his approval.[22]

Meanwhile Mossadeq continued to put pressure on the Shah not to interfere in government affairs. The Shah, who thought that the British had a hand in anything that happened in Iran, had come to believe that they were behind Mossadeq's every action. He thought that British demands for the removal of Mossadeq were simply a camouflage. He even thought that the closing of the British embassy had been engineered by the British themselves in collaboration with Mossadeq.[23] As to the prime minister's pressure on him, the Shah, unaware of the Anglo-American coup plot, attributed it to Britain's desire to "deprive him of his power and prestige." He complained to Henderson that "the British had thrown out the Qajar Dynasty, had brought in his father and had thrown his father out. Now they could keep him in power or remove him in turn as they saw fit. If they desired he should stay. . . . If on the other hand they wanted him to go he should be told immediately so that he could leave quietly."[24]

The Shah's worries were communicated to Churchill, who sent him a personal message through Henderson saying that there were no such schemes and that "we should be very sorry to see the Shah lose his powers or leave his post or be driven out." In reply the Shah, greatly relieved, "expressed gratification." He told Henderson that the exchange of messages should be kept in absolute secrecy.[25] But by asking the British to decide on his fate, the Shah had demonstrated to Britain and the United States that he had no base at home.

Henderson, who was to leave Tehran for Washington for discussions on the coup, asked the Shah whether he would support General Zahedi to replace Mossadeq, though he refrained from mentioning anything about the impending coup plot. The Shah's answer was that the general was neither "an intellectual giant" nor a man likely to carry out a successful military coup. He observed that the Amini brothers were much more powerful among the military and the politicians and could block Zahedi if they desired.[26]

The Americans tried the Amini brothers, but failed to win them over. According to Abol-Qassem Amini, then Deputy Court Minister, an emissary from "a foreign embassy" told him that the "embassy" was prepared to pay $5 million to the Aminis in fees and expenses for Mossadeq's overthrow. He refused the offer.[27]

The British continued to harass Mossadeq by all possible means. Late in April 1953 MI6 Iranian agents kidnapped Major General M. Afshartus, chief of Iran's police, and killed him. Their motive was to indicate that Mossadeq's government was on shaky ground, and at the same time to eliminate an able officer who they felt would effectively oppose any coup attempt. Zahedi, along with Baqa'i and a number of retired officers, was implicated in this assassination. To avoid arrest, Zahedi, who had been released earlier, took refuge in the Majlis, where he could enjoy the cooperation of Kashani and other deputies opposed to Mossadeq.[28]

The assassination of Afshartus was meant to serve notice to the Americans that Mossadeq was not in control, and this led to fears that the communists might exploit the situation. On June 25 at a high-level meeting at the State Department attended by, among others, the Dulles brothers, Secretary of Defense Charles Wilson, Walter Bedell Smith, and Kermit Roosevelt, it was agreed to proceed with Operation Ajax. Henderson and Byroade, who attended the meeting, were neither for nor against the scheme. The prime mover was John Foster Dulles, who considered Mossadeq's neutrality a sign of his weakness toward the communists. Eisenhower, who generally relied on Dulles's and Smith's judgment, approved the scheme.[29] As to the possible Soviet reaction to the coup, it was felt that since Stalin had died in March and the new leadership in Moscow had not yet consolidated itself, the Soviet Union would avoid involvement in Iran. However, as an emergency measure, the U.S. Joint Chiefs of Staff decided on "the general composition of the forces which might be deployed to southern Turkey and to the vicinity of Basra, Iraq, in the event of a Tudeh coup in Iran."[30]

The components of the Anglo-American coup plan were four: to start a political and propaganda campaign in which Mossadeq was to be portrayed as a crypto-communist, to encourage the opposition to create disturbances, to press the Shah to dismiss Mossadeq and appoint Zahedi as his replacement, and to obtain the support of military officers for Zahedi's appointment. These activities were to be conducted by the CIA in cooperation with MI6, both of whom had employed Iranian agents. Wilber and Roosevelt prepared propaganda material against Mossadeq, which was translated into Persian and passed on to the CIA. "Given high priority, it poured off the Agency's press and was rushed by air to Tehran."[31]

Meanwhile Zahedi and his men, backed by the Shah, prompted the opposition in the Majlis to intensify their attacks on Mossadeq. Government supporters, finding that Kashani was spearheading the aims of the opposition, voted him out of his position as speaker of the Majlis and replaced him with Abdollah Moazzami, a National

Front supporter. This infuriated Kashani, who decided, with other opposition deputies, to block the approval of any bill that Mossadeq presented to the Majlis outside his emergency powers. Finding that the Majlis had come to a standstill, twenty-seven deputies of the National Front announced their resignation on July 14, 1953; they were followed by twenty-five from other caucuses. This left the Majlis with just over twenty deputies, and it could not function anymore.

On July 22, vast demonstrations took place in Tehran urging the dissolution of the Majlis. What made these demonstrations significant was the strength of the Tudeh crowd as contrasted with the weak showing of the National Front and its supporters. The British lost no time in contending that Mossadeq's supporters were mainly communists. The fact was that Kashani and Baqa'i, who were skillful crowd organizers, did not favor dissolving the Majlis while Tudeh did.

On July 27, in a broadcast to the nation, Mossadeq stated that some foreign powers were bent on overthrowing him to install their own supporters and that a group in the Majlis had assisted them in their schemes. He then announced that he planned to ask the people through a referendum whether or not they wanted the continuation of the current term of such a Majlis, adding that if they did he would resign. In the subsequent referendum the majority voted to dissolve the Majlis, leading to British and American accusations that Mossadeq had terminated the Majlis with communist support. When he held a meeting with the Soviet ambassador to discuss the expansion of trade with Russia, they accused him further of selling Iran to the Russians. Actually, he had earlier rejected a demand that Iran renew the Soviet concession in the Caspian fisheries.

In the state of confusion and bewilderment in Iran over the assassination of Afshartus, the closing of the Majlis, and the division in the ranks of National Front members, the CIA found the soil fertile for the execution of the coup. But the Shah had not yet been told of the coup plot and the need for his support. Henderson was away and the message had to be conveyed to the Shah by someone whom he fully trusted. Roosevelt decided to use the Shah's twin sister, Princess Ashraf, who had been exiled for her subversive activities against Mossadeq's government and lived in France.

To pass the message to Ashraf, he felt he had to find someone who appealed to her. Roosevelt selected for the job an American officer "who regarded himself as the lady-killer of the twentieth century."[32] He and an MI6 officer went to Paris, where they asked the princess to go to Tehran and persuade her brother to cooperate in the execution of the Anglo-American coup plot. Ashraf agreed to do so after being promised that if the coup failed the United States would give her sufficient financial support to go on living abroad in the style to which she was accustomed.[33] On July 25, 1953, Ashraf went to Tehran and told her brother about the contemplated plot. He could not decide whether or not to support the scheme. Meanwhile the princess, suspected of scheming against the government, was told to leave the country.

To persuade the Shah to cooperate in the coup, the CIA director chose General H. Norman Schwarzkopf, who had previously served in Iran as adviser to the Iranian Gendarmerie, the rural police force. Schwarzkopf, a graduate of the U.S. Military Academy and a former head of the New Jersey police, had gone to Iran as a colonel in 1942. During his six years of service in Iran, he successfully trained the Gendarmerie and internal security forces and was active in subduing communist infiltration, particularly in northern Iran. The reasons for using him in 1953 were that he knew the Shah well and that he had many friends among both the Iranian officers and the American military advisers stationed in Iran.[34]

Schwarzkopf arrived in Tehran on August 1 "armed with a diplomatic passport and a couple of large bags [containing] millions of dollars." He met the Shah and assured him that America would give him full support if he cooperated in the coup. He also conferred with Zahedi, who was in hiding, as well as old Iranian and American friends in the military.

These meetings paved the way for the execution of the coup, whose aim was to overthrow Mossadeq and reestablish the Shah's authority so that he would in turn secure Western control over Iranian oil.[35] It is ironic that thirty-eight years later, in 1991, the general's son, General H. Norman Schwarzkopf, Jr., was in the same region commanding a huge force engaged in another oil war—this time to dislodge Iraqi forces from Kuwait so that Saddam Hussein would not become the arbiter of the supply and price of Arab oil.

The elder Schwarzkopf met Roosevelt, who had earlier entered Iran under the name of James Lockridge, and reported to him on his visits with the Shah and others. He urged Roosevelt to meet personally with the Shah and work out with him the execution of Operation Ajax.

On midnight of August 1–2, by arrangements made through the Rashidians, Roosevelt met with the Shah in secret and discussed his plans, telling him that he represented both Eisenhower and Churchill. The Shah did not take him seriously, particularly because he suspected that the Americans were on Mossadeq's side. His doubts, however, were removed when Eisenhower stated at a conference in Seattle on August 4 that Mossadeq, in his drive to get rid of the Parliament, was supported by Iran's communist party and that this was "very ominous for the United States" and the free world. Mossadeq's effort "must be blocked now," said Eisenhower.[36]

The coup plan that Roosevelt spelled out for the Shah included an alliance with some religious leaders, who had asked "huge sums of money"; gaining the support of Iranian military officers; and a program of psychological warfare against Mossadeq. The Shah was told to issue *firmans* dismissing Mossadeq as prime minister and replacing him with Zahedi. Roosevelt assured the Shah that he had ample funds for the operation; his safe was "jam-packed with stacks of rial notes . . . the equivalent of about one million dollars." He then met Zahedi, "who was concealed in a house in the American Embassy compound," and informed him of his discussions with the Shah. Roosevelt reported his activities to Washington through the British relay in Cyprus.[37]

The Shah promised to sign two *firmans* on August 9 dismissing Mossadeq and appointing Zahedi, after which he would leave for his Caspian resort so that he would be away from Tehran during the operation. Instead he flew in panic to the Caspian with his wife, Soraya, before issuing the *firmans*. Roosevelt sent an Iranian agent to the Caspian to obtain the required *firmans*, and the agent returned on August 12 with two sheets signed by the Shah and bearing the Crown emblem but otherwise blank. These sheets were filled in above the signature as Roosevelt instructed.

On August 15 at about midnight, Colonel N. Nassiri, commander of the Imperial Guards, escorted by three truckloads of armed soldiers and four armored cars, went to Mossadeq's house to deliver the Shah's *firman* dismissing him. The plan was to arrest Mossadeq while other officers of the Imperial Guards would arrest Cabinet ministers and the Chief of the Army Staff. But things did not work out that way. Mossadeq, finding it odd that someone should call on him at midnight, did ask the colonel in, and the officers in charge of guarding his house overwhelmed Nassiri's forces and arrested them without a shot being fired. The other plotting officers managed only to arrest two Cabinet ministers and a National Front leader, who were released the following morning. The Imperial Guards were disarmed, fourteen officers suspected of collaborating with Zahedi were arrested, and the government offered a reward to anyone who could locate Zahedi himself.[38]

Upon hearing the news of the abortive coup, the Shah panicked and fled with his wife on their private plane to Bagdad. The CIA drew up contingency plans to fly Zahedi, Roosevelt, and his chief Iranian collaborators out of the country on the U.S. military attaché's plane.[39]

In Tehran, the press berated the Shah, saying that his flight should be viewed as his abdication. The Tudeh party issued a statement demanding the proclamation of a republic. Mossadeq's government announced that there was no intention of changing the regime, but this did not make Shah Mohammad Reza immune. On August 16 there were vast anti-court demonstrations during which Foreign Minister Fatemi, who had been released by the plotters earlier that day, addressed the crowd. The Shah, said Fatemi, had fled to Bagdad "to reach the nearest British Embassy."[40]

In fact the Shah, on his arrival in Bagdad, was anxious to discuss his situation with the British ambassador. Not wanting to "complicate matters" by meeting him in person, the Shah sent word to him asking what he should do. The reply he received was that the question would be put to the Foreign Office. Next the Shah, "tired and perplexed," had a "clandestine meeting" with the U.S. ambassador, from whom he wanted "urgent guidance." The ambassador gave the routine reply that he would refer the matter to Washington.[41]

The Shah's inability in 1953 to make decisions affecting his own fate and that of his country, and his requests that the British and

American ambassadors decide for him, were an exact replica of his actions in 1978, twenty-five years later, when Ayatollah Khomeini fomented a rebellion against him. In that year, too, he wanted the ambassadors of Britain and the United States to tell him what to do.

Having lost hope of regaining his throne, the Shah urged the American embassy to arrange the sale of his plane. But since the Iranian embassy wanted the Iraqi authorities to hand over the aircraft to them, the Americans, as well as the British, avoided getting involved.[42] Meanwhile there was confusion in London and Washington over what should be their advice to the Shah. At the Foreign Office, Assistant Under Secretary of State Reginald Bowker weighed the alternatives. Should he urge the Shah to abdicate or not to abdicate? Analyzing various options, he said: "It may be argued that the Shah by running away with so little dignity . . . cannot be relied upon at any future time to exercise effective leadership, [and thus] it is no use keeping him as a possible leader or focus of loyalty." He felt, however, that Britain should follow the American recommendation, which was to have the Shah insist that he was Iran's legal sovereign. Since he doubted that Mossadeq could be removed at any time soon, he suggested that the Shah be advised to remain somewhere in the Middle East for the time being.[43]

Not receiving a satisfactory answer from the British and American embassies, the Shah and his wife flew by British commercial plane on August 18 to Rome, where the Italian press talked of "the staffless, baggageless, moneyless royal couple." On arrival, the Shah stated that he did not intend to ask Italy for political asylum, but the *Daily Telegraph*'s Rome correspondent predicted, "He will probably join the small colony of exiled monarchs already in Rome." The Shah told his queen that he might instead go to the United States, where his mother and one of his sisters were living.[44]

Meanwhile, Under Secretary of State Walter Bedell Smith told the British in Washington that the Americans were "inclined to make attempts to improve their relations with Musaddiq."[45] Furthermore, he sent a radio message to Kermit Roosevelt telling him to give up the scheme and get out. But since the flight of the Shah, Roosevelt had taken a series of measures to revive the coup and the prospects looked bright to him.

The day after the Shah's flight to Bagdad, CIA and MI6 local agents, assisted by Zahedi's men, distributed vast numbers of copies of the Shah's *firman* appointing Zahedi prime minister. They consolidated the opponents of Mossadeq, who consisted of retired army officers, some active officers loyal to the Shah, old-guard politicians who had lost their influence and power under Mossadeq, and a number of big businessmen whose profits had been badly hurt as a result of the oil embargo. They also contacted two leaders of the Qashqa'i tribe, who were Mossadeq's allies, and offered to pay them $4 million provided the tribe led a revolt against Mossadeq and recognized Zahedi as prime minister. The two rejected the offer, saying that they were not prepared to stab Mossadeq in the back.[46]

Roosevelt knew that his most difficult problem was Mossadeq's wide popularity. In an effort to discredit the prime minister, Roosevelt's men flooded Tehran with clandestine papers carrying articles that categorically described Mossadeq as a communist collaborator and a fanatic. In addition, with the help of the Rashidian brothers, he hired a large crowd of people at a cost of $50,000 and told them to act as if they were Tudeh members. On August 17, the "rented" crowd, shouting communist slogans, threw rocks at mosques and Moslem clergymen. The crowd, later joined by credulous Tudeh members passing by, tore down statues of the Shah and his father and denounced both of them.[47] The author, who witnessed these events, was puzzled by them. But Roosevelt, who knew what was going on, enjoyed the potential impact of what his hired mob did. "I recognized," he said, "that this was the best thing we could have hoped for. The more they shouted against the Shah, the more the army and the people recognized them as the enemy."[48]

According to Richard Cottam, the "people we had under our control . . . were more than just provocators, they were shock troops." What they did was to inspire fears of a communist takeover and create an atmosphere that compelled onlookers to choose between Mossadeq—who was portrayed as the one who had let the communists loose—and the monarchy, an established institution.[49] The result was that Mossadeq's popularity waned while hostility to the Shah turned into indifference.

Mossadeq, unhappy at seeing the Shah's statues torn down, instructed the police to suppress the Tudeh, thinking they were the real instigators. Furthermore, at the request of U.S. ambassador Loy

Henderson, who had flown back to Tehran after the Shah's flight, Mossadeq ordered full protection for the Americans. He was aware of the coup plot, however, and of those Iranians, widely known to be British agents, who were working for his overthrow. Nur ed-Din Kianuri, the Tudeh party leader, who had learned about the impending coup through the party's intelligence network, wanted Mossadeq to take countermeasures by appealing to the people and by providing arms to the Tudeh to stand against the plotters; but Mossadeq refused. He did not want people to risk their lives to keep him in power, nor did he want to rely on the Tudeh.[50]

This left the way open for Roosevelt, who was soon joined by General Robert McClure, chief of the U.S. military mission to Iran. McClure took up the task of dealing with the Iranian Army. In an effort to keep Brigadier General Taqi Riahi, Iran's chief of staff, away from Tehran while a second coup was tried, McClure invited Riahi to join him for a few days of rest and fishing. When Riahi declined the invitation, McClure observed that since the U.S. advisory mission was to the Shah's court, he had no responsibilities toward Mossadeq, adding that they both had to support the Shah. Riahi rejected his suggestion, saying that they both had to serve Iran.

McClure decided to contact army commanders personally. On August 16 he flew to Isfahan, where he asked General M. Davallu, commander of the Isfahan garrison, to distribute among his officers copies of the Shah's decree appointing Zahedi prime minister. Furthermore he bluntly instructed Davallu to send forces to Tehran to subdue the supporters of Mossadeq's government, which he considered illegal. He said that he had already contacted Colonel Teymur Bakhtiar, commander of Kermanshah garrison, and that Bakhtiar had agreed to send forces to Tehran. Davallu replied that he was responsible to Prime Minister Mossadeq and the Army staff, not to an American officer. McClure ended the meeting by saying, "I will kick Mossadeq out of office."[51]

McClure and his men had better success in Tehran, where they cooperated with retired officers to bring a number of active officers to the Shah's side with cash and promises of promotion; among these were commanders of a tank battalion and two infantry regiments. In addition, to prevent the police from opposing planned riots by hired mobs, Brigadier General M. Daftari, an officer close to Zahedi, talked Mossadeq into giving him command of the police force, claiming that he would faithfully serve him.[52]

With every preparation made by CIA and MI6 men, Kermit Roosevelt set the date of the second coup attempt for August 19, 1953. Since the outcome was unpredictable and the Americans did not know whether or not the Tudeh would play an active role against the coup, precautionary measures were taken in Washington. The National Security Council asked for recommendations from the Joint Chiefs of Staff on "courses of military action in Iran, in support of a non-communist Iranian Government" in case the Shah requested "some degree of military support." Subsequently, the Joint Chiefs considered "the outline of possible emergency military actions" in support of the Shah, and the exigency plans for the deployment of "ground, air, and naval forces to Iran."[53]

On the morning of August 19, groups of paid thugs appeared in various sections of Tehran. They stopped all cars, giving the drivers pictures of the Shah to stick in their windows and telling them to put on their lights. If anyone resisted, he was beaten and the windows of his car were broken. Soon the center of Tehran was flooded with cars carrying the Shah's picture. Meanwhile from the city center a large mob of weight lifters, wrestlers, and others equipped with clubs, chains, sticks, and knives, headed by Sha'ban Ja'fari, known as "Sha'ban the brainless," marched toward Mossadeq's house shouting "Long live the Shah." In front of the group were jugglers, tumblers, and bazaar barkers. The mob leaders had used CIA funds to provide "every entertainment that money could buy" so as to attract passersby to join the mob.[54]

The same mob that two days earlier had pretended to be communists demanding the Shah's overthrow was now proclaiming its revulsion to those demands and asking for Mossadeq's overthrow. Cottam concedes that it was "a mercenary mob. It had no ideology. That mob was paid for by American dollars." And it was protected by truckloads of policemen and soldiers whose commanders were promised money and promotion to join the Shah's supporters. When General Riahi sent a column to suppress the mob, Police Chief Daftari, who as we have seen was in fact on Zahedi's side, told the officers of the army column: "We are colleagues and brothers all faithful to the Shah and should not fire at each other." Pro-Mossadeq crowds began to move in but found that they were no match for armed mobs protected by the military. There were no signs of the Tudeh party, some of whose members had been clubbed by the police the day before at Mossadeq's orders.[55]

The hired mob, now joined by some police and army units, set fire to the buildings of pro-Mossadeq and Tudeh newspapers and political parties that supported Mossadeq. Another group occupied the Tehran Radio Station. Zahedi moved out of hiding and was driven on a tank to the radio station, where he announced his takeover. When a corps of the Shah's Imperial Guards attacked Mossadeq's house with Sherman tanks, bazookas, and artillery, Colonel E. Momtaz, who was in charge of the forces protecting the house, moved Mossadeq and his aides out over the back wall. His forces then began their counterattack. A long, bitter battle ensued in which some 300 people were killed. Among them were some members of the hired mob, in whose pockets were found 500-rial banknotes paid to them by the CIA men that morning for their participation. Mossadeq's house was subsequently stormed and ransacked.[56]

On the same day Zahedi installed himself as prime minister. Mossadeq and his colleagues gave themselves up on the following day. Many government ministers, National Front leaders, and army officers loyal to Mossadeq, as well as a large number of Tudeh leaders, were arrested by Zahedi's men, and those detained by Mossadeq during the abortive coup were released. General Zahedi's son, Ardeshir, asked Ambassador Henderson if there was anything he wanted Zahedi to do. Henderson's reply was that he wanted to make sure that no bodily harm came to Mossadeq. Zahedi in turn assured the press that "not a hair of his head would be harmed."[57]

Zahedi and Roosevelt cabled the Shah in Rome, telling him to return. He flew back on August 23 on a chartered Dutch plane along with twenty foreign correspondents. As a precaution, his arrival was not previously announced, and the road leading from the airport to his palace was lined with tanks, armored cars, and troops.

With an expenditure of $7 million,[58] the CIA ended Mossadeq's popular nationalist movement and with it the hopes of Iranians to manage their own affairs without the interference of foreign powers. The Americans thus performed with their own funds the job that Britain had been seeking ways to perform for over two years.

The news of Mossadeq's fall reached Eden while he was convalescing on a Mediterranean cruise, and he "slept happily that night."[59] The British press, which never even hinted that the coup had been plotted by Britain and the United States, gave the whole credit to the "royalists." Mossadeq's house was described as "fortified by a bunker-like structure built of steel and concrete,"[60] a structure "reminiscent of Hitler's last days."[61] That Mossadeq had an ordinary house with no fortifications is attested by the author, who then lived on the same street.[62]

The London *Times*, however, reminded its readers that General Zahedi, the new prime minister, had been kidnapped in 1942 by British officers in Iran at a time when "he was suspected of planning with the German high command a rising against the allied occupation forces in Persia." Fitzroy Maclean, who during the war was in charge of this kidnapping and belittled Zahedi,[63] now sought to make amends. In a broadcast over the BBC World Service on August 20, he said that in the course of the 1942 kidnapping he had "pressed a Colt automatic into the lower ribs of the prime minister of Persia." Happily the general had not resisted; otherwise he would have had to shoot him, depriving Iran of "a charming . . . loyal and patriotic officer . . . [who] would not have been there to carry out the remarkable coup" against Mossadeq. Although Mossadeq "had put himself into the arms of the Russians," he said, there was "no earthly reason to suppose that the Americans had anything to do with General Zahedi's success."

At a British Cabinet meeting on August 25, 1953, Churchill, who himself had had a major share in involving the Americans in the coup, showed concern about the consequences of their involvement. He said that now "it would be easy for the Americans, by the expenditure of a small amount of money, to keep all the benefits of many years of British work in Persia."[64] He was right to be concerned: the Americans did indeed replace Britain in Iran after the coup. That was the price Britain had to pay for her impossibly high-handed behavior during her years in Iran.

21

An Oil Consortium Takes Over

The success of the Anglo-American coup delighted the British, who had longed for such an event for over two years. They were now eager to reach a favorable settlement with Zahedi's government but unwilling to help it financially. The U.S. government, however, decided to back the new prime minister by giving him $45 million in emergency aid, and Henderson suggested that further assistance be given.[1]

The British were not happy about this development. Dixon noted that "if he [Zahedi] can get money out of the Americans . . . he will be less inclined to come to a reasonable settlement of the oil dispute." Furthermore he was concerned that the Americans, as part of the process of giving aid to Iran, might take the initiative in solving the dispute and impose their terms on the British. Lord Salisbury, who in the absence of Eden was in charge of the Foreign Office, felt that "if we give the impression in Washington that we are only concerned with our oil to the exclusion of the necessity of keeping Persia in the anti-communist camp, we may lose all control over American action." In spite of these considerations, British ambassador Sir Roger Makins requested Secretary of State Dulles not to give any further aid to Zahedi lest the resulting financial relief cause him to relax his efforts to settle the oil dispute.[2]

With Mossadeq gone, AIOC chairman Sir William Fraser insisted that the company be permitted to return to Iran without delay. But Sam Falle, who had participated in the coup plot, observed: "The A.I.O.C. are capable of any bêtise. I trust it is fully and universally understood that the A.I.O.C. stink in Persia and any attempt to reinstate them, in whatever guise or form, is bound to fail."[3] The Foreign Office, too, felt that AIOC could never recover its monopoly and should instead make arrangements for participation with American oil companies in exploiting Iranian oil; after all, it was the direct intervention of the United States in Iran that had brought about Mossadeq's downfall. But Fraser worried that AIOC's "prestige" would suffer if Americans were let in.[4]

Meanwhile the State Department looked for someone who could work out a solution to the oil problem. Assistant Secretary of State Henry Byroade suggested Walter Levy, but Dulles himself chose Herbert Hoover, Jr., the son of a former U.S. president, who headed the Consolidated Engineering Corporation and had long experience in the oil business. He was appointed in mid-September 1953 as assistant to Dulles on the Iranian oil problem.[5]

Hoover argued that since Iran's oil exports had been replaced by oil from other sources, the only way to export large quantities of Iranian oil was to get the cooperation of the entire petroleum industry. Furthermore, he contended that no reputable oil company would take part in such an operation without being given effective management control, and also that Iran should not expect to get better terms than other producers. Dulles was persuaded. He cabled U.S. Ambassador Henderson to say that the February proposals made to Mossadeq were no longer workable, and that he should see if Iran would agree to having a new operating concern owned by AIOC, Shell, and American companies with "title to or lease of all producing and refining facilities" for at least forty years, paying Iran 50 percent of the profits.[6]

Henderson cabled back that if such a settlement were imposed, "friends of the west in Iran . . . would consider that they had been deceived and betrayed by their British and American friends." The general public would say that the "greatest danger to Iranian independence was from direction of western imperialists who now in their moment of triumph were insisting that Iran agree for [a] period of another forty years to suffer under the yoke [of] foreign oil concessionaires." Henderson thought it "not unlikely [that] Zahedi's Government would resign at once" rather than sign such an agreement," and that the "Shah in despair would abdicate."[7]

Anthony Eden, who had returned to work after months of illness, sent a message to John Foster Dulles praising Henderson for "the admirable way in which [he] had handled matters" to Britain's satisfaction and asking Dulles to let Henderson know "how grateful

I am for the part he has played." Eden added that the immediate aim should be for Britain to reestablish relations with Iran. That way the two countries could discuss things directly rather than through intermediaries, "however trusted and well briefed" they might be. In other words, he did not want the Americans to conduct negotiations in the absence of the British. He then asked Dulles to tell Hoover to stop in London on his way to Tehran.[8]

Dulles did not want Hoover to be seen at the Foreign Office lest the Iranians suspect collusion between the Americans and the British. Instead Allen Dulles of the CIA arranged a clandestine meeting in Amsterdam between Hoover, Neville Gass, and Basil Jackson of AIOC. Hoover assured Gass and Jackson that he would not ignore AIOC's interests and would make certain that Iran did not get better terms than other producers.[9]

Hoover went to Tehran late in October 1953 and met with various authorities there, giving them each a paper he had prepared in consultation with some U.S. oil companies that emphasized the world oil surplus and the need to bring in major oil companies to enable Iranian oil to flow back to world markets. The Shah agreed with this analysis but warned Hoover that the British and the Americans should not press the government to the "extent which would strengthen impression among Iranians [that] it is subservient to great powers of [the] West."

Zahedi felt the same way, telling Henderson that he did not wish his government to "appear to be a puppet of the United States and United Kingdom Governments."[10] He told Hoover that any solution involving foreign control and equal division of profits would create difficulties for his government. Iran was different from other Middle Eastern producers, he said, because the capital invested by the British in Iranian oil had been recovered many times over through "exorbitant profits realised by the AIOC." Furthermore, said Zahedi, if the goal was to settle on a 50-50 basis, he saw no reason for Iran to pay compensation.[11]

The Iranian government was against AIOC's having a major share in a consortium of oil companies, and it was against foreign control. A note from Nasrollah Entezam, Iran's foreign minister, informed Henderson that AIOC was hated in Iran. The government of Iran was prepared to negotiate "for the sale of oil" with a group of major international oil companies, but not a group in which the British oil companies had a major share.[12]

Secretary of State Dulles was delighted that the Iranians had rejected AIOC majority holding. He cabled Henderson that this was "absolutely best thing that has happened so far. . . . Fact that Iran took aggressive initiative [on AIOC] was of great psychological importance." When Dulles informed Eden that he could not support an AIOC majority,[13] Eden replied that AIOC's minimum participation should be 51 percent, a figure clearly implying effective management control.[14] On learning of this proposal, Henderson cabled Dulles that no U.S. company should be asked to run the risk of investing in a consortium in which 51 percent of the shares were British-owned.[15]

When the United States rejected AIOC majority participation, the British suspected that the American oil companies were intent on grabbing their oil interests in Iran. It was also suspected that Hoover and Byroade were in league with the American companies. D. Greenhill of the Foreign Office noted that "there can be little doubt that Mr. Hoover is persona grata with the [U.S.] oil boys."[16] According to the *Sunday Observer* of October 19, 1953, Henderson, too, had been influenced by the oil lobby, and American diplomacy was working overtime to establish solid influence in Iran before diplomatic relations between Iran and Britain could be resumed.

The Americans, for their part, were suspicious of the British. According to Byroade, "many Persians . . . feared that HM Government might work for the overthrow of the present Government if they could not extract a satisfactory oil agreement with them." Eden, upset by this assertion, noted that "Byroade is either very stupid or mischievous."[17] But Zahedi himself, who had been kidnapped and imprisoned by the British during the war, could not help being suspicious of them.

In an effort to create an atmosphere conducive to the resumption of relations with Britain and the conclusion of an agreement with a group of foreign oil companies, the Iranian government, funded by the United States, fed the press with articles criticizing Mossadeq's past policies and tactics.[18] One paper went so far as to claim that Mossadeq had nationalized the oil industry in collusion with Britain: "beyond doubt, the British themselves forced nationalization on Iran as they did not need our oil or the Abadan refinery."[19]

Such statements did not go unchallenged. In an open letter to the prime minister, Makki called on the government not to distort facts and to proceed according to the oil nationalization law. He opposed the resumption of relations with Britain, warning that this would enable the British "to send their agents and spies back to Iran to pave the way for an oil settlement worse than the 1933 Concession." Kashani, who had supported Zahedi's rise to power and had been left unrewarded, stated in a broadcast message, "I shall not allow the revival of the former British oil company and of imperialism in Iran."[20] Zahedi welcomed such statements, which helped him argue that the Iranian public could not accept the return of AIOC.

In December 1953, Zahedi, who had by then tightened his grip over Iran, informed Henderson that his government was prepared to resume diplomatic relations with Britain provided that the British first showed their goodwill by such measures as lifting the oil embargo; otherwise his action would appear to the public as capitulation. On Henderson's urging, Zahedi resumed relations without waiting for any sign of goodwill. However, he told Vice President Richard Nixon, who was in Tehran in the second week of December, that he had taken a "dangerous step"; if the British remained intransigent, his government could not survive.[21]

While awaiting a decision on the choice of an ambassador to Iran, Eden sent Denis Wright to Tehran as chargé d'affaires. According to Eden, Wright had "acute intelligence and a considerable knowledge of economic matters, including the problems of the oil industry."[22] He had served as head of the Economic Relations Department at the Foreign Office. AIOC chairman Fraser was annoyed that Eden had not consulted him on this appointment. Wright arrived in Tehran late in December, fourteen months after the embassy was closed, with a team of fourteen people. He was followed several weeks later by Sir Roger Stevens, ambassador in Sweden, whom Eden chose as ambassador to Iran because of his economic knowledge.

The day after Wright's arrival, two emissaries of the Shah handed him a *bout de papier* from the sovereign, which said that all questions of high policy on oil should be cleared with him first. Wright promptly informed Iran's foreign minister about this clandestine approach, thus gaining the confidence of Zahedi's government. But the Shah was upset that he had been exposed as not trusting his prime minister.[23]

Wright soon found that "there is much latent support for Musaddiq throughout the country." He informed Eden that although Zahedi's "Government appear to be well in control . . . they lack popular support." He added that AIOC "would be courting disaster" if it returned to Iran. His advice was that Britain should genuinely show her good faith to Iran and that "a reasonable settlement will do more than any words."[24]

Meanwhile, Herbert Hoover, Jr., pursued his consortium idea, which ran against U.S. antitrust laws. In fact the U.S. Justice Department on April 21, 1953, had filed a civil complaint against some of the very same American oil companies that Hoover had in mind for his consortium. It was alleged that these companies "have unlawfully . . . monopolized trade and commerce in petroleum and products," and that they had fixed oil prices while dividing world markets among themselves.[25] There were ways to obtain antitrust immunity, however, by the use of such catchwords as "the threat of communism" and "the security interests of the free world." Backed by President Eisenhower and the National Security Council, Hoover obtained clearance from Herbert Brownell, the U.S. attorney general, to proceed with the formation of a consortium to run Iran's oil industry.[26] He followed this up by holding discussions with some major U.S. oil companies, telling them that their cooperation was considered essential by the National Security Council.[27]

Fraser, who had come to realize that AIOC could no longer operate alone in Iran, invited the presidents of seven major oil companies to London for discussions on the formation of a consortium. As if he considered these corporation heads below his rank, Fraser's invitation was signed by Eric Drake, his deputy.[28]

In mid-December, Hoover and the representatives of eight major oil companies—Standard Oil of California, Standard Oil of New Jersey, Texaco, Gulf, Socony-Vacuum, Compagnie Française des Pétroles (CFP), Shell, and AIOC—met for three days in AIOC's offices in London. Fraser, who opened the meeting, stated that in any future arrangement he wanted AIOC to have 50 percent participation; other companies desiring to have a share in Iran's oil industry should pay adequate compensation to AIOC for their participation. Hoover opposed AIOC having so large a share in the consortium, saying that it was politically unrealistic. Dulles strengthened his hand by hinting that "the present Persian government had been put in office by the Americans."[29] It followed that the initiative should remain in American hands and that Britain and AIOC would do better to keep a low profile.

After much wrangling, AIOC agreed to accept 40 percent, leaving 40 percent to U.S. oil companies and 12 percent to Shell. Fraser offered the remaining 8 percent to CFP, but the Americans objected; because the French company was subject to British domination, the proposed arrangement would give AIOC working control over the consortium. Agreement was finally reached at the end of March when CFP consented to take no more than 6 percent. This increased Shell's share from 12 percent to 14 percent.[30]

The next step was to arrive at a financial deal with Fraser, which proved to be a formidable task. On March 12, 1954, Hoover and the representatives of the consortium met again in London, where Fraser divulged his thoughts on what he expected the other companies to pay AIOC for their participation. He said one approach to the problem was to calculate how much AIOC had lost by being deprived of Iran's oil reserves, which he estimated at 5.5 billion tons. Considering these reserves to be the property of his company, he stated that their value underground at 20 cents per barrel would amount to over $8 billion. Rather than ask for so much, however, he proposed that the companies pay AIOC 10 cents per barrel for a certain amount of production as well as cash totaling $1.267 billion, based on 100 percent participation. In addition he expected Iran to pay compensation "for rupture of agreement" by providing AIOC with 110 million tons of free oil over a 20-year period. At the then current price of $1.90 per barrel this came to $1.463 billion, an amount that Fraser did not consider "burdensome to Iran's economy." Fraser thus sought, in addition to 10 cents a barrel on oil produced by new participants, a total of $2.73 billion (on a 100 percent basis) as compensation for AIOC's losses in Iran.[31] It is worth noting that the company's annual statement for 1951 had valued its installations in Iran at $94 million.

The American oil companies and Shell submitted counterproposals arguing that any payments made to AIOC in consideration of its rights and interests in Iran should be based on the commercial value of those rights and not on Iran's reserves. Furthermore, they argued that if AIOC sold its rights, it could not at the same time claim compensation of $1.463 billion in free oil from Iran. They suggested that payments to AIOC (on a 100 percent basis) should total $800 million.[32] This was the amount that Walter Levy had estimated to be the total value of AIOC's enterprise in Iran.

When Fraser stuck to his proposal, Hoover cabled Dulles that if the consortium were to negotiate a 50-50 type arrangement with Iran, there was no reason for Iran to pay compensation to AIOC. Furthermore, he argued that AIOC, as a participant in the consortium, would not be deprived of any future operating profits because it would be getting as much Iranian oil as it could market; thus "it is not giving up or selling out anything which would cut back its present business." Hoover called Fraser's proposals "absolutely unacceptable."[33] Henderson agreed, calling Fraser's demand for payment of compensation by Iran "fantastic." He pointed out that Iran had hundreds of millions of dollars of counterclaims, most of which were considered valid by French and Belgian jurists. In his opinion AIOC's best course was to cancel these counterclaims by ignoring its own claims.[34]

Irritated by Fraser's exorbitant demands, Dulles cabled Winthrop Aldrich, U.S. ambassador in London, asking him to tell Eden that unless Fraser drastically changed his attitude American companies would break off negotiations. He added: "Such a development would undoubtedly . . . force us to reconsider our whole attitude toward the Iranian oil question since it would appear impossible ever to obtain a reasonable solution to the Anglo-Iranian oil dispute in the face of such obstacles. It might ultimately force us, with great reluctance, to review the whole scope of our Middle East relationships."[35]

This was an ultimatum that Eden could not ignore. To calm nerves in Washington, he advised the State Department that if Iran accepted a 50-50 arrangement, all that AIOC would ask in compensation would be "a net sum in the order of £100 million [$280 million]" and not the $1.463 billion worth of oil demanded by Fraser. With regard to payment by participants, Eden informed

Aldrich that he had told Fraser to find an acceptable medium between his figure and that of the American group. An agreement was finally reached on March 19, when AIOC reduced its claim to $1 billion (on a 100 percent basis). This meant that the five U.S. majors, Shell, and the French company had to pay to AIOC $600 million for their 60 percent participation. Of this amount, $150 million had to be paid in cash and the balance at the rate of 10 cents per barrel over twenty-four years.[36]

What remained unsettled was the sum of £100 million that Britain expected Iran to pay as compensation. Henderson cabled both Dulles and Hoover that paying compensation would cause Iran to receive less income per barrel than other oil-producing countries. Moreover, an agreement giving Iran no control over her oil industry, dividing the profits equally between Iran and the consortium, and forcing the country to pay compensation as well "will generally be considered in Iran despite all face saving devices as national capitulation." Byroade, too, considered it absurd for AIOC to claim anything from Iran. But the British insisted. To keep Iran in isolation and deprive her of U.S. support, the British government proposed that the amount of compensation be left to Britain to negotiate directly with Iran. Hoover and Aldrich yielded to this proposal when they found that the whole consortium deal would collapse if they did not.[37]

Early in April 1954, the London negotiations ended with a memorandum of understanding entitled "Basis for Settlement with Anglo-Iranian." The eight signers agreed to form an oil consortium composed of AIOC with a 40 percent share, American companies 40 percent, Shell 14 percent, and CFP 6 percent. The five American companies, with a share of 8 percent each, were Standard Oil of New Jersey, Standard Oil of California, Socony-Vacuum, Texaco, and Gulf.

Before the consortium representatives left for Tehran, Ambassador, Sir Roger Stevens, sent Eden a report on the political situation in Iran. "Nationalistic principles remain sacred," he told Eden, and the government "cannot afford an agreement which does not look presentable." Mossadeq's legacy, he said, could not be simply ignored; indeed, it would haunt the impending negotiations. He added:

It will be no ordinary trial of wits. I should compare it rather to a meeting of co-executors of the estate of an elderly crank as troublesome in death as in life. He has left an eccentric will to which the settlement must outwardly conform, but the executors are really engaged together in a conspiracy to interpret the will liberally enough to enable the monies to be invested in such a way as to bring maximum profit to all the beneficiaries.[38]

The negotiators began their discussions in Tehran in mid-April 1954. The British government sent David Serpell of the Treasury and Angus Beckett of the Ministry of Fuel and Power to Tehran to monitor the negotiations. Beckett had an additional job: to "trail" Hoover and report on his every word and move. To this end he booked a room in the same hotel as Hoover and tried repeatedly to engage him in conversation. But he found little to report to his superiors about Hoover "except for an occasional crack at the British" and a tendency "to sneak off to bed."[39]

To smooth negotiations with Iran after twenty-eight months of open hostility on the part of the British, Eden stated in the House of Commons on April 12 that Britain welcomed the establishment of the consortium and that his government's policy was "to do all in their power to ensure the well-being and prosperity of Persia." As we have seen, this was far from the truth. Moreover, not everyone in Britain was happy about a mixed consortium taking over oil operations in Iran. The *Sunday Express* wrote on April 18:

With Mosadeq . . . pushed out, you might expect our full legal rights to be restored to us. If you do you underestimate the power of American oil interests. After months of secret negotiations, there is to be a "cut-up". . . . The carve-up means that Britain will no longer have exclusive control over any oil territory in the world, except Brunei in Borneo. . . . The lion is not only having his tail twisted; he is being skinned. And the British Government . . . is acquiescing tamely in the skinning.

Negotiations in Tehran were conducted by Orville Harden, chairman of Jersey Standard, on behalf of the U.S. oil companies; H. E. Snow, a director of AIOC; and John Loudon, president of Shell. F. R. Berbigier of CFP attended as an observer. On the Iranian side was a committee of three headed by Finance Minister Dr. Ali Amini, a French-educated economist who was an in-law of Mossadeq's and had served briefly in his Cabinet. No less important was an Iranian subcommittee of four that dealt with technical and legal details and met with its counterparts from the consortium.[40]

For help in the negotiations Iran originally employed two consultants, but Ambassador Stevens disapproved of both men and persuaded the Iranians to replace them with Torkild Rieber, a former president of Texaco, who had been suggested by Hoover. It is interesting to note that before making this suggestion Hoover consulted Eden, who endorsed it but cautioned that his endorsement should not be made known to Iran.[41] As Eden expected, Rieber and his assistant Wortham Davenport, an American lawyer, furthered the consortium's aims rather than Iran's. For example, when the Iranians asked the two men how much oil they might be able to sell without bringing in foreign oil companies, they replied, "As much as you can pour in your hat."[42]

On behalf of the British government Stevens, Wright, Serpell, and Beckett attended the negotiations as observers. Other observers were Henderson and William Rountree of the U.S. embassy and the Dutch minister in Tehran.[43]

The consortium representatives began their negotiations with an effort at deception. They submitted a proposal that in reality gave the participating companies full managerial and operational control of the Iranian oil industry and yet "one which would not make it appear as though Iran Government had, contrary to nationalization law and deeply felt desire of Iran public, removed itself from control of industry." The Iranians rejected the proposal, saying that they expected the consortium to function as an agent of NIOC. The consortium representatives argued that such an arrangement would encourage other oil-producing countries in which they operated to nationalize and ask for similar terms.[44]

Other differences became apparent among the consortium members themselves. The British, as a matter of prestige as well as a desire to maintain maximum control, wanted the nationality of the consortium company and its managers to be British, its place of registration in London, and its location at AIOC headquarters in the British capital. The Iranians were "hysterically antagonistic" to

U.K. registration and management. Shell and the American companies opposed British management, preferring Dutch, and wanted the company's location to be Iran so as to minimize British interference. Fraser opposed Dutch registration and management "unless they were purely 'brass plate' companies and steps were taken to ensure that the real business was controlled in London."[45]

The consortium was intent on giving Iran 50 percent of the net profits, but the Iranian government feared that "undisguised 50-50 profit sharing" would lead the public to accuse it of capitulation. Furthermore, there was the question of the currency in which payments to Iran would be made. The British wanted payments to be in pound sterling so as to bring Iran's foreign expenditures under British exchange controls.

The five American oil companies, all of which had access to major oil supplies in the Middle East and elsewhere, had joined the consortium "in the interest of the policy of the United States Government." They were not prepared, however, to make any arrangement that was not beneficial to them. Thus, whenever AIOC tried to impose its will or Iran did not accept their conditions, the American companies simply threatened to pull out.[46]

All these differences brought the negotiations to a stalemate, and the consortium representatives decided to leave Tehran for consultations with their principals. In addition, the U.S. oil companies considered it essential to consult the U.S. administration. At a high-level meeting in Washington on May 21, 1954, attended by, among others, Secretary of the Treasury Humphrey, Deputy Secretary of Defense Charles Anderson, and the representatives of the five American companies, the company representatives made it clear that in their judgment any arrangement with Iran should be on a 50-50 basis, payments to Iran should be made chiefly in the form of Iranian income tax so as to exempt this money from American taxes, the duration of the agreement should be the same as that of the AIOC concession, and the consortium should have "full and effective management of all oil operations." The U.S. government officials supported the companies' position. They argued that "failure to achieve a settlement would not only threaten US commercial interests in the Middle East but . . . would threaten US national security," which necessitated saving Iran from communist control."[47]

Meanwhile, in Tehran, Zahedi's problems were not confined to the oil question. Hoping to remove him from office with American consent, the Shah asked Henderson who he thought should be prime minister if Zahedi failed to reach an oil agreement within the framework of the nationalization law. Henderson replied that a solution could be found within a "liberal interpretation" of the law, and that it was unwise to change the Cabinet in the middle of oil negotiations. Henderson asked the British, too, to advise the Shah against a change of government at this juncture, and the Foreign Office complied. As Aldrich noted, however, the British avoided "specific endorsement of Zahedi (regarding whom they evidently have some reservations)."[48]

All this time the British were pressing Iran on the question of compensation. In a note to the Iranian government, Ambassador Stevens said the consortium negotiations could not come to a successful end until the compensation issue was settled. In a disingenuous attempt to portray AIOC as magnanimous, Stevens's note said that the company did not intend to claim compensation for the loss of future profits or for assets to be used by the consortium. It did intend to claim compensation for having been deprived of 100 million tons of Iranian oil between 1951 and 1954, during which time it had been "forced to incur abnormal expenditure" to purchase oil for its customers from other sources. And it intended to claim compensation for the Kermanshah refinery, the Nafti-Shah oil field, and the internal distribution facilities that were to be left to the Iranian government. In the course of discussions, the British revealed that all these claims added up to £263 million.[49]

The Iranians rejected AIOC's pretense of magnanimity in overlooking future profits and the cost of installations; plainly, they said, the company could not claim compensation from Iran for these interests and at the same time sell them to the consortium. They also rejected the claim that the company had been deprived of Iranian oil for three years, saying that Iran had repeatedly offered to sell oil and that AIOC had refused to buy it. They then enumerated in detail Iran's counterclaims, which added up to more than £300 million. These included unpaid royalties and taxes, Iran's share in AIOC's reserves and dividends, and finally a sum of £50 million to repay damage attributable to the British oil boycott. In the course of eighteen sessions of hard bargaining, a settlement was reached at the end of July 1954 in which Iran agreed to pay a net compensation of £25 million in ten yearly installments of £2.5 million beginning in 1957.[50]

Regarding the currency in which the consortium would pay Iran, Finance Minister Amini believed that the best arrangement would be for each member company to pay in the currency of its own country. The British, as we have seen, insisted on sterling, which would compel Iran to import items from the sterling area even when such items were not competitively priced. The French had earlier threatened to withdraw from the group if they were compelled to "pay for oil in sterling convertible only at the pleasure of the British who would be in [a] position [to] give British firms preference over the French." Henderson, too, considered it unfair to give Britain a "whip hand over Iranian foreign trade," and Secretary of the Treasury Humphrey noted that such an arrangement would discriminate against U.S. exports. It was finally agreed that payments to Iran would be made in sterling, but that Britain would convert 40 percent of Iran's receipts from the consortium to other currencies needed in Iranian trade.[51]

The second round of consortium negotiations began on June 22, 1954. In this round the chief representative of the U.S. oil companies was Howard Page, vice president and director of Jersey Standard, replacing Harden, who had taken ill. Page, who had joined Jersey Standard twenty-five years earlier, had shown his shrewd negotiating ability on various occasions. Furthermore, he had excellent credentials with the British for having wholeheartedly backed the Iranian oil boycott.

During the course of negotiations, the Iranians continued to resist allowing the consortium to take full control of management and pay Iran 50 percent of the profits. But they were not in a strong position. The government, installed by an Anglo-American coup, could not stand against the companies supported by the coup makers. Amini's only hope was to obtain terms that would not look humiliating to the Iranian public. In the opinion of John Loudon, president of Shell, who attended the meetings, "Amini was a good negotiator and was honest in his argumentation of Iran's case," but he knew that Iran was in a weak position and thus "did not try hard to bargain for more than 50% of the profits." The other side, fully exploiting Iran's weakness, made its offer and said "Take it or leave it." As Amini recalled, "Whenever I pressed on for better terms, Page would say, 'The U.S. Government has asked us to find markets for your oil; if you don't like our terms we will go back home.' "[52]

By mid-July the problem had boiled down to "reaching agreement on language." On the one hand, it was necessary to satisfy the demands of the consortium regarding the management and control of Iran's oil industry; on the other hand, it was necessary to convince the Iranian public that Iran's nationalization of oil had not been nullified. The legal counsel of the eight participating companies, in consultation with Iranian delegates, worked out the wording and on August 4 drew up a "Heads of Agreement" embodying the principles agreed upon.

On the following day President Eisenhower sent a flattering message to the Shah asking his support for the agreement. Although he knew that the Shah had hardly played a role in the negotiations, the president praised him for making "a valuable contribution" to their success. To the sovereign who had fled his country twelve months earlier, the president said, "I have watched closely your courageous efforts, your steadfastness over the past difficult years." And now the oil settlement would be "a significant step in the direction of the realization of your aspirations for your people."[53] Delighted by the president's message, which was publicized on the same day, the Shah urged the Majlis to approve the consortium agreement.

The agreement in its detailed form was completed on August 29, 1954, and initialed by Amini and Page. To forestall legal problems the agreement was passed on to Attorney General Brownell, who assured President Eisenhower that it did not violate antitrust laws and would serve the national security interests of the United States. As we have seen, Brownell's predecessor, James McGranery, had reported in January 1953 that the oil cartel's domination of the world oil markets was "a serious threat to our national security."[54] Four days later "The Iranian Consortium Agreement and Related Documents" were signed by Amini and Morteza-Quli Bayat, managing director of NIOC.

The agreement gave NIOC nominal ownership of the Iranian oil industry's assets. But it provided for the establishment of two operating companies in Iran, one for exploration and production and the other for refining, both of them wholly owned by the consortium and both given full powers on behalf of NIOC to manage and control all operations. Furthermore, these powers could not be revoked or modified by any "general or special legislative or administrative measures or any act whatsoever of or emanating from Iran." The period of the agreement was for twenty-five years, and it could be renewed, if the consortium desired, for up to three five-year terms. This brought the total period to forty years ending in 1994, which more or less coincided with the termination of AIOC's concessionary agreement of 1933. Iran was to receive 50 percent of the net profits under a complicated formula designed to make the division of profits appear more favorable to the Iranians. Payments to Iran were to be in the form of taxes to the Iranian government so that the companies could get tax credits from their governments against their payments to Iran.[55]

The consortium members were not prepared to sign the agreement in Tehran lest doing so make any arbitration of differences between the signatories subject to the interpretation of Iranian laws. Thus copies of the agreement were flown by chartered plane to London, where they were signed on September 20 by AIOC, Shell, and CFP. On the same day they were flown to New York and signed by the chairmen of the five U.S. oil companies.

The terms of the agreement were no more favorable than those of concessionary arrangements elsewhere, nor did Iran have any say in the management of her oil industry. But to give NIOC the appearance of usefulness, it was allowed to be in charge of "non-basic" operations such as housing, health, and education. To overcome the differences concerning the nationality of the consortium and its management and location, a multinational creature was hatched whose organs were scattered in various countries. The two operating companies were incorporated under the laws of the Netherlands but registered in Iran. The shares of these companies were held by Iranian Oil Participants, a consortium holding company incorporated in London. The operating companies had a board of seven members, two of them Iranian; and the general management was Dutch.[56]

No less important was a secret agreement between the participating companies that established a scale for the amount of oil to be produced by each in Iran and tied this to production levels in other countries in which the consortium members operated. Thus Iran's oil income was at the mercy of the consortium, which could limit her production if it so decided. By such monopolistic practices the cartel controlled the production of oil and consequently its price in world markets.

On September 21, 1954, Amini presented a bill to the Majlis endorsing the agreement. Prime Minister Zahedi, who shared the fears of Loy Henderson and Denis Wright that any agreement perceived as invalidating nationalization would not be approved, had taken precautionary measures well in advance. Months earlier, Mossadeq and a number of other National Front leaders had been tried by a military tribunal and sentenced to death or imprisonment (see Chapter 22). Furthermore, martial law had been imposed, and the military governor had arrested anyone thought likely to be critical of a consortium agreement. Among those arrested was Mostafa Fateh, a former senior executive of AIOC, who was most knowledgeable on Iranian oil.

To eliminate any worries about the Majlis, Zahedi had taken the precaution of arranging for new elections in which the ballot boxes produced most of the government-sponsored candidates. In the words of one CIA official who was on the spot at the time, "Zahedi selected his own candidates and bulldozed the elections."[57] In addition, a long publicity campaign had been carried out to discredit Mossadeq's handling of nationalization and to persuade the public that Zahedi's government had achieved the same purpose through the consortium.

Even so, National Front supporters in Abadan and Tehran staged demonstrations against the proposed agreement. Moreover, Mossadeq, who was then in jail, did not remain silent. Under the pretext of demanding a review of the military tribunal's verdict, he wrote a twenty-nine-page petition of which twenty-seven pages concerned the oil dispute and the consortium deal. The petition, which was passed on to his lawyer and clandestinely distributed, said that the government, in open defiance of the Nationalization Act and the interests of the nation, had agreed to place Iran's oil industry in the hands of foreigners for another forty years while NIOC, which should have been in charge, was left with such trivial duties as housing and transportation in oil areas. Moreover, he said, the government had created an environment in which no one was allowed to criticize its "disastrous action." As for the West, if it was serious about fighting communism, it should avoid greedy exploitation of the weak. He concluded that it was now clear to all why he had been imprisoned: it was because he refused to compromise the sovereignty of Iran.[58]

The local papers did not dare to voice any criticism of the consortium agreement. But Hassan Sadr, one of Mossadeq's lawyers, published in his newspaper an article reproaching Britain and the United States for showing concern over communist threats to Iran while doing everything they could to force her into leaving her oil industry in their hands. "If they were genuinely interested in our independence," he said, "was it not fairer to get compensation from us as they did in Mexico, and give us the freedom to run our oil industry?" This was the last issue of his paper. The next day Zahedi's government stopped its publication.[59]

The Majlis began debating the consortium bill on October 10, 1954. The opposition was confined to five members, among them M. Darakhshesh, president of the Teachers' Union, who was greatly upset when hundreds of his colleagues were arrested for opposing the bill. Darakhshesh stated that the agreement was clear evidence that Iran's ruling class sought its selfish aims through collaboration with foreign interests. He criticized the agreement in legal and financial detail while stressing that it ran contrary to nationalization law and the long-held aspirations of the people. He revealed that his speech was based on materials dropped over the wall to his house by well-informed experts who feared arrest if they personally criticized the bill.

His and others' attacks on the bill had no impact. The Shah, pleased at having received the personal backing of President Eisenhower, put his weight behind the bill, telling deputies that he would regard a vote against it as a vote against his person. On October 21 the Majlis ratified the "Consortium Agreement" by 113 to 5 with 10 abstentions; a week later the Senate ratified it with 4 against and 4 abstentions. The Shah endorsed it on October 29.[60]

The consortium members, knowing in advance that the bill would be passed, had sent tankers to Abadan, and they began loading on the following day. The first tanker was AIOC's—a symbolic gesture to demonstrate that the company was alive and active in Iran. As an added symbol of its power in Iran, H. E. Snow, one of its directors, was appointed general manager of Iranian Oil Participants. This holding company, which had been established in London by the consortium, was entrusted with overall policy decisions on Iranian oil.

Not all problems, however, had been solved. The American independent oil companies were angry at being excluded from the consortium. Months before the agreement was concluded, a public relations firm wrote a letter on their behalf to John Foster Dulles saying that "the State Department is a party . . . to the creation of a monopoly in the sale and distribution" of Iranian oil. They accused the department of siding with AIOC against Iran's nationalization by preventing the sale of Iranian oil to American independents, while assisting in the formation of a cartel to pull "England's investment chestnuts out of fire." They pointed out that AIOC as a partner in the consortium was the "de facto Foreign Office of the British Government where its own interests are involved." Above all, they wanted to buy oil from Iran "without paying tribute to another Government or one of her agents."[61]

Realizing that if the independents were left out they would create a major row, the State Department, "for no other reason than a desire to pay lip-service to free competition," persuaded the five U.S. companies in the consortium each to relinquish, at cost, one eighth of their share to "qualified" U.S. independents. Their shares were accordingly reduced from 8 percent to 7 percent to make room for nine U.S. independents, who formed a group called Iricon with a 5 percent share in the consortium.[62]

In response to the ratification of the consortium agreement AIOC stock rose to about four times its level at the time of the 1951 oil crisis. In November AIOC changed its name to that of one of its subsidiaries, British Petroleum. At the same time the company gave its shareholders a bonus of 400 percent by providing four shares to the owner of each ordinary share, saying that this was done "in accordance with the growth and wealth of the Company and now that it is free from the uncertainty of Iranian involvement." Four months later, on February 15, 1955, R. A. Butler, the Chancellor of the Exchequer, told the House of Commons that "the value of the Government's holding [in the former AIOC] at the close of business yesterday was just over £233,000,000." The British government had paid £5 million for these shares. In the words of John Strachey, Secretary of State for War in Attlee's Cabinet, "this last British empire, the empire of oil, has 'paid' better than any other."[63]

At the same time, however, AIOC's excessive greed, as personified by its chairman, Sir William Fraser, made no small contribution to the decline of this empire. The British government, which had witnessed Fraser's disastrous handling of the Iranian oil dispute, finally looked for some face-saving way of replacing him as the company's chairman. Late in 1954 he was falsely acclaimed as the architect of the consortium deal, but in 1956 he was removed from the chairmanship while being honored with the title of Baron Strathalmond of Pumpherstone. The oil magnate Calouste Gulbenkian commented that he should have been called Lord Crude of Abadan.[64] Fraser died in April 1970.

Iran paid heavily for going after a shadow of nationalization under the consortium agreement. All that was in fact nationalized and transferred to Iran was the country's internal distribution facilities, the Nafti-Shah oil fields, and the Kermanshah refinery, whose products were not exported. These were worth at most £10 million, yet in return for them Iran paid £25 million and was forced to waive over £100 million of indisputable claims.[65] The sums Iran paid and the claims she waived, made her oil income considerably less than the 50 percent envisaged in the consortium agreement.

Instead of going after the appearance of nationalization, Zahedi's government would have done better to tell the Iranian people the truth: namely, that given the prevailing situation, Iran's best course was to accept an equal division of profits and wait for a better opportunity in the future to nationalize her oil industry. Had the government chosen this course, it could have gained more than 50 percent of the net profits because under the 1933 concession it could also claim 20 percent of AIOC's worldwide profits. In fact, in August 1951, when Lord Stokes tried his hand at settling the oil dispute, he was under instructions from the British government to try to get Iran to agree to a 50-50 split of the profits, and to settle Iran's 20 percent interest in AIOC's worldwide profits by offering "a down payment to buy them off."[66] Stokes never had a chance to make this offer because Iran at that point would consider nothing but nationalization.

It is surprising, however, that during the consortium negotiations the Iranians never raised this claim as a bargaining point when they gave up the idea of nationalization. Apparently the obsession with achieving even the merest show of nationalization had been so powerful as to destroy their ability to distinguish between illusion and reality.

In the United States and Britain there was jubilation at the settlement of the oil dispute. Secretary of State Dulles praised Hoover for his "remarkable contribution" to the consortium negotiations. British ambassador Stevens lauded Howard Page for his "brilliant combination of industry and imagination," but had little praise for Hoover, whom he considered "affable, intelligent, forceful" but "unscrupulous and fundamentally dishonest." He applauded the settlement as bringing "the return of AIOC to Persia as 40% members of the Consortium and a revival of British prestige and influence all through this area."[67]

Sir Eric Drake, AIOC's general manager and later chairman of British Petroleum, believes in retrospect that AIOC could not have operated alone in Iran as before. "Things could have been delayed if the Company had settled the dispute earlier, but they could not be stopped altogether." He believes that "the consortium agreement was to the Company's benefit as it took the load off our back." The load he refers to was the work of Fraser, who he concedes was shortsighted and narrow-minded.[68]

Mossadeq's view, reflected in his memoirs, was that the government's acceptance of the consortium agreement was "an open and disastrous treachery to the nation. . . . As long as the Iranians have no control over their own oil industry they would not be able to achieve freedom and independence."[69] Other Iranian nationalists felt the same way.

Some outside views are also of interest. Edith Penrose, known for her writings on the role of international firms, rightly states that under the consortium agreement, the Iranians were "in no better position to intervene directly in their price, offtake or investment arrangements than are the governments of other producing countries." Jerald Walden agrees: the establishment of the consortium "represented a resounding triumph for the British and the International Petroleum Cartel and a catastrophic defeat for the national aspirations of Iran." Anthony Sampson has written that the formation of the consortium marked "the apogee of the influence of the seven sisters [the seven major oil companies] both with the Middle East governments and with their own home governments." David Painter believes that the consortium "helped the major oil companies maintain their control over the world oil economy." A. H. Frankel observes that "any stake in that [consortium] venture was like getting 'a licence to print money.'"

By contrast, the Iranian economist F. Fesharaki finds some consolation for his countrymen. In his view, "Perhaps the most significant consequence of the nationalization was the creation of the NIOC . . . the first national oil company in a major oil producing country." This company, by observing the operations of the consortium, gradually obtained a great deal of experience and knowhow, which enabled it later to operate globally on its own.[70]

Few of these analysts make what might be the most important point of all: that the transition from an all-British monopoly to one in which U.S. companies owned a major share reflected the realities of American power—a power that was to play a major role in Iran for the following twenty-five years.

22

The Coup's Aftermath

With Mossadeq's government overthrown and nationalist leaders imprisoned, it remained for the British, with American backing, to make sure that there would be no popular challenge to General Zahedi's government and its consortium deal. The Shah, humiliated by Mossadeq and others who had exposed his collaboration with the British, was more than willing to help. To serve his own purposes as well as those of his Anglo-American allies, he subjected his imprisoned adversaries to a military trial.

Zahedi's government took every precautionary measure to ensure that there would be no public reaction to Mossadeq's trial. The trial took place at a time when martial law was imposed, demonstrations banned, newspapers sympathetic to the National Front suppressed, and nationalist and Tudeh leaders jailed. Indeed, many persons deemed hostile to the regime were summarily executed.

Mossadeq's trial began in the second week of November 1953. The Shah personally appointed General Nasrollah Mogbeli as chief judge and Major General Hossein Azmudeh as military prosecutor. As Mossadeq's attorney the court appointed Colonel Jalil Bozorgmehr, who proved to be less tractable than expected.

In his bill of indictment, Azmudeh accused Mossadeq of malicious intent to traduce Iran's constitution; it was alleged that he had sought to eradicate the monarchy and replace it with a republic. To this end he had disobeyed the Shah's order for his dismissal and instigated the people against the Shah. Telling the court that Mossadeq's actions constituted treason to the monarchy and the state, Azmudeh asked for the death penalty.[1]

Mossadeq rejected these allegations. What the people of Iran were witnessing, he said, was a trial staged by foreigners to serve their aims. Not only was he not against monarchy, but if anyone had demonstrated his disregard for the constitution it was the Shah, who had had no constitutional right to issue an order for his dismissal. In fact, said Mossadeq, he was still the prime minister, and if there were any allegations against him they should be raised in the civil court specifically set up for the trial of government officials.

The prosecutor replied by attacking Mossadeq, calling him "a vile liar" and a man with "a doctoral degree in treachery and crime." He went so far as to claim that Mossadeq, under the facade of fighting against colonialism, had exerted all his effort to derail the anticolonial movement pioneered by none other than the Shah. Worse yet, Mossadeq was the enemy of Islam and "does not believe in the day of divine creation and the day of judgement."

Mossadeq in turn denounced the prosecutor. To slander a constitutionally elected prime minister, he said, was to slander the Iranian people who had elected him. As for the accusation of being irreligious, was the prosecutor's aim to arrange for someone to kill him and then simply say that the assassin was a religious fanatic? In response to the allegation that he had thwarted the Shah's anticolonial movement, Mossadeq reminded the court that the sovereign's father had come to power with Britain's blessing and that his own opposition to Reza Shah was well-known.

A memorable scene at the trial, witnessed by the writer, occurred when Mossadeq stated that he disagreed with the Shah in cases where the monarch disregarded the constitution. To be sure, he said, disagreements between kings and prime ministers were nothing new; witness the differences between King Edward VIII of Britain and Stanley Baldwin. Before he could finish, the prosecutor shouted: "Shut up and sit down. How could a prime minister allow himself to disagree with his sovereign? This can in no way happen." Mossadeq sat down and, as if wanting to take a nap, put his head on his attorney's shoulder. After repeated demands by the judge to resume his defense, he told the court in a sarcastic tone, "Since I enjoy the statements of the military prosecutor, I prefer that he does all the talking." As Elwell-Sutton put it, "the old man by sheer resourcefulness and audacity turned [the trial] into a complete farce."[2]

Mossadeq's trial took place during the consortium negotiations, which he was eager to derail. He repeatedly brought up the subject of oil, saying that it would be open treachery to ignore Iran's nationalization law and conclude a contract on the basis of an equal division of profits, giving half of Iran's oil revenues to the wealthiest companies in the world. He pointed out that when certain foreign powers had come to realize that he was not going to place Iran's sovereignty and resources at their disposal, they had used every possible means to effect his downfall. He belittled the court for trying to condemn someone who had successfully defended Iran's case at the U.N. Security Council and the World Court. He sharply contrasted the fairness of international tribunals with that of a "foreign" court at home. His most telling statement, one that sums up his political perception and the reasons for his downfall, was made in his final defense. He said:

> In the course of Iran's constitutional history, this is the first time that a legally elected prime minister has been subjected to imprisonment and burdened with accusations. . . . Numerous sins have been attributed to me, but I know that I have committed no more than one, and that is that I have not yielded to the whims of foreigners. Throughout the course of my prime ministership I had only one objective in both domestic and foreign policy, and that was to have the nation command its own destiny. . . . I have come to the conclusion that without securing freedom and independence it will not be possible for the Iranians to overcome the numerous obstacles on their way to prosperity and greatness. I did the best I could in this regard. . . .
>
> It is a fact that [by treating me in this fashion] they want to give a lesson to others. . . . My only wish, however, is that the Iranian nation should fully realize the immensity and importance of its [independence] movement and that it should under no circumstances shrink from the pursuit of its honorable goal.
>
> . . . For over a century the destructive and fatal policies of foreigners have affected the fate of our homeland . . . [I refer] particularly [to] the political and economic interference of the British imperial power and the open and covert domination of its former oil company, which for half a century deprived us of opportunities of honorable revival.
>
> The way my colleagues and I are treated here . . . will demonstrate to the world that the magnitude and scope of the

power which foreigners still wield in this country are much greater than was imagined. . . .

. . . My trial is not dissimilar to that of Marshal Pétain. . . . Like him I am put on the stand of the accused in old age, and maybe I will be convicted like him. But . . . there is an outstanding difference between the two cases, since Pétain was tried by the French for having collaborated with the enemy of France, whereas I am being tried by the agents of foreigners for having fought against the enemy of Iran.[3]

Throughout the course of the trial, Mossadeq defended himself with dignity, never deviating from his principles in an effort to buy himself acquittal. The Shah wished Mossadeq to be hanged for having panicked him into his humiliating flight to Bagdad and Rome. But this was beyond the Shah's powers. Mossadeq was still popular at home and respected abroad for his determined stand against foreign domination. On the heels of his detention in August 1953 a number of foreign dignitaries, including representatives at the U.N. Security Council and judges of the World Court, had sent messages to Iran in Mossadeq's praise; and U.S. ambassador Henderson, speaking for the State Department, made it clear to Zahedi that Mossadeq's life should be spared. Well before the end of the trial, the Shah decided that Mossadeq should be sentenced to three years' imprisonment and revealed this decision to Kermit Roosevelt.[4] This was exactly the sentence imposed by the military court. When the chief judge announced the sentence, Mossadeq stated: "The verdict of this court indeed augments my honor in history."

The court also tried and convicted many of Mossadeq's aides, among them his foreign minister, Hossein Fatemi, who was sentenced to death. Before his execution by a firing squad, he told Azmudeh, "My death will be an honorable one, one that teaches the young generation to defend their homeland with their blood and not to let foreigners govern their country. . . . When I closed the doors of the British Embassy, I was unaware of the fact that while this royal court functions, Britain does not need an embassy here."[5]

The Iranian drive toward freedom from foreign domination had been defeated. "For a brief euphoric moment Iranians had deluded themselves into believing that they could assert their independence," but they soon realized that "this had been a dream and that the British once again, this time working through the Americans, had demonstrated their ability to turn back even the strongest Iranian challenge."[6] Iranian liberals were particularly disillusioned. Before the coup, they had perceived the United States as heading up a new postwar world order that promoted the freedom of nations.

Today as always relations between nations are governed chiefly by interest and power. Attempts are made to modify the thrust of power by establishing certain international legal principles, but when a dispute arises between the strong and the weak, it is power, rather than moral and legal principles, that determines the outcome. Ebrahim Khajenuri, an Iranian political writer, warned his countrymen long ago not to be fooled by the aura of righteousness and fairness exhibited by some foreign powers, but to be on the watch for the sort of tricky games they play in the name of politics.[7]

The question remains whether the American intervention in Iran was in the long-term interest of the United States. Few today would claim that it was. As George McGhee put it, the coup in Iran resulted "in a great loss of confidence in us by other nations," particularly those struggling for freedom and independence.[8] Nations that looked upon the United States as the defender of freedom and democracy were disillusioned when America took the opposite course in Iran. As Justice William O. Douglas observed, "[Mossadeq], whom I am proud to call my friend, was a democrat in the LaFollette-Norris sense of the term. We united with the British to destroy him; we succeeded and ever since our name has not been an honored one in the Middle East."[9]

The United States destroyed Mossadeq, who had given his people a feeling of national dignity for the first time in decades and who had established the foundations of a constitutional democracy. Worse yet, the United States took the role of protector and guarantor of an autocratic Shah. Not until the Iranian revolution of 1978 did the United States come to see that this policy had been basically wrong. Today Paul Nitze is only one of many who believe that America made a "mistake" in tying herself to "Chiang Kai-Shek in China and the Shah in Iran."[10]

In his comprehensive study *The Tragedy of American-Iranian Relations*, James Bill rightly contends that the U.S. covert operations of August 1953 crippled American credibility. It "alienated important generations of Iranians from America" and "left a running wound that bled for twenty-five years."[11] The anti-American and anti-Shah revolution of 1978–79 showed that "the crises of today are often current outbursts of deep and enduring social or political tides from the past."[12]

The United States by her action inadvertently drove the nationalists, among other groups, toward extremism and revenge. When Ayatollah Khomeini pioneered the fight against the Shah, calling him an American stooge, millions were attracted to the Muslim leader without considering what he stood for. The 1953 coup in fact planted the seeds of the later revolution.[13] There is no doubt that the Americans as well as the British bear a heavy responsibility for what is taking place in Iran today.

What, then, did the United States gain from the coup? One might argue that the American oil companies obtained a 40 percent share in Iran's oil industry and thus made billions in profits. But this did not require a coup, since Mossadeq had repeatedly urged McGhee and Henderson to encourage U.S. oil companies to come to Iran and run her oil industry, replacing AIOC, within the framework of nationalization.

Britain, too, had more attractive options than a coup. Had she stopped treating Iran as a colony and immediately followed Aramco's lead in contracting for an equal division of profits, the Iranians would not have been so keen to nationalize their oil industry. But Britain, having been a colonial power for over a century, was in no mood to accept nationalization, and the Iranians could see no other way to free themselves from British bondage. The resulting impasse led to Britain's loss of the AIOC concession and the surrender of 60 percent of AIOC's interests to other oil companies. This in turn resulted in the loss of over half of the revenues that AIOC would have received from 1953 to 1978, the year of the final expropriation of foreign oil interests in Iran. From late 1973 to 1978, the price of Persian Gulf oil ranged from $10 to over $30 per barrel, and Iranian production from the former area of the AIOC rose to 5.5 million barrels per day. Thus the $600 million that AIOC obtained for the transfer of 60 percent of its interests could have been recouped within a matter of weeks had Fraser agreed to a 50-50 division of profits in 1951. Even after nationalization there were a number of occasions when the company was offered the opportunity to operate as the sole purchasing agent for Iranian oil with 35 percent discount, but such chances were lost when the company and the British government held out for nothing less than full control.

What Britain gained from the coup was an expanded trade with Iran and development contracts, which "the Shah personally controlled." Sir Anthony Parsons, the last British ambassador to Tehran before the 1978–79 revolution, writes, "we gambled on the Shah and, for many years, our gamble paid off."[14] But these gains are dwarfed by the enormous loss of AIOC profits, some tens of billions of dollars, owing to the surrender of 60 percent of the company's interests.

Also to be considered are the losses due to the rapid decline of Iran's economy after the 1978–79 revolution, which led to a sharp reduction in Iran's imports from Britain, among other Western nations. The economic as well as political costs of the 1953 coup will live on for quite some time. C. M. Woodhouse of MI6, one of the main architects of the coup and later a member of Parliament, admits that the consequences of the British action were not foreseen. "At that time," he says, "we were simply relieved that a threat to British interests had been removed."[15] The cost of such a short-term view has been very high for Britain.

There were mistakes on the Iranian side, too. Mossadeq was an idealist who did not compromise with the realities of world power. With his Jeffersonian ideas on morality and politics, he believed that since there was nothing legally wrong with his oil nationalization drive, he could win his fight against the British by appealing to America's moral values and her anticolonial stand. U.S. prodding had been a major consideration in the British postwar withdrawal from India, Burma, Malaya, and Palestine. Mossadeq felt that the United States, in the same spirit, would help free Iran from British economic exploitation, the more readily because such exploitation made the country's deprived masses receptive to communism. But he underestimated the underlying strength of Anglo-American relations, the cohesion of the oil cartel, and the malleability of America's moral values, the last having been repeatedly demonstrated in Latin America.

Mossadeq also underestimated the role that the Shah, with British prompting, could play against him; nor could he imagine that the Shah would support British interests at the expense of his own people. At the same time he overestimated the cohesion, endurance, and resilience of his own people in pursuit of their national aspirations. To mobilize these aspirations and to advance his ideals, Mossadeq needed a properly organized political party; instead, he stood above party politics. He relied primarily on popular support and secondarily on the National Front, a loose coalition of parties and groups composed of such diverse classes as the intelligentsia, the clergy, and the bazaar merchants. Although these groups had certain common goals, their divergence on other aims and interests later led to factionalism, which was exploited by the British and their proxies. In the end Mossadeq had nothing to rely on but popular support.

In 1945 the British military attaché in Tehran observed, "The Persian, though capable of spasmodic feats of bravery, is not renowned for that dogged brand of courage which sustains prolonged resistance in adverse circumstances."[16]

Mossadeq was not such a Persian. Against overwhelming odds, he remained faithful to his ideals and determined to free Iran from foreign domination. He knew that the British would give him no quarter. So, as Dean Acheson put it, "he took the declaration of a fight to the finish with dignity."[17]

Mossadeq's policy was not dictated by real-politik. Instead he seemed to follow Max Weber's dictum that "all historical experience confirms the truth—that man would not have attained the possible unless time and again he had reached out for the impossible." Weber in his time saw the main danger to his nation as coming from the emperor's personal rule and his lack of political accountability. Mossadeq found the same faults with the Shah, who by meddling in Iran's domestic and foreign affairs impeded his nation's progress toward parliamentary democracy and freedom from foreign domination.

Mossadeq's great hope was "to establish a polity which would be impervious to corruption and would, therefore, enhance the credibility of the government and ultimately give substance and meaning to citizenship and political participation."[18] Without such a development, he believed, Iran would continue to fall prey to local autocracy and foreign exploitation. Mossadeq was "a devoted proponent of Enlightenment values"; he hoped to establish in Iran a system that was, "in its central particulars, the same system that Americans and western Europeans claimed as their own." Thus it is "ironic in the extreme," as Richard Cottam put it, that his "regime should be brought down by the self-proclaimed leaders of what they call the 'free world.'"[19]

Mossadeq could not have been brought down by an internal coup because his opponents had neither adequate power nor a popular base. The CIA itself had judged a Tudeh takeover unlikely. When Britain and the United States decided to stage a coup, they found it expedient to talk of an impending Tudeh coup and to call Mossadeq a crypto-communist; but neither government's officials believed in these accusations. Kermit Roosevelt, who was the key figure in implementing the coup, agrees with a State Department intelligence report calling Mossadeq "strongly anti-communist." Roosevelt adds that "the British were very stupid in negotiations with Mossadegh. . . . They did not make any gesture that he could accept" to avoid "this whole blowup."[20]

George McGhee, the American who knew Mossadeq best, says that as a Western-educated aristocrat with a conservative background, he "had no reason to be attracted to socialism or communism." He was "basically . . . a patriotic Iranian nationalist whose lifelong aim was to free Iran from what he perceived to be foreign domination," whether British or Russian.[21] Many others in the Truman administration expressed similar views and approved wholeheartedly of Mossadeq's national movement. But when Eisenhower took over, his men took a different approach, and it was this view that led to the coup.

The most important issue for the Eisenhower administration was that Mossadeq's idea of oil nationalization might spread throughout the Middle East and elsewhere, endangering the interests of American oil companies. Since it was politically impossible to say that Mossadeq's government should be overthrown for the purpose of protecting Anglo-American oil interests, the United States found it expedient to join Britain on the pretext of preventing an imminent takeover of Iran by the communists.

As we have seen, the British among themselves did not seriously accuse Mossadeq of communist tendencies, but they found other faults with him. Sam Falle, who was involved in the coup, blamed him for wanting to end the British domination of Iran. To Donald Logan such an intention, even today, looks unforgivable: "We had to use force to bring Iran to sanity."[22]

Although Mossadeq was overthrown, his movement had a major impact on Iran and the third world. He succeeded in breaking AIOC control over Iran's oil industry. Furthermore, the dissemination of his concepts on the sovereignty of nations and their right to control their national resources encouraged other third-world producers to disentangle themselves from the control of the Western oil cartel. This led in 1961 to the formation of the Organization of Petroleum Exporting Countries (OPEC), whose first Secretary General was Fuad Rouhani, Deputy Director of Iran's national oil company. As OPEC's membership grew from 5 to 13, it took under its control 90 percent of the world's export of crude oil, while deciding on its own price and production levels dictated earlier by the oil cartel.

After Gandhi, Mossadeq was no doubt the one who most passionately propagated the idea of eliminating foreign domination. Churchill and Eden, by their shrewd schemes, succeeded in overthrowing Mossadeq, but they could not stop the spread of his concepts.

Among those influenced by Mossadeq was President Gamal Abdel Nasser of Egypt in his drive to nationalize the Suez Canal in 1956. The failure of Anthony Eden's attempt to overthrow Nasser by arranging an Anglo-French-Israeli military attack on Egypt was followed by pressure for independence brought by colonial people on every continent. In the following decade, Britain "was hustled and harried out of most of her old colonies."[23] Soon afterward the West lost its control over the oil resources of third world countries, which formed their own producing cartel in OPEC and tamed the companies that had ruled over them. The last oilmen from the Anglo-American–dominated consortium left Iran shortly after Ayatollah Khomeini took power in early 1979.

As for Mossadeq, after serving his three-year term in solitary confinement, he was placed under house arrest and watched by SAVAK, the Shah's secret police, who allowed no one except close relatives to visit him. The National Front went underground in Iran, but intensified its activities in the West. Its lobbying in the United States during the Kennedy administration led in 1962 to American demands that the Shah extend some degree of freedom to his opponents. When the Shah complied, the National Front responded by holding demonstrations in which 100,000 participated calling for the return of Mossadeq. But soon their leaders were arrested for endangering the security of the state.

Mossadeq, in poor health, confided to his relatives that he wished to be buried in the "cemetery of freedom" alongside those who had been killed by the Shah's troops in the July 1952 uprising in his favor (see Chapter 16). When he died at the age of 85 on March 5, 1967, the government did not allow a funeral or honor his burial wishes. He was buried instead in the dining room of his house in Ahmad Abad, outside Tehran, and only his relatives were allowed to visit his grave. Years earlier, when Reza Shah forbade the public from visiting a certain grave, Mossadeq had remarked: "Dictatorship is so all-encompassing that it has to assert itself even over the dead."[24]

On Mossadeq's death the Iranian media, being under tight government control, were silent. The foreign press, however, paid him glowing tribute, praising him for his singlemindedness and devotion to democracy and freedom from foreign exploitation.[25] Twelve years later, in March 1979, one million people from all over the country converged on Ahmad Abad to visit his grave on the anniversary of his death. This was possible for the first time because the revolution had forced the Shah out of the country.

Mossadeq's "defence of Iran's independence, his defiance of AIOC, his charisma and his overthrow with American and British support helped make him an enduring hero"[26] and restored him "to the standing that only a man who is somewhat unworldly can attain."[27]

"Seen in retrospect," Albert Hourani writes, "the brief years of Musaddiq's rule have had a deep and lasting significance. His was the most determined attempt to create a strong executive power in Iran, upheld by popular support, and to use it in order to obtain not simply an improved position within the [British] imperial system but complete independence. . . . Inside Iran, his memory remained as a symbol of independence."[28]

The 1953 coup was a tragic chapter in the history of Iran and the Middle East as a whole since it halted the march toward liberal democracy in the area. Moreover, the assumption that reinstating the autocratic Shah, and arming him, would serve the strategic and energy interests of the United States in the Persian Gulf proved wrong. What the coup produced instead was the Iranian revolution, the rise of Islamic fundamentalism that abhorred the West, and the resulting American and Arab support of Saddam Hussein that led to his delusions of grandeur and his invasion of Iran and later Kuwait. Although the United States' intervention in the Gulf war made her a friend of main Arab oil producers and thus a de facto member of OPEC with a say in the price and production of oil, this is an empty privilege in the absence of democracy and thus stability in the area. As a commentator observed after the Gulf war, "The region continues to be largely a horror show of autocracy and despotism pacified by state violence."[29]

The two greatest democracies of the world aborted the birth of democracy in a distant land for what they wrongly conceived to be in their self-interest. By doing so, they helped to unleash a chain of traumatic events in Iran and the rest of the Middle East, while gravely damaging their own interests. All that can be said of such a tragedy is what Dean Acheson says in his book at the end of the chapter on Iran: "Once again one reflects on Oxenstierne's question: 'Dost thou not know, my son, with how little wisdom the world is governed?'"[30]

Notes
Bibliography
Index

Notes

Complete authors' names, titles, and publishing information on publications cited in short form in the Notes will be found in the Bibliography.

1.—The Age of Autocracy and Concessions

1. See E. Teymuri, *Asré bi-Khabari*, 4th ed. (Tehran, 1363/1985), p. 106.

2. F. Kazemzadeh, *Russia and Britain in Persia, 1864–1914: A Study in Imperialism* (New Haven, 1968), p. 103.

3. S. Gopal, *British Policy in India, 1858–1905* (Cambridge, U.K., 1965), p. 243.

4. R. L. Greaves, *Persia and the Defence of India, 1884–1892* (London, 1959), p. 25.

5. R. W. Ferrier, *The History of the British Petroleum Company*, Vol. I, *The Developing Years, 1901–1932* (Cambridge, U.K., 1982), hereafter cited as "Ferrier, *B.P.*," p. 28. Ferrier is the B.P. historian.

6. Kazemzadeh, *Russia and Britain*, p. 108. G. Jones, *Banking and Empire in Iran: The History of the British Bank of the Middle East*, Vol. I (Cambridge, U.K., 1986), p. 11.

7. G. N. Curzon, *Persia and the Persian Question*, Vol. I (London, 1892), p. 480.

8. Kazemzadeh, *Russia and Britain*, p. 13.

9. Ibid., pp. 122, 127; Teymuri, *Asré*, p. 107.

10. Jones, *Banking*, pp. 22–23. For the text of the Bank Concession see Appendix I, pp. 341–54.

11. E'etemad ol-Saltaneh, *Ruznameh Khaterat* (Tehran, 1356/1977), p. 616.

12. E. G. Browne, *The Persian Revolution of 1905–1909*, new imp. (London, 1966), p. 33.

13. Ibid., p. 45. On the character of Afghani see N. R. Keddie, *Sayyid Jamal ad-Din "al-Afghani": A Political Biography* (Los Angeles, 1972). Also M. Tabataba'i, *Namehayé Afghani* (Tehran, 1349/1970).

14. Browne, *Persian Revolution*, pp. 18–19.

15. Ibid., p. 57.

16. Jones, *Banking*, p. 53.

17. Browne, *Persian Revolution*, p. 66.

18. Mostafa Fateh, *Panjah Sal Nafté Iran*, 2d ed. (Tehran, 1358/1979), p. 249; Teymuri, *Asré*, p. 211.

19. L. P. Elwell-Sutton, *Persian Oil: A Study in Power Politics* (London, 1955), p. 13; Fateh, *Panjah Sal*, pp. 250–51.

20. Ferrier, *B.P.*, p. 252.
21. FO60/640, Hardinge to Lansdowne, May 12, 1901.
22. Fateh, *Panjah Sal*, p. 254; Ferrier, *B.P.*, p. 38.
23. Ibid., quoted by Ferrier from B.P. document H 17/47.
24. Ibid., pp. 640–43.
25. FO48/733, D'Arcy to Lansdowne, June 27, 1901.
26. See N. S. Fatemi, *Oil Diplomacy: Powder Keg in Iran* (New York, 1954), p. 357.
27. W. Mineau, *The Go Devils* (London, 1958), p. 21.
28. Fateh, *Panjah Sal*, p. 254.
29. Mineau, *Go Devils*, p. 32.
30. For details of the concessions syndicate see Ferrier, *B.P.*, pp. 70–71.
31. FO371/715, Sir G. Barclay to Sir Edward Grey, Oct. 25, 1909.
32. Browne, *Persian Revolution*, p. 133.
33. Ibid., p. 150; Kazemzadeh, *Russia and Britain*, p. 499.
34. Mineau, *Go Devils*, p. 39–47.
35. Ferrier, *B.P.*, pp. 103–4.
36. Ibid., p. 107.
37. Elwell-Sutton, *Persian Oil*, pp. 19–20.
38. Browne, *Persian Revolution*, pp. 133–71; E. Abrahamian, *Iran Between Two Revolutions* (Princeton, N.J., 1982), pp. 50–101.
39. J. Bozorgmehr, *Taqriraté Mossadeq Dar Zendan* (Tehran, 1359/1980), pp. 11–12.
40. Browne, *Persian Revolution*, pp. 321–26.
41. Elwell-Sutton, *Persian Oil*, pp. 20–21.
42. Fateh, *Panjah Sal*, pp. 259–62; Mineau, *Go Devils*, pp. 59–62.
43. *The Times* (London), Nov. 22, 1918.
44. Ferrier, *B.P.*, p. 202.
45. FO371/91620, Admiralty to Kenneth Younger, June 15, 1951.
46. Winston Churchill, *The World Crisis, 1911–1918*, Vol. I (London, 1938), pp. 102–5.
47. Ferrier, *B.P.*, pp. 291–94, 217–19.
48. Ibid., pp. 230, 673.
49. Elwell-Sutton, *Persian Oil*, pp. 26–27.
50. Fateh, *Panjah Sal*, pp. 274–78.
51. Z. Mikdashi, *A Financial Analysis of Middle Eastern Oil Concessions, 1901–1965* (New York, 1966), pp. 18–19, 37–38; Elwell-Sutton, *Persian Oil*, pp. 28–33.
52. Ibid. (both citations).
53. Ibid.
54. Ibid.

2.—Reza Shah and the 1933 Concession

1. *Documents on British Foreign Policy, 1919–1939*, Vol. IV, 1st series (London, 1952), pp. 1119–21.
2. The abortive 1919 Anglo-Persian agreement is reproduced in Harold Temperly, "The Liberation of Persia," part v of *A History of the Peace Conference of Paris* (London, 1924).
3. The two were Sarem od-Dowleh Mas'ud, Minister of Finance, and Nos-

rat od-Dowleh Firuz, Minister of Foreign Affairs. See Denis Wright, *The English Amongst the Persians During the Qajar Period, 1787–1921* (London, 1977), pp. 178–80. Also Denis Wright, *The Persians Amongst the English: Episodes in Anglo-Persian History* (London, 1985), pp. 193–94, 205.

4. Ibid. (both citations).

5. See N. S. Fatemi, *Diplomatic History of Persia, 1917–1923: Anglo-Russian Power Politics in Iran* (New York, 1952), pp. 257–58.

6. Lord Ironside, *High Road to Command: The Diaries of Major-General Sir Edmund Ironside, 1920–1922* (London, 1972), pp. 152–61. See also Wright, *The English*, pp. 181–82.

7. M. T. Bahar, *Tarikhé Mokhtasaré Ahzabé Siassi*, Vol. I (Tehran, 1323/1944), pp. 61–68, 106–16. According to Bahar, Zia is quoted as saying that he distributed 20,000 Tomans among the Cossacks, including their commander, Reza Khan, giving the latter an additional bonus of 2,000 Tomans. See also Y. Dowlat-Abadi, *Hayaté Yahya*, Vol. IV, 3d ed. (Tehran, 1361/1982), pp. 227–28. Dowlat-Abadi was at the time a member of the Majlis.

8. Ironside, *Diaries*, p. 117.

9. Donald N. Wilber, *Riza Shah Pahlavi, The Resurrection and Reconstruction of Iran* (Hicksville, N.Y., 1975), p. 48.

10. FO371/6403, Norman to Curzon, March 1, 1921. See also Nance Kittner, "Issues in Anglo-Persian Diplomatic Relations, 1921–1933" (Ph.D. diss., University of London, 1981), p. 35. This paper gives a well-documented account of relations between Reza Shah and the British.

11. Fatemi, *Diplomatic History*, text of Anglo-Soviet Treaty, pp. 263–66.

12. FO416/73, Loraine to Curzon, May 28, 1923.

13. FO371/8051, Loraine to Curzon, July 16, 1921. G. Waterfield, *Professional Diplomat, Sir Percy Loraine of Kirkharle, 1880–1961* (London, 1973), p. 82.

14. FO416/72, Loraine to Curzon, May 5, 1923; FO416/73, Loraine to Curzon, May 28, 1923; FO416/9043, India Office to F.O., May 16, 1923.

15. Wright, *The Persians*, p. 192.

16. Waterfield, *Professional Diplomat*, p. 122.

17. Majlis Proceedings, Oct. 31, 1925.

18. Elwell-Sutton, *Persian Oil*, p. 67.

19. Ferrier, *B.P.*, pp. 596, 601–3.

20. John Rowland and Basil Cadman, *Ambassador for Oil: The Life of John First Baron Cadman* (London, 1960), p. 115; FO371/11498, Loraine to Oliphant, June 1, 1926.

21. Fateh, *Panjah Sal*, p. 286.

22. *Setareh Iran*, Nov. 25, 1928.

23. Ferrier, *B.P.*, pp. 604–8; Fateh, *Panjah Sal*, p. 287.

24. FO371/16933, Concession Revision and Royalty Payments, APOC, April 1929–May 1932.

25. Ferrier, *B.P.*, pp. 616–22.

26. M. Q. Hedayat, *Khaterat va Khatarat*, 3d ed. (Tehran, 1361/1982), pp. 395–96. Hedayat was then Iran's prime minister.

27. Fateh, *Panjah Sal*, p. 292.

28. FO371/16078, F.O. to Hoare, Dec. 1, 1932.

29. CAB23/73, Cabinet Conclusions 65(32)3, Dec. 7, 1932.

30. FO371/16079, Opinion by the Law Offices of the Crown, Dec. 7, 1932; Hoare to F.O., Dec. 13, 1932.

31. CAB23/73, Cabinet Conclusions 67(32)3, Dec. 14, 1932; FO371/16079, Minute by Rendel, Dec. 14, 1932; F. P. Walters, *A History of the League of Nations* (London, 1952), p. 572.

32. League of Nations, *Official Journal XIV* (1933), Memorandum submitted by Persian government to the League's Secretary-General, Jan. 18, 1933, and Minutes of the Third Meeting, 17th Session, Jan. 26, 1933, pp. 289–303.

33. League of Nations, *Official Journal XIII* (1932), Memorandum submitted by the British government to the League's Council, Dec. 19, 1932, pp. 2298–2305, and ibid., XIV (1933), pp. 198–204. See also FO371/16935, Minutes of the Council's Third Meeting, 17th Session, Jan. 26, 1933.

34. Fateh, *Panjah Sal*, p. 295.

35. Rowland and Cadman, *Ambassador for Oil*, p. 123.

36. Ibid., pp. 123–26; F. Rouhani, *Tarikhé Melli Shodané San'até Nafté Iran* (Tehran, 1352/1973), p. 65.

37. Rowland and Cadman, *Ambassador for Oil*, pp. 126–28; FO371/16937, Cadman to Simon, Apr. 21, 1933.

38. Rowland and Cadman, *Ambassador for Oil*, p. 129.

39. Ibid., p. 130.

40. Ibid., p. 131.

41. See Majlis Proceedings, Taqizadeh's statement, Jan. 27, 1948.

42. Rowland and Cadman, *Ambassador for Oil*, p. 132. The text of the 1933 concession is reproduced in the League of Nations *Official Journal*, No. 12, 77th Session, Dec. 1933, pp. 1653–60.

43. AIOC Annual Report and Accounts as at 31st Dec., 1950.

44. Fatemi, *Oil Diplomacy*, pp. 159, 180; Ali Vossuq, *Chahar Fasl dar Tafannon va Tarikh* (Tehran, 1361/1982), p. 69; Rowland and Cadman, *Ambassador for Oil*, p. 121.

45. Majlis Proceedings, Jan. 27, 1948.

46. Mostafa Elm, "Governmental Economic Planning in Iran" (Ph.D. diss., Syracuse University, 1959), p. 10.

47. Ibid., pp. 236–82; K. Farmanfarmayan, "Social Change and Economic Behaviour in Iran," *Explorations in Entrepreneurial History*, IX, No. 3 (February 1957), p. 180.

48. Donald N. Wilber, *Iran Past and Present*, 7th ed. (Princeton, N.J., 1975), p. 131.

49. Ashraf Pahlavi, *Faces in a Mirror: Memoirs from Exile* (Englewood Cliffs, N.J., 1980), p. 39.

50. Wilber, *Iran*, p. 131.

51. H. Longhurst, *Adventure in Oil: The Story of British Petroleum* (London, 1959), p. 96; Elwell-Sutton, *Persian Oil*, p. 105.

52. Sir Reader Bullard, *Letters from Tehran: A British Ambassador in World War II Persia* (London, 1991), p. 69.

53. Longhurst, *Adventure in Oil*, pp. 99–100.

54. Wright, *The Persians*, quoting from the diary of Oliver Harvey, private secretary to Anthony Eden, p. 213.

55. Ibid., quoting from the diaries of Amery and Nicholson, pp. 213–14; interview with Prince Hamid Qajar, London, Mar. 25, 1985.

56. Wright, *The Persians*, p. 214.

57. Hossein Fardust, *Khaterat: Zohur va Soghuté Saltanaté Pahlavi*, Vol. I (Tehran, 1369/1990), pp. 39–60.

58. For the Shah's character see Marvin Zonis, *Majestic Failure: The Fall of the Shah* (Chicago, 1991).

59. Fitzroy Maclean, *Eastern Approaches* (London, 1949), pp. 265–75. The author explains in detail how he abducted General Zahedi with the assistance of John Gault, the British consul in Isfahan, Professor Laurence Lockhart, a Persian linguist, and a group of commandos. On dissatisfaction with the occupying forces see Barry Rubin, *Paved with Good Intentions: The American Experience in Iran* (New York, 1980), pp. 20–21.

3.—Iran Defies Russia and Britain

1. For further details on the composition of the Majlis, see Abrahamian, *Iran*, pp. 199–224.

2. Majlis Proceedings, Oct. 29 and Dec. 2, 1944.

3. Edward R. Stettinius, Jr., *Roosevelt and the Russians: The Yalta Conference* (Westport, Conn., 1970, ©1949), p. 175.

4. FO371/40241, Minute by C. F. Warner, Oct. 18, 1944.

5. James F. Byrnes, *Speaking Frankly* (New York, 1947), p. 119.

6. For a detailed account see: G. Lenczowski, *Russia and the West in Iran, 1918–1948: A Study in Big Power Rivalry* (Ithaca, N.Y., 1949).

7. FO371/52673, Memorandum by Howe, Apr. 16, 1946.

8. Ibid., "Memorandum on Persia," Apr. 13, 1946; FO371/52710, British Military Attaché, Tehran, to F.O., May 22, 1946; FO371/52706, Cabinet Conclusions, July 4, 1946.

9. Conversation with Jahanshah Samsam, a Bakhtiari tribal chief, at the Police Headquarters detention center, Tehran, Oct. 28, 1946. Samsam told me that he had discussed the Qashqa'i-Bakhtiari scheme for the occupation of southern Iran with John Gault, the British consul in Isfahan, before its execution.

10. Rubin, *Good Intentions*, p. 33.

11. Interview with Aga Khan Bakhtiar, then a Majlis deputy and confidant of Qavam, London, Oct. 5, 1984.

12. See Majlis Proceedings, Oct. 22, 1947. The full English text of the act appears in Elwell-Sutton's *Persian Oil*, pp. 118–19.

13. See Fateh, *Panjah Sal*, pp. 385–86, on his discussions with the British ambassador.

14. Elwell-Sutton, *Persian Oil*, p. 102.

15. I was in Abadan during this revolt and by chance witnessed the bloody clashes that occurred there.

16. FO371/39988, Minute by Hankey, Nov. 29, 1943; FO371/52735, Minute by Bevin, July 20, 1946.

17. Fateh, *Panjah Sal*. All through his book, Fateh blames the shortsightedness of the company and British envoys in Iran as well as the corruption and timidity of Iranian officials who submitted to the company's wishes.

18. A. Pahlavi, *Faces in a Mirror*, pp. 89–90.

19. For a study of the Shah's efforts to establish an authoritarian state, see H. Ladjevardi, "The Origins of U.S. Support for an Autocratic Iran," *International Journal of Middle East Studies*, XV (1983), pp. 225–39.

20. For further details see Elm, "Governmental Economic Planning in Iran."

21. The text of this memorandum is given in Majlis Proceedings, July 25, 1949.

22. Iran claimed that, under the concession, the company's sterling payments should be based on the real market value of gold—then £11.25 per ounce—and not on the "artificial" value of £8.40 set by the Bank of England.

23. Majlis Proceedings, July 25, 1949.

24. Golsha'ian's report to Sa'ed, June 8, 1949, in Fateh, *Panjah Sal*, pp. 390–91.

25. Ibid., Minute by Golsha'ian, May 10, 1949, pp. 391–92.

26. Private letter from Fateh to Taqizadeh, June 14, 1949. Fateh gave me a photocopy of the letter.

27. The main points of the supplemental agreement were briefly as follows: (1) AIOC to increase royalties and taxes per ton to 7/– as of 1948; (2) Iran's 20 percent share in dividends and reserves be paid annually by AIOC as of 1947 without subjecting these payments to the British government's dividend limitation and U.K. taxes; (3) annual payments to Iran on these accounts to be no less than £4 million; (4) AIOC to give a 20 percent discount on the price of oil products sold for local consumption.

28. Cyrus Ghani, *Yaddashthayé Dr. Qassem Ghani*, Vol. IX (London, 1982), quoting Golsha'ian, pp. 621–23.

29. FO371/91534, Gass to Butler, May 8, 1951.

30. FO371/91524, Minutes of meeting at F.O., Jan. 16, 1951.

31. Majlis Proceedings, July 23–26, 1949.

32. FO371/75500, Bevin to Le Rougetel, Oct. 26, 1949; Sa'ed, London, to Royal Court, Oct. 21, 1949, in Fateh, *Panjah Sal*, p. 402.

33. Hossein Makki, *Ketabé Siah*, Vol. III, Part I (Tehran, 1360/1981), pp. 39–45.

34. Ibid.

35. For a detailed account of Mossadeq's life see: Dr. Mohammad Mossadeq, *Khaterat va Ta'allomat* (Tehran, 1365/1986); F. Diba, *Mohammad Mossadegh: A Political Biography* (London, 1986); B. Afrasiabi, *Mossadeq va Tarikh* (Tehran, 1360/1981); Bozorgmehr, *Taqriraté Mossadeq*.

36. M. Mossadeq, "Capitulassion va Iran," in *Mossadeq va Masaléyé Hoquq va Siassat*, ed. Iraj Afshar (Tehran, 1357/1978), p. 67.

37. George McGhee, *Envoy to the Middle World: Adventures in Diplomacy* (New York, 1983), pp. 61–79. McGhee, who participated in many of the Shah's meetings in Washington, gives an illuminating account of the Shah's discussions.

38. U.S. Department of State, *Foreign Relations of the United States* (hereafter cited as *FR-US*), 1950, Vol. V, Memorandum of conversation with Hossein Ala, Jan. 26, 1951.

39. For the United States–Iranian Agreement of Oct. 6, 1947 concerning the U.S. military mission and its revisions and extensions in 1949 and 1950, see "U.S. Treaties and Other International Agreements," *FR-US*, 1950, Vol. I.

40. McGhee, *Envoy*, pp. 22–24.

41. *FR-US*, 1950, Vol. V, Discussions with AIOC officials, pp. 13–15.

42. Majlis Proceedings, June 20, 1950.

43. *FR-US*, 1950, Vol. V, Wiley to Secretary of State, Jan. 30, 1950, pp. 459–63, and May 26, 1950, pp. 558–59.

44. FO371/75464, Minute by Wright, Feb. 9, 1949; Le Routegel to Strang, Nov. 12, 1949.

45. FO371/82313, Shepherd to Bevin, Dec. 17, 1950.

46. FO371/91448, Shepherd to Bevin, Report of events in Persia in 1950, Feb. 19, 1951.

47. "Précis of Message sent to Mr. Northcroft by Prime Minister through Dr. Jalali," June 20, 1950, in E. Ra'in, *Asnadé Khané Seddon* (Tehran, 1358/1979), p. 170.

4.—The General's Mission

1. Majlis Proceedings, June 27, 1950.

2. *FR-US*, 1950, Vol. V, Memo by Richard Funkhouser to McGhee, Sept. 14, 1950, pp. 97–99.

3. McGhee, *Envoy*, p. 325.

4. *FR-US*, 1950, Vol. V, Grady to Secretary of State, July 13, 1950, pp. 556–57; Secretary of State to U.S. Embassy, London, July 14, 1950, p. 569.

5. FO371/82375, Minute by L. Barnett, Aug. 3, 1950; Minutes of meeting at F.O., Aug. 2, 1950.

6. McGhee, *Envoy*, p. 333.

7. *FR-US*, 1950, Vol. V, Memo from Rountree to McGhee, Dec. 20, 1950, pp. 634–35.

8. Ibid., Grady to Secretary of State, July 20, 1950, pp. 174–75.

9. Ibid., U.S. Delegation at London's Foreign Ministers Meeting to Acting Secretary of State, May 16, 1950, p. 546; U.S. Ambassador in London to U.S. Embassy, Tehran, Aug. 18, 1950, p. 585.

10. Ibid., Grady to U.S. Embassy, London, Aug. 15, 1950, pp. 581–82; Grady to Secretary of State, Oct. 21, 1950, p. 607.

11. Ibid., U.S. Ambassador in Moscow to Acting Secretary of State, Sept. 14, 1950, pp. 588–89.

12. Ibid., Memo from Funkhouser to McGhee on "Discussions with British on AIOC," Sept. 14, 1950, pp. 97–99.

13. Ibid., "Middle East Oil," Paper prepared by Funkhouser, Sept. 1950, pp. 76–96.

14. Ibid., Informal US-UK discussions, London, Sept. 21, 1950, pp. 593–600.

15. Ibid., Acheson to Bevin. Nov. 20, 1950, pp. 616–17; interview with George McGhee, London, Sept. 18, 1985.

16. *FR-US*, 1950, Vol. V, Grady to Acheson, Oct. 31, 1950, pp. 612–13; Acheson to Grady, Nov. 18, 1950, pp. 613–14.

17. AIOC, Tehran, to AIOC, London, July 2, 1950, in Ra'in, *Asnadé*, pp. 251–55.

18. Ibid., AIOC Information Office, Tehran, to AIOC London, pp. 273–75; AIOC Report on the Company's Public Relations Activities in Iran, Mar. 14, 1951, pp. 48–54.

19. McGhee, *Envoy*, p. 74.

20. *FR-US*, 1950, Vol. V, U.S. Chargé d'Affaires, London, to Secretary of State, Dec. 14, 1950, p. 632.

21. Majlis Proceedings, Oct. 19, 22, 24, and 26, 1950. See also Rouhani, *Tarikhé Melli Shodané*, p. 84.

22. *FR-US*, 1950, Vol. V, Memo from Rountree to McGhee, Dec. 20, 1950, pp. 634–35.

23. FO371/91521, Franks to F.O.; Acheson's message to Bevin, Nov. 29, 1950.

24. Ibid., Shepherd to F.O., Dec. 7, 1950.

25. Ibid., Minute by Furlonge, Dec. 21, 1950.

26. Majlis Proceedings, Dec. 26, 1950.

27. FO371/91448, Shepherd to Bevin, Feb. 19, 1951.

28. FO371/91521, Shepherd to Bevin, Dec. 29, 1950; FO371/91522, Sir R. Hay, Bahrain, to F.O., reporting on his trip to Tehran, Feb. 16, 1951.

29. FO371/91521, Shepherd to Bevin, Dec. 31, 1950.

30. Ibid., Burrows to Furlonge, Jan. 3, 1951.

31. *Time* magazine: "Iran-Troubled Oil," Jan. 8, 1951.

32. FO371/91759, Memorandum by Fry on "Anglo-American Relations in Saudi Arabia," Feb. 7, 1951.

33. The nationalization proposal, tabled earlier on Nov. 29, 1950, was signed by Mossadeq, Haeri-Zadeh, Shayegan, Saleh, and Makki. It was tabled again on Jan. 11, 1951.

34. Elwell-Sutton, *Persian Oil*, p. 204.

35. FO371/91524, Record of meeting at F.O., Jan. 16, 1951.

36. FO371/91522, Military branch of the Admiralty to Rothnie, F.O., Feb. 12, 1951.

37. FO371/91522, Record of meeting held in Sir William Strang's Office with Treasury and AIOC officials, Jan. 23, 1951.

38. Elwell-Sutton, *Persian Oil*, p. 271.

39. McGhee, who held a B.S. degree in geology from the University of Oklahoma and a doctorate from Oxford, was employed by various oil companies in the early 1930s as a geologist. In 1940 he established his own oil-producing firm. Max Thornburg was formerly with Standard Oil of California and later petroleum adviser to the State Department.

40. FO371/91522, British Embassy, Tehran, to F.O., Feb. 1, 1951.

41. FO371/91573, Fateh to Elkington, Jan. 27, 1951; FO371/91577, Minute by Logan, July 7, 1951.

42. *FR-US*, 1951, Vol. V, Conference of Middle East Chiefs of Mission, Istanbul, Feb. 14–21, 1951, pp. 60–71.

43. FO371/91522, Shepherd to F.O., Feb. 10 and 11, 1951.

44. Ibid., Shepherd to F.O., Feb. 21, 1951; FO371/91523, Shepherd to F.O., Feb. 26, 1951.

45. FO371/91522, Shepherd's confidential report to Bevin, Feb. 10, and to F.O., Feb. 15, 1951.

46. Ibid., Text of prepared parliamentary question and answer, Feb. 21, 1951.

47. FO371/91523, Shepherd to F.O., Feb. 26, 1951.

48. Ibid., L. A. C. Fry, F.O., to D. R. Serpell, Treasury, and Victor Butler, Ministry of Fuel and Power, Mar. 1, 1951; Serpell to Fry, Mar. 1, 1951; Shepherd to F.O., Mar. 3, 1951.

49. Ibid., English text of Persian broadcast of Mar. 4, 1951, entitled "Persian Oil Nationalisation—The British View," said to be written by David Mitchell.

50. FO371/91524, Northcroft to Gass, Mar. 8, 1951.

51. FO371/91522, F.O. to British Embassy, Tehran, Feb. 23, 1951.

52. FO371/91523, Shepherd to Razmara, Feb. 23, 1951.
53. Interview with A. H. Ebtehaj, London, June 5, 1985.
54. FO371/91523, Shepherd to Razmara, Feb. 23, 1951.
55. Ibid., Shepherd to Bevin, Feb. 26, 1951.
56. Ibid., Shepherd to F.O., Mar. 1, 1951; Record of meeting on Persian oil at F.O., Mar. 2, 1951.
57. Ibid., F.O. to Shepherd, Mar. 2, 1951.
58. Ibid., British Embassy, Tehran, to F.O., Mar. 2 and 4, 1951.
59. I worked in the AIOC Information Office in Tehran during 1949–51 and heard this often from some members of the British staff at the time.
60. One who made this claim was Colonel H. Deyhimi, then head of the Shah's Military Bureau. According to Deyhimi the royal court knew about Tahmassebi's assassination plot but were uncertain that it would succeed; thus Assadollah Alam, the Shah's confidant, arranged with a sergeant to do the job. See Colonel G. Mossavar-Rahmani, *Kohné-Sarbaz: Khateraté Siassi va Nezami* (Tehran, 1366/1987), pp. 353–58. See also "Interview with Dr. M. Baqa'i," *Iranian Oral History Collection* (Harvard University Center for Middle Eastern Studies, 1987).

5.—The Oil Nationalization Act

1. William Roger Louis, *The British Empire in the Middle East, 1945–1951* (Oxford, 1984), p. 649.
2. FO371/91525, Bolton to Makins, quoting William Iliff, Mar. 3, 1951.
3. Elwell-Sutton, *Persian Oil*, p. 199.
4. FO371/91524, Shepherd to F.O., Mar. 14, 1951; FO371/91525, Minute by Pyman, Mar. 14, 1951.
5. FO371/91524, Shepherd to Morrison, Mar. 19, 1951; FO371/91526, Shepherd to F.O., Mar. 27, 1951.
6. FO371/91524, Shepherd to F.O. (two communications), Mar. 18, 1951.
7. Ibid., F.O. to Tehran, Mar. 23, 1951; Shepherd to F.O., Mar. 24, 1951.
8. FO371/91525, Shepherd to F.O., Mar. 28, 1951.
9. Ibid., Record of meeting held at F.O., Top Secret, Mar. 20, 1951.
10. Ibid.
11. Ibid.
12. FO371/91470, F.O. to British Embassy, Washington, Mar. 24, 1951; FO371/91454, Franks to F.O., Mar. 27, 1951.
13. FO371/91525, Minute by Fry giving the views of Noel-Baker, Mar. 31, 1951.
14. FO371/91524, Franks to F.O., Mar. 27, 1951; FO371/91525, Shepherd to F.O., Apr. 2, 1951.
15. FO371/91524, Minute by Rothnie, Mar. 29, 1951.
16. FO371/91470, F.O. to British Embassy, Tehran, Apr. 4, 1951.
17. FO371/91527, Minute by Strang on his meeting with Fraser, Apr. 19, 1951.
18. FO371/91524, Shepherd to F.O., Mar. 18, 1951.
19. McGhee, *Envoy*, pp. 326–27.
20. *FR-US*, 1951, Vol. V, Secretary of State to U.S. Embassy, London, Mar. 31, 1951, pp. 296–97.
21. FO371/91470, Meeting at F.O., Apr. 2, 1951.

22. McGhee, *Envoy*, p. 333.

23. Ibid., pp. 329–30.

24. FO371/91470, Morrison to Franks, Apr. 6, 1951; Franks to Morrison, Apr. 28, 1951.

25. Ibid., Bowker to Strang, Brief for U.K. Delegation to Washington, Apr. 6, 1951.

26. Ibid., Franks to F.O., Apr. 10, 1951.

27. Ibid.

28. *New York Times, Washington Post, Wall Street Journal*, Apr. 7, 1951.

29. FO371/91471, British Embassy, Washington, to Eastern Department, F.O., Apr. 7, 1951; McGhee, *Envoy*, pp. 337–38; Parliamentary Debates, House of Commons, June 21, 1951.

30. FO371/91555, Franks to F.O., July 5, 1951.

31. FO371/91562, C. E. Steel, British Embassy, Washington, to Roger Makins, F.O., July 5, 1951.

32. Ibid., Minute by Makins, July 5, 1951.

33. FO371/91525, Shepherd to F.O., Apr. 1, 1951.

34. FO371/91522, Minute by Fry on his conversation with Leggett, Feb. 6, 1951.

35. FO371/91527, Leggett to Strang, Apr. 14, 1951.

36. FO371/91621, Mountbatten of Burma to First Sea Lord, Apr. 5, 1951; Philip Ziegler, *Mountbatten: The Official Biography* (London, 1985), pp. 499–501.

37. FO371/91526, Strang to Shepherd, Apr. 5, 1951; Fergusson to Bridges, Apr. 12, 1951.

38. FO371/91528, Shepherd to F.O., Apr. 27, 1951.

39. For the full text of the act see Majlis Proceedings, Apr. 28, 1951. English translation of the act in Elwell-Sutton, *Persian Oil*, pp. 216–17.

6.—Forces at Work in Iran, Britain, and the United States

1. Makki, *Ketabé Siah*, Vol. III, Part I, pp. 35–44; Abrahamian, *Iran*, pp. 254–55.

2. Abrahamian, *Iran*, pp. 253–61.

3. Makki, *Ketabé Siah*, Vol. III, Part I, pp. 47–53.

4. FO371/98620, Shepherd to Eden and its enclosures, Jan. 14, 1952.

5. FO371/98607, Middleton to F.O. sending Bolland's report, Aug. 4, 1952.

6. Interview with Henry Byroade, Washington, Sept. 30, 1985. *FR-US*, 1951, Vol. V, Conclusions and Recommendations of the Conference of the Middle East Chiefs of Mission at Istanbul, Feb. 14–21, 1951, pp. 70–72.

7. Correlli Barnett, *The Pride and the Fall: The Dream and Illusion of Britain as a Great Power* (New York, 1986), p. 304.

8. FO371/91575, Notes on Persian oil, July 31, 1951.

9. Ibid. Also FO371/91608, Report of the Official Working Party on Persian Oil, Oct. 29, 1951.

10. State Department Bulletin, Apr. 24, 1943.

11. *The Times* (London), Mar. 22, 1951. The anonymous author of the article, according to Professor Roger Louis, was Ann Lambton of the School of Oriental Studies, London University.

12. *The Economist*, Apr. 21, 1951.

13. Fateh, *Panjah Sal*, pp. 102–20, 500.

14. *Baltimore Sun*, June 21, 1951, reporting on the Senate hearings of June 20; *U.S. News and World Report*, Sept. 28, 1951.

15. *Washington Post*, Apr. 7 and June 22, 1951.

16. *New York Times*, Nov. 8, 1951.

17. FO953/1163, B. Burrows, British Embassy, Washington, to American Department, F.O., June 16, 1951; P. H. Gore-Booth to F.O., June 15, 1951.

18. FO953/1163, Slessor's report to F.O., "Spreading the British Point of View in America," May 15, 1951.

19. Ibid., Minister of State for Foreign Affairs to Slessor, May 23, 1951; Gore-Booth to F.O., June 20, 1951. Interview with Sir Oliver Franks, Oxford, Jan. 21, 1988.

20. FO371/91529, Franks to Strang, Apr. 21, 1951; FO371/91584, J. V. Kelly, Moscow, to Furlonge, Aug. 31, 1951.

21. Interview with Sir Eric Drake, London, Oct. 30, 1986; FO371/91522, Minute by L. A. C. Fry on his conversation with Leggett, Feb. 6, 1951.

22. FO371/91628, Noel-Baker to Bevin, Nov. 15, 1950.

23. Ibid., British Legation, Tel Aviv, to F.O. sending the *Jerusalem Post* article by Soleh Boneh, July 6, 1951.

24. FO371/91628, Noel-Baker to Bevin, Nov. 15, 1950.

25. Anthony Sampson, *The Seven Sisters: The Great Oil Companies and the World They Made* (London, 1975), pp. 134–35.

26. The AIOC Annual Report for the year ending Dec. 31, 1950.

27. McGhee, *Envoy*, pp. 322–26.

28. John Strachey, *The End of Empire* (London, 1959), p. 173.

29. FO371/91607, Minutes of meeting in Sir Edward Bridges's room, Oct. 23, 1951.

30. FO371/91547, R. S. Cairey, Rangoon, to F.O., June 16, 1951.

31. *FR-US*, 1951, Vol. V, "National Intelligence Estimate," Jan. 8, 1951, pp. 268–76.

32. Ibid., Richard Funkhouser on "Middle East Oil," Sept. 1950, pp. 76–96.

7.—Iran Takes Over the Company

1. AIOC Annual Report and Accounts as at 31st Dec. 1950; FO371/91611, Minute by Strang, "Some Notes on the Persian Oil Dispute and its Implications," Oct. 23, 1951; FO371/91574, "Notes for Lord Privy Seal's Mission" attached to Minute by Berthoud, Aug. 3, 1951.

2. FO371/91523, C. E. Loombe, Bank of England, to Eastern Department, F.O., Feb. 28, 1951.

3. *FR-US*, Vol. V, 1950, State Department paper entitled "Middle East Oil," Sept. 1950, pp. 76–96; *FR-US*, Vol. V, 1951, "National Intelligence Estimate" prepared by CIA, Jan. 8, 1951, pp. 268–76. Although British documents gave Iran's oil production in 1950 as 32 million tons and the capacity of Abadan as 20 million tons a year, the above U.S. reports give Iran's production as 700,000 barrels a day (35 million tons in 1950) and Abadan's capacity as 27 million tons in that year.

4. Ibid. (both citations).

5. FO371/91611, Minute by Makins, Nov. 9, 1951.

6. FO371/91458, Ministry of Defence to GHQ, Middle East Land Forces, Top Secret, May 2, 1951.

7. FO371/91529, Shepherd to F.O., May 2, 1951.

8. FO371/91534, Shepherd to F.O., May 7, 1951.

9. FO371/91533, Aide-mémoire handed to Morrison by Iran's ambassador in London, May 8, 1951.

10. FO371/91535, Shepherd to Furlonge, May 2, 1951.

11. The members from the Senate were Dr. Ahmad Matin-Daftari, former prime minister; Morteza-Qoli Bayat, former prime minister and finance minister; Abul-Qasem Najm, former finance minister and foreign minister; Mohammad Soruri, former Minister of the Interior and Justice; and Dr. Reza-Zadeh Shafaq, university professor and often a delegate to the United Nations. The members from the Majlis were Allahyar Saleh, former Minister of Finance and Justice; Dr. Abdollah Moazzami, Professor of International Law, Tehran University, and former member of the Supreme Economic Council; Dr. Ali Shayegan, former education minister and a lawyer; Nasser-Qoli Ardalan, economic expert; and Hossein Makki, former civil servant.

12. FO371/91534, Shepherd to Morrison, May 12, 1951; Elwell-Sutton, *Persian Oil*, pp. 222–23.

13. FO371/91535, F.O. to Shepherd, May 14, 1951; FO371/91534, British Embassy, Paris, to F.O., May 15, 1951.

14. FO371/91535, F.O. to British Embassy, Tehran, Seddon to Varasteh, May 25, 1951.

15. FO371/91528, Franks to F.O., Apr. 29, 1951; FO371/91533, Franks to F.O., May 12, 1951.

16. FO371/91534, Minute by M. R. Starkey, F.O., recording his conversation with Attlee, May 14, 1951.

17. FO371/91535, Morrison to Franks, May 18, 1951.

18. FO371/91538, Shepherd to F.O., May 30, 1951; FO371/91542, British Embassy, Tehran, to D. A. Logan, Eastern Department, F.O., June 2, 1951.

19. FO371/91538, Remarks by Acheson at his press conference on May 23, 1951; Brief for Cabinet meeting prepared by Furlonge, May 28, 1951; FO371/91531, Bowker to Shepherd giving Morrison's views, May 5, 1951.

20. House of Commons Debates, May 29, 1951.

21. FO371/91542, Truman's message to Mossadeq, May 31, 1951; FO371/91543, Truman's message to Attlee, May 31, 1951.

22. McGhee, *Envoy*, pp. 389–90.

23. *Wall Street Journal*, June 5, 1951; *Dad*, June 4, 1951.

24. FO371/91540, Shepherd to F.O., June 1, 1951.

25. FO371/91541, Attlee to Walter Gifford conveying his message to President Truman, June 5, 1951.

26. "Asnadé Naft," Iran's Foreign Ministry Publications (1330/1951), Mossadeq's message to Truman, pp. 116–19.

27. FO371/91540, F.O. to Shepherd, June 2, 1951.

28. FO371/91549, Berthoud's minute on his conversation with Levy, May 22, 1951, and Furlonge's notes on the same minute.

29. *Wall Street Journal*, June 9, 1951.

30. Rouhani, *Tarikhé Melli Shodané*, pp. 146–47.

31. FO371/91547, Shepherd to F.O., June 19, 1951; Fateh, *Panjah Sal*, pp. 529–30.

32. FO371/91550, Morrison's statement in the House of Commons, June 20, 1951.

33. *The Times* (London), June 23, 1951.

34. Interview with Mehdi Sami'i, who accompanied the two Iranian missions to Abadan, London, June 1, 1985.

35. FO371/91543, Shepherd to F.O., June 11, 1951.

36. FO371/91544, Capper to F.O., June 14, 1951.

37. FO371/91548, F.O. to Capper, Fraser's message to Drake, June 20, 1951; FO371/91548, F.O. to Franks, June 23, 1951; FO371/91550, Franks to F.O., June 25, 1951.

38. Rouhani, *Tarikhé Melli Shodané*, pp. 157–59; FO371/91551, Shepherd to F.O., June 26, 1951.

39. FO371/91551, H.M.S. *Wren* to F.O., Message from Drake to Fraser, June 26, 1951.

40. FO371/91553, Shepherd to F.O., June 29, 1951.

41. FO371/91537, Record of conversation with Fraser at Chiefs of Staff Committee Meeting, Top Secret, May 23, 1951.

42. FO371/91554, British Embassy, Tehran, to F.O., from Seddon to Gass, July 3, 1951; FO371/91555, F.O. to British Embassy and Seddon, Tehran, July 7, 1951.

43. FO371/91554, Shepherd to F.O., July 2 and 3, 1951; F.O. to Shepherd, July 5, 1951.

44. FO371/91557, Capper to F.O., July 6, 1951.

45. FO371/91555, Shepherd to F.O., July 4, 1951.

46. FO371/91562, Frigate *Flamingo* to Admiralty, July 7, 1951; FO371/91563, Shepherd to F.O., July 12, 1951.

47. I was taken with some other translators from the dissolved AIOC Information Office to Seddon's residence to translate the company's confidential papers into Persian.

48. Ra'in, *Asnadé*, pp. 315, 321.

49. Ibid., "Précis of message sent to Mr. Northcroft by the Prime Minister [A. Mansur] through Dr. Jalali," p. 170; Rice to Northcroft, May 2, June 22 and 28, 1950, pp. 260–69. See p. 318 on guilds.

50. Ibid., Northcroft to AIOC, London, Mar. 14, 1951, pp. 48–54.

51. *Sheipuré-Marde-Emruz*, No. 22, reprinted in Ra'in, *Asnadé*, pp. 309–12.

52. Majlis Proceedings, July 1 and 3, 1951.

53. FO371/91563, Shepherd to F.O., July 12, 1951.

54. FO371/91564, Parliamentary Debate, July 12, 1951.

55. FO371/91547, U.K. High Commission in India to Commonwealth Relations Office, London, June 12, 1951; FO371/91576, U.K. High Commission in India to British Embassies in Tehran and Washington, July 17, 1951.

56. FO371/91538, CBS broadcast, May 20, 1951.

57. FO371/91535, Minute by Rothnie, May 18, 1951; FO371/91568, British Legation, Amman, to Morrison, July 16, 1951.

58. FO371/91571, British Embassy, Tehran, to F.O., giving the text of Baqa'i's speech, Aug. 1, 1951.

59. *New York Herald Tribune*, July 15, 1951.

8.—The Harriman and Stokes Missions

1. Dean Acheson, *Present at the Creation: My Years in the State Department* (New York, 1969), pp. 505–7.
2. FO371/91553, Musaddiq's message to Truman, June 28, 1951; F.O. to British Embassy, Tehran, June 28, 1951.
3. Acheson, *Creation,* p. 507.
4. Ibid., pp. 507–8.
5. FO371/91555, Franks to F.O., July 4, 1951.
6. Ibid., Message from Morrison to Acheson, July 7, 1951.
7. FO371/91560, Franks to F.O., text of Truman's message of July 8 to Musaddiq, July 9, 1951; FO371/91562, Musaddiq's reply to Truman, attached to Minute by Furlonge, July 16, 1951.
8. *New York Herald Tribune,* Homer Bigart's report from Tehran on Shepherd's press conference, July 13, 1951; FO371/91562, F.O. to Shepherd, July 13, 1951.
9. FO371/91561, Morrison to Franks, message to Acheson, July 12, 1951.
10. Acheson, *Creation,* p. 505; FO371/91562, Franks to F.O. giving the text of Harriman's press statement, July 12, 1951.
11. FO371/91601, Jebb, New York, to F.O. giving summary of conversation between Middleton and Wilkinson of Asiatic Petroleum Company on Harriman's talks with U.S. oil companies, Oct. 13, 1951.
12. FO371/91562, F.O. to British Embassies in Tehran and Washington reporting on Gaitskell's discussions with Harriman, July 14, 1951.
13. Elwell-Sutton, *Persian Oil,* p. 244.
14. CAB128/20, Cabinet Conclusions 52(51) and 53(51), July 16 and 19, 1951.
15. FO371/91565, House of Commons Debates, July 17, 1951.
16. FO371/91564, Shepherd to F.O., July 17, 1951.
17. Vernon Walters, *Silent Missions* (New York, 1978), pp. 241–63.
18. FO371/91566, Shepherd to F.O., July 18, 1951.
19. The five members were Minister of Finance Varasteh and four members of the Majlis and the Senate: Matin-Daftari, Reza-Zadeh Shafag, Shayegan, and Allahyar Saleh.
20. Rouhani, *Tarikhé Melli Shodané,* pp. 190–91.
21. FO371/91567, Shepherd to F.O., July 20, 1951.
22. Ibid., Shepherd to F.O., July 22, 1951; FO371/91568, Shepherd to F.O., July 24, 1951.
23. FO371/91571, Minute by Sarner on meeting between Gifford and Strang, July 25, 1951; FO371/91570, British Embassy, Tehran, to F.O., July 29, 1951.
24. Rouhani, *Tarikhé Melli Shodané,* pp. 191–92; FO371/91568, Shepherd to F.O., July 24, 1951.
25. FO371/91568, F.O. to British Embassies in Tehran and Washington, July 23, 1951; FO371/91571, F.O. to Shepherd, July 26, 1951.
26. FO371/91568, Shepherd to F.O., July 24 and 25, 1951; FO371/91569, Shepherd to F.O., July 29, 1951; British Embassy, Washington, to F.O., July 26, 1951.
27. *Baltimore Sun,* July 28, 1951.

28. FO371/91569, F.O. to Shepherd, July 27, 1951.

29. *New York Times*, July 30, 1951.

30. CAB128/20, Cabinet Conclusions 56(51) and 57(51), July 30 and Aug. 1, 1951.

31. FO371/91575, Notes of meeting held with Levy, July 29, 1951; FO371/91573, Minute by Strang for Morrison, July 29, 1951.

32. FO371/91575, AIOC paper entitled "Agenda for a Working Basis of Cooperation Between the Iranian Government and Anglo-Iranian," sent by Gass to Bowker, July 31, 1951.

33. FO371/91573, Minute by Strang for Morrison, July 29, 1951.

34. Other members of the Stokes mission were Dr. W. Nuttal, technical adviser of the Ministry of Fuel and Power, M. T. Flett of the Treasury, P. Ramsbotham of the Foreign Office, and five AIOC representatives headed by E. H. O. Elkington.

35. FO371/91574, "Notes for Lord Privy Seal's Mission," attached to Minute by Berthoud, Aug. 3, 1951.

36. Ibid. Also FO371/91525, F.O. to Shepherd, Apr. 5, 1951.

37. FO371/91575, Record of a meeting held between the Chancellor of the Exchequer, Lord Privy Seal, and officials of the Ministry of Fuel and Power, the Treasury, and the Foreign Office, July 21, 1951.

38. FO371/91576, Record of conversation between Lord Privy Seal and Dr. Musaddiq prepared by Ramsbotham, Aug. 5, 1951.

39. FO371/91577, Minutes of the meeting by Ramsbotham, Aug. 5, 1951.

40. Ibid., Shepherd to F.O., Aug. 5, 1951.

41. FO371/91577, Stokes to F.O., Minute by Nuttal, Aug. 8, 1951; Elwell-Sutton, *Persian Oil*, p. 250.

42. FO371/91575, F.O. to British Embassy, Tehran, reporting Capper's statement to the press, Aug. 6, 1951; FO371/91578, Shepherd to F.O., Aug. 17, 1951; FO371/91576, Capper to F.O., Aug. 10, 1951.

43. FO371/91580, Capper to F.O., repeated for information to Middle East Air Forces and War Office, Aug. 23, 1951.

44. FO371/91574, Shepherd to F.O. on meeting of the Stokes mission with the Iranian delegation, Aug. 9, 1951.

45. FO371/91578, Minute by Ramsbotham on the third meeting between Lord Privy Seal and Musaddiq, Aug. 9, 1951.

46. FO371/91576, Lord Privy Seal to Secretary of State, Aug. 13, 1951.

47. FO371/91575, Lord Privy Seal to Secretary of State, Aug. 12, 1951; FO371/91573, Shepherd to F.O. on Levy's views, Aug. 7, 1951.

48. FO371/91578, Memorandum of the British delegation, Aug. 11, 1951.

49. Ibid., Stokes to F.O., Aug. 14, 1951.

50. FO371/91577, Shepherd to F.O., Aug. 15, 1951.

51. Acheson Papers, "Princeton Seminars," May 15–16, 1954, p. 1624.

52. Interview with Walter Levy, New York, Sept. 26, 1985.

53. FO371/91580, Meeting of Lord Stokes and Pyman with Sayyid Zia at the British Embassy residence in Gulhak, Aug. 15, 1951; FO371/91587, Stokes's note to Foreign Secretary, Top Secret, Sept. 6, 1951.

54. FO371/91579, Minute by Furlonge, Aug. 15, 1951; FO371/91577, Shepherd to F.O. on Lord Privy Seal's meeting with Kashani, Aug. 11, 1951.

55. Elwell-Sutton, *Persian Oil*, p. 252.

56. FO371/91578, Lord Privy Seal to F.O., Text of the reply of the Iranian delegation, Aug. 19, 1951.

57. Ibid. Also FO371/91577, Shepherd to F.O., from Lord Privy Seal, Aug. 14, 1951; FO371/91580, Minutes of the 8th meeting of U.K.–Iran Delegations, Aug. 19, 1951.

58. FO371/91580, Ramsbotham to Logan, Aug. 20, 1951.

59. FO371/91579, Shepherd to F.O., from Lord Privy Seal, Aug. 20 and 21, 1951.

60. Majlis Proceedings, Aug. 22, 1951.

61. FO371/91580, Ramsbotham to Logan, Aug. 20, 1951.

62. FO371/91579, Shepherd to F.O., from Lord Privy Seal, three communications, Aug. 21, 1951.

63. FO371/91580, Shepherd to F.O., Text of Musaddiq's memorandum to Lord Privy Seal, Aug. 22, 1951.

64. FO371/91580, F.O. to British Embassy, Tehran, giving the details of ministerial discussions on Iran, Aug. 22, 1951.

65. FO371/91581, F.O. to Franks, Message from Attlee to Truman, Aug. 23, 1951.

66. Ibid., Franks to F.O., Aug. 23, 1951.

67. *Washington Post*, Aug. 27, Aug. 28, and Sept. 11, 1951.

68. *New York Times*, Aug. 28 and Sept. 22, 1951.

69. FO371/91582, Minute by Malcolm, Aug. 23, 1951; FO371/91584, Minute by Berthoud, Aug. 30, 1951; FO371/91586, Minute by Strang, Sept. 6, 1951.

70. FO371/91584, Minute by Berthoud on his meeting with Levy, Aug. 28, 1951; FO371/91585, Record of meeting between V. Butler and Walter Levy, July 29, 1951.

71. FO371/91586, Minute by Berthoud, Sept. 1, 1951.

72. FO371/91587, Fergusson to Strang, Sept. 5, 1951.

9.—The Oil Cartel's Stranglehold

1. CAB21/983, Ministry of Fuel and Power to Cabinet, June 20, 1951.

2. FO371/91601, U.K. delegation, New York, to F.O., on conversation between Middleton and heads of a number of U.S. international oil companies, Oct. 13, 1951.

3. U.S. Congress, *The International Petroleum Cartel, the Iranian Consortium and U.S. National Security*, Report prepared for Subcommittee on Multinational Corporations (Washington, 1974), pp. 14, 15. (Hereafter cited as *Cartel.*)

4. Ibid., p. 15.

5. John M. Blair, *The Control of Oil* (London, 1977), p. 62.

6. FO371/91546, AIOC note attached to minute by Logan, June 6, 1951.

7. FO371/91601, E. Goad, Ministry of Transport, to V. Butler, Ministry of Fuel and Power, Oct. 9, 1951.

8. FO371/91538, Logan to Gass, AIOC, May 28, 1951; FO371/91613, Logan to Secretary of State, Nov. 15, 1951; Note by Persian (Official) Committee, Nov. 15, 1951.

9. FO371/91613, Text of AIOC advertisement, Sept. 5, 1951.

10. FO371/91565, Capper to F.O., from Mason to Fraser and Seddon, July 18, 1951; FO371/91568, F.O. to Franks, July 18, 1951.

11. FO371/91613, AIOC to Rothnie, Nov. 16, 1951; FO371/91617, AIOC to Rothnie, Dec. 12, 1951.

12. FO371/91618, Sir V. Mallet, British Embassy, Rome, to F.O., Dec. 27, 1951; Minute by Sarell on his discussions with the Italian Chargé d'Affaires in London, Jan. 3, 1952; FO371/91613, British Embassy, Lisbon, to F.O., Dec. 8, 1951.

13. FO371/104620, F.O. to U.K. High Commission in India, Apr. 11, 1953.

14. FO371/104617, British Embassy, Ankara, to F.O., Jan. 13, 1953; RG59, Box 5510, Memo of conversation of Henry Arnold and Rear Admiral Thomas Kelly with William Baxter of the Office of Greek, Turkish and Iranian Affairs, Aug. 5, 1953.

15. FO371/91557, F.O. to British High Commission in Wahnerheide, West Germany, July 2, 1951; FO371/91559, British High Commission, Wahnerheide, to F.O., July 7, 1951; FO371/91618, British High Commission, Wahnerheide, to F.O., Dec. 19, 1951.

16. FO371/91535, F.O. to British Embassy, Paris, May 21, 1951; FO371/91553, British Embassy, Rome, to F.O., June 28, 1951; Minute by Bowker on his conversation with Cafra of AGIP, July 25, 1951.

17. FO371/91613, Coldrick to Eden, Nov. 16, 1951; Anthony Nutting to Coldrick, Nov. 29, 1951.

18. FO371/91563, British Embassy, Washington, to F.O., July 12 and 16, 1951.

19. FO371/91564, British Embassy, Washington, to F.O., July 10, 1951.

20. FO371/91554, Shepherd to F.O., July 4, 1951.

21. FO371/91561, Pakenham to Morrison, Top Secret, July 4, 1951.

22. Senate Proceedings, Sept. 6, 1951.

23. FO371/91586, Shepherd to F.O., Sept. 6, 1951.

24. Ibid., Shepherd to F.O., Sept. 7, 1951; Minute by Strang on the discussions of the Working Party on Persian Oil, Sept. 8, 1951.

25. Fateh, *Panjah Sal*, pp. 565–66.

26. FO371/91589, Franks to F.O., Sept. 21 and 22, 1951.

27. FO371/91591, Shepherd to F.O., Sept. 21, 1951.

28. FO371/91586, Minute by Bowker, Sept. 4, 1951; FO371/91584, Shepherd to F.O., Aug. 25, 1951.

29. FO371/91589, F.O. to Shepherd, Sept. 22, 1951; Middleton to Sarner, Sept. 18, 1951; FO371/91592, Shepherd to Ala, Sept. 22, 1951.

30. FO371/91590, Working Party paper on "Approach to a New Persian Government," Sept. 21, 1951.

31. Ibid., Shepherd to F.O., Sept. 25, 1951.

32. FO371/91580, Attlee to Mason, Aug. 23, 1951.

33. FO371/91590, F.O. to Shepherd, Sept. 25, 1951; FO371/91591, Shepherd to F.O., Sept. 27, 1951.

34. FO371/91590, F.O. to Franks, Personal message from Attlee to Truman, Sept. 25, 1951.

35. FO371/91591, Franks to F.O., Sept. 26, 1951.

36. Ibid.

37. Ibid., Truman's reply to Attlee, Sept. 26, 1951.

38. *Keyhan* and *Bakhtar*, Sept. 26, 1951.

39. FO371/91591, F.O. to Capper, Sept. 26, 1951.

10.—British Plans for the Occupation of Abadan

1. *FR-US*, 1950, Vol. V, U.S.-U.K. Political-Military Conversations, Washington, Oct. 26, 1950, pp. 233–37.

2. Ibid., p. 236.

3. FO371/91525, Bolton to Makins sending report dated Feb. 28, 1951, of C. E. Loombe on "Persian Threat to Nationalise A.I.O.C.," Mar. 3, 1951.

4. FO371/91524, Furlonge to Ministry of Defence, Mar. 20, 1951.

5. FO371/91458, Ministry of Defence to GHQ, Middle East Land Forces (MELF), May 2, 1951; GHQ-MELF to Ministry of Defence, May 3, 1951; Chiefs of Staff Committee Meeting, May 4, 1951; GHQ-MELF to Ministry of Defence, May 8, 1951. DEFE4/45, Chiefs of Staff Committee Meeting, July 11, 1951.

6. CAB128/19, Cabinet Conclusions 35(51), May 10, 1951; CAB21/1982, Chiefs of Staff Committee Meeting, May 23, 1951.

7. FO371/91534, Franks to Morrison, May 17, 1951.

8. FO371/91535, Morrison to Franks, May 18, 1951.

9. *Wall Street Journal*, Apr. 7, 1951; *Philadelphia Inquirer*, Aug. 28, 1951.

10. *Washington Post*, June 22, 1951.

11. FO371/91538, British Embassy, Washington, to F.O. reporting Howard K. Smith broadcast, May 20, 1951.

12. FO371/91549, Minute by Berthoud on his conversation with Levy, May 22, 1951.

13. FO371/91537, Record of discussions with Fraser at Chiefs of Staff Committee Meeting, May 23, 1951; CAB21/1982, Chiefs of Staff Committee Meeting, May 29, 1951.

14. FO371/91458, GHQ-MELF, to Ministry of Defence, May 21, 24, and 27, 1951; Ministry of Defence to GHQ-MELF, May 18, 23, 25, and 28, 1951; CAB21/1982, Chiefs of Staff Committee Meeting, May 29, 1951; Joint Planning Staff Paper, May 29, 1951; Defence Committee Meeting, June 4, 1951.

15. Ibid. Also DEFE4/45, Chiefs of Staff Committee Meeting, July 11, 1951.

16. FO371/91548, Fergusson to Lieutenant-General Sir Kenneth McLean, June 18, 1951.

17. FO371/91555, Notes of meeting to discuss Persia, June 27, 1951.

18. FO371/91559, Churchill to Truman, June 29, 1951.

19. FO371/91615, British Embassy, Tehran, to F.O. reporting Stewart Alsop's interview with Kashani, Nov. 26, 1951. FO371/91571, Minute by Furlonge, June 26, 1951; Logan to Bowker, July 13, 1951; Millar to Dixon, June 22, 1951.

20. Herbert Morrison, *An Autobiography* (London, 1960), p. 281; CAB21/1982, Chiefs of Staff Committee Meeting, May 21, 1951; DEFE4/45, Annex to Minutes of the Meeting of the Chiefs of Staff Committee, July 17, 1951; K. O. Morgan, *Labour in Power, 1945–1951* (Oxford, 1984), p. 471.

21. CAB21/1982, Chiefs of Staff Committee Meeting, May 21 and 29, 1951.

22. FO371/91550, Minute by Berthoud, June 21, 1951; CAB21/1983, Conclusions of a meeting of the Cabinet at 10 Downing Street, June 25, 1951.

23. FO371/91541, Minute by Furlonge, Brief for Secretary of State, May 31, 1951; FO371/91459, Morrison to Franks, June 8, 1951.

24. FO371/91554, Minute by Strang on his meeting with Holmes, June 20, 1951.

25. FO371/91548, Morrison to Shepherd, June 20 and 22, 1951; FO371/91458, GHQ-MELF, to Ministry of Defence, May 24, 1951; Ministry of Defence to GHQ-MELF, May 25, 1951; DEFE4/45, Chiefs of Staff Committee Meeting, Aug. 1, 1951.

26. FO371/91552, Shepherd to F.O., June 25, 1951; FO371/91548, Minute by Berthoud on his conversation with Elkington, Aug. 28, 1951.

27. CAB128/19, Cabinet Conclusions 48(51), July 2, 1951.

28. Ibid.

29. Ibid. Also FO371/91559, Minute by Strang on discussions of Attlee and Morrison with leaders of the opposition, July 5, 1951.

30. CAB51/200, Memorandum by Morrison, July 11, 1951; DEFE4/45, Annex to Conclusions of Chiefs of Staff Committee Meeting, July 11, 1951; FO371/91555, Franks to Morrison, July 5, 1951.

31. CAB128/20, Cabinet Conclusions 51(51), July 12, 1951; CAB51/212, Memorandum by Morrison, July 20, 1951.

32. Ibid., Cabinet Conclusions 53(51), July 19, 1951.

33. Ibid. Also Cabinet Conclusions 54(51), July 23, 1951; FO371/91568, Minute by Bowker, July 18, 1951.

34. FO371/91590, F.O. to Shepherd, Sept. 25, 1951; F.O. to Capper, Sept. 26, 1951.

35. CAB128/20, Cabinet Conclusions 60(51), Sept. 27, 1951.

36. Longhurst, *Adventure in Oil*, pp. 143–44.

37. FO371/91594, Ministry of Defence to GHQ-MELF, Top Secret, Oct. 4, 1951.

38. *The Times* (London), Oct. 22, 1951.

39. Morgan, *Labour in Power*, p. 471.

40. F. Williams, *A Prime Minister Remembers: The War and Post-War Memoirs of the Rt. Hon. Earl Attlee* (London, 1961), p. 255.

41. Kenneth Harris, *Attlee* (London, 1982), p. 472.

11.—The Oil Dispute Taken to the United Nations

1. FO371/91571, Minute by C. C. Parrot, July 6, 1951.

2. FO371/91592 and 91691, F.O. to U.K. delegation to the United Nations, New York, Sept. 27 and 28, 1951.

3. FO371/91592, Morrison to Franks, Sept. 28, 1951.

4. Ibid., Franks to Morrison, Sept. 28, 1951.

5. Ibid., Franks to Morrison, Secret, Sept. 29, 1951; Morrison to Franks, Sept. 30 and Oct. 1, 1951.

6. FO371/91598, F.O. to Franks, Morrison's message to Acheson, Sept. 30, 1951.

7. U.N. Security Council Official Records, 559th Meeting, Oct. 1, 1951. The nonpermanent members of the Security Council were Brazil, Ecuador, India, the Netherlands, Turkey, and Yugoslavia.

8. Ibid.

9. FO371/91593, Shepherd to F.O., Sept. 30, 1951.

10. Ibid., Shepherd to F.O. from Seddon to Fraser, Oct. 3, 1951; FO371/91598, Minute by Rothnie, Oct. 10, 1951.

11. FO371/91602, R. H. Arnold, AIOC, London, to L. C. Rice, AIOC, New York, Oct. 11, 1951.

12. FO371/91597 and 91598, Shepherd to F.O., Oct. 6 and 8, 1951; FO371/91602, Stokes to Morrison, Oct. 8, 1951.

13. FO371/91597, British Embassy, Mexico City, to F.O., Oct. 2, 1951.

14. *Evening Standard* (London), Oct. 15, 1951.

15. FO371/91602, U.K. High Commissioner in India to F.O., Oct. 6, 1951; *Keyhan*, Oct. 4 and 8, 1951.

16. FO371/91594, Jebb to F.O., Oct. 2, 1951; Minute by Furlonge, Oct. 5, 1951; Military Branch of the Admiralty to Furlonge, Oct. 9, 1951; F.O. to Jebb, Oct. 10, 1951.

17. FO371/91602, Morrison to Franks, Oct. 12, 1951.

18. FO371/91598, Acheson to Morrison, Oct. 5, 1951; FO371/91595, Morrison to Franks, Oct. 6, 1951.

19. FO371/91597, Franks to F.O., Oct. 7, 1951; FO371/91598, Jebb to F.O., Oct. 9, 1951.

20. The main members of the Iranian delegation accompanying Mossadeq were four members of the Joint Parliamentary Oil Committee: Dr. Matin-Daftari and S. Bayat of the Senate, Allahyar Saleh and Dr. Ali Shayegan of the Majlis. Other members from the Majlis were Dr. M. Baqa'i, Abbas Mas'udi, and Mostafa Mesbah-Zadeh; the last two were chief editors of leading papers. Also in the delegation were Hossein Fatemi, Deputy Prime Minister and editor of a leading daily; Karim Sanjabi, Minister of Education; and Javad Bushehri, Minister of Roads.

21. RG59, Box 5509, "McGhee-Mosadeq Conversations" (hereafter cited by its title alone), Oct. 8, 1951. This extensive paper contains Mossadeq's discussions with various officials during his stay in the United States.

22. FO371/91592, F.O. to Franks, Sept. 30, 1951.

23. U.N. Security Council Official Records, 560th Meeting, Oct. 15, 1951.

24. Ibid., 561st Meeting, Oct. 16, 1951. Part of Mossadeq's speech was read by Allahyar Saleh.

25. Ibid.

26. U.N. Security Council Official Records, 561st, 562nd, 563rd, 564th, and 565th Meetings, Oct. 16–19, 1951. The statements made by various speakers are broken down on each issue and put together with the relevant replies.

27. FO371/91603, Jebb to F.O., Oct. 16, 1951.

28. Acheson, *Creation*, p. 510.

29. FO371/91600, U.K. delegation at the U.N. to Eastern Department, F.O., Oct. 8, 1951.

30. U.N. Security Council Official Records, 565th Meeting, Oct. 19, 1951.

31. FO371/91605, Jebb to F.O., Oct. 19, 1951; FO371/91606, Shepherd to F.O., Oct. 23, 1951.

32. *Financial Times* (London), Oct. 22, 1951.

12.—Mossadeq's Discussions in the United States

1. Ivision S. Macadam, ed., *The Annual Register, 1951*, p. 62.

2. Ibid., Churchill's speech at Guildhall, p. 67.

3. FO371/91597, Jebb to F.O., Oct. 8, 1951; FO371/91601, Franks to F.O., Oct. 13, 1951.

4. McGhee, *Envoy*, pp. 395–96.

5. "McGhee-Mosadeq Conversations," Oct. 9, 1951.

6. *New York Times*, Oct. 12, 1951.

7. McGhee, *Envoy*, p. 397.

8. "McGhee-Mosadeq Conversations," Meeting at Blair House, Oct. 23, 1951.

9. Ibid.

10. Ibid.

11. David S. Painter, *Private Power and Public Policy: Multinational Oil Corporations and U.S. Foreign Policy, 1941–1954* (London, 1986), pp. 182–83.

12. FO371/91607, Franks to F.O. giving the State Department's calculations on the breakdown of the price of oil and a 50-50 division of profits based on the data received from American oil companies, Oct. 3, 1951. Gross profit was calculated as follows:

Production cost per barrel	25	cents
Per barrel capital investment in oil fields	20	"
Total cost	45	"
Posted price per barrel	$1.75	
Cost per barrel as given above	.45	
Gross profit	$1.30	

Half of the gross profit, or 65 cents, was to be Iran's share, to which was added the 45 cents cost per barrel because Iran had to bear such costs.

13. "McGhee-Mosadeq Conversations," meetings on Oct. 24 and 29, 1951.

14. FO371/91607, Franks to F.O., Text of U.S. proposals, Oct. 30, 1951.

15. Ibid., Paper by Persian Oil Working Party, F.O., Nov. 1, 1951; FO371/91609, Minute by Ramsbotham on the Nov. 6 meeting of the Persian Oil Working Party, Nov. 8, 1951.

16. FO371/91609 and 91611, Minutes by Strang, Oct. 23, Nov. 1, and Nov. 3, 1951; FO371/91609, Prime Minister's office to F.O., Nov. 3, 1951.

17. FO371/91608, Minutes of meeting held at Eden's office, Nov. 1, 1951; FO371/91612, Brief prepared by F.O. for presentation of HMG's case by Eden at meetings with Acheson and Harriman in Paris, Nov. 6, 1951; FO371/91610, Fergusson to Eden, Nov. 6, 1951.

18. FO371/91609, Sir Herbert Williams, M.P., to Anthony Nutting, F.O., Nov. 7, 1951; FO371/91612, Minute by Furlonge, Nov. 13, 1951.

19. *New York Times*, Nov. 8, 1951.

20. Acheson, *Creation*, p. 511.

21. FO371/91608, Eden, Paris, to F.O., Nov. 5, 1951; Anthony Eden, *Full Circle: The Memoirs of Anthony Eden* (London, 1960), pp. 200–201.

22. Robert Rhodes James, *Anthony Eden* (London, 1986), p. 346; FO371/91609, Churchill to Eden, Paris, Nov. 8, 1951.

23. FO371/91608, F.O. to Eden, Paris, Nov. 6 and 7, 1951.

24. FO371/91609, Eden to F.O., Nov. 8 and 9, 1951.

25. McGhee, *Envoy*, p. 403. Also "McGhee-Mosadeq Conversations," Nov. 8 and 9, 1951.

26. "McGhee-Mosadeq Conversations," Memorandum of conversation between Mossadeq and Warne, Nov. 9, 1951. William Warne was with the U.S. Department of the Interior for sixteen years dealing with water resources and was Assistant Secretary for Water and Power in that department for four years before being appointed to serve in Iran.

27. FO371/91612, Minute by Dixon, Nov. 14, 1951.

28. See FO371/91611, Franks to F.O., Nov. 14, 1951.

29. "McGhee-Mosadeq Conversations," Nov. 15, 1951.

30. Ibid., Nov. 17, 1951.

31. *Al-Ahram*, Nov. 20–24, 1951.

32. FO371/91474, British Embassy, Cairo, to Eden, Dec. 3, 1951.

33. *Shahed*, Nov. 25, 1951.

13.—Britain Manipulates the World Bank

1. FO371/91610, Franks to F.O., Nov. 10, 1951. See also Elwell-Sutton, *Persian Oil*, p. 274.

2. FO371/91612, Franks to F.O. giving text of the World Bank memorandum, Nov. 17, 1951.

3. FO371/91610, F.O. to Franks, Nov. 16, 1951; FO371/91615, British Embassy, Rome, to F.O., Nov. 16, 1951.

4. FO371/91614, Eden to Franks, Dec. 7, 1951.

5. FO371/91616, Franks to F.O., Dec. 12, 1951; *Shahed*, Dec. 2, 1951.

6. FO371/91616, Minute by Makins, record of conversation with Black, Dec. 13, 1951.

7. FO371/91617, Franks to Eden, Dec. 15, 1951; Eden to Franks, Dec. 17, 1951.

8. Ibid., Franks to Eden, Dec. 17, 1951; Eden to Franks, Dec. 18, 1951.

9. FO371/91616, Middleton to F.O., Dec. 8 and 12, 1951; FO371/91618, Middleton to F.O. on his conversation with Henderson, Dec. 19, 1951; FO371/91617, F.O. to Franks, Dec. 20, 1951.

10. FO371/91619, Franks to Eden, Dec. 29, 1951; FO371/98646, Minute by Makins, Dec. 30, 1951.

11. Ibid. (both citations).

12. Ibid., Letter from World Bank to Persian Prime Minister, dated Dec. 28, 1951, handed to him on Jan. 2, 1952.

13. FO371/98647, Middleton to Sarell, Jan. 7, 1952.

14. FO371/98646, Letter from Persian Prime Minister to Mr. Garner, Jan. 3, 1952.

15. FO371/98647, Minute by Ramsbotham, Jan. 14, 1952.

16. FO371/98646, F.O. to Franks, Jan. 5, 1952.

17. Letter to the London *Times* by L. S. Emery, a Conservative elder statesman, Jan. 1, 1952.

18. "Official Conversations and Meetings of Dean Acheson, 1949–1953," in *The Presidential Document Series* (Microfilm Division, Princeton University Library), Reel 5, June 23, 1983.

19. Ibid. See also Acheson, *Creation*, p. 599.

20. FO371/98647, Minute by Makins, Jan. 7, 1952; Franks to F.O., Jan. 10, 1952.

21. FO371/98608, Record of meeting between Eden and Acheson at the State Department, Jan. 9, 1952.

22. FO371/98646, Eden to F.O., Jan. 10, 1952.

23. FO371/98608, Record of meeting held in Bowker's room, F.O., Feb. 19, 1952.

24. FO371/98684, Eden to Franks, Jan. 26, 1952.

25. FO371/98647, Shepherd to F.O., reporting on Rieber's views given to the U.S. Embassy, Tehran, Jan. 18, 1952; Minute by Makins, Jan. 29, 1952.

26. FO371/98685, Acheson's message to Eden, Feb. 8, 1952; Franks to F.O., Feb. 5, 1952.

27. Ibid., Eden to Franks, Feb. 9, 1952.

28. FO371/98608, Meeting at the State Department regarding the World Bank mission to Persia, Feb. 11, 1952.

29. FO371/98648, Burrows to Ross, Eastern Dept., F.O., Feb. 9, 1952.

30. FO371/91616, Franks to F.O., Dec. 12, 1951; FO371/98674, Minute by Makins, Jan. 29, 1952.

31. FO371/91617, Minute by Makins, record of conversation with Eugene Black, Dec. 13, 1951; Franks to F.O., Dec. 17, 1951.

32. FO371/91616, Eden to Franks, Dec. 14, 1951. FO371/91617, Record of meeting of Secretary of State with Eugene Black, Dec. 14, 1951; Minute by Makins, Record of conversation with Black on his discussions with the chairman of Standard Oil of N.J., Dec. 13, 1951.

33. Interview with Sir Oliver Franks, Oxford, U.K., Jan. 5, 1988.

34. FO371/98648, Middleton to Ross on his conversation with a Majlis deputy, Feb. 11, 1952.

35. FO371/98608, U.K./U.S. Meeting held at F.O., Feb. 14, 1952; Minute by Strang, Feb. 16, 1952; Minute by Ramsbotham, Feb. 14, 1952.

36. FO371/98647, Middleton to F.O., Feb. 13, 1952; F.O. to Franks, Jan. 15, 1952.

37. FO371/98648, Henderson to U.S. Embassy, London, Feb. 17, 1952; Minute by Ramsbotham, Feb. 21, 1952.

38. FO371/98647, Middleton to F.O., Feb. 17, 1952. The price formula put forward by the World Bank was as follows:

Persian Gulf posted price per barrel of crude		$1.75
33⅓ percent rebate to bulk buyer	.58	
21⅛ percent to be kept in trust	.37	
Production and investment costs	.30	1.25
Balance to be paid to Iran		$0.50

39. Ibid., Middleton to F.O., Feb. 13, 1952; FO371/98648, Henderson to State Department, Feb. 17, 1952.

40. FO371/98648, Strang to Eden through U.K. delegation, NATO, Lisbon, Feb. 21, 1952.

41. FO371/98649, Minute by Bowker, conversations with Mr. Garner at Minister of State's dinner, Feb. 28, 1952; F.O. to British Embassy, Tehran, Feb. 29, 1952.

42. Ibid., F.O. to Middleton, Mar. 1, 1952.

43. FO371/98650, Middleton to F.O., from Prudhomme to AIOC, Mar. 11,

1952; F.O. to Middleton, from AIOC, London, to Prudhomme, Tehran, Mar. 12, 1952.

44. Ibid., Middleton to F.O., Mar. 13, 1952.

45. FO371/98686, Middleton to F.O., Mar. 11, 1952.

46. FO371/91616, Conversation between Secretary of State and the Persian ambassador, Dec. 11, 1951.

47. Rouhani, *Tarikhé Melli Shodané*, p. 256.

48. I tried to arrange an interview in April 1988 with Eugene Black, who was then living in Florida. I sent him the contents of declassified documents showing that the World Bank was not evenhanded in the Iranian oil dispute. Black declined to give an interview, saying that he did not remember the 1951–52 negotiations with Iran. He sent my inquiries to a former colleague of his, whose explanations I found unconvincing.

14.—Judgment at the World Court

1. Hassan Sadr, *Defa'é Dr. Mossadeq az Naft dar Zendané Zerehi* (Tehran, 1357/1978), pp. 29–32.

2. International Court of Justice, The Hague, *IJC Pleadings, Anglo-Iranian Oil Company Case (United Kingdom v Iran)*, 1952, p. 427.

3. FO371/91562, Shepherd to F.O., July 12, 1951.

4. FO371/91537, Memorandum by Soskice, May 25, 1951.

5. FO371/98679, Minutes by Rothnie, Apr. 9 and May 17, 1952.

6. Elwell-Sutton, *Persian Oil*, p. 265.

7. FO371/98680, Butler to Eden, June 25, 1952.

8. The World Court judges were from Great Britain, El Salvador, the United States, Poland, Norway, Chile, Egypt, Canada, the Republic of China, Brazil, Yugoslavia, Uruguay, and France, plus an ad hoc judge from Iran. The judge from the Soviet Union was absent owing to illness. Sir Benegal Rau of India could not attend because he had earlier participated in the U.N. Security Council debate on the same dispute.

9. *IJC Pleadings, 1952*, pp. 437–42.

10. FO371/98680, Butler to Eden, June 25, 1952.

11. *IJC Pleadings, 1952*, pp. 445–99.

12. FO371/98679, Minute by Beckett, May 19, 1952.

13. *IJC Pleadings, 1952*, pp. 509–81.

14. FO371/98680, Beckett to Strang, June 24, 1952.

15. FO371/91537, Memorandum by Soskice, May 25, 1951.

16. FO371/98680, Butler to Eden, June 25, 1952.

17. International Court of Justice, The Hague, *IJC Reports of Judgments, Advisory Opinions and Orders, 1952*, pp. 94–114.

18. FO371/98680, Minute by Beckett, July 23, 1952.

15.—British Attempts to Overthrow Mossadeq

1. FO371/91524, Shepherd to F.O., Mar. 18, 1951.

2. FO371/91459, Shepherd to Furlonge, May 6, 1951; Shepherd to Morrison, May 21, 1951.

3. FO371/91529, Furlonge to Morrison, Apr. 29, 1951.

4. FO371/91459, Shepherd to Morrison, May 21, 1951.

5. FO371/91548, Minute by Berthoud, June 15, 1951; FO371/91550, Minute by Berthoud, June 21, 1951.

6. FO371/91539, Minute by Furlonge, May 30, 1951.

7. FO371/91464, Shepherd, "A Comparison Between Persian and Asiatic Nationalism in General," Oct. 2, 1951.

8. FO371/91454, Shepherd to Morrison, Mar. 15, 1951.

9. Ibid., Shepherd to Morrison, July 2, 1951.

10. Acheson, *Creation*, p. 509.

11. As related to me by Sir George Middleton in the course of an interview, London, Jan. 29, 1986.

12. Louis, *The British Empire*, pp. 658–59.

13. FO371/91542, Shepherd to Bowker, May 28, 1951; FO371/91547, Shepherd to F.O., June 18, 1951; Shepherd to Morrison, June 18, 1951.

14. FO371/91459, Shepherd to Furlonge, F.O., May 6, 1951.

15. George McGhee, "Recollections of Dr. Mohammad Musaddiq," in James A. Bill and Wm. Roger Louis, eds., *Musaddiq, Iranian Nationalism, and Oil* (London, 1988), pp. 297–98.

16. As related by one of his colleagues at the British embassy in Tehran. See also Louis, "Musaddiq and the Dilemmas of British Imperialism," in Bill and Louis, eds., *Musaddiq, Nationalism*, p. 236.

17. C. M. Woodhouse, *Something Ventured* (London, 1982), p. 111; FO371/91584, Shepherd to F.O., Aug. 25, 1951.

18. FO371/91556, Minute by Strang, June 23, 1951.

19. FO371/91583, Shepherd to F.O., Aug. 30, 1951.

20. FO371/91551, Shepherd to F.O., June 26, 1951; F.O. to Shepherd, June 28, 1951.

21. FO371/91462, Minute by Pyman, Sept. 8, 1951; Minute by Jackson, Dec. 13, 1951.

22. FO248/1524, Minute by Shepherd, Sept. 22, 1951; FO248/1531, Minute by Pyman, Jan. 17, 1952.

23. FO248/1531, Minute by Zaehner, June 1952.

24. FO371/91565, Minute by George Rogers on his meeting with Shafia, June 21, 1951; FO371/91570, Minute by Barclay, F.O., on his conversation with Clement Davis about his discussions with Horace Emery, July 4, 1951.

25. FO371/91551, Minute by Logan on his conversation with Haig Galustian, June 23, 1951. Interview with Sir George Middleton, London, Jan. 29, 1986.

26. FO371/91541, Burrows, British Embassy, Washington, on his conversation with Dr. Berger Voesendorf, to Eastern Dept., F.O., May 28, 1951.

27. FO371/91589, F.O. to Shepherd, Sept. 22, 1951; FO371/91593, Shepherd to F.O., Sept. 29, 1951.

28. FO371/91589, Middleton to Sarner, Sept. 18, 1951.

29. FO371/91584, Lord Privy Seal Note on Tehran talks, Aug. 22, 1951; FO371/91590, Lord Privy Seal Notes on Iranian oil situation, Sept. 22, 1951; FO371/91591, Stokes to Younger, Sept. 24, 1951.

30. FO371/91572, Gordon Waterfield, BBC, to Furlonge, enclosing Elwell-Sutton's statement of July 12, 1951, on Persian oil dispute, July 13, 1951.

31. FO371/91527, Leggett to Strang, Apr. 14, 1951; FO371/91610, Sir Ralph Glyn, M.P., to Eden enclosing a letter from Leggett, Oct. 24, 1951; FO371/91522, Minute by L. A. C. Fry, Feb. 6, 1951.

32. CAB128/20, Cabinet Conclusions 51(51), July 12, 1951.

33. *Wall Street Journal*, June 9, 1951.

34. FO953/PG14537, P. H. Gore-Booth, British Embassy, Washington, to F.O., June 15 and 20, 1951.
35. FO371/91473, Shepherd to Strang, Sept. 11, 1951; FO371/91606, Shepherd to Morrison, Oct. 23, 1951.
36. FO371/91535, Shepherd to Furlonge, May 14, 1951; FO371/91544, Shepherd to Furlonge, June 7, 1951.
37. FO371/91537, Franks to F.O. on his conversation with McGhee, May 25 and 26, 1951.
38. *FR-US*, 1951, Vol. I, Memorandum by Special Assistant to Secretary of State Acheson, July 31, 1951.
39. FO371/91589, Franks to F.O., Sept. 21, 1951; FO371/91592, Franks to F.O., Sept. 29, 1951.
40. FO371/91591, Franks to F.O., Sept. 26, 1951.
41. Ibid., Shepherd to F.O., Sept. 21, 1951; FO371/91582, Minute by Bowker, Aug. 25, 1951; FO371/91606, Shepherd to F.O., Oct. 23, 1951.
42. FO371/91550, Minute by Berthoud, June 21, 1951.
43. Ibid. In 1907 Britain and Russia signed an agreement dividing Iran into two zones of influence.
44. FO371/91584, Shepherd to F.O., Aug. 25, 1951.
45. FO371/91560, Shepherd to Furlonge, July 2, 1951.
46. Ibid., Furlonge to Shepherd, July 21, 1951.
47. FO371/91571, Middleton to F.O., Aug. 1, 1951.
48. FO371/91550, Minute by Bowker, June 20, 1951.
49. FO371/91586, Shepherd to F.O., Sept. 6 and 10, 1951.
50. *Tolu*, Aug. 29, Sept. 6, and Sept. 18, 1951; *Dad*, Sept. 13, 1951.
51. *Shahed*, Sept. 6 and 18, 1951; *Keyhan*, Aug. 30, Sept. 6, and Sept. 18, 1951.
52. FO371/91615, Franks to F.O. giving a survey of U.S. press, Nov. 20, 1951.
53. *U.S. News and World Report*, "An Interview with the Prime Minister of Iran," July 25, 1951.
54. FO371/91589, Shepherd to Younger, Sept. 15, 1951.
55. *New York Times*, Sept. 23, 1951.
56. FO371/91607, Minutes of meeting in Sir Edward Bridges's room, Oct. 23, 1951.
57. FO371/91555, Notes of a meeting at the House of Commons on Persia attended by Attlee, Morrison, Churchill, and Eden, June 27, 1951.
58. FO371/91610, Sir Ralph Glyn, M.P., to Eden, sending Leggett's letter of Oct. 17, 1951, Oct. 24, 1951; Anthony Nutting to Glyn, Nov. 5, 1951.
59. FO371/91608, Minutes of a meeting chaired by Eden at the Foreign Office, Nov. 1, 1951; Logan to R. J. W. Stacy, Board of Trade, sending a report of the Official Working Party on Persian Oil containing Shepherd's views, Nov. 1, 1951.
60. FO371/91609, Minute by Berthoud on his conversation with Lambton, Nov. 2, 1951. Britain's Special Operations Executive (SOE) was the equivalent of the American Office of Strategic Services (OSS).
61. FO371/91540, Shepherd to F.O., June 4, 1951; FO371/91530, Shepherd to F.O., May 3, 1951; FO371/91525, Minute by Pyman, Mar. 14, 1951; FO248/1514, Minutes by Pyman, Aug. 28 and 30, 1951.

62. FO371/91554, British Embassy, Rome, to Eastern Department, F.O., June 29, 1951; FO371/91555, British Embassy, Rome, to Bowker, F.O., June 29, 1951.

63. FO371/91536, Minute by Furlonge, May 11, 1951.

64. F. Bostock and G. Jones, *Planning and Power in Iran: Ebtehaj and Economic Development under the Shah* (London, 1989), pp. 107–8.

65. FO371/91536, Oliver Harvey, Paris, to Furlonge, May 18, 1951; FO371/91555, British Embassy, Paris, to Bowker, June 28, 1951.

66. Elwell-Sutton, *Persian Oil*, p. 200.

67. FO371/98608, Minute by Sarell, Jan. 22, 1951.

68. Ibid., UK-US meeting at F.O., Feb. 14, 1952. British participants: Ross, Sarell, Ramsbotham, Rothnie, and Cornwallis. American participants: Nitze and Linder of the State Department and Palmer of the U.S. embassy, London.

69. Ibid., F.O. to Middleton, Feb. 15, 1952.

70. Ibid., Middleton to F.O., Feb. 17, 1952.

71. Ibid., Logan, Washington, to F.O., Feb. 11, 1952.

72. Ibid., Minute by Strang on Nitze's meeting with British ministers, Feb. 16, 1952; F.O. to Franks, Feb. 19, 1952.

16.—Qavam's Prime Ministership and the Communist Threat

1. FO371/91565, Minute by George Rogers on his discussions with Shafia, June 21, 1951.

2. FO371/91559, Morrison to Churchill, July 3, 1951; Minute by Bowker on his meeting with Conservative MPs Fitzroy Maclean, Christopher Soames, and Julian Amery, July 5, 1951.

3. FO371/91610, Amery to Bowker enclosing letter of Oct. 28, 1951, from Shafia to Colonel Mavrodi, Nov. 6, 1951.

4. FO248/1514, Minute by Zaehner, Nov. 10, 1951.

5. FO371/91612, Middleton to F.O., Secret, Nov. 18, 1951.

6. *Khabar*, Nov. 11, 1951.

7. FO371/91612, Minute by Logan, Nov. 19, 1951; FO371/91613, Minute by Matthews, Nov. 13, 1951.

8. FO371/98683, Middleton to Sarell, Jan. 7, 1952.

9. Ibid., Anthony Nutting (in the absence of Eden) to J. Amery, Feb. 19, 1952.

10. Ibid., Kenneth de Courcy to Anthony Nutting, Feb. 13, 1952.

11. Ibid.

12. Ibid., Amery to Selwyn Lloyd, Mar. 25, 1952; Interview with Prince Hamid Qajar, London, Mar. 25, 1985.

13. Ibid.

14. Ibid., Minute by Ross, Apr. 5, 1952.

15. Ibid., Note by Eden, Apr. 11, 1952.

16. Ibid., Bowker to Middleton, Apr. 16, 1952.

17. FO371/98688, Franks to F.O., Apr. 10 and 16, 1952.

18. FO248/1531, Minutes by Falle, Apr. 28 and June 30, 1952.

19. Ibid., Minute by Middleton, June 11, 1952.

20. Ibid., Minute by Zaehner, June 23, 1952.

21. FO371/98686, Middleton to F.O., Mar. 11, 1952.

22. FO371/98615, John Walker, British Embassy, Tehran, to F.O. on talks with the Shah, May 19, 1952.

23. Interview with Henry Byroade, Washington, Sept. 30, 1985.

24. FO371/98689, Middleton to F.O., May 14, 1952.

25. FO371/98690, Brief for Eden by Ross, June 23, 1952.

26. *Shahed*, Oct. 29 and Nov. 5, 1951.

27. FO371/98731, W. E. Thomas, British Embassy, Tehran, to Sir G. Myrddin-Evans, Ministry of Labour, Dec. 17, 1951, and Feb. 4, 1952; F. C. Mason to Myrddin-Evans, Jan. 16, 1952; Minute by Mason, Jan. 9, 1952.

28. RG 59, Box 5509, "McGhee-Mosadeq Conversations," Nov. 5, 1951.

29. FO371/98615, Minute by Ross, Mar. 24, 1952.

30. FO248/1531, Minute by Falle, July 13, 1952.

31. FO371/1531, Minute by Logan, May 14, 1952.

32. FO371/98601, Middleton to Ross, July 21, 1952. Hassan Arsanjani, "Yaddashthayé Siasié-man," *Bamshad*, June 11–Nov. 26, 1956, pp. 45–46.

33. FO371/98691, Minute by Fergusson, July 18, 1951, with notes by Eden on the margin.

34. Ibid., Minute by Makins, July 1952; FO371/98683, Fergusson to Makins, July 19, 1952, with notes by Eden on the margin.

35. Ibid. (both citations).

36. G. R. Nejati, *Jonbeshé Melli Shodané San'até Nafté Iran* (Tehran, 1364/1985), Qavam's statement of July 18, 1952, pp. 218–19.

37. *Keyhan*, Kashani's statement, July 18, 1952.

38. Nejati, *Jonbeshé*, pp. 221–22; *Keyhan*, July 21 and 22, 1952. Reports on the number of dead and wounded ranged from 60 to 800.

39. FO371/98691, Middleton to F.O., July 27, 1952.

40. Ibid., Minute by Ross, July 27, 1952; Middleton to F.O., July 27, 28, and 29, 1952.

41. FO371/98692, Henderson to State Dept., Aug. 2, 1952.

42. FO371/98607, Secret report by Bolland, Aug. 4, 1952.

43. *Shahed*, Oct. 29 and Nov. 5, 1951.

44. *Ettela'at*, quoting Tabari, Feb. 19, 1985.

45. FO371/98683, de Courcy to Nutting, Feb. 13, 1952.

46. FO371/91550, Minute by Berthoud, June 21, 1951.

47. FO371/98691, Franks to F.O., July 29, 1952.

48. Interview with General M. Jam, who was a member of the committees in charge of purging the Iranian army, London, Feb. 18, 1988. Nejati, *Jonbeshé*, pp. 224–25.

49. Abrahamian, *Iran*, pp. 272–73.

50. Mossadeq, *Khaterat*, p. 211.

17.—Churchill's Games with Truman

1. The amount claimed by Iran was £49,987,440, which consisted mainly of unpaid balances of Iran's 20 percent share in AIOC's general reserves and adjustments on royalties under the 1949 Supplemental Agreement. The sum in fact was approximately equal to the amount set aside for Iran in reserves carried in the AIOC statement of Dec. 31, 1951.

2. FO371/98691, Middleton to F.O., July 27 and 28, 1952.

3. Ibid., Franks to Eden, July 31, 1952.

4. Ibid., Eden's message to Acheson, Aug. 9, 1952.

5. FO371/98693, Franks to Eden, Secret, Aug. 12, 1952; RG 59, Box 5509, "An Account of the Iranian Oil Controversy" (hereafter cited as "Oil Controversy"), Vol. II, p. 14.

6. Interview with Sir Oliver Franks, Jan. 4, 1988.

7. "Oil Controversy," Vol. II, Middleton's discussions with Mossadeq on Aug. 14, 1952.

8. Ibid., Appendix B-6, Personal and Secret Message from Churchill to Truman, Aug. 16, 1952.

9. Ibid., Appendix B-7, Personal and Secret Message from Truman to Churchill, Aug. 18, 1952.

10. Ibid., Appendix B-8, Personal and Secret Message from Churchill to Truman, Aug. 20, 1952.

11. Ibid., Appendix B-9, Churchill's draft of a joint message to Mossadeq, Aug. 20, 1952.

12. Ibid., p. 17.

13. Ibid., Appendix B-10, Truman to Churchill, Aug. 21, 1952.

14. Ibid., Appendix B-11, Churchill to Truman, Aug. 22, 1952.

15. Ibid., Appendix B-12, Joint Truman-Churchill Proposals handed to Mossadeq on Aug. 27, 1952.

16. Ibid., p. 20.

17. Ibid., Appendix B-17, Truman to Churchill, Aug. 28, 1952.

18. *The Times* (London), Sept. 6, 1952, Letter to the Editor from R. R. Stokes, House of Commons, dated Sept. 5, 1952.

19. Majlis Proceedings, Sept. 16, 1952.

20. "Oil Controversy," Vol. II, Appendix B-20, Mossadeq to Churchill and Truman, Sept. 24, 1952.

21. Ibid., Appendix B-21, Churchill to Truman, Sept. 29, 1952.

22. Ibid., Appendix B-23, Acheson to Mossadeq, Oct. 5, 1952; Appendix B-24, Eden to Mossadeq, Oct. 5, 1952; Appendix B-25, Mossadeq to Acheson, Oct. 7, 1952; Appendix B-26, Mossadeq to Eden, Oct. 7, 1952.

23. Ibid., Appendix B-27, British government's note to the Iranian government, Oct. 14, 1952.

24. CAB129/55, C(52) 341, Cabinet Paper dated Oct. 17, 1952, being Middleton's report to F.O., Oct. 13, 1952.

25. FO371/98621, Middleton to F.O., Oct. 18, 21, and 22, 1952.

26. "Oil Controversy," Vol. II, Appendix B-28, Note from Iran's Foreign Minister to British Chargé d'Affaires, Oct. 22, 1952.

27. Eden, *Full Circle*, p. 208.

28. *Frankfurter Neue Press*, Oct. 17, 1952.

29. Acheson, *Creation*, pp. 681–82.

30. Ibid.

31. "Oil Controversy," Vol. II, Memorandum of Conversations, Oct. 8, 1952, pp. 30–31; Painter, *Private Power*, pp. 185–87.

32. U.S. Congress, *Cartel*, 1974, pp. III–IV.

33. NSC 136, Statement of Policy, Nov. 6, 1952.

34. NSC 136/1, Statement of Policy, Nov. 7, 1952.

35. "Oil Controversy," Vol. II, p. 34.

36. Ibid., Appendix B-31, British paper handed to U.S. Embassy in London, Nov. 18, 1952.

37. FO371/98603, Burrows to Bowker on discussions with Bohlen, July 30, 1952; FO371/98703, Sir Gladwyn Jebb, New York, to F.O. reporting Eden's discussions with Acheson, Nov. 21, 1952.

38. Ibid., Greenhill, F.O., to Flett, Treasury, enclosing a paper on the conclusions of Persia (official) Committee, Nov. 28, 1952.

39. Dwight D. Eisenhower, *The White House Years: Mandate for Change, 1953–1956* (New York, 1963), p. 57.

40. *FR-US*, 1952–54, Vol. I, Memorandum by the Secretary of State of a meeting between President Truman and General Eisenhower on Nov. 18, 1952, pp. 22–27.

41. "Oil Controversy," Vol. II, Appendix E-4, U.S. Government Statement of Dec. 6, 1952.

42. Acheson, *Creation*, p. 684. Interview with Henry Byroade, Washington, Sept. 30, 1985. Interview with Paul Nitze, Washington, May 8, 1984. Byroade and Nitze accompanied Acheson at these meetings, along with David Bruce, Under Secretary of State.

43. FO371/98704, F.O. to British Embassy, Paris, for Eden, Dec. 12, 1952.

44. Ibid., British Embassy, Paris, to F.O., Dec. 15, 1952.

45. Ibid., Steel to F.O., Dec. 18, 1952; Eden, Paris, to Steel, Dec. 19, 1952; FO371/98652, Franks to F.O., Nov. 10, 1952.

46. FO371/98704, Steel to F.O., three communications, Dec. 16, 1952.

47. Ibid., Steel to F.O., Dec. 23, 1952.

48. CAB129/58, C(53)1, Note by Eden on a report received from U.S. Embassy, London, on Henderson's discussions with Mossadeq, Jan. 1, 1953.

49. FO371/104606, U.S. Embassy, London, to F.O., on Henderson's discussions with Mossadeq, Dec. 31, 1952, and Jan. 2, 1953.

50. Ibid., Memorandum from Byroade to Dixon along with two draft agreements, Jan. 3, 1953.

51. Ibid., Minute by Ross, Jan. 3, 1953; CAB129/58, C(53)6, Memorandum by Eden on "Musaddiq's Position," Jan. 6, 1953.

52. FO371/104606, Henderson's memorandum, Jan. 4, 1953; Henderson's message to Byroade, Jan. 6, 1953.

53. FO371/104607, Fitzmaurice's note on "Proposed Terms of Reference of Arbitral Tribunal" with comments by Ross, Jan. 1, 1953.

54. Ibid., Henderson to State Dept. and U.S. Embassy, London, Jan. 9 and 11, 1953.

55. FO371/104608, Acheson to Byroade, London, Jan. 13, 1953; FO371/104609, Minute by Fitzmaurice, Jan. 13, 1953.

56. FO371/104608, Henderson to State Dept. and U.S. Embassy, London, Jan. 13, 1953.

57. FO371/104612, Letter to Musaddiq signed by Eden and dated Jan. 16, 1953, which was never sent.

58. FO371/104610, F.O. to British representatives in Bagdad, Cairo, Bahrain, Jedda, Amman, Damascus, Beirut, Jakarta, Rangoon, and Caracas, Jan. 17, 1953.

59. FO371/104608, Eden to Churchill, Jan. 14, 1953.

60. FO371/104609, Letter from Eden to Walter Gifford enclosing two draft agreements, Jan. 14, 1953.

61. Ibid., U.S. Embassy, London, to F.O. giving the details of Henderson's discussions with Mossadeq, Jan. 15, 17, and 18, 1953.

62. Ibid., U.S. Embassy, London, to F.O., Jan. 19, 1953; FO371/104610, Minute by Ross, Jan. 16, 1953.

18.—Iran's Oil-less Economy

1. G. W. Stocking, *The Middle East Oil: A Study in Politics and Economic Controversy* (Nashville, Tenn., 1970), p. 154.

2. FO371/904617, "The Rose Mary Case," Dec. 31, 1952.

3. FO371/104618, Minute by Ross for Minister of State, Feb. 3, 1953.

4. FO371/104617, Treasury to F.O., Jan. 28, 1953.

5. FO371/104620, Dixon's brief for Eden, Mar. 30, 1953.

6. FO371/104625, Record of conversation at F.O. between Dixon, Bowker, and Signor del Balzo of the Italian Foreign Ministry, June 24, 1953.

7. Ibid., Note by Churchill for Eden, Mar. 27, 1953.

8. FO371/104638, Minute by Fitzmaurice, June 9, 1953.

9. FO371/104620, British Embassy, Tokyo, to F.O., Apr. 13, 1953.

10. RG59, Box 5509, American Embassy, Tehran, to State Dept., June 27, 1953.

11. Ibid., Henderson to State Dept., Mar. 14, 1953.

12. FO371/104612, Makins to F.O., Feb. 10, 1953; State Dept. to U.S. Embassy, London, Feb. 11, 1953; F.O. to British Embassy, Washington, Feb. 18, 1953.

13. FO371/105165, Dixon to Makins, Apr. 2, 1953.

14. Ibid., Minute by Ramsbotham, "Think Piece" on future policy regarding the Persian oil problem, Apr. 14, 1953.

15. FO371/105166, Memorandum by Ramsbotham on "Oil Policy," June 24, 1953; Shell Memorandum on "Current Middle East Political Situation," June 26, 1953.

16. *Ettela'at*, articles by Hassibi, Feb. 12 and Apr. 30, 1953. RG59, Box 5509, Secret Security Information, Memorandum on "Scope of Sale of Persian Oil," May 12, 1953.

17. FO371/98627, Bank Melli Iran to Bank of England, Nov. 15, 1951; Eden to Chancellor of the Exchequer, Jan. 22, 1952; FO371/98627, J. Walker, British Commercial Counselor, Tehran, to M. Heddy-Miller, Treasury, Feb. 11, 1952; FO371/98634, British Embassy, Tehran, to Rothnie, July 14, 1952.

18. *Ettela'at*, June 30, 1952.

19. Majlis Proceedings, Dec. 14, 1952.

20. "Oil Controversy," Vol. II, p. 44.

21. International Monetary Fund, *International Financial Statistics*, Vol. VIII, No. 1 (Jan. 1955), p. 155.

22. Ibid., Vol. VII, No. 7 (July 1954), pp. 110–11.

23. For further details on Iran's economy under Mossadeq, see Julian Bharier, *Economic Development in Iran, 1900–1970* (London, 1971), chap. 3; Homa Katouzian, "Oil Boycott and the Political Economy: Musaddiq and the Strategy of Non-oil Economics," in Bill and Louis, eds., *Mussadiq, Nationalism*, pp. 203–27; Rouhani, *Tarikhé Melli Shodané*, chap. 27; and Fateh, *Panjah Sal*, pp. 643–46.

24. Habib Ladjevardi, "Constitutional Government and Reform under Musaddiq," in Bill and Louis, eds., *Musaddiq, Nationalism*, pp. 69–90.

19.—Eden's Games with Eisenhower

1. Robert H. Ferrell, ed., *The Eisenhower Diaries* (London, 1981), pp. 221–24; Stephen E. Ambrose, *Eisenhower*, Vol. II (New York, 1984), pp. 19–21.
2. FO371/104607, Eden to Makins, Jan. 20, 1953; FO371/104610, Eden to Makins, Jan. 23, 1953.
3. FO371/104611, Minute by Ramsbotham, Jan. 31, 1953; Minute by A. D. M. Ross, Jan. 26, 1953.
4. Ibid., Minute by Ross, Jan. 28, 1953.
5. Ibid., Memorandum by Fitzmaurice, Jan. 27, 1953.
6. Ibid., Henderson to State Dept., Jan. 28 and Feb. 3, 1953.
7. *Ettela'at*, interview with Hassibi, Feb. 5 and 25, 1953.
8. Francis Williams, *A Prime Minister Remembers: The War and Post-War Memoirs of the Rt. Hon. Earl Attlee* (London, 1961), letter dated 14 Sept. 1951 from Lord Stokes to Prime Minister Clement Attlee, pp. 249–51.
9. FO371/104612, Minute by Ramsbotham on his telephone conversation with Gutt, Feb. 13, 1953.
10. FO371/104612, State Dept. to U.S. Embassy, London, Feb. 11, 1953; Henderson to U.S. Embassy, London, Feb. 15, 1953.
11. Ibid., Eden to Makins, Feb. 18, 1953.
12. FO371/104613, Draft Compensation Agreement and Heads of Government Agreement, Feb. 20, 1953.
13. FO371/104612, Makins to F.O., Feb. 18, 1953; F.O. to Makins, Feb. 19, 1953.
14. FO371/104613, Henderson to State Dept., Feb. 20, 1953.
15. Ibid., Minute by Ross containing notes by Dixon, Feb. 21, 1953.
16. Ibid., Makins to F.O. on Henderson's discussions with Mossadeq, Feb. 23 and 24, 1953; FO371/104614, Makins to F.O., Mar. 4, 1953.
17. FO371/104608, Minute by John Colville, Jan. 6, 1953; FO371/104610, Makins to F.O., Jan. 26, 1953.
18. FO371/104614, Ministerial visit to the U.S.: Record of meeting with President Eisenhower, Mar. 6, 1953.
19. Ibid. Also Eden, *Full Circle*, pp. 212–13.
20. Eden, *Full Circle*, pp. 212–13. Also James, *Eden*, p. 360.
21. FO371/104614, State Department Statement of Mar. 6, 1953; Communiqué on United States–United Kingdom Political Talks, Mar. 7, 1953.
22. *Dad*, Apr. 5, 1953; *Jebhé-Azadi*, May 5, 1953.
23. FO371/104614, Henderson's discussions with Mossadeq, Mar. 9, 1953.
24. Ibid., Henderson's discussions with Mossadeq, Mar. 18, 1953. Interview with Loy Henderson, Washington, Apr. 26, 1984.
25. Ibid., Ross's brief on "Line Chosen for News Department" on Mossadeq's forthcoming speech, Mar. 19, 1953.
26. Mossadeq's broadcast on Tehran Radio, Mar. 20, 1953.
27. FO371/104615, Henderson's meeting with Mossadeq, Apr. 4, 1953.
28. Ibid., Minute by Dixon, Apr. 9, 1953.
29. FO371/104636, Gass to Bowker sending the draft of the AIOC annual statement with notes by Rothnie and Ramsbotham, Apr. 9, 1953.

30. Ibid., J. H. Clos to Walter Bedell Smith, May 5, 1953.
31. Ibid., Memorandum of conversation between F. McCollum and J. J. Cosgrove of Continental Oil and Byroade, Nitze, and Akins of State Dept., May 11, 1953.
32. FO371/104615, Makins to F.O., Apr. 23, 1953; Jebb to F.O., Apr. 22, 1953; F.O. to Makins, Apr. 29, 1953.
33. Ibid., Personal message from Butler to Humphrey, May 5, 1953.
34. FO371/104616, Minute by Dixon, May 15, 1953; FO371/105166, Minute by Ramsbotham, May 20, 1953.
35. FO371/104613, British Embassy, Paris, to F.O. on discussions with Pierre Charpentier, Under Secretary for Economic Affairs at Quai d'Orsay, Feb. 14, 1953.
36. RG59, Box 5509, Petroleum Administration for Defense (PAD) to Linder, Feb. 4, 1953.
37. Ibid., U.S. Embassy, Tehran, to State Dept., June 5, 1953.
38. Ibid., Richards, Office of Greek, Turkish, and Iranian Affairs, GTI, to Byroade quoting Henderson, June 9, 1953.
39. FO371/104635, British Embassy, Bern, to F.O., Mar. 7, 1953; Minute by Dixon, Mar. 10, 1953.
40. RG59, Box 5509, American Embassy, Bonn, to Secretary of State, Mar. 26, 1953; State Dept. to American Embassy, Bonn, Mar. 27, 1953.
41. RG59, Box 5510, R. L. Taylor to the President, July 31, 1953; Gordon Mattison, U.S. Embassy, Tehran, to State Dept., June 26, 1953.
42. RG59, Box 5509, Lyndon Johnson to State Dept., June 29, 1953.
43. RG59, Box 5511A, Levy to John F. Fergusson of Policy Planning Staff, State Dept., May 25, 1953.
44. RG59, Box 5510, Memorandum of conversation between Levy and Jernegan, July 21, 1953.
45. RG59, Box 5509, Mossadeq to Eisenhower, May 28, 1953.
46. Ibid., Memorandum of conversation at Matthew's office, State Dept., June 19, 1953.
47. Ibid., Eisenhower to Mossadeq, June 29, 1953.
48. Interviews with Dr. Ali Amini, Paris, May 22, 1983; Shapur Bakhtiar, Paris, May 25, 1983; Loy Henderson, Washington, Apr. 26, 1984; M. H. Qashqa'i, London, Apr. 15, 1985; George McGhee, London, Sept. 18, 1985.

20.—The Coup

1. The three Rashidian brothers were named Seyfollah, Assadollah, and Qodratollah.
2. Woodhouse, *Something Ventured*, pp. 116–18.
3. Ibid.
4. Donald N. Wilber, *Adventures in the Middle East: Excursions and Incursions* (Princeton, N.J., 1986), pp. 111, 157.
5. Brian Lapping, *End of Empire* (London, 1985), p. 218.
6. Robert Scheer, "How CIA Orchestrated '53 Coup in Iran." *Los Angeles Times*, Mar. 29, 1979.
7. Woodhouse, *Something Ventured*, pp. 121–23; Lapping, *End of Empire*, p. 215.

8. Interview with M. H. Qashqa'i, London, Apr. 16, 1985. Qashqa'i, then a Majlis deputy, spoke to Mossadeq about Kashani's demand for funds.

9. Interview with Colonel M. Matin, London, Jan. 4, 1984. In 1953 Matin was adjutant to the commander of Isfahan garrison.

10. Bozorgmehr, *Taqriraté Mossadeq*, pp. 128–31.

11. FO371/10562, F.O. to Secretary of State, Mar. 3, 1953.

12. FO371/98603, Middleton to F.O., Aug. 28, 1952; FO371/98606, British Embassy, Washington to F.O., Dec. 24, 1952.

13. RG59, Box 5509, Secret Security Information, Memorandum for the President on "The Iranian Situation," Mar. 1, 1953.

14. Kermit Roosevelt, *Countercoup: The Struggle for the Control of Iran* (New York, 1979), p. 121.

15. Mark Gasiorowski, "The 1953 Coup D'Etat in Iran," *International Journal of Middle East Studies*, XIX (Aug. 1987), pp. 261–86.

16. FO371/104614, Eden, Washington, to F.O., Mar. 9, 1953.

17. FO371/98606, Note of an informal meeting between Middleton and the representatives of four Commonwealth governments, Nov. 25, 1952.

18. FO371/104561, Note by Rothnie for Director of Military Intelligence, Jan. 1953.

19. FO371/104615, Brief for the Minister of State, Apr. 20, 1953.

20. James, *Eden*, pp. 262–63.

21. Gasiorowski, who has interviewed several former CIA officers then active in Iran, says that the CIA bribed Baqa'i and M. T. Falsafi. See his article "The 1953 Coup," p. 269 and footnotes 42 and 45.

22. Roosevelt, *Countercoup*, p. 155; interview with Donald Wilber, Princeton, Oct. 15, 1985; Wilber, *Adventures*, pp. 187–89. Wilber considers himself the principal planner of operation Ajax. On p. 8 of his book he reproduces a letter of Jan. 30, 1954, from Allen Dulles commending him for his "outstanding contribution" to the operation.

23. FO248/1531, Minute by Zaehner, June 4, 1952; FO371/98605, Middleton to F.O., Oct. 22, 1952.

24. FO371/104659, Makins to F.O. relating Henderson's message to the State Dept., May 21, 1953.

25. Ibid., F.O. to Makins sending Churchill's message to the Shah for transmission through the State Dept., May 28, 1953; Makins to F.O. on Henderson's audience with the Shah, June 2, 1953.

26. Ibid. The Amini brothers were the sons of Princess Fakhr od-Dowleh, the daughter of Mozaffar ed-Din Shah. Brigadier General Mahmud Amini, a Saint-Cyr-educated officer, headed the Gendarmerie. Ali Amini had previously held ministerial posts. Abol-Qassem Amini was at the time Acting Court Minister.

27. *Bakhtaré-Emruz*, July 1978 issue, quoting from a written statement made by Abol-Qassem Amini on June 15, 1961.

28. *Keyhan*, Apr. 26, 1953.

29. Separate interviews in Washington with Kermit Roosevelt and Loy Henderson on Apr. 26, 1984, and with Henry Byroade on Sept. 30, 1985.

30. RG218, CCS092 Iran (4-23-48) Sec. 8 S.O., Memorandum by Lieut. General F. F. Everest, USAF, Director, Joint Staff, to Secretary of Defense, June 19, 1953.

31. Wilber, *Adventures*, pp. 188–89.

32. Roosevelt, *Countercoup*, p. 145.

33. Gasiorowski, "The 1953 Coup," p. 273.

34. A. Pahlavi, *Faces in a Mirror*, pp. 134–40.

35. Roosevelt, *Countercoup*, pp. 147–49.

36. *Public Papers of the Presidents of the United States: Dwight D. Eisenhower, 1953* (Washington, 1954), p. 541.

37. Lapping, *End of Empire*, pp. 219–20; Roosevelt, *Countercoup*, pp. 163–66.

38. Nejati, *Jonbeshé*, pp. 363–85. Nejati, who interviewed most of the officers involved in the abortive coup of August 15, gives a detailed account of events.

39. *The Times* (London), Aug. 17, 1953; Gasiorowski, "The 1953 Coup," p. 273.

40. *Bakhtaré-Emruz*, Aug. 16, 1953.

41. FO371/104659, British Embassy, Bagdad, to F.O., Aug. 17, 1953.

42. Ibid., Aug. 19, 1953.

43. Ibid., Bowker's internal note, Aug. 19, 1953.

44. *Daily Telegraph* (London), Aug. 19, 1953.

45. FO371/104659, Makins to F.O., Aug. 18, 1953.

46. Interview with M. H. Qashqa'i, London, Apr. 16, 1985; in 1953 Qashqa'i was a Majlis deputy. Drew Pearson, "CIA Chief Next to Kennedy in Power," *Washington Post*, Jan. 29, 1962.

47. Gasiorowski, "The 1953 Coup," p. 274.

48. Roosevelt, *Countercoup*, p. 180.

49. Lapping, *End of Empire*, p. 220.

50. *Bessuyé-Ayandeh*, Aug. 9, 1953; F. M. Javanshir, *Tajrobeyé 28 Mordad* (Tehran, 1359/1980), p. 312; Lapping, *End of Empire*, p. 215.

51. Interview with Colonel M. Matin, London, Jan. 4, 1984. Matin attended the meeting between General Davallu and General McClure. Nejati, *Jonbeshé*, relating his interview with Riahi, p. 404.

52. Nejati, *Jonbeshé*, p. 413.

53. RG218, CCS092 Iran (4-23-48) Sec. 9, Arthur W. Radford, Chairman, Joint Chiefs of Staff, to General Twining, General Ridgway, and Admiral Carney, Aug. 19, 1953.

54. Nejati, *Jonbeshé*, pp. 409 and 418; Lapping, *End of Empire*, p. 221.

55. Nejati, *Jonbeshé*, pp. 409 and 418.

56. Ibid. For Nejati's interviews with most of the officers involved on both sides of the coup, see *Jonbeshé*, pp. 407–29.

57. Interview with Loy Henderson, Washington, Apr. 26, 1984.

58. Kermit Roosevelt says that he had $1 million at his disposal for the coup operation, but spent only $75,000 and gave the rest later to the Shah (*Los Angeles Times* interview with Roosevelt, Mar. 29, 1979). In his book, *Countercoup*, Roosevelt gives the same low figure of $75,000 so as to give the impression that a spontaneous uprising in favor of the Shah rendered further CIA financing unnecessary. (It is known that the Shah's men read the manuscript of Roosevelt's book before publication and made modifications in the Shah's favor.) Henderson, by contrast, says that millions of dollars were paid by the CIA to army officers, mullahs, and mob leaders (interview with Henderson, Washington, Apr. 26, 1984). Among the expenditures was $2 million paid to General Zahedi (*Bakhtaré-Emruz*, July 1978, quoting Abol-Qassem Amini,

Acting Court Minister in the first half of 1953). Nikki Keddie, who interviewed parties involved in the coup, believes the cost of the operation totaled "several million dollars"; see her *Roots of Revolution: An Interpretive History of Modern Iran* (New Haven, 1981), note 69 of chap. 6.

59. Eden, *Full Circle*, p. 214.

60. *The Times* (London), Aug. 20, 1953.

61. *Daily Telegraph* (London), Aug. 20, 1953.

62. At the time of the coup, I lived half a mile north of Mossadeq.

63. Maclean, *Eastern Approaches*, pp. 263–76.

64. C.C.50(53), Cabinet Conclusions, Aug. 25, 1953.

21.—An Oil Consortium Takes Over

1. RG59, Box 5511A, Henderson to Secretary of State, Sept. 21, 1953.

2. FO371/104577, Minute by Dixon, Aug. 21, 1953; Minute by Salisbury, Aug. 22, 1953. RG59, Box 5511A, Memorandum of conversation between Makins and Dulles, Sept. 4, 1953.

3. FO371/104584, Falle to Baker, Aug. 26, 1953.

4. FO371/98695, Minute by Bowker on his conversation with Fraser, Aug. 26, 1953.

5. RG59, Box 5511A, Byroade to Dulles, Sept. 5, 1953; Dulles to Henderson, Sept. 11, 1953.

6. Ibid., Dulles to Henderson, Sept. 23, 1953.

7. Ibid., Henderson to Secretary of State, Sept. 25, 1953.

8. Ibid., Eden's message to Dulles, Oct. 7, 1953.

9. Ibid., Dulles to Henderson, Oct. 7, 1953; FO371/104642, Beeley, Washington, to Dixon, Oct. 19, 1953.

10. FO371/104585, Minute by Gandy, Oct. 13, 1953; RG59, Box 5511A, Henderson to State Dept., Oct. 22 and 29, 1953.

11. Ibid., Henderson to State Dept., Oct. 29, 1953.

12. Ibid., Note in Persian handed by Entezam to Henderson and Hoover, Nov. 1, 1953.

13. Ibid., Dulles to U.S. Ambassadors in Tehran and London, Nov. 9, 1953.

14. FO371/104643, Minute by Dixon, Nov. 13, 1953.

15. RG59, Box 5511A, Henderson to Secretary of State, Nov. 6, 1953.

16. FO371/104643, Minute by Greenhill, Nov. 17, 1953.

17. FO371/104643, Notes by Eden on Foreign Office cable to British Embassy, Washington, Nov. 14, 1953; FO371/104644, Minute by Dixon on "Persia," Secret, Dec. 8, 1953.

18. Interview with Ali Amini, Paris, May 22, 1983. RG59, Box 5511A, Henderson to State Dept., Oct. 2, 1953.

19. *Azad*, Nov. 7, 1953.

20. *Shahed*, publishing Makki's open letter; Kashani's message broadcast on Radio Tehran, Nov. 3, 1953.

21. RG59, Box 5512, Henderson to State Dept., Dec. 9 and 11, 1953.

22. Eden, *Full Circle*, p. 240.

23. Interview with Sir Denis Wright, Buckinghamshire, England, July 5, 1985. FO371/110059, Wright to Eden, Jan. 7, 1954.

24. Ibid., Wright to Eden, Feb. 13, 1954.

25. U.S. Congress, *Cartel*, pp. 35–46.

26. RG59, Box 5511A, Memorandum of conversation between Hoover and the Attorney General, Nov. 12, 1953.

27. RG59, Box 5512, Memorandum of conversation between Hoover and legal staff members of Socony-Vacuum and Standard Oil of N.J., Nov. 24, 1953.

28. Ibid., Drake's letters to seven oil companies, Dec. 3, 1953.

29. Ibid., U.S. Embassy, London, to State Dept., Dec. 18, 1953; FO371/110047, Makins to Dixon, Jan. 22, 1954.

30. RG59, Box 5512, John Foster Dulles to U.S. Embassies, London and Tehran, Feb. 24, 1954; U.S. Embassy, London, to State Dept., Mar. 12, 1954.

31. Ibid., U.S. Embassy, London, to State Dept., Mar. 13 and 15, 1954.

32. Ibid., Hoover to State Dept., Mar. 13 and 15, 1954.

33. Ibid., Hoover to State Dept., Mar. 16, 1954.

34. Ibid., Henderson to State Dept., Mar. 16, 1954.

35. Ibid., Dulles to Aldrich, London, and Henderson, Tehran, Mar. 17, 1954.

36. Ibid., Aldrich to State Dept., Mar. 18, 1954; Memorandum of conversation between the officials of the British Embassy and State Dept., Mar. 19, 1954.

37. Ibid., Henderson to Secretary of State, Mar. 20, 1954; Memorandum of conversation at the State Dept., Mar. 22, 1954.

38. FO371/110060, Stevens to Eden, Mar. 13, 1954.

39. FO371/110063, Stevens to Fry, May 12, 1954.

40. The other two members of the Iranian committee were S. Bayat, Managing Director of Plan Organization, and F. Nuri-Esfandiari, member of the Plan High Council. The members of Iran's oil subcommittee were F. Rouhani, A. Ettehadieh, F. Nafici, and R. Fallah.

41. RG59, Box 5509, "Oil Controversy," Vol. III, p. 17.

42. Rouhani, *Tarikhé Melli Shodané*, pp. 426–37, and *Zendegié Siasié Mossadeq* (London, 1366/1987), p. 593.

43. RG59, Box 5512, Hoover to Secretary of State, Mar. 31, 1954.

44. Ibid., Hoover to Secretary of State, Apr. 26, 1954.

45. FO371/110065, Minute by Belgrave, June 12, 1954; RG59, Box 5512, Jernegan to Murphy, May 15, 1954.

46. PREM 11/726, Makins to Eden, Feb. 19, 1954; Makins to Caccia, Mar. 23, 1954.

47. Ibid., Memorandum of conversation at the State Dept., May 21, 1954.

48. Ibid., Henderson to State Dept., May 29, 1954; Aldrich to State Dept., May 31, 1954.

49. Ibid., Henderson to Secretary of State, Apr. 30, 1954.

50. Rouhani, *Tarikhé Melli Shodané*, pp. 486–502. RG59, Box 5509, "Oil Controversy," Vol. III, pp. 41–47.

51. RG59, Box 5512, Henderson to State Dept., Mar. 21 and May 4, 1954; Dulles to Aldrich and Henderson, Apr. 7, 1954; Butterworth to State Dept., May 20, 1954.

52. Interview with John Loudon, London, Nov. 27, 1986; interview with Amini, Paris, May 22, 1983.

53. "Oil Controversy," Vol. III, Appendix D-8, Letter from the President to the Shah, Aug. 5, 1954.

54. U.S. Congress, *Cartel*, Report of the Attorney General to the National Security Council, pp. 29–33.

55. "Oil Controversy," Vol. III, pp. 61–65.

56. Ibid. See Appendices B-11 to B-14 for details of the consortium agreement.

57. Interview with a CIA official who wishes to remain anonymous, Washington, Nov. 8, 1984.

58. Sadr, *Defa'é Mossadeq*, pp. 44–73.

59. *Qiamé Iran*, Aug. 23, 1954; the article is reproduced in Sadr, *Defa'é Mossadeq*, pp. 83–87.

60. Majlis Proceedings, Oct. 10–12, 21, 1954. RG59, "Oil Controversy," Vol. III, p. 57.

61. RG59, Box 5513, E. S. Akers of the public relations firm of Ernest L. Klein, representing U.S. independents, to John Foster Dulles, June 2, 1954.

62. On April 29, 1955, the five U.S participants each relinquished one-eighth of their holdings in the consortium, allocating them to the following U.S. independents: Richfield 25 percent; American Independent Oil Co., a consortium of ten U.S. independents, 16.66 percent; Getty, Atlantic, Signal, Hancock, Standard of Ohio, Tidewater, and San Jacinto each 8.33 percent. Later mergers changed this composition.

63. Strachey, *End of Empire*, p. 173.

64. Sampson, *Seven Sisters*, p. 148.

65. Rouhani believes that Iran, by paying £25 million, by wiping out its indisputable claims, and by being forced to pay a disproportionate share of the depreciation of assets, in fact paid £146 million in compensation. He argues further that Iran, as the owner of the oil resources, and not AIOC, should have received $600 million for granting seven new companies a share in the country's oil wealth. See Rouhani's *Tarikhé Melli Shodané*, pp. 502–4, and *Zendegié Siasié Mossadeq*, pp. 602–4. See also Benjamin Shwadran, *The Middle East, Oil and the Great Powers*, 3d ed. (New York, 1973), p. 148.

66. FO371/91574, "Notes on Lord Privy Seal's Mission" attached to minute by Berthoud, Aug. 3, 1951.

67. Quoted from Stevens Papers, Stevens to his parents, Aug. 2, 1954, by William Roger Louis in "Musaddiq, Oil and the Dilemmas of British Imperialism," paper presented at the Conference on Iranian Nationalism and the International Oil Crisis of 1951–54 at the University of Texas, Austin, Sept. 26–27, 1985.

68. Interview with Sir Eric Drake, London, Oct. 30, 1986.

69. Mossadeq, *Khaterat*, pp. 396–97.

70. Edith T. Penrose, *The Large International Firm in Developing Countries: The International Petroleum Industry* (London, 1968), pp. 215–16; Jerald L. Walden, "The International Petroleum Cartel in Iran: Private Power and the Public Interest," *Journal of Public Law*, XI (Spring 1962), pp. 51–52; Sampson, *Seven Sisters*, p. 151; Painter, *Private Power*, pp. 197–98; Paul H. Frankel, *Mattei, Oil and Power Politics* (New York, 1966), p. 96; Fereidun Fesharaki, *Development of the Iranian Oil Industry: International and Domestic Aspects* (New York, 1976), pp. 59–60.

22.—The Coup's Aftermath

1. For a detailed account of Mossadeq's trial see Jalil Bozorgmehr, *Mossadeq dar Mahkameyé Nezami* in two volumes (Tehran, 1364/1985). For a study

of Mossadeq's reflections in jail, see Bozorgmehr, *Taqriraté Mossadeq dar Zendan* (Tehran, 1359/1980).

2. Elwell-Sutton, *Persian Oil*, p. 315.

3. Bozorgmehr, *Mossadeq*, Vol. I, pp. 166–67.

4. Roosevelt, *Countercoup*, p. 200.

5. Nejati, *Jonbeshé*, p. 445.

6. Richard Cottam, *Nationalism in Iran* (Pittsburgh, 1979), p. 231.

7. Ebrahim Khajenuri, *Bazigarané Asré Tala'i: Davar, Teymurtash et al.*, new ed. (Tehran, 1357/1978), pp. 60–61.

8. George McGhee, "Recollections of Dr. Muhammad Musaddiq," in Bill and Louis, eds., *Mussadiq, Nationalism*, p. 304.

9. William O. Douglas, "The U.S. and Revolution," in K. E. Boulding et al., *The U.S. and Revolution* (Santa Barbara, Calif., 1961), p. 10.

10. Paul H. Nitze, "America: An Honest Broker," *Foreign Affairs* (Fall 1990), p. 7.

11. James A. Bill, *The Eagle and the Lion: The Tragedy of American-Iranian Relations* (New Haven, 1988), pp. 85–91.

12. William Pfaff, "American Leaders Ought to Read History," *International Herald Tribune*, Dec. 4, 1986.

13. Bill, *The Eagle and the Lion*, pp. 91–95.

14. Anthony Parsons, *The Pride and the Fall: Iran, 1974–1979* (London, 1984), pp. 140–41.

15. Woodhouse, *Something Ventured*, p. 131.

16. FO371/45458, British Military Attaché, Tehran, to F.O., Dec. 21, 1945.

17. Acheson, *Creation*, p. 511.

18. F. Azimi, *Iran: The Crisis of Democracy, 1941–1953* (London, 1989), p. 334.

19. Richard Cottam, "Nationalism in Twentieth Century Iran," in Bill and Louis, eds., *Mussadiq, Nationalism*, pp. 23, 35.

20. *Los Angeles Times*, Mar. 29, 1979.

21. McGhee, "Recollections," in Bill and Louis, eds., *Mussadiq, Nationalism*, p. 302.

22. *End of Empire: Iran*, Granada Television Series, 1985.

23. B. Porter, *The Lion's Share: A Short History of British Imperialism, 1850–1970* (London, 1975), p. 335.

24. Diba, *Mossadegh*, pp. 193–95.

25. *New York Times*, Mar. 5, 1967; *Daily Telegraph*, Mar. 6, 1967; *Le Monde*, Mar. 7, 1967; *Frankfurter Allgemeine*, Mar. 6, 1967.

26. Lapping, *End of Empire*, p. 224.

27. Keddie, *Roots of Revolution*, p. 141.

28. Albert Hourani, "Conclusion," in Bill and Louis, eds., *Musaddiq, Nationalism*, p. 339.

29. Rami G. Kouri, "For a Common Arab and Semitic Home," *New York Times* (*IHT*, Aug. 3, 1991).

30. Acheson, *Creation*, p. 685.

Bibliography

Unpublished Primary Sources

Documents at the British Public Record Office, London

CAB21	Cabinet Office: Registered Files	1916–54
CAB23	Cabinet Minutes	1916–39
CAB128	Cabinet Minutes and Conclusions	1945–54
CAB129	Cabinet Memoranda	1945–54
CAB131	Defence Committee	1950–54
C.C.50(53)	Cabinet Conclusions	1953
DEFE4	Chiefs of Staff Committee: Minutes of Meetings	1947–54
DEFE5	Chiefs of Staff Committee: Memoranda	1947–54
FO60	General Correspondence before 1906: Persia	1900–1905
FO248	Embassy and Consular Archives—Iran: Correspondence	1907–54
FO371	General Correspondence: Political	1906–54
FO416	Confidential: Persia	1900–1954
FO953	Foreign Publicity	1947–54
PREM	Records of the Prime Minister's Office	1945–55

Records at the U.S. National Archives, Washington, D.C., for the Years 1950–54

NSC. National Security Council Numbered Papers.

Record Group 59. Records of the State Department, including those of the Petroleum Division and the Bureau of Intelligence and Research.

Record Group 218. Records of the Joint Chiefs of Staff.

Record Group 253. Records of the Petroleum Administration for War.

Record Group 304. Records of the National Security Resources Board.

Record Group 330. Secretary of Defense Office Files.

Published Documents

– Alexander, Y., and A. Nanes, eds. *The United States and Iran: A Documentary History.* Frederick, Md.: University Publications of America, 1980.

Asnadé Naft (Documents on Oil). Tehran: Iranian Ministry of Foreign Affairs Publications, 1951.

– *Documents of the National Security Council, 1947–1977.* Washington, D.C.: University Publications of America, 1980.

Documents on British Foreign Policy, 1919–1939, 1st series, Vol. IV. London: Government Printing Press, 1952.

International Court of Justice, The Hague. *IJC Pleadings, Anglo-Iranian Oil Company Case (United Kingdom v Iran)*, 1952.

———. *IJC Reports of Judgements, Advisory Opinions and Orders*, 1952.

International Monetary Fund, Washington, D.C. *International Financial Statistics*, Vol. VII, 1954; Vol. VIII, 1955.

Iranian Oral History Collection. Harvard University Center for Middle Eastern Studies. Cambridge, Mass., 1987.

League of Nations Official Journal, Vol. XIII, 1932; Vol. XIV, 1933.

Macadam, Ivision S., ed. *The Annual Register: A Review of Public Events at Home and Abroad*, volumes relating to the years 1949–1954. London: Longmans, Green, 1950–55.

Mozakeraté Majlisé Sena (Senate Proceedings). *Ruznameyé Rasmyé Keshvar.* Tehran, 1950–52.

Mozakeraté Majlisé Showrayé Melli (Majlis Proceedings). *Ruznameyé Rasmyé Keshvar.* Tehran, 1941–54.

"Official Conversations and Meetings of Dean Acheson, 1949–1953." The Presidential Document Series. Microfilm Division, Princeton University Library.

Parliamentary Debates (Hansard). *House of Commons Official Report.* Sessions 1948–54. 5th Series, Vols. 470–529. London: H.M. Stationery Office, 1949–54.

Public Papers of the Presidents of the United States: Dwight D. Eisenhower, 1953. Washington, D.C.: GPO, 1954.

Public Papers of the Presidents of the United States: Jimmy Carter, 1977. Washington, D.C.: GPO, 1978.

Temperley, Harold, ed. *A History of the Peace Conference of Paris*, Vol. V. London: Henry Froude and Hodder & Stoughton, 1924.

United Nations, New York. *UN Security Council Official Records, 1951.*

U.S. Congress. Senate. Committee on Foreign Relations. Subcommittee on Multinational Corporations. *The International Petroleum Cartel, the Iranian Consortium and U.S. National Security.* Washington, D.C.: GPO, 1974.

U.S. Department of State. *Foreign Relations of the United States*, volumes relating to the years 1950–54. Washington, D.C.: GPO, 1980–86.

Memoirs, Diaries, and Biographies

Acheson, Dean. *Present at the Creation: My Years in the State Department.* New York: Norton, 1969.

Alavi, Bozorg. *Varaq Pareyé Zendan* (Torn Prison Notes). Tehran: n.p., 1942.

Arfa, H. *Under Five Shahs.* London: John Murray, 1964.

Arsanjani, H. *Yaddashthayé Siassi* (Political Memoirs). Tehran: Atesh Pbls., 1956.

Bozorgmehr, Jalil. *Mossadeq dar Mahkameyé Nezami* (Mossadeq in the Military Court), 2 vols. Tehran: Nashré Tarikhé Iran, 1985.

———. *Taqriraté Mossadeq dar Zendan* (Mossadeq's Statements in Jail). Tehran: Sazmané Ketab, 1980.

Bullard, Reader. *Letters from Tehran: A British Ambassador in World War II Persia.* London: I. B. Tauris, 1991.

Byrnes, James F. *Speaking Frankly.* New York: Harper, 1947.

Churchill, Winston S. *The World Crisis, 1911–1918,* 4 vols. London: Odhams Press, 1938.

Curzon, George Nathaniel. *Persia and the Persian Question,* 2 vols. London: Longmans, Green, 1892.

– Diba, Farhad. *Mohammad Mossadegh: A Political Biography.* London: Croom Helm, 1986.

Dowlat-Abadi, Yahya. *Hayaté Yahya* (The Life of Yahya), 3d ed., 4 vols. Tehran: Attar Pbls., 1982.

– Dulles, Allen W. *The Craft of Intelligence.* New York: Harper and Row, 1963.

Eden, Anthony. *Full Circle: The Memoirs of Anthony Eden.* London: Cassell, 1960.

E'etemad ol-Saltaneh, *Ruznameh Khaterat* (Journal of Memoirs), 2d ed. Tehran: Amir Kabir Pbls., 1977.

– Eisenhower, Dwight D. *The White House Years: Mandate for Change, 1953–1956.* Garden City, N.Y.: Doubleday, 1963.

Fardust, Hossein. *Khaterat: Zohur va Soghuté Saltanaté Pahlavi* (Memoirs: The Rise and Fall of Pahlavi's Reign). Tehran: Ettela'at, 1990.

Farrokh, M. *Khateraté Siassié Farrokh* (The Political Memoirs of Farrokh). Tehran: Sahami Pbls., 1969.

– Ferrell, Robert H., ed. *The Eisenhower Diaries.* London: Norton, 1981.

Ghani, Cyrus. *Yaddashthayé Dr. Qassem Ghani* (The Memoirs of Dr. Qassem Ghani), 12 vols. London: Ithaca Press, 1980–85.

Hardinge, Arthur H. *A Diplomat in the East.* London: Jonathan Cape, 1928.

– Harris, Kenneth. *Attlee.* London: Weidenfeld and Nicolson, 1982.

Hedayat, Mehdi-Qoli. *Khaterat va Khatarat* (Memoirs and Perils), 3d ed. Tehran: Zavvar Pbls., 1982.

Ironside, Lord. *High Road to Command: The Diaries of Major-General Sir Edmund Ironside, 1920–1922.* London: Leo Cooper, 1972.

James, Robert Rhodes. *Anthony Eden.* London: Weidenfeld and Nicolson, 1986.

Kasravi, A. *Zendeganié Man* (My Life). Tehran: Peyam Pbls., 1946.

Maclean, Fitzroy. *Eastern Approaches.* London: Jonathan Cape, 1949.

Makki, Hossein. *Ketabé Siah* (Black Book), 4 vols. Tehran: Bongahé Tarjomeh va Nashré Ketab, 1981.

– McGhee, George. *Envoy to the Middle World: Adventures in Diplomacy.* New York: Harper and Row, 1983.

– Morrison, Herbert. *An Autobiography.* London: Odhams Press, 1960.

Mossadeq, Mohammad. *Khaterat va Ta'allomat* (Memoirs and Agonies). Tehran: Elmi Pbls., 1986.

Mossavar-Rahmani, Colonel Gholamreza. *Kohné Sarbaz: Khateraté Siassi va Nezami* (Old Soldier: Political and Military Memoirs). Tehran: Khadamaté Farhanguié Rassa, 1987.

Pahlavi, Ashraf. *Faces in a Mirror: Memoirs from Exile.* Englewood Cliffs, N.J.: Prentice-Hall, 1980.

Pahlavi, Mohammad Reza. *Mission for My Country.* London: Hutchinson, 1961.

Parsons, Anthony. *The Pride and the Fall: Iran, 1974–1979.* London: Jonathan Cape, 1984.

Roosevelt, Kermit. *Countercoup: The Struggle for the Control of Iran.* New York: McGraw-Hill, 1979.

Rowland, John, and Basil Cadman. *Ambassador for Oil: The Life of John First Baron Cadman.* London: Jenkins, 1960.

Sadr, Hassan. *Defa'é Dr. Mossadeq az Naft dar Zendané Zerehi* (Dr. Mossadeq's Defense on Oil at the Military Prison). Tehran: Offset, 1978.

Seyyed Javadi, Ali Asqar Haj. *Daftarhayé Enqelab* (Notes on the Revolution). Tehran: Jonbesh Pbls., 1980.

Stettinius, Edward R., Jr. *Roosevelt and the Russians: The Yalta Conference.* Westport, Conn.: Greenwood Press, 1970, ©1949.

Truman, Harry S. *Years of Trial and Hope, 1946–1952.* Garden City, N.Y.: Doubleday, 1956.

Vossuq, Ali. *Chahar Fasl dar Tafannon va Tarikh* (Four Chapters in Fun and History). Tehran: Golgasht, 1982.

Vossuq, Sepahbod Ahmad. *Dastané Zendegani: Khaterat az Panjah Sal* (The Story of Life: Memoirs of Fifty Years). Tehran: n.p., n.d.

Walters, Vernon A. *Silent Missions.* Garden City, N.Y.: Doubleday, 1978.

Waterfield, Gordon. *Professional Diplomat: Sir Percy Loraine of Kirkharle, 1880–1961.* London: John Murray, 1973.

Williams, Francis. *A Prime Minister Remembers: The War and Post-War Memoirs of the Rt. Hon. Earl Attlee.* London: Heinemann, 1961.

Wilson, Arnold T. *Persia: Letters and Diaries of a Young Political Officer, 1907–1914.* London: Readers Union Edition, 1942.

Woodhouse, C. M. *Something Ventured.* London, Granada, 1982.

Ziegler, Philip. *Mountbatten: The Official Biography.* London: Collins, 1985.

Books, Articles, and Dissertations

Abrahamian, Ervand. *Iran Between Two Revolutions.* Princeton, N.J.: Princeton University Press, 1982.

Adamiyat, F. *Fekré Azadi va Moqadamé Nehzaté Mashrutiaté Iran* (The Concept of Freedom and the Beginning of the Constitutional Movement in Iran). Tehran: Sukhan, 1961.

Afrasiabi, Bahram. *Mossadeq va Tarikh* (Mossadeq and History). Tehran: Nilufar, 1981.

Ambrose, Stephen E. *Eisenhower, Vol. 2: The President.* New York: Simon and Schuster, 1984.

———. *Ike's Spies: Eisenhower and the Espionage Establishment.* Garden City, N.Y.: Doubleday, 1981.

Amirsadeghi, H., and R. W. Ferrier, eds. *Twentieth Century Iran.* London: Heinemann, 1977.

Amuzegar, Jahangir. "The Oil Story: Facts, Fiction and Fair Play," *Foreign Affairs,* July 1973.

———. "Oil Wealth: A Very Mixed Blessing," *Foreign Affairs,* Spring 1982.

Azimi, Fakhreddin. *Iran: The Crisis of Democracy, 1941–1953.* London: I. B. Tauris, 1989.

Bahar, Mohammad Taqi (Malek ol-sho'ara). *Tarikhé Mokhtasaré Ahzabé Siassi: Enqerazé Qajarieh* (A Short History of Political Parties: The Fall of the Qajars), Vol. I. Tehran: Amir Kabir, 1944.

Bakhash, S. *Iran: Monarchy, Bureaucracy and Reform under the Qajars, 1858–1896.* London: Ithaca Press, 1978.

Barnett, Correlli. *The Pride and the Fall: The Dream and Illusion of Britain as a Great Nation.* New York: Free Press, 1986.

Bharier, Julian. *Economic Development in Iran, 1900–1970.* London: Oxford University Press, 1971.

— Bill, James A. *The Eagle and the Lion: The Tragedy of American-Iranian Relations.* New Haven: Yale University Press, 1988.

— Bill, James A., and Wm. Roger Louis, eds. *Mussadiq, Iranian Nationalism, and Oil.* London: I. B. Tauris, 1988.

Binder, Leonard. *Iran: Political Development in a Changing Society.* Berkeley: University of California Press, 1962.

- Blair, John. *The Control of Oil.* London: Macmillan Press, 1977.

- Block, J., and P. Fitzgerald. *British Intelligence and Covert Action.* Kerry, Ireland: Brandon Book Publishers, 1983.

Bostock, E., and G. Jones. *Planning and Power in Iran: Ebtehaj and Economic Development under the Shah.* London: Frank Cass, 1989.

Browne, Edward G. *The Persian Revolution of 1905–1909,* new imp. London: Cambridge University Press, 1966.

Chubin, Shahram, and Sepehr Zabih. *The Foreign Relations of Iran.* Berkeley: University of California Press, 1974.

Cottam, Richard. *Nationalism in Iran.* Pittsburgh: University of Pittsburgh Press, 1979.

- ———. "The United States, Iran, and the Cold War," *Iranian Studies,* III (Winter 1970).

Elm, Mostafa. "Governmental Economic Planning in Iran." Ph.D. diss., Syracuse University, 1959.

———. "Oil Negotiations: A View from Iran," *Columbia Journal of World Business,* VI, No. 6 (Nov.–Dec. 1971).

———. "Who is Helping Whom in the Mirage of Foreign Aid," *Columbia Journal of World Business,* III, No. 4 (July–Aug. 1968).

- Elwell-Sutton, L. P. *Persian Oil: A Study in Power Politics.* London: Lawrence and Wishart, 1955.

Engler, Robert. *The Politics of Oil: Private Power and Democratic Directions.* Chicago: University of Chicago Press, 1961.

- Eveland, Wilbur C. *Ropes of Sand: America's Failure in the Middle East.* New York: Norton, 1980.

Farmanfarmayan, Khodadad K. "Social Change and Economic Behaviour in Iran," *Explorations in Entrepreneurial History,* IX, No. 3 (Feb. 1957).

Fateh, Mostafa. *Panjah Sal Nafté Iran* (Fifty Years of Persian Oil), 2d ed. Tehran: Pyam Pbls., 1979.

Fatemi, Nasrollah S. *Diplomatic History of Persia, 1917–1923: Anglo-Russian Power Politics in Iran.* New York: Russel F. Moore, 1952.

———. *Oil Diplomacy: Powder Keg in Iran.* New York: Whittier Books, 1954.

Ferrier, R. W. *The History of the British Petroleum Company,* Vol. I: *The Developing Years, 1901–1932.* Cambridge, U.K.: Cambridge University Press, 1982.

Fesharaki, Fereidun. *Development of the Iranian Oil Industry: International and Domestic Aspects.* New York: Praeger, 1976.

Ford, Alan W. *The Anglo-Iranian Oil Dispute of 1951–1952: A Study of the Role of Law in Relations of States*. Berkeley: University of California Press, 1954.

— Frankel, Paul H. *Mattei, Oil and Power Politics*. New York: Praeger, 1966.

———. *Oil: The Facts of Life*. London: Weidenfeld and Nicolson, 1962.

— Gasiorowski, Mark. "The 1953 Coup D'Etat in Iran," *International Journal of Middle East Studies*, XIX (1987).

Ghani, Cyrus. *Iran and the West: A Critical Bibliography*. London and New York: Kegan Paul International, 1987.

Ghoreishi, Ahmad. "Soviet Foreign Policy in Iran, 1917–1966." Ph.D. diss., University of Colorado, 1965.

Gopal, Sarvepalli. *British Policy in India, 1858–1905*. Cambridge, U.K.: Cambridge University Press, 1965.

Graham, Robert. *Iran: The Illusion of Power*. London: Croom Helm, 1978.

Greaves, R. L. *Persia and the Defence of India, 1884–1892*. London: Athlone Press, 1959.

Halliday, Fred. *Iran: Dictatorship and Development*. New York: Penguin, 1979.

— Hartshorn, J. E. *Politics and World Oil Economics: An Account of the International Oil Industry in Its Political Environment*. New York: Praeger, 1962.

Issavi, C., and M. Yeganeh. *The Economics of Middle Eastern Oil*. New York: Praeger, 1962.

Javanshir, F. M. *Tajrobeyé 28 Mordad* (The Experience of the August 19 Coup). Tehran: n.p., 1980.

Jones, Geoffrey. *Banking and Empire in Iran: The History of the British Bank of the Middle East*, Vol. I. Cambridge, U.K.: Cambridge University Press, 1986.

Katoozian, Homa. *The Political Economy of Modern Iran, 1926–1979*. New York: New York University Press, 1981.

Kazemi, F. *Poverty and Revolution in Iran*. New York: New York University Press, 1980.

Kazemzadeh, Firuz. *Russia and Britain in Persia, 1864–1914: A Study in Imperialism*. New Haven: Yale University Press, 1968.

Keddie, Nikki R. *Religion and Rebellion in Iran: The Tobacco Protest of 1891–1892*. London: Frank Cass, 1966.

———. *Roots of Revolution: An Interpretive History of Modern Iran*. New Haven: Yale University Press, 1981.

———. *Sayyid Jamal ad-Din "al-Afghani": A Political Biography*. Los Angeles: University of California Press, 1972.

Khajenuri, Ebrahim. *Bazigarané Asré Tala'i* (Players of the Golden Age): *Davar, Teymurtash et al.*, new ed. Tehran: Entesharate Javidan, 1978.

Kia-Nuri, Nureddin. *Hezbé Tudeh Iran va Dr. Mohammad Mossadeq* (Iran's Tudeh Party and Dr. Mossadeq). Tehran: Tudeh Party Pbls., 1980.

Kittner, N. "Issues in Anglo-Persian Diplomatic Relations, 1921–1933." Ph.D. diss., University of London, 1981.

— Ladjevardi, Habib. "The Origins of U.S. Support for an Autocratic Iran," *International Journal of Middle East Studies*, XV (1983).

Lambton, Ann K. S. *Qajar Persia: Eleven Studies*. London: I. B. Tauris, 1987.

Lapping, Brian. *End of Empire*. London: Granada, 1985.

- Ledeen, M., and W. Lewis. *Debacle: The American Failure in Iran*. New York: Alfred A. Knopf, 1981.

Leeman, Wayne A. *The Price of Middle East Oil: An Essay in Political Economy*. Ithaca, N.Y.: Cornell University Press, 1962.

Lenczowski, George. *The Political Awakening in the Middle East*. Englewood Cliffs, N.J.: Prentice-Hall, 1970.

———. *Russia and the West in Iran, 1918–1948: A Study in Big Power Rivalry*. Ithaca, N.Y.: Cornell University Press, 1949.

Levy, Walter J. *Oil Strategy and Politics, 1941–1981*. Boulder, Col.: Westview Press, 1982.

Logrigg, Stephen H. *Oil in the Middle East: Its Discovery and Development*, 3d ed. Oxford: Oxford University Press, 1968.

Longhurst, Henry. *Adventure in Oil: The Story of British Petroleum*. London: Sidgwick and Jackson, 1959.

Louis, Wm. Roger. *The British Empire in the Middle East, 1945–1951*. Oxford: Oxford University Press, 1984.

Lubell, Harold. *Middle East Oil Crises and Europe's Energy Supplies*. Baltimore: Johns Hopkins Press, 1963.

Mahmud, M. *Tarikhé Ravabeté Siassié Iran va Engelis* (A History of the Political Relations of Iran and Britain), 5 vols. Tehran: Eqbal, 1949–53.

Mikdashi, Zuhayr. *A Financial Analysis of Middle Eastern Oil Concessions, 1901–1965*. New York: Praeger, 1966.

- Millspaugh, Arthur C. *Americans in Persia*. Washington, D.C.: Brookings Institution, 1946.

Mineau, Wayne. *The Go Devils*. London: Cassell, 1958.

Morgan, K. O. *Labour in Power, 1945–1951*. Oxford: Clarendon Press, 1984.

Mosely, Leonard. *Power Play: Oil in the Middle East*. New York: Random House, 1973.

Mossadeq, Mohammad. "Capitulassion va Iran" (Capitulation and Iran), in *Mossadeq va Mas'aleyé Hoquq va Siassat* (Mossadeq and the Problems of Law and Politics), ed. Iraj Afshar. Tehran: Zamineh, 1979.

———. "Entekhabat dar Orupa va Iran" (Elections in Europe and Iran), in *Mossadeq va Mas'aleyé Hoquq va Siassat* (Mossadeq and the Problems of Law and Politics), ed. Iraj Afshar. Tehran: Zamineh, 1979.

———. *Le Testament en Droit Musulman* (*Secte Chyite*). Paris, 1914.

———. *Notqha va Mozaheraté Dr. Mossadeq dar Dowrehayé Panjom va Sheshomé Majlis Showrayé Melli* (Speeches and Discussions of Dr. Mossadeq During the Fifth and Sixth Sessions of the Majlis). Paris: Entesharaté Mossadeq, 1971.

Nejati, Col. Gholam-Reza. *Jonbeshé Melli Shodané San'até Nafté Iran* (The Movement for Nationalization of Iran's Oil Industry). Tehran: Sherkaté Sahami Enteshar, 1985.

- Nitze, Paul H. "America: An Honest Broker," *Foreign Affairs*, Fall 1990.

- Painter, David S. *Private Power and Public Policy: Multinational Oil Corporations and U.S. Foreign Policy, 1941–1954*. London: I. B. Tauris, 1986.

- Penrose, Edith T. *The Large International Firm in Developing Countries: The International Petroleum Industry*. London: Allen and Unwin, 1968.

Pirnia, Hossein. *Dah Sal Kushesh dar Rahé Hefz va Basté Hoquqé Iran dar Naft* (Ten Years of Struggle to Preserve and Maintain Iran's Rights in Oil). Tehran: n.p., 1952.

Porter, Bernard. *The Lion's Share: A Short History of British Imperialism, 1850–1970.* London and New York: Longmans, 1975.

Ra'in, Esma'il. *Asnadé Khané Seddon* (The Documents at Seddon's Residence), 2d ed. Tehran: Bongah Tarjomeh va Nashré Ketab, 1979.

Ramazani, Rouhullah K. *Iran's Foreign Policy, 1941–1973.* Charlottesville, Va.: University Press of Virginia, 1975.

——. ———. *The United States and Iran: The Patterns of Influence.* New York: Praeger, 1982.

Rouhani, Fuad. *Tarikhé Melli Shodané San'até Nafté Iran* (A History of the Nationalization of the Iranian Oil Industry). Tehran: Ketabhayé Jibi, 1973.

———. *Zendegié Siasié Mossadeq* (The Political Life of Mossadeq). London: Paka Print, 1987.

Rubin, Barry. *The Great Powers in the Middle East, 1941–1947: The Road to the Cold War.* London: Frank Cass, 1980.

——. ———. *Paved with Good Intentions: The American Experience in Iran.* New York: Oxford University Press, 1980.

Safa'i, Ebrahim. *Rahbarané Mashrutiyat* (The Leaders of the Constitution). Tehran: Javidané-Elmi, 1965.

Sampson, Anthony. *The Seven Sisters: The Great Oil Companies and the World They Made.* London: Hodder and Stoughton, 1975.

Shwadran, Benjamin. *The Middle East, Oil and the Great Powers,* 3d ed. New York: Wiley, 1973.

— Sick, Gary. *All Fall Down: America's Tragic Encounter with Iran.* New York: Random House, 1985.

Stocking, George W. *The Middle East Oil: A Study in Politics and Economic Controversy.* Nashville, Tenn.: Vanderbilt University Press, 1970.

— Stoff, Michael B. *Oil, War, and American Security.* New Haven: Yale University Press, 1980.

Strachey, John. *The End of Empire.* London: Gollancz, 1959.

Tabataba'i, M. *Namehayé Afghani* (The Letters of Afghani). Tehran: n.p., 1970.

Tanzer, Michael. *The Political Economy of International Oil and the Underdeveloped Countries.* London: Temple Smith, 1969.

Tavanyan-Fard, H. *Dr. Mossadeq va Eqtessad* (Dr. Mossadeq and Economics). Tehran: Alavi, 1953.

Teymuri, Ebrahim. *Asré bi-Khabari* (The Age of Ignorance), 4th ed. Tehran: Eqbal, 1985.

Walden, Jerald L. "The International Petroleum Cartel in Iran: Private Power and the Public Interest," *Journal of Public Law,* XI (Spring 1962).

Walters, F. P. *A History of the League of Nations.* London: Oxford University Press, 1952.

Wilber, Donald N. *Adventures in the Middle East: Excursions and Incursions.* Princeton, N.J.: Darwin, 1986.

———. *Iran Past and Present,* 7th ed. Princeton, N.J.: Princeton University Press, 1975.

———. *Riza Shah Pahlavi: The Resurrection and Reconstruction of Iran.* Hicksville, N.Y.: Exposition Press, 1975.

Williams, William A. *The Tragedy of American Diplomacy*, rev. ed. New York: Dell, 1962.

Wright, Denis. *The English Amongst the Persians During the Qajar Period, 1787–1921*. London: Heinemann, 1977.

———. *The Persians Amongst the English: Episodes in Anglo-Persian History*. London: I. B. Tauris, 1985.

Yergin, Daniel. *The Prize: The Epic Quest for Oil, Money, and Power*. New York and London: Simon and Schuster, 1991.

Zabih, Sepehr. *The Communist Movement in Iran*. Berkeley: University of California Press, 1966.

———. *The Mossadegh Era: Roots of the Iranian Revolution*. Chicago: Lake View Press, 1982.

Zonis, Marvin. *Majestic Failure: The Fall of the Shah*. Chicago: University of Chicago Press, 1991.

———. *The Political Elite of Iran*. Princeton, N.J.: Princeton University Press, 1971.

Newspapers and Weeklies

The dates of issue of papers and weeklies consulted are given in the notes.

Al-Ahram (Cairo)
Bakhtar (Tehran)
Bakhtaré-Emruz (Tehran, later Munich)
Baltimore Sun
Bamshad (Tehran)
Bessuyé-Ayandeh (Tehran)
Dad (Tehran)
Daily Telegraph (London)
The Economist (London)
Ettela'at (Tehran)
Evening Standard (London)
Financial Times (London)
Independent (London)

International Herald Tribune (Paris)
Keyhan (Tehran)
Los Angeles Times
New York Herald Tribune
New York Times
Philadelphia Inquirer
Setareh Iran (Tehran)
Shahed (Tehran)
Time (New York)
The Times (London)
U.S. News and World Report (New York)
Wall Street Journal (New York)
Washington Post

Index

Abadan, 14–15, 16–17, 50, 96, 108, 357n.3; British naval presence in, 47, 84, 157; British plans to occupy, 26, 128, 155–56, 160–61, 163–64; World War II occupation of, 40–41
Abdullah, King (Jordan), 122
Acheson, Dean, 60, 62, 87, 89, 102, 343; and American oil company fears, 105; and arbitration proposals, 248, 249, 251, 254; briefing of Eisenhower by, 259–60; and British complaint to United Nations, 170, 173, 181; and British schemes to oust Mossadeq, 224, 239, 294; and Churchill's visit to the United States, 198, 199; and economic assistance to Iran, 69, 199, 203, 248; and eviction of AIOC's British staff, 153–54; and Harriman mission, 124–26, 127; and joint Truman-Churchill message, 251, 254; lump-sum compensation proposal of, 257–58, 260–61; mediation attempts by, 174, 184, 185–86, 188–90, 191; opinion of Mossadeq, 246, 339; opinion of Shepherd, 218; opposes use of force, 158, 165; recognizes Iran's right to nationalize, 85, 112, 113; and Supplemental Oil Agreement, 66, 72; warning to Eden, 258–59; World Bank proposal of, 200–201
Aden, 267–68
Adenauer, Konrad, 288
Admiralty, British, acquisition of AIOC shares by, 15–17; Iran's demands for disclosure of AIOC sales to, 65, 74; presence of its naval forces off Iran, 47, 84, 157; proposed intervention of tankers by, 146. *See also* Navy, British
Afghani. *See* Assad-Abadi, Seyyed Jamal
Afshartus, M., 298–99
AGIP. *See* Italian National Oil Company
Ahmad Shah, 14, 24, 25, 27, 41

AIOC. *See* Anglo-Iranian Oil Company
Ala, Hossein, 34, 39, 138, 152, 218; and expulsion of AIOC's British staff, 171; as prime minister, 81, 82, 83, 91; resignation of, 92, 215
Alam, Assadollah, 81, 230, 355n.60
Aldrich, Winthrop, 317, 318
Alexander II, Tsar, 2
Aliabadi, M. H., 209
Amery, Julian, 236–37, 238
Amery, Leopold, 41, 237
Amini, Abol-Qassem, 298, 380n.26
Amini, Ali, and oil consortium negotiations, 320, 323–24, 326, 380n.26
Amini, Mahmud, 380n.26
Amin ol-Soltan, Ali Asgar, 4, 6, 11
Anderson, Charles, 321
Anglo-Egyptian Treaty (1936), 193
Anglo-Iranian Oil Company (AIOC), 138, 221, 242, 374n.1; American companies' cooperation with, 103, 190, 223, 260; and American proposal to World Bank, 200–201; and American settlement proposals, 186, 187, 257–58, 262–64, 265, 266; assets of, 100, 107–8; and boycott, 144–45, 146–47, 267–68, 269; British criticism of, 90–91, 102–4, 310; and British interests in Iran, 83, 87, 99, 104–5, 108–9; and consortium agreement, 325, 328–29; and consortium negotiations, 286, 312–13, 315–18, 319, 321; coup proposal from, 293–94, 297; dispossession of, 116–19; distrust of American oil companies, 75; exports of, 144, 145, 270; expulsion of British staff of, 149–51, 152–54, 166–68, 171, 226; financial position at time of nationalization, 107–9; and Harriman mission, 125, 130, 132–33; illusions of, 81; interception of NIOC communications by, 146–47; interference in Iranian politics

397

Oil, Power, and Principle
was composed in 10.5 / 13 Sabon
with Futura display by Keystone Typesetting, Inc.,
Orwigsburg, Pennsylvania; printed and bound over
binder's boards in ICG Arrestox by Braun-Brumfield, Inc.,
Ann Arbor, Michigan; with dust jackets printed in 2 colors
by Braun-Brumfield, Inc.; designed by Kachergis Book
Design, Pittsboro, North Carolina; and published by
Syracuse University Press, Syracuse,
New York 13244-5160.

 Contemporary Issues in the Middle East

This well-established series continues to focus primarily on twentieth-century developments that have current impact and significance throughout the entire region, from North Africa to the borders of Central Asia.

Recent titles in the series include: